Progressive Evangelicals
and the Pursuit of Social Justice

Progressive Evangelicals
and the Pursuit
of Social Justice

BRANTLEY W. GASAWAY

The University of North Carolina Press 🕮 *Chapel Hill*

This book was published with the assistance of the
Thornton H. Brooks Fund of the University of North Carolina Press.

© 2014 THE UNIVERSITY OF NORTH CAROLINA PRESS

Complete cataloging information for this
title is available from the Library of Congress.

ISBN 978-1-4696-1772-5 (pbk.: alk. paper)
ISBN 978-1-4696-1773-2 (ebook)

A portion of this book was published, in somewhat different form, as
"'Glimmers of Hope': Progressive Evangelical Leaders and Racism, 1965–2000,"
in *Christians and the Color Line: Race and Religion after Divided by Faith*, edited
by J. Russell Hawkins and Phillip Luke Sinitiere (New York: Oxford
University Press, 2013). By permission of Oxford University Press, USA.

To Katie

Contents

Acknowledgments

I am grateful to have had such a wonderful network of support—both professional and personal—as I worked on this project over the past decade. Without the wisdom and encouragement of the people below, this book would not have been possible.

My academic mentors deserve especial thanks. First and foremost, Yaakov Ariel shaped this book from its conception to completion. His generosity of time, good cheer, wise counsel, continual engagement, and confidence in my abilities were crucial at each step. Both Laurie Maffly-Kipp and Randall Styers read early versions of this project and provided insightful feedback. Grant Wacker encouraged my interests, pushed me to think and to write clearly, and made invaluable suggestions regarding the book's structure and style. I also benefited immeasurably from the probing questions and perceptive advice of Jason Bivins, who continued to support this work through its final stages. Finally, I want to thank my earliest academic advisors, David Holmes and Peter Williams, for their guidance and friendship.

Other friends offered moral and intellectual support in the early stages of this project. Reid Neilson, Jeff Wilson, and Ben Zeller shared their wit and wisdom throughout our years in graduate school. I am particularly indebted to Seth Dowland, Matt Harper, and Sarah Ruble, who read initial drafts and helped me to envision what this work could become. My ongoing friendship and collaboration with Seth remain some of the best parts of my job.

My colleagues at Drake University and then Bucknell University provided welcoming environments that encouraged and enabled me to complete this book. Renee Cramer, Brad Crowell, Jennifer Harvey, Jennifer McCrickerd, and Tim Knepper supported my pedagogical and scholarly development while I was at Drake. At Bucknell, Maria Antonaccio, Karline McLain, Paul Macdonald, Rivka Ulmer, Stuart Young, and Carol White have offered both direct and indirect assistance. I am grateful to have found a professional home among such dedicated and collegial faculty.

Additional scholars and friends also read significant portions of the manuscript: Randall Balmer, Rusty Hawkins, John Inazu, Michael James, David Martino, Steven Miller, Scott Morrison, Josh Reitano, Michael Schmidli, Phil Sinitiere, and David Swartz. Their comments and corrections improved the book.

For generous funding and resources that supported my research, I thank the University of North Carolina at Chapel Hill Graduate School and Department of Religious Studies; the Louisville Institute; and Bucknell University. I am also grateful to the staffs of many libraries, including Davis Library at the University of North Carolina at Chapel Hill; Duke Divinity School Library; Cowles Library at Drake University; Bertrand Library at Bucknell University; Murray Library at Messiah College; and the Billy Graham Center Archives and Buswell Memorial Library at Wheaton College. Finally, for bringing this book to publication, I thank my editor, Elaine Maisner, and all of the dedicated and talented staff at the University of North Carolina Press.

Throughout the years, I have been blessed by the love and support of my family: my parents, Phil Gasaway and Joan Smith; my stepfather, David Smith; my brother, Sonny Gasaway, and his wife, Whitley; and my in-laws, Danny and Ellen Krease, Julie and Brodie Theis, and Kevin Krease. My daughters, Eleanor, Anna, and Carolyn, were born at different stages in this project, and their playfulness and love have provided a welcome counterbalance to the demands of the academic life. I thank each of them for her patience—and yes, Daddy has finally finished his book.

Above all, I am indescribably thankful to my wife, Katie. Her partnership, endurance, and constant love not only made this work possible but also make my life a joy. It is to her that I dedicate this book.

Progressive Evangelicals
and the Pursuit of Social Justice

Introduction

As the nearly 1,000 participants in Sojourners' "Peace Pentecost 1985" gathering marched through the streets of Washington, D.C., they punctuated their singing of "This Little Light of Mine" with stops for prayer. Eventually the procession of progressive evangelicals and their ecumenical allies arrived across from the White House and prepared to protest. "Let your light shine around this city!" exhorted Jim Wallis, head of the progressive evangelical organization Sojourners. Participants divided into separate groups and marched to six sites that symbolized their idiosyncratic set of political priorities. Outside the White House, demonstrators prayed for "an end to the arms race and for the poor, its primary victims." In front of the Supreme Court, a group protested the "barbaric practice" of the death penalty while also praying for crime victims. At the State Department, protesters pleaded for the American government to "stop its promotion of violence and terror" in Central America and "instead join in peaceful resolution of the conflicts in that embattled region." Outside the South African embassy, another group prayed "on behalf of freedom and democracy and in protest of our own government's accommodation to apartheid." At the same time, demonstrators at the Soviet embassy "prayed on behalf of the people of Afghanistan, whose country has been brutally invaded by another arrogant superpower." Finally, protesters at the Department of Health and Human Services prayed for unborn children, called for increased alternatives so that "desperate women would not be driven to have abortions," and gathered in the formation of the women's symbol in order "to show that respect for unborn life also requires respect for women."[1]

1

Progressive evangelical leaders designed this range of ritualized protests to challenge both the political right and left, for they believed that neither side offered a consistent and comprehensive defense of human life. "We're showing that we are willing to pay the price, to sacrifice, to go to jail, if necessary, to draw attention to all the assaults on human life that are now so abundant," Jim Wallis declared after 248 Peace Pentecost participants were arrested for civil disobedience of demonstration regulations. "We hope to serve notice that whenever there are policies of violence, militarism and injustice, they will be resisted by the churches."[2]

Media coverage of Sojourners' Peace Pentecost protests focused on the unconventional combination of progressive evangelicals' political positions. By 1985 most observers regarded the Religious Right's political conservatism and support for Republicans as standard for evangelicals. In a profile of Sojourners, the *Los Angeles Times* acknowledged that "conservative fundamentalist groups capture the headlines" while the evangelical left was only "quietly exerting influence." Therefore, when progressive evangelicals did manage to attract media attention with events such as Peace Pentecost, reporters often seemed surprised. "Although the Sojourners consider themselves evangelicals and are theologically conservative, they espouse many beliefs that are politically left-wing," the *Philadelphia Inquirer* reported. At the same time, the *Chicago Tribune* highlighted how the Peace Pentecost's "protests differed from other peace rallies," for "many of the protestors carried signs opposing abortion, a position that does not sit well with mainstream peace organizations and pro-choice women's groups." In an article examining the leading representatives of evangelical progressivism—Sojourners, Evangelicals for Social Action, and the "radical-evangelical magazine" *The Other Side*—the *Wall Street Journal* concluded that progressive evangelicals were difficult to classify, for they "don't fit comfortably anywhere on the modern U.S. political spectrum."[3]

While journalists portrayed the progressive evangelical movement as unusual, spokesmen for the Religious Right condemned its leaders as unorthodox for challenging political conservatism. "I think these men are theological liberals," Moral Majority founder Jerry Falwell said on the eve of Sojourners' Peace Pentecost 1985. "They're entitled to their point of view, but they shouldn't pretend it's an evangelical point of view." Despite this dismissal, Falwell felt threatened enough by the media's attention to progressive evangelicals that he scheduled a press conference to coincide with the end of the their protests. He called demonstrators "pseudo evangelicals" and declared that Jim Wallis "is to evangelicalism what Adolf Hitler was to the Roman Catholic Church." After the event, a spokesman for Falwell assured reporters that Wallis, Evangelicals for Social Action president Ron Sider, and other evangelical progressives "are on the lunatic fringe of the evangelical movement" and "no threat" to the Religious Right's political ascendancy.[4]

Yet the Peace Pentecost protests successfully demonstrated that the progressive evangelical movement represented a viable alternative form of religiously inspired politics. Leaders countered the theological interpretations, political priorities, and partisan proclivities of the Religious Right. But they also broke from the political left by opposing abortion, championing conservative sexual morality, and defending the robust role of religion in public life. As part of Peace Pentecost 1985, evangelical progressives reiterated what they had been proclaiming for well over a decade: the Bible calls Christians to work for a comprehensive vision of social justice that transcends what Wallis described as "the selective and inconsistent morality of both the Right and the Left." While their sympathy for many politically liberal positions infuriated Christian conservatives such as Falwell, leaders insisted that they were not a leftist reaction to the Religious Right. "If we follow the Bible, sometimes that will put us to the left of center and sometimes to the right," Ron Sider argued. "We do not have a left-wing agenda, but a biblical agenda." In fact, Wallis contrasted the Religious Right's role as "court chaplains" for Republicans with progressive evangelicals' own sense of political homelessness. "There's no political option on the landscape that represents our vision and view and values," he claimed. Although their unconventional political agenda left progressive evangelical leaders marginalized in partisan politics, they refused to moderate any part of their stated commitment to defend "the sacred dignity of human life" whenever threatened by "war, poverty, racism, abortion, tyranny, and injustice."[5]

This book describes how and explains why the progressive evangelical movement offered a significant alternative to both the Religious Right and the political left from the 1970s into the twenty-first century. Despite their minority status within American evangelical circles, evangelical progressives forged a dynamic religious and political movement. Through sustained activism, a network of leaders devoted themselves to the common cause of persuading evangelicals and other Christians to prioritize social justice in their public engagement. They published journals, wrote books, organized conferences, issued manifestos, and sought additional means for promoting their ideals. The leadership of and contributors to two organizations—Sojourners and Evangelicals for Social Action—as well as a magazine titled *The Other Side* served as the primary public voices of progressive evangelicalism. Through the writings and activities of these representatives, this book analyzes how the movement's broad political agenda and underlying public theology clashed with both conservatives and liberals, Republicans and Democrats, in America's dualistic partisan politics.

Progressive evangelical leaders constantly framed their partisan independence and their anomalous combination of political positions as marks of biblical faithfulness. "It is essential that we never abandon the search to let biblical norms rather than secular values become the decisive source of our political value judgments," Evangelicals for Social Action president Ron Sider declared. Therefore, he insisted, evangelical progressives have "no commitment to ideologies of left or right." Neither liberals' preoccupation with "peace, justice, and racial equality" nor conservatives' narrow focus on "freedom, family, and the sanctity of human life" faithfully incorporated the "balance of concerns that we see disclosed in the Scriptures," Sider concluded. Instead, because "God seems to be concerned both with peacemaking and the family, both with justice and life," he argued that evangelical progressives must promote "a multi-issue agenda" that straddles the respective platforms of the political left and right. Likewise, Sojourners' Jim Wallis portrayed progressive evangelicalism as "a real alternative in American religious life" to both the "Religious Right and secular left." Though often "unrecognized by the media," Wallis claimed, this movement "relates biblical faith to social transformation; personal conversion to the cry of the poor; theological reflection to care of the environment; core religious values to new economic priorities; the call of community to racial and gender justice; morality to foreign policy; spirituality to politics; and, at its best, transcends the categories of liberal and conservative that have captivated both religion and politics." Indeed, the title of Wallis's 2005 best-selling book *God's Politics: Why the Right Gets It Wrong and the Left Doesn't Get It* epitomized progressive evangelicals' conviction that neither political ideology faithfully reflected "the politics of the Bible." With a vision for public engagement that proved too politically liberal for Christian conservatives yet too theologically and socially conservative for political liberals, progressive evangelical leaders regularly found themselves caught in the crossfire of partisan conflicts and culture war debates.[6]

Contemporary evangelical progressivism is not a historical anomaly. To be sure, over the past several decades many observers and even evangelicals themselves have assumed an inherent connection between conservative theology and political conservatism. The *Los Angeles Times* went so far as to suggest that Jim Wallis seemed an apparent "contradiction in terms" for being "an evangelical Christian who proselytizes progressive politics." But popular perceptions of evangelicals' right-wing predilections do more than miss the diversity within modern evangelicalism; they also ignore the rich record of evangelical progressivism in previous periods of American history. In fact, the sharp decline in evangelicals' social reform activism during the early twentieth century marked a notable departure from previous attitudes and actions—and it was the consequences of this change that the founders of the contemporary progressive evangelical movement hoped to reverse.[7]

Beginning in the early nineteenth century, evangelicals across denominational lines—particularly in the North—participated in numerous progressive and sometimes radical campaigns to combat social problems. Galvanized by periodic waves of religious revivalism, they formed and fueled an array of benevolent societies dedicated to such causes as expanding literacy and enhancing education, championing temperance, advocating prison reforms, promoting peace, alleviating poverty, and opposing slavery. These evangelicals remained dedicated to crusading for personal religious conversions and piety. But they also believed that Christian benevolence required corresponding commitments to improve people's temporal welfare and to redress social problems. In the 1830s the intensity of evangelicals' social activism increased under the influence of Charles Grandison Finney, the leading evangelist of the mid-nineteenth century. Finney promoted the doctrine of "entire sanctification," urging converted Christians to pursue not only a perfected personal life but also a perfected society. "The great business of the church is to reform the world—to put away every kind of sin," he declared. "The church of Christ was originally organized to be a body of reformers," and thus Christians must labor "to reform individuals, communities, and governments ... until every form of iniquity shall be driven from the earth." Finney's influence spread through his revivals and his role as professor and then president at Oberlin College, which became a breeding ground for progressive causes—especially radical abolitionism and women's rights. The commitment to promoting both revivalism and reform also ran strong in Methodist and other evangelical circles. Although not all antebellum evangelicals shared this reformist impulse, compassion for sinful and suffering people led many to join progressive campaigns. "Liberalism on social issues, not reaction, was the dominant note which evangelical preachers sounded before 1860" as they "played a key role in widespread attacks on slavery, poverty, and greed," concluded Timothy Smith in his history of nineteenth-century progressive evangelicalism.[8]

As social problems grew rather than abated with increasing urbanization, industrialization, and immigration in the later nineteenth and early twentieth centuries, evangelical progressivism remained an important force in American public life. Numerous groups continued to combine evangelistic and reform efforts. The establishment in 1850 of New York's Five Points Mission by Phoebe Palmer—the most prominent leader of the holiness movement that spread within Methodism and beyond—inspired hundreds of individual churches and interdenominational societies to develop urban ministries that offered food, clothing, housing, employment assistance, and medical aid. By the turn of the century, notable examples of successful evangelical social work included the broad campaigns of the Salvation Army, the spread of rescue missions through the advocacy of Jerry McAuley and S. H. Hadley, and the urban ministries of the Christian and Missionary Alliance. In working closely with the poor, gospel welfare workers recognized the impoverishing effects of not only individual choices but also oppressive conditions. Therefore, they joined more liberal and secular activists in advocating a wide range of progressive reforms. On a more popular level, Frances Willard, the influential leader of the predominantly evangelical Woman's Christian Temperance Union, broadened the group's reformist causes to include improved public education, prison reforms, support for labor unions, and even endorsement of women's suffrage and ordained religious leadership. In the political realm, no one embodied evangelical progressivism as visibly as William Jennings Bryan. The Democratic presidential candidate in three elections and secretary of state under President Woodrow Wilson, Bryan emphasized the practical and progressive dimensions of evangelical faith. "Christ is not only a guide and friend in all the work that man undertakes," he declared, "but his name can be invoked for the correction of every abuse and the eradication of every evil, in private and public life." Thus Bryan promoted a wide range of populist policies and reforms designed to aid both the common people and the poor, suffering, and oppressed.[9]

While many evangelicals remained politically and socially conservative, these examples demonstrate how evangelical Christianity contains resources—biblical materials and theological traditions—that have inspired progressive activism within particular social and historical contexts. Nineteenth-century progressive evangelicals emphasized biblical commands to love others, especially the poor and oppressed, as well as biblical interpretations of racial and gender egalitarianism. Many Calvinistic evangelicals during this time believed themselves charged by God to exercise control over society, ensuring that it reflected Christian morality and mores. Among those with a Wesleyan heritage, the quest for perfectionism—both personal freedom from sin and practical love of neighbor—also inspired campaigns to sanctify society. Finally, postmillennial expectations common to the majority of nineteenth-century Protestants produced optimism that religious revivals and public reforms would help to inaugurate the anticipated kingdom of God. Most evangelicals thus believed that a "Christian America" required not only the redemption of individuals but also the reformation of society. As part of their own movement, contemporary progressive evangelical leaders discovered in these historical precedents a "usable past" that helped to justify their own activism. For example, from 1974 to 1975 the magazine that became *Sojourners* published a ten-part series on nineteenth-century evangelical progressivism—which became the basis for Donald Dayton's 1976 book *Discovering an Evangelical Heritage*—in order to demonstrate that their progressive political engagement was restoring a venerable but forgotten tradition. "I am a nineteenth-century evangelical born in the wrong century," Jim Wallis regularly declared, for at that time Christians were "fighting for social justice."[10]

In the early twentieth century, however, an individualistic social ethic began to displace most evangelicals' commitment to progressive social reforms. They came to regard the spiritual renewal and moral transformation of individuals as the proper means for reforming the social order as a whole. This shift—what several sympathetic scholars have labeled the "Great Reversal"—occurred in the context of divisive theological controversies. Identifying themselves as "fundamentalists," evangelical leaders defended traditional "fundamentals" of Christianity against theologically liberal "modernists." These Protestant liberals reinterpreted or occasionally rejected historical doctrines in light of new scientific developments and biblical criticisms, and most embraced the Social Gospel movement. Social Gospel advocates emphasized "the sinfulness of the social order" and prioritized progressive reforms of social injustices over individual regeneration, remaining optimistic that such reforms would further the realization of the kingdom of God. Fundamentalists were aghast. They accused Protestant liberals of apostasy and Social Gospel proponents of heresy for belittling the importance of personal conversion. In addition, most fundamentalist evangelicals adopted the recently developed eschatology of premillennial dispensationalism—a pessimistic theology of the end times in which inevitable cultural decline would lead to the "rapture" of true Christians from earth before Jesus returned to defeat "the antichrist" and establish God's millennial kingdom. Thus, fundamentalist evangelicals believed, not only did social reform and political activism threaten to distract from the vital work of personal evangelism, but such efforts also could not stem the social decay that they expected to occur before Jesus's imminent second coming. Ultimately, the association of political progressivism with theological liberalism caused religiously conservative evangelicals to shun both.[11]

By the late 1920s the social reform impulse within evangelicalism had atrophied. Fundamentalist evangelicals largely forgot how previous generations had promoted both evangelism and progressive social concern. To be sure, they remained troubled by social problems and the secularization of American culture. Yet when fundamentalists did attempt to redress social ills, they turned almost exclusively to religious campaigns to redeem individuals through personal spiritual and moral renewal. Unable to vanquish either theological liberalism or secularizing trends in society, fundamentalist evangelicals largely retreated into a separatist subculture and built institutions dedicated to preserving conservative theology and to promoting revivals.[12]

In the mid-twentieth century, a group of fundamentalist leaders grew dissatisfied with this separatism and sought to reengage with the broader American culture. Identifying their movement as the "new evangelicalism" and reclaiming the self-designation of "evangelicals," they wanted to enhance the appeal of theologically conservative Christianity by gaining intellectual respectability and cultural relevancy. Leaders used the newly formed National Association of Evangelicals, the creation of *Christianity Today* magazine, and especially the successful revivals of Billy Graham to build a broad coalition of conservative Protestants under the banner of "evangelicalism." Yet their fundamentalist heritage and zeal for personal conversions continued to relegate social concern to a secondary status. Except for supporting anticommunism, evangelical leaders remained mostly distant from direct political activism in the 1950s and 1960s and primarily devoted themselves to religious issues and winning converts. Confidence in their individualistic social ethic continued to justify the conviction that evangelism itself represented the ultimate expression of social concern. "There is no redeemed society apart from redeemed men," wrote an editor in *Christianity Today* in 1965. "The greatest and most radical solution" to social problems lies in "the transformation of the human heart through the grace and Gospel of the Lord Jesus Christ." Suspicious of progressive reforms, religious conservatives had developed a deep affinity for social and political conservatism as well. As a result, most evangelicals responded coolly to the rising tide of social protests and progressive campaigns in the 1960s and early 1970s.[13]

But beginning in earnest in the mid-1960s, a small group of leaders from within this evangelical network began to reevaluate their attitudes toward social and political activism. A number of theologians, evangelists, and academics produced books that outlined biblical mandates concerning not only evangelism but also social justice and political responsibilities. Most important, two journals dedicated to progressive social action appeared. In 1965 Baptist minister Fred Alexander, his wife, Anne, and his son, John, began publishing *Freedom Now* to confront the blatant racism they perceived in fundamentalist evangelical circles. After several years John Alexander took primary leadership of the magazine, broadened its concern to all forms of injustice and suffering, and changed its name to *The Other Side* in order to identify with the oppressed and marginalized. In 1971 Jim Wallis and several fellow students at Trinity Evangelical Divinity School outside of Chicago formed the People's Christian Coalition and began to publish the *Post-American*. The group protested what members interpreted as American imperialism in Vietnam and the complicity of American Christians in racism and economic injustice. Several years later they renamed both their community and magazine *Sojourners* and moved to Washington, D.C., to live and to minister among the poor. *The Other Side* and the *Post-American* created forums for a growing network of like-minded evangelicals to explore and to promote social justice.

By 1973 evangelicals dedicated to campaigning against injustice and inequalities became a self-conscious minority within larger evangelical circles. Several leading proponents convened a workshop in order to unite sympathizers further and to challenge fellow evangelicals to rebalance commitments to both personal and social transformation. At the 1973 Thanksgiving Workshop on Evangelicals and Social Concern in Chicago, a small group of evangelical leaders came together to draft a statement defending progressive social action and political reform. The resulting Chicago Declaration of Evangelical Social Concern outlined the primary convictions of the emergent movement by including confessions of the evangelical community's sins of omission and commission in areas of justice such as racism, sexism, economic exploitation, and militaristic nationalism. Overall, the endorsers identified social justice as a political imperative. "We call on our fellow evangelical Christians to demonstrate repentance in a Christian discipleship that confronts the social and political injustice of our nation," read the declaration. In an effort to sustain the momentum created by this initial meeting, Ron Sider led the formation of Evangelicals for Social Action, an organization that joined *The Other Side* and Sojourners as the most visible representatives of the progressive evangelical movement. Above all, the Chicago Declaration of Evangelical Social Concern symbolized the coalescence of contemporary evangelical progressivism and marked what signers considered a renewal of evangelicalism's rich tradition of social responsibility and political engagement. To both these leaders and outside observers, the progressive evangelical movement seemed poised to direct the future of evangelicalism in the public sphere.[14]

In the late 1970s, however, a markedly different form of evangelical political engagement arose and quickly overshadowed progressive evangelicalism. Led by a separate, more extensive, and well-financed network of Christian conservatives, the new Religious Right emerged in reaction to perceived attacks on America's "Christian heritage" and traditional "family values." Like progressive evangelicals, leaders of the Religious Right such as the Moral Majority's Jerry Falwell, author Tim LaHaye, and Focus on the Family's James Dobson urged evangelicals to abandon their skepticism of social and political engagement. But these Christian conservatives built their movement not around efforts to redress injustices and inequalities but rather around campaigns to reverse the secularization of public culture and to combat abortion, feminism, and gay rights activism. As they allied themselves with Republican politicians, Religious Right leaders also intensified their dedication to economic conservatism and American militarism. Their support for Ronald Reagan's 1980 presidential election captured the media's attention, and this new visibility and apparent influence of the Religious Right quickly established the popular, long-lasting perception of evangelicals as staunch political conservatives. Though progressive leaders had helped guide evangelicals back to social and political activism, the glare of the Religious Right obscured their movement.[15]

Yet evangelical progressives refused to fade quietly into the background. Leaders consistently vied for attention and promoted their commitment to social justice as the "truly evangelical" alternative to the Religious Right. As early as 1981, for example, Jim Wallis protested that "the public image of evangelicalism in this country is a distortion of the best of that tradition." To be sure, he claimed, the Religious Right's "problem is not in mixing faith and politics" since "biblical faith does have political meaning." But by promoting right-wing ideology and neglecting issues of injustice, the Religious Right betrayed the heritage of evangelical social concern and sullied evangelicals' reputation. In response, Wallis declared, progressive evangelicals "want to restore the true meaning of the word evangelical"—namely, that the ministry and message of Jesus is "good news to all the afflicted"—by "organizing for economic justice, working against racism, standing up for women, and speaking out for peace."[16]

Similarly, in the mid-1990s Wallis, Ron Sider, and prominent progressive evangelical leader Tony Campolo founded Call to Renewal, a network created as an explicit "alternative to the Religious Right" and promoting "the vital link between spiritual renewal and social transformation." Writing in *Sojourners*, Campolo described evangelical progressives as "ideologically homeless" in American religion and politics. "Politically conservative evangelical Christians" have "stolen the 'evangelical' label" and effectively associated it with "right-wing Republicanism," he complained. Wallis leveled similar accusations. "The evangelical Christian movement has been hijacked" by "a combination of fundamentalist preachers and right-wing operatives," he exclaimed. Wallis reiterated that "we do not challenge the Religious Right's 'right' to bring its religious values into the public sphere as some political liberals have." But he contrasted their "ideological" and "partisan" faith with "true evangelical faith" that "transcends the Left and Right." In Call to Renewal's founding statement, progressive evangelical leaders again claimed to move beyond partisan and ideological divisions. "We refuse the false choices between personal responsibility or social justice," "between sexual morality or civil rights for homosexuals, between the sacredness of life or the rights of women, between fighting cultural corrosion or battling racism," they wrote. Even as evangelical progressives defended the Religious Right's appeals to religion in politics against criticism from political liberals, they championed their own anomalous agenda as the biblical ideal.[17]

Although relegated to a modest niche within evangelicalism in the 1980s and 1990s, progressive evangelical leaders began escaping the Religious Right's shadow early in the twenty-first century and recapturing the attention of evangelical audiences, journalists, and even politicians. Prior to the 2004 presidential election, Sojourners widely promoted an advertising campaign titled "God is Not a Republican. Or a Democrat" in which Wallis and other progressive evangelical leaders decried the Religious Right's partisanship. They insisted that Christians must evaluate candidates' positions not only on abortion and gay marriage but also on poverty, peace, racial reconciliation, gender equality, and environmental care. That year Sider helped craft a new statement for the centrist National Association of Evangelicals that pushed evangelicals to include justice for the poor, peacemaking, and environmental stewardship among their civic responsibilities. In 2005 Wallis published *God's Politics: Why the Right Gets It Wrong and the Left Doesn't Get It* and contrasted progressive evangelicals' "prophetic vision of faith and politics" with three groups: "religious right-wingers" who "focus only on sexual and cultural issues while ignoring the weightier issues of justice"; "liberal secularists who want to banish faith from public life"; and "liberal theologians whose cultural conformity and creedal modernity serve to erode the foundations of historic biblical faith." The unexpected success of *God's Politics*—it spent fifteen weeks on the *New York Times'* best-seller list—propelled Wallis into the public eye and opened new opportunities. In addition to many speaking engagements for evangelical and ecumenical audiences, Wallis appeared on Jon Stewart's *The Daily Show*, addressed meetings of Democratic politicians eager to understand religious voters after their recent defeat, and met with international political leaders at annual meetings of the World Economic Forum in Davos, Switzerland. Newspapers ran profiles of Wallis with headlines such as "The Amazing True Story of the Liberal Evangelical" and "The Gospel According to Jim Wallis." Other media outlets featured interviews with Sider and Campolo and reported on the growing concern among evangelicals—especially those under age thirty—for social justice issues.[18]

By the 2008 presidential election season, the progressive evangelical movement had moved into the limelight for the first time in over three decades. Sojourners hosted a CNN forum on faith and politics for the leading Democratic candidates (Republican candidates declined a similar invitation). Wallis released another popular book: *The Great Awakening: Reviving Faith and Politics in Post-Religious Right America.* "During the years dominated by the Religious Right, a 'progressive evangelical' was thought to be a misnomer," he boasted. "But now a new generation of evangelical students and pastors" want "to reunite faith and social justice." Several younger leaders emerged as public faces for the movement, including urban activist Shane Claiborne, *Time* magazine editor Amy Sullivan, and antipoverty advocate Lisa Sharon Harper. Tony Campolo spearheaded another strategic initiative—a new group calling itself "Red Letter Christians"—that brought together these younger representatives with veterans such as Wallis, Sider, emergent church leader Brian McLaren, and Columbia University professor Randall Balmer. Claiming faithfulness to the biblical words of Jesus often printed in red, Red Letter Christians "share an evangelical theology," a "passionate commitment to social justice," and the desire "to avoid partisan politics," wrote Campolo. While journalists highlighted progressive evangelicals' activism during the campaign, leaders received even more attention after Barack Obama's election. Wallis, who had developed a friendship with Obama over the previous decade, and Florida megachurch pastor Joel Hunter joined a small group of spiritual advisers to the new president. In addition, the new Obama administration began regularly consulting other evangelical progressives such as Mercer University scholar-activist David Gushee. "This is a new experience for me," Wallis admitted to a reporter. "I've been forty years in the wilderness, and now it's time to come out." No longer did progressive evangelical leaders toil far from the spotlight. Never had they been in such demand.[19]

While the progressive evangelical movement did not supplant the Religious Right in terms of influence and visibility, popular perceptions of evangelical political engagement began more accurately to reflect its complex and contested nature. Not all theological conservatives were political conservatives. Evangelicals did not monolithically support Republican agendas. And sizable number of evangelicals cared as much about addressing poverty, promoting peace, protecting the environment, and defending human rights as they did about abortion and same-sex marriage. In its list of the top religion stories of 2008, *Time* described the apparent move of many evangelicals away from "the narrow concerns of the Religious Right" as "the birth of the new evangelicalism." Yet the magazine also acknowledged the historical background to this development. "For decades," *Time* noted, "leaders like Jim Wallis, Tony Campolo, and Ron

Sider have pressed their movement to extend its concern beyond classic issues of individual sin" and to promote social justice. Thus the broadened appeal of progressive evangelicalism may have been novel, but the movement itself had provided a passionate and principled yet underappreciated alternative to both the Religious Right and the political left since the early 1970s. This book tells that story.[20]

🕮 This study draws upon the publications and activities of the three most prominent progressive evangelical voices over the past four decades: Sojourners, Evangelicals for Social Action (ESA), and *The Other Side*. Several factors make these two organizations and *The Other Side* effective lenses through which to analyze the development, activism, and animating political philosophy of the contemporary progressive evangelical movement. First, each of these representatives dates to the movement's formative period. *The Other Side*, started as *Freedom Now* in 1965, and *Sojourners*, founded as the *Post-American* in 1971, contributed to the rise of the progressive evangelical movement by offering forums that brought together early leaders and promoted their arguments. ESA formed following the 1973 Thanksgiving Workshop on Evangelicals and Social Concern, a meeting that marked the self-conscious emergence of contemporary evangelical progressivism.

Second, the leaders of and contributors to *The Other Side*, Sojourners, and ESA played central, long-standing roles in organizing and promoting progressive evangelicalism. Many of those affiliated with these groups—including *The Other Side*'s editor John Alexander, Sojourners' head Jim Wallis, and ESA president Ron Sider—helped to coordinate the early collaborative efforts that culminated in the 1973 Thanksgiving Workshop. Along with longtime collaborator Tony Campolo, Wallis and Sider served as the most visible faces of the progressive evangelical movement for well over three decades. In addition to the respective platforms provided by *Sojourners* and ESA's publications, Wallis and Sider wrote popular books, coordinated campaigns, made public appearances, and garnered media attention in efforts to promote progressive evangelical concerns.

Third, Sojourners, *The Other Side*, and ESA produced the most regular and most recognized publications of the movement. After beginning as the *Post-American* in 1971, *Sojourners* became the premier journal of progressive evangelicalism by the end of the decade. The magazine's popularity waxed and waned, with *Sojourners* having its greatest appeal as a counterweight to the prominence of the Religious Right during Republican presidential administrations. Subscriptions rose through the 1970s to almost 40,000; peaked near 60,000 in the mid-1980s; fell to below 25,000 in the late 1990s; and then rebounded to over 45,000 by 2006. In 2013 Sojourners as an organization claimed to reach "more than 1.5 million readers annually in print, online, and email." *The Other Side* began in 1965, under the title *Freedom Now*, as the earliest progressive evangelical journal. While surpassed in prominence by *Sojourners* in the mid-1970s, *The Other Side* remained an important organ for progressive Christians committed to "justice rooted in discipleship" (as the journal's subtitled proclaimed). Subscriptions reached over 16,000 in the early 1980s before settling between 11,000 and 14,000 for the next two decades. As a result of both internal tensions and the financial pressures faced by small, independent publications, however, *The Other Side* ceased publication in 2004. After ESA's origin in 1973 it hosted a series of national workshops before beginning to publish newsletters in 1980 and its own magazine, *Prism*, in 1993. Although ESA's publications never reached a large number beyond its modest membership, the organization exercised influence through separate activities such as hosting workshops on world hunger in the late 1970s, promoting peace efforts and nuclear disarmament in the 1980s, coordinating campaigns against South African apartheid, and helping launch the Evangelical Environmental Network in the 1990s. Most important, the speaking engagements and popular publications by Ron Sider widely disseminated ESA's convictions. Other journals, such as *Right On* and the *Reformed Journal* in the 1970s, and organizations, such as the Association (later Center) for Public Justice beginning in the 1980s, also promoted progressive evangelical perspectives. Yet *Sojourners*, *The Other Side*, and ESA's corpus constituted the movement's longest running, most visible publications.[21]

Finally, a focus on these three representatives reveals progressive evangelicalism as a coherent yet complex religious movement. Like the broader evangelical tradition, the progressive evangelical movement represented an unofficial network of organizations and individuals loosely united by common convictions and cooperative campaigns. While those affiliated with Sojourners, *The Other Side*, and ESA saw themselves as partners in promoting social justice, differences arose in both style and substance. In the 1970s Sojourners and Wallis embraced the fiery language and critiques of the New Left and identified as "radical evangelicals." Even as they adopted a more moderate tone and softened stance toward the United States and its political system, Wallis continued to promote an aggressive brand of "prophetic politics," standing on the margins of mainstream evangelicalism and calling the perceived wayward majority back to "faithful" public engagement. *The Other Side* also published provocative articles, but its editors and authors devoted more attention to integrating personal faith and social justice. At the center of progressive evangelical circles through the mid-1980s, *The Other Side* moved away from its evangelical roots and catered to more ecumenical audiences in the decade before its demise in 2004. ESA remained the most explicitly evangelical group, as its intentional retention of the label "evangelical" suggests. While Wallis was the prophet of progressive evangelicalism, Ron Sider served as its pastor. Under his irenic leadership, ESA sought to work from within mainstream evangelicalism and shepherd the evangelical majority toward progressive political positions. Sider published his books with evangelical presses, wrote as a contributing editor for *Christianity Today*, and attempted more than any other progressive leader to build bridges with the Religious Right. While occasionally frustrating to other evangelical progressives, Sider's measured tones, adoption of some centrist positions, and collaboration with more conservative evangelicals established his identity as the most moderate progressive evangelical leader.

In terms of substance, these leading progressive evangelical voices readily united against racism, sexism, economic injustice, and American militarism. But different biblical interpretations and political strategies produced conflicting responses to abortion and homosexuality, two of the primary issues that differentiated them from the political left. Sojourners and ESA each adopted a "completely pro-life" position but differed with respect to legislative restrictions on abortion. In addition, while both defended the civil rights of gays and lesbians, they concluded that God did not condone same-sex behavior. In contrast to ESA, however, Sojourners muted its position in reaction to criticism from ecumenical supporters and instead promoted dialogue between Christians who disagreed about the morality of covenantal gay and lesbian unions. *The Other Side* broke with Sojourners and ESA on each issue. Regarding abortion as morally ambiguous, its editors refused to identify as either pro-life or pro-choice. *The Other Side* also came to affirm the committed unions of gay and lesbian Christians. By analyzing these internal differences, this study demonstrates the dynamic, multivocal nature of the progressive evangelical movement.

I primarily use the labels "progressive evangelicals" or "evangelical progressives" for leaders of this movement to indicate the combination of their religious identity and political orientation. As evangelicals, the leaders of Sojourners, ESA, and *The Other Side* affirmed a core set of defining theological principles—the primacy of biblical authority, the need for personal conversion and faith in Jesus's atoning work, and a dedication to evangelistic and humanitarian efforts. Throughout their movement's history, progressive leaders' consistent appeals to biblical interpretations as the foundation for their political activism reflected evangelicals' hallmark commitment to the primary authority of the Bible. In addition, these evangelical progressives emerged from within the transdenominational network of theologically conservative Protestants who broke from the separatist subculture of fundamentalism in the mid-twentieth century and adopted the self-identity of "evangelical." As evidenced by the 1973 Chicago Declaration of Evangelical Social Concern, early leaders viewed themselves as reformers within the broader evangelical movement. *The Other Side* explicitly embraced the evangelical label into the 1980s. After John Alexander's resignation as editor in 1984, the journal increasingly incorporated more theologically liberal perspectives and described itself as an "evangelical and ecumenical magazine" through 1988. Subsequently, however, *The Other Side* characterized itself as an "ecumenical magazine" with "deep roots in the evangelical Christian tradition." Even as a few self-identified evangelicals occasionally contributed articles, *The Other Side* had little if any affiliation with the broader evangelical movement over the final decade of its publication.[22]

The leaders of Sojourners and ESA never ceased trumpeting their evangelical identity. "There has never been a doubt that I am an evangelical," asserted Jim Wallis in a 2008 interview with *Christianity Today*. Under his leadership, he argued, Sojourners remained "committed to the central lordship of Jesus Christ and the authority of the Scriptures." At a conference celebrating ESA's thirtieth anniversary, Ron Sider declared, "I am not a social activist. I'm a disciple of Jesus Christ"—a statement intended to demonstrate that his evangelical identity took precedence over and shaped his vocation. "When new opportunities as an evangelical social activist opened up," Sider stated, he committed himself to "grounding my social activism in historic Christian faith and maintaining a strong passion for evangelism." The evangelical credentials of prominent leaders such as Wallis and Sider were displayed in 2008 when centrist evangelicals invited them to join as charter signatories of "An Evangelical Manifesto," a document proclaiming that "evangelicals must be defined theologically and not politically" and are "never completely equated with any party" or "partisan ideology." Though Jerry Falwell and other leaders of the Religious Right periodically charged that their left-leaning politics discredited their evangelical identity, progressive leaders stood within the evangelical tradition.[23]

The designation "progressive" for these evangelicals reflects their foundational commitment to social, political, and economic reforms of injustices and inequalities. At the beginning of their activism in the 1970s, both participants and observers often described the larger movement as "young evangelicals" and Sojourners and The Other Side in particular as "radical evangelicals." By the 1980s, however, these initial designations disappeared as the movement's leadership grew older and radicalism lost its appeal. Sojourners and Wallis in particular accepted pragmatic support for populist and progressive politics, even as they criticized existing political structures and ideologies. In the mid-1990s some leaders as well as journalists began adopting the term "progressive" to describe the movement's distinctive political commitment to social justice and substantive equality for the poor, oppressed, and marginalized. Tony Campolo offered an incisive self-description of the movement soon after joining Wallis and Ron Sider in forming the Call to Renewal network. "We define ourselves as being theologically orthodox but with a progressive social agenda," he wrote in Sojourners, for they "focused on ending racism, sexism, militarism, poverty, and political injustices." Wallis retroactively embraced the description for his whole career as a social justice advocate. "I have always been a progressive evangelical," he claimed in 2008, and he pointed to signs of increased commitment to social justice among young evangelicals as evidence of a renewed progressive evangelical movement.[24]

Journalists and scholars have used "liberal evangelicals," "evangelical left," "Christian left," or "Religious Left" in order to contrast the movement to the Religious Right. And critics within the Religious Right gleefully branded progressive evangelicals as "left" or "liberals" in an effort to discredit them among evangelicals firmly committed to both religious and political conservatism. Yet leaders, especially Wallis, chafed at these descriptions. Because they claimed to promote "biblical" politics that challenged and transcended both the political right and the political left, it remained symbolically and substantively important for progressive evangelicals to resist any suggestion that they were ideologically and politically partisan—the very sin they accused the Religious Right of committing. "People of faith should not be in any party's pockets," Wallis argued. "The Religious Right was a political party, not a religious one. There should not now be a Religious Left." Therefore Wallis explicitly disowned that label. "There is a Religious Left in this country, and I'm not part of it," he insisted to *Christianity Today*. Likewise, Tony Campolo explained the purpose of the Red Letter Christian network as "*not* to create a Religious Left movement to challenge the Religious Right, but to jump-start a religious movement that will transcend partisan politics." Despite such denials, those affiliated with and supportive of Sojourners, ESA, and *The Other Side* have clearly occupied the left side of the evangelical political spectrum since the early 1970s. Their focus on social justice issues traditionally associated with political liberals and their sympathies for left-leaning policies to address these problems produced affinities for the political left. The label "progressive evangelical" has the advantage of respecting the movement's detachment from both the broader *political* left and right. But on a relative map of political engagement *within* evangelicalism, progressive evangelicals operated on the left. At times, therefore, I also describe their movement as representative of "the evangelical left."[25]

While Wallis, Campolo, and other leaders eschewed identification with the Religious Left, progressive evangelicals did often partner with left-leaning Catholics, mainline Protestants, black Christians, and Jewish groups. Such cooperation mirrored that of evangelical leaders of the Religious Right who allied themselves with politically conservative Catholics and Jews. Spurned by the majority within their own religious tradition, the evangelical left regularly collaborated with other religious leaders who shared their social and political agendas. By the end of the 1970s, both *Sojourners* and *The Other Side* began drawing upon ecumenical authors and attracting readers from across Christian traditions. "We are not merely or uniquely an evangelical magazine," *Sojourners'* editors stated. "There will continue to be those who write for and read *Sojourners* who are deeply Christian but may well be non-evangelical." Associate editor Wes Michaelson explained that "the deep failure of the modern evangelical tradition" regarding the proper way "to relate the gospel to political and social realities" left progressive evangelicals searching for other examples. They especially found inspiration in the rich tradition of Catholic social teaching and champions such as Dorothy Day and peace activists Daniel Berrigan and Philip Berrigan (who became contributors to the magazine). "*Sojourners* is still clearly evangelical, but now, one would say, in both the Protestant and Catholic traditions," Wallis wrote in 1981. *The Other Side* also increasingly added non-evangelical Christian contributors, and by the 1990s articles by mainline Protestants exceeded those from the remaining evangelical contributors to the magazine. Even ESA, despite the exclusively evangelical perspective of its publications, joined like-minded Catholics and mainline Protestants in several public campaigns. In its analysis of the progressive evangelical movement's *political* engagement, this book includes articles by non-evangelical contributors to *Sojourners* and *The Other Side* as illustrative of the evangelical left's positions. In analyzing the movement's *theological* foundations, however, this study uses only publications by progressive evangelical leaders themselves.[26]

🕮 This book offers both a thematic history of contemporary progressive evangelicalism and an analysis of the distinctive theological convictions that shaped the movement's public engagement and political positions. I argue that leaders developed an implicit political philosophy—what I label the movement's "public theology of community"—that inspired and integrated their anomalous political agenda and placed the progressive evangelical movement at odds with both the Religious Right and the political left. First, chapter 1 recounts the rise of the contemporary progressive evangelical movement. Influenced by the civil rights movement and the New Left's radical protests, a vanguard of evangelical leaders began to reclaim social concern as a biblical imperative. Two journals—*The Other Side* and the *Post-American*—popularized calls for evangelicals to address social problems not merely through evangelism and individual charity but also through political reforms of injustice. These magazines attracted influential evangelists, academics, and theologians and fostered a network of pioneering progressive evangelicals. Collaborative efforts by these leaders culminated at a workshop in 1973 that issued the Chicago Declaration of Evangelical Social Concern, a manifesto that articulated the core commitment of the emerging evangelical left to combat all forms of injustice.

In chapter 2, I identify and analyze progressive evangelicals' underlying public theology—that is, their theologically and biblically based political philosophy—that held together their unusual combination of political positions. To be clear: this implicit public theology emerged in the course of, not prior to, progressive evangelicals' activism. Leaders did not begin their movement with a systematic theology for public life, and they rarely appealed to the larger framework of their public theology in promoting specific political positions and public policies. Nevertheless, they operated with an inchoate set of biblical interpretations concerning social justice and political ideals. As the progressive evangelical movement matured, leaders such as Jim Wallis and especially Ron Sider devoted more sustained attention to articulating and even to systematizing the theological framework for their public and political praxis. Primarily drawing upon these later works, this chapter summarizes the biblical principles and paradigms that progressive evangelicals determined should guide Christians' public engagement. Because leaders believed that the biblical connotations of community set the terms for justice in the public sphere, I argue that their operative political philosophy represented a "public theology of community." Progressive evangelicals concluded that people have not only individual rights but also communal responsibilities for the common good. Biblical expectations for social justice dictate that all community members have the right to access socioeconomic goods necessary for substantively equal opportunities in communal life. Such access requires that a community fairly allocate its resources, and progressive evangelical leaders concluded that the state—as the organized political community— should promote social justice by encouraging such just distribution. By developing this public theology of community, progressive evangelical leaders became part of larger philosophical debates. They called into question the individualistic foundations and secular expectations of forms of political liberalism associated with advocates ranging from John Locke to John Rawls. Although progressive evangelicals painted themselves as the alternative to the Religious Right, both groups rejected the secularist impulse of the political left.

The majority of the book then comprises chapters that examine how the leaders of Sojourners, ESA, and *The Other Side* responded to pressing social and political issues: racism (chapter 3), feminism (chapter 4), abortion (chapter 5), homosexuality (chapter 6), poverty (chapter 7), and American nationalism and militarism (chapter 8). Within each of these thematic chapters, I adopt a chronological approach in order to interpret the evolving and on occasion conflicting positions of these progressive evangelical representatives from the 1970s into the twenty-first century. I demonstrate how their public theology and dedication to social justice for *all* community members—especially the poor, marginalized, and victimized—underlay and unified progressive evangelicals' respective positions on these social and political issues.

Because in this book I have limited my analysis to the political concerns that most consistently occupied progressive evangelical leaders since the 1970s, I have not devoted a chapter to environmental issues—what many leaders have broadly labeled "creation care." Over the past two decades, progressive evangelicals have further distinguished themselves from the Religious Right by supporting legislative restrictions and political policies designed to protect the environment, care for endangered species, and combat global warming. Ron Sider and ESA helped to launch the Evangelical Environmental Network in 1993, and Jim Wallis and Sojourners also became outspoken advocates for environmental stewardship. Their evolving commitment to environmentalism as a matter of social justice underscores the continued development and broad agenda of evangelical progressivism—a point to which I return briefly in the epilogue.[27]

⊛ Although the overwhelming majority of citizens firmly support the institutional separation of church and state, American politics remain awash in a sea of faith. This book focuses on the complex and contested nature of evangelicals' political engagement, but it also points to the broader salience of religion in the public sphere. Most Americans have not embraced the distinctive combination of theological positions and political proposals advanced by progressive evangelical leaders. Nevertheless, these leaders' public theology of community and dedication to the common good have represented constructive contributions to ongoing debates—both moral and political in nature—concerning the proper balance between individual rights and communal responsibilities in our liberal democracy.

1. The Rise of the Contemporary Progressive Evangelical Movement

Over the Thanksgiving weekend of 1973, a small group of evangelical leaders gathered at the hotel of Chicago's Wabash Avenue YMCA for an unconventional workshop. Their goal—drafting a statement that declared Christians' responsibilities for social action and reform—distinguished participants as a self-conscious minority within the broader evangelical movement. They rejected the prevailing view that Christians should primarily address people's eternal spiritual welfare and social problems through evangelism. Instead, these evangelicals believed that faithfulness to the Bible requires equal concern for people's temporal needs and the pursuit of justice through social and political activism. At the end of the workshop, participants issued a document—the Chicago Declaration of Evangelical Social Concern—that they hoped would change the course of evangelicals' public engagement.

As an evangelical manifesto, the Chicago Declaration was remarkable for its time. The statement called American evangelicals to confession and repentance for failing to confront "social and political injustice." Endorsers acknowledged dissonance between God's love and justice and evangelicals' own apathy toward "those suffering social abuses"— the poor, the oppressed, and racial minorities. In addition to identifying American society as unjust, the declaration criticized evangelicals' complicity in both economic exploitation and militaristic nationalism that compounded global suffering and violence. Endorsers also confessed evangelicals' wrongful support of male domination and female passivity, calling instead for "mutual submission." Thus the overwhelming thrust of the Chicago Declaration centered upon a summons to public engagement on behalf of progressive political and social reforms. Both the tenor and vocabulary pointedly countered the narrow religious preoccupation, apolitical inclinations, and conservative orientation characteristic of most evangelicals. Embodying the core convictions of contemporary progressive evangelicalism, the Chicago Declaration captured the vision of a new movement of evangelicals committed to social justice and progressive politics.[1]

Publication of the 1973 Chicago Declaration culminated the pioneering efforts of early progressive evangelical leaders. Beginning in earnest in the mid-1960s, a vanguard of activists, evangelists, academics, and theologians began to criticize evangelicals' lack of social concern and public engagement. Through magazines, books, conferences, and even political activism, they urged evangelical audiences to fulfill the biblical mandate to promote social justice. In particular, two journals—*The Other Side* and the *Post-American*—became nuclei in the emerging progressive evangelical movement by establishing popular forums for its ideals and attracting sympathetic advocates. The editors and contributors to these journals propelled the rise of contemporary evangelical progressivism by attempting to reform evangelicals' social and political perspectives. Over the previous half century, and in contrast to more liberal Protestants inspired by the Social Gospel movement, evangelicals had channeled almost all of their energies into evangelistic and religious campaigns. While most were not indifferent to social problems, they believed that authentic social change would come only through the spiritual redemption and moral transformation of individuals. Politics seemed to affect only temporal matters and potentially distracted from the more urgent task of saving souls, and thus evangelicals largely eschewed political activism beyond general support for conservative politicians and anticommunism. Yet pioneering progressive evangelicals regarded this religious preoccupation, individualistic social ethic, and apolitical conservatism as unbiblical. They insisted that the Bible calls Christians to forms of public engagement that directly address social problems and advance social justice—tasks, leaders argued, that requires progressive political participation. As *The Other Side* and the *Post-American* popularized these arguments and attracted influential supporters, a network of progressive evangelical leaders emerged in the early 1970s. Their collaborative efforts led to the 1973 Thanksgiving workshop, and the resultant Chicago Declaration of Evangelical Social Concern established the progressive evangelical movement as a recognizable faction within American evangelicalism. While the thunderous rise of the Religious Right at the end of the decade attracted more attention and support, a small coalition of evangelical progressives coordinated the first campaigns to push evangelicals back into the political sphere.

MAGAZINES FOR A MOVEMENT

Two magazines—*The Other Side* and the *Post-American*—played central roles in the rise and trajectory of contemporary progressive evangelicalism. Leaders of social, political, and religious movements regularly create journals in order to disseminate their beliefs and to forge a common sense of purpose and identity among participants. During the twentieth century, notable examples of such religious periodicals included the *Christian Century*, the flagship magazine of mainline Protestantism; *Christianity and Crisis*, founded by Reinhold Niebuhr as a journal of religious and political opinion for Protestant liberals; *Commonweal*, the voice of progressive Catholic public intellectuals; and, more recently, *First Things*, a neoconservative journal uniting like-minded Catholics, Protestants, and Jews. Within modern evangelicalism itself, the most prominent magazine, *Christianity Today*, began as a strategic effort of "new evangelical" leaders to strengthen their movement and to distinguish it from fundamentalist evangelicalism in the mid-twentieth century. While most of these magazines never reached vast numbers of readers, they nevertheless exercised influence in two important respects: these journals positioned themselves as the public voices of their respective movements, and they attracted clergy and lay leaders to their religious and political positions. In the late 1960s and early 1970s, *The Other Side* (founded as *Freedom Now*) and the *Post-American* began to assume this role for progressive evangelicalism. These magazines popularized calls for social justice, brought together a network of advocates for progressive political participation, and offered supporters a sense of shared identity. Thus close inspection of the emergence and evolution of *The Other Side* and the *Post-American* offers insight into the rise of contemporary evangelical progressivism. Other journals such as *Right On*, published by the leftist Christian World Liberation Front, and the scholarly *Reformed Journal* also promoted progressive forms of evangelical public engagement. Yet *The Other Side* and the *Post-American* attracted the most attention and retained reputations as vital organs for evangelical progressivism. Through their regular publication and growing popularity, the two journals served as midwives for the progressive evangelical movement.[2]

Freedom Now for *The Other Side*

By the mid-1960s, Fred Alexander, a pastor in the conservative General Association of Regular Baptists, believed that the times were certainly changing. As a younger fundamentalist evangelical in the early twentieth century, Alexander had regarded attacks by liberal Protestants on traditional interpretations of the Bible as evangelicals' greatest threat. "The problem of the church thirty years ago was theological—proper Biblical doctrine," he wrote. But now Alexander concluded that theologically conservative Christians faced a more pressing "practical" problem: "the proper application of Biblical doctrine to human relations, especially racial relations." Alexander became convinced that whites must demonstrate love for others not only through evangelistic programs but also through practical actions that alleviated racial inequalities. He lamented most evangelicals' lukewarm or even antagonistic reactions to the civil rights movement as a failure before both God and their black neighbors. In response, Fred, his wife, Anne, and their son, John, began in 1965 to publish *Freedom Now*, a twelve-page newsletter designed to convince fundamentalist evangelicals to support blacks' civil rights and equal opportunities as part of their Christian discipleship. Although many liberal Christian leaders had already mobilized for such reform, the majority of evangelicals still believed that social or political activism—including the civil rights movement—distracted and thus undermined the church's foremost task of evangelism. Yet the Alexanders refused to accept that Christians could justifiably address spiritual privation while neglecting physical and economic problems. "To practice the whole gospel of Jesus Christ means, we believe, to have integration, to remove all forms of discrimination, to improve educational facilities, and to fight poverty," Fred Alexander wrote in *Freedom Now*'s initial issue. Over the next several years, the Alexanders' modest newsletter evolved into a provocative magazine. While fundamentalist evangelicals rejected the Alexanders' message, the journal found support among a small but growing group of more socially engaged evangelicals. In the process, *Freedom Now* and its successor *The Other Side* became a leading forum for evangelical opposition to all forms of injustice, enhancing both the appeal and momentum of the nascent progressive evangelical movement.[3]

Personal exposure to the plight of African Americans transformed the Alexanders' interpretation of Christian social ethics. In the early 1960s Fred Alexander began teaching at a black Bible college and moved into an integrated neighborhood in Cleveland, Ohio. His growing awareness of racial inequalities and the inspiration of civil rights leaders led him to reevaluate the standard evangelical belief that religious conversions and moral reforms of individuals would solve socioeconomic problems. "I must confess that most of my life I have isolated Christian responsibility from everything but soul winning and direct Christian activity," he reflected. "I have honestly believed that all we need to do is lead people to Christ and build them up in the faith, and everything else would automatically fall into place." Yet the elder Alexander discovered that a sole focus on evangelism and religious training did little to lessen blacks' inequality; in fact, it allowed evangelicals to "claim an interest in a man's soul" but "neglect his physical welfare." John Alexander reached a similar conclusion. As a student at the evangelical Trinity College in the early 1960s, he became disillusioned with his peers' preoccupation with "winning souls" to the neglect of meeting people's urgent physical needs. After graduating and working with his father for several years, John moved to Chicago to begin graduate work in philosophy at Northwestern University and to teach at one of evangelicalism's premier institutions, Wheaton College. Together the Alexanders hoped to challenge white evangelicals' apparent apathy and naïveté regarding social problems through publishing a periodical.[4]

The journal's title, *Freedom Now*, alluded to Martin Luther King Jr.'s criticism of gradualist approaches to integration and civil rights adopted by many evangelicals, including the celebrated evangelist Billy Graham. But the Alexanders also intended the title to underscore that blacks needed more than eventual religious salvation—they needed immediate deliverance from social and economic problems. To be sure, Fred Alexander explained in the initial issue, "salvation through Jesus Christ" remained the only means to true, eternal freedom. But "the simple message of salvation" would not end segregation and racial injustices. Expeditious rather than eventual freedom from such social problems required the application of "the whole gospel" to "every phase of an individual's life, not just the 'religious' phase." From the magazine's outset, the Alexanders promoted their interpretation of the Christian gospel as both the answer to individual sin and a summons to active social concern.[5]

Because evangelicals associated a commitment to social reform with the heresies of the Social Gospel, early contributors to *Freedom Now* took great pains to distinguish themselves from liberal Protestants who described the purpose of evangelism and salvation in terms of social justice rather than spiritual redemption. The Alexanders insisted that they were neither promoting social action at the expense of evangelism nor conflating the two. "Surely the gospel of Jesus Christ is partly social," Fred Alexander argued, for "being born again means being born again in the whole man, political, social, economical, personal, etc." The editors used the liberal National Council of Churches (NCC) as a foil by quoting one of its officials: "Salvation has more to do with the whole society than with the individual soul," stated the NCC's head of evangelism, and "it is for this reason that contemporary evangelism is moving away from winning souls one by one to the evangelism of the structure of society." The Alexanders unequivocally condemned the NCC's position. Yet they also insisted that such expressions of the Social Gospel did not nullify a *proper* biblical regard for social action. "Because some men confuse social concern with evangelism does not make social concern evil any more than it makes evangelism evil," they argued. "Because they have let the pendulum swing too far in one direction does not mean that we should let it swing too far in the other direction." Yet the editors knew they faced an uphill battle. John Alexander complained that lingering backlash against the Social Gospel and the consequent concentration on spiritual issues made it "very common to hear evangelicals say that social, political, and economic problems have nothing to do with Christianity." According to *Freedom Now*, anxiety about the Social Gospel had become a red herring that prevented evangelicals from rightly expressing love of others through practical social concern.[6]

Although the magazine pressed readers to confront social problems, the legacy of fundamentalist evangelicals' individualistic social ethic initially restricted *Freedom Now*'s own recommended responses. Until early 1968 the magazine largely proposed conservative strategies for social change that depended upon personal transformations rather than on political reforms or public policies. If readers had biblically accurate racial views and deepened familiarity with blacks' experiences, the Alexanders assumed, then they would take individual initiatives to improve African Americans' welfare. Thus the editors printed several exegetical articles that debunked interpretations of the Bible used to support blacks' subordination and segregation.[7] As practical suggestions, *Freedom Now* urged actions such as building friendships with blacks, reading books such as *Black Like Me* by John Howard Griffin, joining the NAACP, and even subscribing to

Ebony magazine. John Alexander also pushed readers to accept considerable blame for African Americans' socioeconomic inequalities. "The reason Negroes have so many problems is precisely because whites have treated them so wretchedly," he wrote. "First we broke their legs, and now we criticize them for limping." Therefore, Alexander expected evangelicals to repent and to take personal responsibility for helping blacks. A few articles did express support for civil rights legislation and protest demonstrations, but early issues of *Freedom Now* focused primarily on reforming Christians' personal beliefs and behaviors that hindered a balanced concern for blacks' spiritual and physical needs. While this broad commitment to social concern and relieving the plight of African Americans marked a departure from most evangelicals' reluctance to support the civil rights movement, these proposals revealed that the Alexanders still viewed personal reforms as sufficient for social change.[8]

Coverage of Martin Luther King Jr.'s assassination in April 1968 marked a turning point in *Freedom Now*'s prescriptions for social action. Following King's death, the editors began offering unequivocal support for civil rights activism and efforts to change social structures. "The time for polite discussion is past," John Alexander wrote. He called upon not only individual readers but also their denominations and political parties "to become involved in a massive action program." The editors admitted that they now viewed most of *Freedom Now*'s previous proposals as far too narrow and inadequate—they "had been fiddling while Rome burned," John Alexander regretted. The memorial issue on King marked the beginning of a more aggressive tone and signaled two critical developments in the progressive orientation of *Freedom Now*.[9]

First, the framework and language of justice began to supersede that of love as the foundation for social concern. In the magazine's earliest years, articles primarily invoked Jesus's command to love one's neighbors as the basis for supporting blacks' civil rights.[10] After King's assassination, *Freedom Now* increasingly appealed to the ideal of social justice. Bill Pannell, a black evangelist with Youth for Christ and contributing editor to the magazine, remembered that as a younger fundamentalist evangelical he "had been schooled to decry any suggestion of the social implication of the Gospel." But King's activist example persuaded him that the Bible taught not only loving reconciliation between individuals but also expectations for a just society. "I began to see that the issue was not love, but justice, and that one is false to the Gospel if he dares preach one concept to the exclusion of the other," wrote Pannell. Likewise, Fred

Alexander renounced his previous criticism of King's confrontational tactics and now agreed that "things like justice and freedom are more important than peace." He pledged to emulate King by protesting against anyone "who is practicing injustice." Building upon these articles, *Freedom Now* proclaimed that Christians must do more than offer personal acts and attitudes of love—they must also seek justice through social reforms. Although he normally "opposed everything the [liberal] World Council of Churches stands for," John Alexander affirmed their statement that "Christian responsibility" may include "revolutionary action to achieve a radical change of social structures or of the political regime" in order "to arrive at a social order based on greater justice." *Freedom Now* soon devoted an issue to the theme "The Old Testament in Today's Society," claiming that evangelicals had neglected for too long guidelines for a just society in the Mosaic laws and Hebrew prophets. "We must make it very clear to those who say Christianity has little to say to society" that they "are in disobedience to God's Word," John Alexander wrote. Thus *Freedom Now* began championing the progressive evangelical conviction that Christians cannot truly express love for others without working for social justice.[11]

This dedication to a just society led to a second development in *Freedom Now*: advocacy for evangelicals' broad political engagement. The magazine previously concentrated on religious and relational obligations, but editors and contributors began promoting evangelicals' political responsibilities for furthering justice. Christians must measure social conditions and public policies by biblical standards of justice, authors argued, and effective reforms of injustices require political activism. Christians should be "judging America by God's Word," Fred Alexander declared, "and then helping it live up to its dream." Indicative of this shift, the editors dedicated the entire September–October 1968 issue to political matters, with articles on the presidential election, the relationship between church and state, and an extended interview with evangelical senator Mark Hatfield of Oregon about his progressive politics. "Members of the church are also members of the state, and as such they must fulfill their responsibilities in the state and not isolate themselves from it entirely," John Alexander claimed. In subsequent issues, authors presented defenses of active political engagement that ranged from descriptions of biblical mandates for "responsible participation in human society" to assurances that Christians who worked for political reforms were not disobeying the Bible by undermining "law and order."[12]

To mainline and liberal Protestants outside of the evangelical subculture, such arguments would have sounded quaint. They had long taken for granted that their Christian faith entailed public responsibilities, and journals such as the *Christian Century* and *Christianity and Crisis* regularly published political analyses and opinions. But the Alexanders recognized that evangelical audiences needed to hear biblical support for public and political engagement. Despite a rich heritage of nineteenth-century activism, most twentieth-century evangelicals had interpreted political activities as a distraction from their paramount religious responsibilities. This pattern persisted through the 1960s into the 1970s. For example, Jerry Falwell, a Baptist minister who later became the most visible leader of the Religious Right, epitomized this repudiation of politics in a 1965 sermon in which he belittled the very campaigns that were inspiring many pioneering progressive evangelicals. "Believing the Bible as I do, I would find it impossible to stop preaching the pure saving Gospel of Jesus Christ and begin to do anything else," including "participating in the civil rights reform," Falwell declared. By the late 1970s, Falwell and other conservative evangelicals changed their minds and promoted political activism to combat legalized abortion, the Equal Rights Amendment, the gay rights movement, and cultural secularization. Yet arguments for evangelicals' robust public engagement came first from early progressive evangelical leaders. As *Freedom Now* encouraged readers to embrace political activism in order to work for social justice, its editors and contributors helped lay the groundwork for the progressive evangelical movement.[13]

The commitments to social justice and political engagement that became central to the magazine shaped its subsequent direction and prompted a change in the journal's name. By 1969 John Alexander had grown frustrated with the conservative ethos at Wheaton College, where *Freedom Now* had been banned from the bookstore. He left his teaching position, assumed editorial leadership of the magazine, and moved to Philadelphia. The magazine also adopted a new name—*The Other Side*—to suggest its broadened concern "about social problems which go beyond the black-white issue." In contrast to prosperous and healthy white Americans, the editors explained, "the other side of America is hungry, defeated and miserable." Representatives resided in "migrant working camps, Indian reservations, inner-city ghettos," and international sites devastated by hunger, war, and tyranny. While *The Other Side* continued regular analyses of racial inequalities, this diversified sensitivity to all suffering resulted in expanding coverage of additional, often interrelated social problems such as poverty, violence, and jingoism. "Our racism, our materialism, our travesty of evangelism, our militarism, our nationalism, our insensitivity to the other side, are open for all to see," Alexander exclaimed. Contributors decried injustices as immoral, analyzed their underlying causes, and pressed readers "to apply the whole gospel of Jesus Christ" through both personal actions and public activism. By identifying forms of social injustice as sinful, *The Other Side* pushed evangelicals to recognize sin manifested not only in individual immorality but also in corrupt cultural values and institutionalized inequalities. Therefore, overcoming both personal and social sins demanded evangelism *and* political action. By the 1973 Thanksgiving Workshop on Evangelicals and Social Concern, *The Other Side* had become a leading voice for evangelical progressivism as it outlined the bases for progressive Christian public engagement. The magazine's circulation had grown to 3,000, a number that would rise to 7,000 in 1977 and to over 16,000 in 1981.[14]

Despite the increasingly progressive and even self-styled "radical evangelical" views expressed within *The Other Side* in the late 1960s and early 1970s, coverage of the most controversial public debate raging through those years—the legitimacy of the Vietnam War—remained largely absent from the magazine's purview. As the war escalated and public support declined from over 50 percent in mid-1967 to 28 percent in mid-1971, other prominent Protestant periodicals readily offered their opinions. Mainline Protestant leaders grew increasingly vocal in their opposition. The *Christian Century* consistently denounced the war as imperialistic. Likewise, after initial internal disagreement, *Christianity and Crisis* promoted antiwar activities as its top priority, with fully 20 percent of its articles addressing Vietnam between 1965 and 1970. In contrast, most evangelicals steadfastly supported the policies and military offensives authorized by Presidents Lyndon B. Johnson and Richard Nixon. They viewed the war as part of America's ongoing moral and necessarily militaristic resistance to the threat of "godless Communism." *Christianity Today* printed editorial endorsements, the Southern Baptist Convention passed supportive resolutions, and Billy Graham expressed "no sympathy for those clergymen who [urge] the U.S. to get out of Vietnam."[15]

Yet *The Other Side* barely mentioned the war, for editors Fred and John Alexander sharply disagreed about the United States' responsibilities and actions. While his father supported America's military campaigns, John helped rally antiwar protests at Wheaton. Their differences led to an awkward silence in the magazine. In 1971 John acknowledged that they had "printed very little (and nothing editorially) about the war in Vietnam." "The factual issues about Vietnam are very complex," he explained, "and we do not feel that Christians are in a special position to decide what the facts are." To be sure, John lambasted the "gross immorality" of President Nixon's statement "that he had ordered the invasion of Cambodia because it would enhance national power and his private honor." But the magazine's leadership failed to reach consensus regarding the morality of America's military involvement in and of itself. *The Other Side*'s inceptive sympathy lay with the civil rights rather than the antiwar movement, and thus the magazine contributed little to the growing disillusionment of some evangelicals with American militarism in Indochina. Instead, fierce opposition to the Vietnam War and American nationalism inspired the development of evangelical progressivism through the pages of another periodical to arise: the *Post-American*.[16]

A *Post-American* Faith

Just after the speaker called for a moment of silence to pray for American troops fighting in Vietnam, faint chanting disturbed the quiet. "Stop the war! Stop the war! Stop the war!" shouted Jim Wallis and other representatives of the People's Christian Coalition. Over 80,000 people who had gathered in the Cotton Bowl turned toward the noise coming from the top of the stadium and saw unfurled banners proclaiming "Christ or Country" and "Cross or Flag." The audience had come to Dallas, Texas, for Explo '72, a weeklong evangelistic training conference in the summer of 1972 sponsored by Bill Bright's Campus Crusade for Christ organization and featuring Billy Graham. On this particular evening, the program had included both a Flag Day ceremony and testimonies by military officers that blended faith and patriotic pride. The evangelical crowd seemed stunned at first by this brazen display but quickly drowned out the small antiwar contingent with thundering boos. Policemen promptly surrounded the protesters, and a Campus Crusade official demanded to know who was in charge. "The Holy Spirit," replied one of the demonstrators. Indeed, those in the People's Christian Coalition—a small group of seminarians from Trinity Evangelical Divinity School led by Wallis—regarded themselves as on a mission from God. Members had traveled to the conference in order to challenge evangelicals' enthusiastic support for American militarism and perceived indifference to social justice. Distribution of literature on Christian peacemaking and the "ruckus" created by their antiwar protest made them conspicuous anomalies among the 206 evangelical groups participating in Explo '72. "The People's Christian Coalition was more radical in its approach to the Gospel," observed *Time* magazine. "They reflected a feeling among a minority of evangelicals at the conference that Bright's brand of Christianity is lacking in social concern." As the negative response to the group's public witness at Explo '72 dramatized, members of the People's Christian Coalition were swimming against the tide of evangelicals' passionate patriotism and political conservatism.[17]

A year earlier, the group had begun publishing a magazine, the *Post-American*, and described its goals in prophetic terms. The People's Christian Coalition sought to free Christianity in the United States—especially mainstream evangelicalism—from an apparent cultural imprisonment. "The American captivity of the church has resulted in the disastrous equation of the American way of life with the Christian way of life," Wallis exclaimed in the first issue. American Christianity has become "so enculturated, domesticated, and lifeless that our generation easily and naturally rejects it as ethically insensitive, hypocritical, and irrelevant to the needs of our times." Yet the group saw itself at the forefront of "a new generation of radical Christians" who were "committed to the revolutionary Christian message"—a message that both "changes men's lives and generates an active commitment to social justice." Evangelicals needed to recover this biblical balance and work for social and political reform, the People's Christian Coalition believed. "Christians must be active in rejecting the corrupt values of our culture" and "prophetic in our resistance and activism against the injustice of a racist society, warfare state, and exploitative system," the group wrote in its mission statement. Under the leadership of Wallis, the *Post-American* and its successor, *Sojourners*, grew to become the flagship journals of evangelical progressivism.[18]

The evolution of Wallis's own faith and politics guided the founding of the People's Christian Coalition and eventually shaped the progressive evangelical movement as a whole. Born in 1948 and reared in a middle-class neighborhood outside of Detroit, Wallis described himself as "a son of the American dream" and experienced a youthful evangelical conversion. As a teenager, however, he became disillusioned with both the suburban lifestyle and conservatism of his all-white community. The plight of black Americans particularly troubled Wallis, and he was appalled by the apparent apathy and patronizing attitude of his Plymouth Brethren congregation. "Christianity has nothing to do with racism; that is a political issue, and our faith is personal," a church elder told him. Yet Wallis refused to accept this apolitical focus on religious rather than social concerns. He ventured into inner-city Detroit to interact with black communities, building relationships with many African Americans whose stories of suffering and oppression indelibly shaped his perspectives on injustice. "They showed me the other America, the America that is wrong and mean and hateful; the America that we white people accept," Wallis remembered. In repeated conversations, the refusal of white Christians to acknowledge that racism contributed to black suffering in general and to the violence of Detroit's 1967 race riot confirmed for Wallis the hypocrisy of the church. As with Fred and John Alexander, the meager response of white evangelicals to injustices faced by African Americans transformed Wallis's understanding of Christians' social and political responsibilities.[19]

As Wallis studied at Michigan State University, involvement in the antiwar movement completed his alienation from his childhood faith. The evangelicals he met on campus again offended him by claiming that "Christian faith had nothing to do with the questions that were creating such a passion in me: racism, poverty, and war." Wallis abandoned the church and channeled his passion into radical student protests. He became attracted to Marxist analysis and the New Left's critique that both oppression of the poor and political self-interest defined American public policy and the power elite. Yet toward the end of his collegiate studies, Wallis began questioning the basic assumptions of the New Left. He witnessed different expressions of exploitation and apparent assent to violence, power manipulation, and condescension toward the poor. The New Left seemed "unable to generate enough vision or resources for spiritual and political transformation" and therefore "had an inadequate basis for both protest and affirmation," he concluded.[20]

As a result, Wallis reconsidered the possibility that the Christian gospel could transform both personal and political life. Rereading the New Testament, he claimed to discover "the wholeness of the gospel message for the first time." The Sermon on the Mount now appeared to him a "manifesto of Christ's new social order." More important, Jesus's identification with the poor and oppressed as described in Matthew 25 served as his "conversion passage." "To find our way back to Jesus means a pilgrimage into the world of the hungry, the homeless, the disenfranchised," Wallis determined. "Contrary to the message I had received from the church, Jesus's message was as political as it was personal, as economic as it was spiritual, having as much to do with public life as individual devotion." Thus Christian discipleship—following Jesus—seemed not to preclude but actually to prescribe progressive social action. In this way, Wallis integrated his youthful biblical faith and more mature cultural criticism, embracing his evangelical identity but rejecting his tradition's apolitical tendencies. Drawn to more sustained theological study, he enrolled in Trinity Evangelical Divinity School in suburban Chicago in the fall of 1970. It did not take long, however, for Wallis's seminary education to become secondary to his leadership of the People's Christian Coalition and advocacy for evangelical progressivism.[21]

Within weeks of his arrival, Wallis found a handful of other seminarians who shared his disappointment with evangelicals' support for the Vietnam War and seeming indifference to racism. The small group gathered for Bible studies and intense discussions that reconfirmed participants' sense that the church had lost its prophetic voice and relevance. Defining the group's commitment to "radical discipleship," Wallis crafted a statement that displayed an ambitious agenda for evangelicals' progressive public engagement. "The Scriptures are clear in condemning social and economic injustice, oppression, racism, hypocrisy, environmental destruction, and the kind of chauvinistic nationalism that gives rise to aggression, imperialism, and endless war," the declaration announced. "Biblical instruction is clear in teaching that faith divorced from social justice is a mockery." Distribution of the statement at the seminary and its neighboring denominational college immediately caused controversy and earned the group the reputation of "radical." As rumors circulated of militant activism at the normally staid seminary, complaints from alumni and financial withholding from donors predictably disturbed the administration. The board of trustees even summoned Wallis to hear his testimony of personal faith in Jesus, presumably to verify his evangelical bona fides. Nevertheless, the People's Christian Coalition (as the group christened itself) received encouragement from defenders such as Trinity professor Clark Pinnock and from students at other campuses and conferences that members began visiting. Their zeal and optimism swelled, for they felt themselves part of nothing less than a new reformation of the church. In the fall of 1971, participants in the People's Christian Coalition—or the Post-Americans, as they also began calling themselves—embodied their aspirations in a magazine that they hoped would become a vehicle for a new movement of biblical Christians committed to social justice.[22]

Combining biblical interpretations with leftist critiques of the United States, the *Post-American* attacked the apparent injustices embedded within American society. The magazine's staff members eschewed subtlety. On the cover of the initial issue, they placed an image of Jesus during his Passion, slumped over and wearing a crown of thorns. Yet Jesus was draped with an unconventional robe—the American flag—and the caption underneath proclaimed "... and they crucified Him." Thus the Post-Americans identified American culture as the adversary and executioner of authentic Christianity. "We have become disillusioned, alienated, and angered by an American system that we regard as oppressive," Wallis wrote in the lead editorial. Throughout its early years, the *Post-American* carried a provocative polemic against a nation whose sinfulness its contributors compared to the "fallen" city of Babylon (Rev. 14-18). "America in 1972," fumed Wallis, "is a society blatantly manifesting violence and racism and resigned to the dictates of a corporate-military complex, a people drunkenly worshiping the idolatrous gods of American nationalism, pride, and power, a culture where values of wealth, property, and security take top priority." Articles adopted the strident rhetoric of the New Left in its damning assessment of "the system" and "the establishment" that represented America's unjust power structures. The group's 1971 bibliography of recommended readings reflected this influence as it included works by Herbert Marcuse, C. Wright Mills, Tom Hayden, Noam Chomsky, William Appleman Williams, and other leftist authors. "The analysis of the injustice of our society made by the 'new left' is fundamentally correct," Clark Pinnock wrote in the first issue. "The contemporary revolutionary student movements represent a secular response to very legitimate moral concerns." However, while the Post-Americans believed that the New Left correctly diagnosed American injustice, they regarded its "secular response" as inadequate. Ultimately, Wallis insisted, only "the Gospel of Jesus Christ brings human liberation which effects a radical transformation of values, which makes new men, and ushers new powers of life, justice, and freedom into human society."[23]

Yet American Christianity no longer preached this liberating gospel, the Post-Americans claimed, but had tragically devolved into a docile civil religion. They particularly complained that evangelicals conflated Christianity and patriotism—blessing "the American Way of Life," baptizing the nation's foreign policies, and conforming to rather than challenging the sinfulness of American society. As a result, Christians were silent on social justice and subservient to America's political and economic self-interest. "By its implication in the American status quo, by partici-pating in the anti-Christian mindset of our society (racism, materialism, nationalism), the church has lost its ethical authority and has become the chaplain of the American nation," Wallis claimed. No one seemed more implicated in civil religion than Billy Graham, the most respected and vis-ible evangelical leader. *Post-American* authors rebuked Graham not only for aligning himself with President Nixon and wealthy businessmen but also for urging Christians to honor America. Instead, they argued that evangelical leaders should act as prophets condemning injustices rather than as priests consecrating American policies. "The more I study the Scriptures, the more I sense how dangerous it is to merge piety with our patriotism," concluded Oregon senator Mark Hatfield, an early supporter who became a *Post-American* contributing editor. "A church that is the captive of the culture or a message that merely echoes the values of the society cannot be truly evangelistic, or truly biblical." The magazine's leadership hoped to inspire its audience to "live by the values and ethical priorities of Jesus Christ and His Kingdom in the midst of the indifference and injustice of the American church and state."[24]

Thus the Post-Americans championed an evangelical progressivism that translated the New Left's demands for social change into the idioms of evangelical Christianity. They argued that Christianity offered both the moral foundation and the moral imperative for opposing injustice. "The Gospel is where personal transformation and the struggle for justice find their basis and motivating power," Wallis stated. Like contributors to *The Other Side*, *Post-American* authors criticized evangelicals' tendency to emphasize the personal but not the social implications of the biblical message and framed the fight for social justice as a biblical obligation. "The false dichotomization of the gospel into spiritual and social is an illegitimate interpretation of Christ to the world," wrote staff member Peggy Herbert. Wallis rejected such a dichotomy as "a narrow orthodoxy," for "the gospel demands political involvement that addresses the needs of people, that is directed against all these things that bind and oppress people, that confronts the political and economic causes of human hurt." Throughout its first two years, the *Post-American* developed and defended theological justifications for public engagement and progressive social action.[25]

In turn, the magazine highlighted a wide range of specific injustices that demanded a Christian response. Several articles addressed systemic racism and supported black liberation. A biblical parody by black pastor

Donald Oden typified the magazine's view of America's racist culture. "The white man has always been my shepherd. I have always been in want," began "Psalm 23 of the Black Man." "He maketh me lie down in welfare and poverty. He leadeth me into the noisy, rat-infested ghetto. He despiseth my soul." The *Post-American* also denounced sexism and women's inequality while challenging Christians to advance "the liberation of women from economic exploitation." References to economic injustice and capitalism's oppressive tendencies abounded, and the Post-Americans endorsed such causes as boycotts led by Cesar Chavez. Above all, the *Post-American* kept opposition to the Vietnam War at the forefront of its concerns. "On the basis of our commitment to the gospel of Jesus Christ, we as Christians in America must recognize the terrible human suffering caused by U.S. policies, repent of our silence and complicity in American nationalism and power, and, as messengers of the gospel of reconciliation and peace, resist the unjust and immoral American involvement in South East Asia," Wallis declared. Their broad agenda for social justice and peace was reflected in the list of topics for seminars taught by the Post-Americans in the summer of 1973: "violence, militarism and war, American nationalism and civil religion, institutional sexism and racism, the structure of American wealth and power, [and] the challenge of U.S. globalism."[26]

By the end of 1973, the *Post-American* was well on its way to becoming the premier journal for evangelical progressivism. The magazine's staff members had left seminary, moved into an intentional community in Chicago, and devoted themselves full-time to publishing and spreading their message. Wallis traveled throughout the country to speak at colleges, conferences, and churches. The Post-Americans actively sought to build a movement of "radical Christians," and they promoted other progressive evangelical groups, activities, and literature in a regular column titled "Signs of a New Order." They viewed *The Other Side* as a partner, not only praising that journal's pioneering work in "developing a Biblically-directed social concern and activism" but also recruiting John Alexander as a contributing editor for their own magazine. In turn, Wallis joined *The Other Side*'s editorial board. The *Post-American* received a particularly notable endorsement from British clergyman John Stott, one of the world's most prominent evangelical leaders. He enhanced the magazine's credibility by likening its combination of theological conservatism and social radicalism to Jesus's own ministry. "Far from resenting or resisting cultural change, we should be in the forefront of those who propose and work for it, provided of course that our critique of culture is made from a sound biblical perspective," Stott wrote. "I thank God for the *Post-American* and for its witness to this truth." While the *Post-American* attracted only a modest 1,200 subscribers in its first two years, its popularity and visibility soon soared. After those on the staff relocated to Washington, D.C., in 1975 and renamed both their community and periodical *Sojourners*, the magazine's circulation grew to 23,000 in 1976, 35,000 in 1978, and 55,000 by 1982.[27]

Together, the *Post-American* and *The Other Side* galvanized contemporary progressive evangelicalism. In the pages of these pioneering magazines, leaders presented theological and pragmatic arguments to persuade evangelicals that progressive social action represented a duty rather than a diversion. Their development of an evangelical theology for public engagement represented an important step, for contributors to these journals constructed a middle ground between what they deemed two unacceptable alternatives: most evangelicals' preoccupation with individual religious conversions and apolitical separatism, and the Social Gospel emphasis on societal transformation and justice that continued as a force within liberal Protestantism. "A faith rooted in Biblical data must stress *both* personal liberation and dynamic commitment to social justice," Wallis proclaimed. Authors attacked sin as both a personal and social phenomenon, stressing the inadequacy of exclusively evangelistic strategies that depended upon the cumulative effect of individuals' spiritual renewal and moral reform. Instead, they argued that resolving inequality and injustice required social and political action. Thus *The Other Side* and the *Post-American* propelled the rise of evangelical progressivism by becoming primary voices for the burgeoning movement. In the process, the journals also helped to nurture a network of leaders dedicated to transforming evangelicals' public engagement.[28]

A PROGRESSIVE EVANGELICAL NETWORK

The Other Side and the *Post-American* increased the momentum of progressive evangelicalism by connecting early advocates within a supportive network. Magazines often shape and strengthen movements they represent by attracting influential proponents. As these leaders identify with a magazine and the movement's goals, they enhance its reputation and bolster its activism. In the late 1960s and early 1970s, sympathetic evangelists, academics, theologians, and even politicians joined *The Other Side* and the *Post-American* as writers, editors, and advisers. Many of these leaders championed evangelical progressivism in separate books or essays that criticized most evangelicals' narrow religious concerns and apolitical conservatism. But they also joined these journals in popularizing calls for social justice and progressive reforms. As these leaders affiliated with *The Other Side* and the *Post-American*, a self-conscious network of pioneering progressive evangelicals evolved. This network became the core of a broader coalition that organized collaborative efforts—including direct political activism in the 1972 presidential campaign—that culminated in the Thanksgiving Workshop on Evangelicals and Social Concern. An analysis of prominent leaders who identified with *The Other Side* and the *Post-American* reveals how the journals helped to unite scattered critics of evangelicals' conservative public engagement into a progressive evangelical chorus.

The Other Side and the *Post-American* ensured that notable African American leaders within the overwhelmingly white circles of evangelicalism would provide pivotal contributions to the progressive evangelical movement. Bill Pannell, a staff evangelist with Youth for Christ, became a contributing editor and author for both magazines. In his popular book *My Friend, the Enemy*, Pannell challenged his white evangelical "friends" to realize how practical apathy toward injustices faced by blacks made them de facto "enemies." He used his regular columns in *The Other Side* to promote progressive public engagement as a better solution "than the usual evangelical cop-out that posits responsibility for change with the individual Christian working within the system." Tom Skinner, the most popular black evangelist in the 1960s following his conversion from gang leadership in Harlem to evangelical Christianity, also joined *The Other Side* as a contributing editor and writer. He published two books with evangelical presses—*How Black Is the Gospel?* and *Words of Revolution*—that outlined Christians' responsibilities to combat injustices. In *The Other Side*, Skinner lampooned evangelicals' reflexive conservatism as a stumbling block to politically and economically powerless people. "For the whites who will read this," Skinner wrote, "I trust it will open your eyes to the fact that the gospel that you have historically preached is not relevant and has not been to the overwhelming majority of black people." He explained how blacks would reject Jesus when evangelicals "wrapped him up in the American flag" and "made him chairman of the Republican Party, head of the Pentagon, [and] founder of capitalism." In addition to Pannell and Skinner, *The Other Side* featured numerous articles by National Black

Evangelical Association president William Bentley and Mississippi activist John Perkins. Perkins subsequently became a regular columnist for *Sojourners* and gained significant attention from mainstream evangelicals for his work in community development and racial reconciliation. Thus the *Post-American* and particularly *The Other Side* drew black leaders into the growing progressive evangelical network.[29]

Both magazines also attracted support from a number of academics who were publishing scholarly and theological defenses of evangelical progressivism. For example, David Moberg, a sociology professor at Marquette University, became a contributing editor for *The Other Side* and the *Post-American*. In two influential books—*Inasmuch: Christian Social Responsibility in the Twentieth Century* and *The Great Reversal: Evangelism versus Social Concern*—he drew upon sociological arguments and theological insights from liberal Protestants such as Ernst Troeltsch, Walter Rauschenbusch, and Reinhold Niebuhr to argue that evangelicals must engage in the public and political actions necessary to combat social sins. Likewise, Richard Pierard, a history professor at Indiana State University, joined both journals as a contributing editor and author. In *The Unequal Yoke: Evangelical Christianity and Political Conservatism*, Pierard criticized evangelicals for uncritically promoting capitalism and American nationalism and demanded that they "no longer sit on the sidelines of the current struggle for social justice." Pierard also coedited two volumes of essays by evangelical scholars that promoted progressive public engagement: *Protest and Politics: Christianity and Contemporary Affairs* and *The Cross and the Flag*. "Eleven of us who are displeased with this calloused indifference on the part of so many of our fellow evangelicals to the vital political, social, and economic problems of the day have decided to speak out in protest," the editors wrote in *Protest and Politics*. Authors urged a range of unconventional stands for evangelicals such as opposition to American militarism, extension of welfare assistance, acknowledgment of Palestinians' just grievances, and endorsement of feminism. Several contributors to these volumes also wrote articles for *The Other Side*, including Calvin College political scientist Paul Henry and Trinity College professor of English Nancy Hardesty. In addition, Calvin College philosopher Nicholas Wolterstorff and Messiah College professor Ron Sider joined *The Other Side* as authors and contributing editors.[30]

The emerging progressive evangelical movement offered a supportive community for these professors and other highly educated evangelicals whose graduate training challenged their tradition's individualistic social ethic and politically conservative instincts. As part of their efforts in the mid-twentieth century to distance themselves from the cultural separatism of their fundamentalist heritage, increasing numbers of "new" evangelicals began pursuing graduate work in secular programs. Indeed, nearly all of the academics affiliated with *The Other Side* and the *Post-American* received doctorates from major research universities, most after attending evangelical colleges. In the transition from evangelical backgrounds to more liberal academic contexts, these scholars encountered alternative theologies and political philosophies. For example, Richard Mouw, a philosophy professor at Calvin College (and future president of Fuller Theological Seminary), graduated from the evangelical Houghton College in 1961 before completing his Ph.D. at the University of Chicago. Mouw described how in the mid-1960s he became "sensitized to issues of justice and peace by the witness of the civil rights movement" and then "convinced that the United States' military involvement in Southeast Asia was seriously misguided." Yet he admitted in his book *Political Evangelism* that "my training within the environs of 'conservative-evangelical' Christianity did not provide me with a theological framework adequate to deal with the concerns over social injustice, racism and militarism that were so much a part of the years I spent doing graduate study at secular universities." Like Jim Wallis, Mouw joined the radical student movement after rejecting the "political passivity" of most evangelicals. But he too abandoned the New Left because of its apparent spiritual shallowness. Even as Mouw made "a cautious re-entry into the evangelical community following graduate school," he incorporated the political ideas and examples of non-evangelical Christians such as Abraham Kuyper, Dietrich Bonhoeffer, Martin Luther King Jr., and Catholic activist Daniel Berrigan. Mouw became an active participant in the early progressive evangelical network and joined the *Post-American* as a contributing editor. Evangelical progressivism allowed many academics like Mouw to retain their core conservative theology while integrating more liberal and secular analyses of injustice.[31]

Several prominent theologians also affiliated with the leading progressive evangelical journals. In the late 1960s, Vernon Grounds, a senior evangelical leader and president of Conservative Baptist Theological Seminary, joined efforts to reverse evangelicals' social indifference and ineffectiveness. In both the Old and New Testaments, he argued in *Evangelicalism and Social Responsibility*, God "demands that injustice be fought" and "righteousness be established in society." While affirming the church's primary task of personal evangelism, he also contended that the church, "living under the law of holy love, is divinely obligated to maximize love by maximizing justice"—a task that necessitated "Christian political action." Grounds joined *The Other Side*'s advisory board and later became president of Evangelicals for Social Action. Among its own contributing editors and authors, the *Post-American* counted Clark Pinnock, Jim Wallis's mentor at Trinity Evangelical Divinity School, and Wheaton College professor Robert Webber. The most influential theologian for the staffs of *The Other Side* and the *Post-American* was Mennonite scholar John Howard Yoder. Yoder's Anabaptist convictions inspired many young evangelical progressives to view the church as an ideal countercultural alternative to unjust worldly societies. His most influential book, *The Politics of Jesus*, offered a forceful rebuttal to interpretations of Jesus and New Testament writings as apolitical. Yoder argued that Jesus resisted state violence and social injustice and that contemporary Christians should follow his social ethic and create an alternative political paradigm in which Christian communities embrace pacifism and establish justice for the marginalized and oppressed. The *Post-American* especially adopted this Anabaptist countercultural vision that coincided with its sympathies for the New Left, and Yoder joined the magazine as an editor and author.[32]

No one embodied the combination of evangelical theology and progressive politics envisioned by *The Other Side* and the *Post-American* more than Mark Hatfield. As the Republican governor of Oregon from 1960 to 1966, Hatfield supported civil rights legislation and cast the lone dissenting vote among other Republican governors in a referendum to support the Vietnam War. After his election to the Senate, Hatfield continued to support progressive public policies and to criticize the war. In *Conflict and Conscience*, the senator urged evangelicals to translate their faith into political concerns for social justice. "We as evangelicals must regain sensitivity to the corporateness of human life," addressing not only "issues of private morality" but also "issues of social morality" such as "war, poverty, and racial antagonism." Hatfield identified with the progressive evangelical movement by becoming not only an adviser to *The Other Side* but also an enthusiastic supporter of the *Post-American*. Indeed, the senator was so impressed by the first issue of the *Post-American* that he telephoned the group to offer his encouragement, became a contributing editor and author, and developed a collaborative friendship with Jim Wallis. In addition, Hatfield's executive assistant Wes Michaelson also became part of the *Post-American*'s editorial board and subsequently joined the renamed *Sojourners* magazine as full-time managing editor. Thus *The Other Side* and the *Post-American* helped to bring Hatfield and Michaelson into the network of other early progressive evangelical advocates.[33]

This network became increasingly visible as progressive evangelical leaders expanded their collaborative activism outside the pages of these journals and into uncharted waters. Theologically conservative Christians had a long history of coordinated evangelistic campaigns and conferences, but ones promoting political engagement signaled a turning point in the development of evangelical progressivism. In 1972 a minority of progressive leaders formed the first evangelical political action committee to support a presidential candidate. Disappointed or disgusted by the policies of Richard Nixon, they banded together as "Evangelicals for McGovern" (EFM) in order to back Democratic senator George McGovern of South Dakota. Ron Sider served as the group's principal organizer, and the leadership team included a number of contributors to *The Other Side* and the *Post-American*: John Alexander, Tom Skinner, Richard Pierard, David Moberg, and Robert Webber. EFM officials sought to persuade other evangelicals that McGovern's platform more closely aligned with biblical principles. "Evangelicals should be concerned about social justice," EFM chairman Walden Howard told *Christianity Today*. "I just don't believe social justice is a high priority with Nixon. But it's the heart of McGovern's motivation." In a circular letter sent to 8,000 evangelical leaders, EFM contrasted Nixon's regrettable track record with McGovern's support for poverty relief, racial justice, and peace in Vietnam. "Let's end the outdated stereotype that evangelical theology automatically means a politics unconcerned about the poor, minorities, and unnecessary military expenditures," the group wrote. While EFM aspired to make social justice evangelicals' paramount election criterion and to present $100,000 to McGovern's campaign as proof of evangelical support, leaders privately expected far less success. *Christianity Today* rightly predicted that most evangelicals would follow Billy Graham's example after he endorsed Nixon and anticipated that the incumbent "will probably go down in history as one of the country's greatest presidents." Indeed, Nixon won 84 percent of the evangelical vote, contributing to his landslide victory—61-38 percent in the popular vote and 520-17 in the electoral vote—over McGovern. Ultimately, EFM succeeded in raising a mere $5,762 from 358 donors.[34]

But these meager numbers did not diminish the momentousness of EFM for participants. The organization's active support for a liberal Democratic candidate represented a clear repudiation of evangelicals' apolitical, conservative inclinations, and both evangelical and mainstream media covered EFM's unexpected campaign. Most important, the group further strengthened a sense of solidarity within the growing progressive evangelical network. "To see the words 'Evangelicals for McGovern' actually in print was an experience of sweet vindication," Richard Mouw later attested. In a postelection letter, Ron Sider reassured contributors that EFM had attained its fundamental objective by underlining the biblical emphasis on justice. More and more evangelicals heard progressive evangelicals' core message: "If we are listening to all that Biblical revelation says about justice in society, our politics must reflect a concern not just about pubs, pot, and pornographic literature, but also about racism, poverty, and the grossly unjust distribution of wealth here and abroad." Sider believed that EFM had revealed "a rising tide of theologically orthodox Christians who are not chained to conservative politics." Building upon the efforts and lessons of EFM, leaders met at a conference in the spring of 1973 and considered how best to sustain their momentum.[35]

The inaugural "Conference on Christianity and Politics" at Calvin College proved significant on two fronts. First, an influential group of evangelicals gathered to discuss not evangelism but rather political engagement. Organized by Calvin professors Richard Mouw and Paul Henry, sessions explored both theological and practical issues of Christian political participation and featured prominent participants within the progressive evangelical network. As the *Post-American* noted approvingly, the conference "was the first organized effort by evangelicals to confront the questions of legitimate political involvement." Second, during the conference several EFM leaders met and decided to organize another major gathering explicitly devoted to evangelicals' social concern. Coordinated by Ron Sider, a planning committee formed that included a majority associated with *The Other Side* or the *Post-American*. Preparing for a proposed workshop in Chicago just after Thanksgiving, the group subsequently met several times to send out invitations and to compose preliminary drafts of an attention-grabbing statement that could set the course for evangelicals' future public engagement.[36]

The influence of *The Other Side* and the *Post-American* as nuclei in the emerging progressive evangelical movement became fully apparent at the 1973 Thanksgiving Workshop on Evangelicals and Social Concern. In addition to the planning committee, the majority of the original endorsers of the declaration produced by the workshop served as editors, advisers, or contributors to one or both of these magazines. As Richard

Mouw affirmed, the journals helped bring together those whose "political involvement did not fit well within the dominant mood of evangelicalism" in the late 1960s and early 1970s. "It became clear that many of us had been engaged in a lonely effort to reconcile evangelical convictions with an activist spirit," Mouw remembered. "We found each other, and a new kind of evangelical witness was expressed through the 1973 Chicago Declaration of Evangelical Social Concern, magazines like *The Other Side* and the *Post-American*, and the Evangelicals for Social Action organization" that would form following the Thanksgiving workshop.[37]

THE CHICAGO DECLARATION OF EVANGELICAL SOCIAL CONCERN

In late November 1973, over fifty leaders met in Chicago for the workshop. The planning committee limited invitations to evangelicals with known sympathy for social action and justice. Committee members also hoped to gather participants diverse in denominational affiliations, geographic locales, age, race, and gender. Yet the leadership committee itself included no women and only one African American, Bill Pannell. The attention to diversity reached only so far in other ways as well. As Richard Pierard later noted, almost all of those in attendance "were people from more articulate walks of life—theologians, college professors, journalists, evangelists, [and] denominational executives." John Alexander, Jim Wallis, and Post-Americans Joe Roos and Boyd Reese represented younger activists. Participating professors included Pierard, Ron Sider, David Moberg, Richard Mouw, Paul Henry, John Howard Yoder, Lewis Smedes of Fuller Theological Seminary, and Stephen Mott of Gordon-Conwell Theological Seminary. Pannell, William Bentley, and John Perkins stood out among the few black participants. The small number of evangelical women included Nancy Hardesty, black activist Wyn Wright Potter, and Sharon Gallagher, editor of Christian World Liberation Front's *Right On* magazine. Peruvian InterVarsity leader Samuel Escobar alone represented an evangelical from outside North America. To buttress the coalition's credibility, the planning committee secured participation from supportive "evangelical elder statesmen" such as Vernon Grounds, World Vision vice president Paul Rees, theologian Bernard Ramm, and Carl F. H. Henry. Henry was the most recognized and respected evangelical in attendance, and his presence offered a symbolic imprimatur for the workshop. As one of the key architects of "new" evangelicals' rejection of fundamentalist separatism in the mid-twentieth century, Henry previously had helped to establish

Fuller Theological Seminary and served as the first editor of *Christianity Today*. His 1947 book *The Uneasy Conscience of Modern Fundamentalism* had voiced the earliest criticism of fundamentalist evangelicals who had become "increasingly inarticulate about the social reference of the Gospel." Although vague in his political proposals, Henry consistently emphasized the necessity of social justice. By drawing Henry and other older leaders into a coalition with "younger, more 'radical' evangelical voices," organizers hoped to enhance the impact of the declaration issued by the workshop.[38]

Yet reaching consensus on a statement that described social and political action as an evangelical imperative proved neither quick nor easy. Prior to the meeting, the planning committee composed a draft for delegates to discuss and to amend as necessary. Almost as soon as the workshop began on Friday, strong objections arose. Feeling underrepresented, both African Americans and women expressed frustrations with the perceived hollowness of the proposed statement's respective content regarding racism and sexism. Speaking for members of the historic peace churches, John Howard Yoder also protested the absence of a condemnation of war. A sense of pessimism and divisiveness prevailed at the end of the first day. The next morning, a new drafting committee—this one containing two blacks yet still no women—prepared another proposal. During lively discussions of the new statement throughout Saturday afternoon, a gradual agreement developed on most points of the declaration. Although acknowledged differences remained regarding how best to rectify injustices, the group discovered increasing unity with respect to each section's descriptive analysis and call for evangelical response. After an additional session Sunday morning, most participants signed what became known as the Chicago Declaration of Evangelical Social Concern.[39]

The traditional language and references within the Chicago Declaration reflected the desire to persuade evangelical audiences of the legitimacy of Christian social responsibility. The signers immediately sought to establish their credentials by identifying themselves "as evangelical Christians committed to the Lord Jesus Christ and the full authority of the Word of God." The declaration then affirmed "that God lays total claim upon the lives of his people" and "requires love" and "justice." Yet endorsers quickly confessed that evangelicals had neither "demonstrated the love of God to those suffering social abuses" nor "proclaimed and demonstrated his justice to an unjust American society," thus establishing grounds for the subsequent calls for penance and amends. In addition, the statement proclaimed, "God abounds in mercy" and "forgives all who repent and turn from their sins." But signers used this fundamental Christian tenet to suggest transforming not personal but rather social sins: "We call our fellow evangelical Christians to demonstrate repentance in a Christian discipleship that confronts the social and political injustice of our nation." Recognizing the unconventional nature of their message, endorsers strategically asserted its orthodoxy. "We proclaim no new gospel," the declaration insisted, "but the gospel of our Lord Jesus Christ, who, through the power of the Holy Spirit, frees people from sin so that they might praise God through works of righteousness." In this case, works of righteousness connoted efforts to end suffering and social injustice. Finally, the signers denied any partisan motivations and framed its message as religiously rather than politically inspired. "By this declaration," they claimed, "we endorse no political ideology or party, but call our nation's leaders and people to that righteousness which exalts a nation."[40]

In succinct fashion, the declaration described several inequalities that produced suffering and marked American society as unjust. Economic disparity received particular criticism. Contending that "the Lord calls us to defend the social and economic rights of the poor and oppressed," supporters urged opposition to the results of America's economic system: "We must attack the materialism of our culture and the maldistribution of the nation's wealth and services." In light of worldwide need and hunger, the declaration continued, Christians should question their own standards of living and work for economic justice in global contexts. The initial concerns of black participants also manifested themselves in strong denunciations of racism and its consequences. Signers lamented evangelicals' history of racism, ongoing support of "the personal attitudes and institutional structures" that segregated Christians, and failure "to condemn the exploitation of racism at home and abroad by our economic system." Perhaps the most controversial passage regarded supporters' diagnosis of evangelicals' sexism. "We acknowledge that we have encouraged men to prideful domination and women to irresponsible passivity," the declaration read. "So we call both men and women to mutual submission and active discipleship." To evangelicals steeped in hierarchical assumptions regarding male headship, this statement would have appeared repugnant.[41]

The criticisms of injustice harbored in American society culminated in a rejection of nationalism and its repercussions. Although signers acknowledged their "Christian responsibilities of citizenship," they did not believe that responsible citizenship entailed patriotic piety and uncritical allegiance. Thus, the declaration proclaimed, "we must resist the temptation to make the nation and its institutions objects of near-religious loyalty." In particular, supporters pointed to the militarism and economic imperialism produced by inordinate nationalism. "We must challenge the misplaced trust of the nation in economic and military might—a proud trust that promotes a national pathology of war and violence which victimizes our neighbors at home and abroad." Closing with hope for the coming of the kingdom of God, the declaration implied that primary loyalty to God's kingdom should temper enthusiasm for the United States of America. By employing familiar theological language to describe Christians' responsibility for social justice, the Chicago Declaration of Evangelical Social Concern represented both a manifesto and an apology for the emergent progressive evangelical movement.[42]

Optimism abounded among many participants after the Thanksgiving workshop. "A rapidly growing movement of biblical social concern is emerging among evangelicals in the seventies," Ron Sider announced, and "the moment when it reaches full flower may be at hand." Sider and other young leaders, "whose increasing dismay at the lack of social concern had been approaching despair," believed that the endorsement of participating "patriarchs of contemporary evangelicalism" could prove decisive in transforming evangelicals' public engagement. "The attack on the social indifference of evangelicalism no longer comes from just a minority of prophetic critics," Paul Henry proclaimed. Black evangelicals also expressed hope. The Chicago Declaration "could herald the end of the beginning of white evangelical involvement in the pressing social issues of our day," William Bentley stated. "Although the declaration would not be adequate for a purely black constituency," he conceded, "it has to be, in my judgment, about the strongest that has so far come from white evangelicalism." Jim Wallis even believed that the declaration portended the rise of evangelicals as the new vanguard of American progressivism. "With the decline of the New Left and other movements for social change present in the sixties, along with the spreading radical Christian consciousness," he wrote in the *Post-American*, "it is highly probable that the strongest thrusts toward prophetic witness and social justice may well spring from those whose faith is Christ-centered and [who] hold an unapologetic biblical faith." Although fundamentalist evangelicals criticized the Chicago Declaration, it received relatively positive coverage in mainstream evangelical journals. More liberal Protestants and the secular press also took favorable notice. "Someday," one reporter speculated in the *Chicago Sun-Times*, "American church historians may write that the most significant church-related event of 1973 took place last week at the YMCA hotel on S. Wabash." Indeed, another journalist reported in the *Washington Post*, the workshop and the declaration "could well change the face of both religion and politics in America."[43]

The relationship between religion and American politics did change dramatically after 1973, but the overwhelmingly conservative forms that most evangelical social and political action took in the ensuing years surprised secular journalists and disheartened the workshop participants. Evangelicals did not become known for their commitment to social justice; they became known for supporting right-wing Republicans and driving the culture wars against abortion, feminism, gay rights, and secularism. Two developments undermined progressive evangelicals' ambitions.

First, the evangelical left coalition that had gathered for the Thanksgiving Workshop on Evangelicals and Social Concern proved fragile. Although the sanguine Ron Sider sought to capitalize on the momentum by founding Evangelicals for Social Action (ESA) and organizing subsequent workshops, he admitted that leaders had "substantial differences" on specific issues. In follow-up conferences and other communications, these differences divided potential progressive evangelical allies and diminished their collective impact. Older, moderate evangelicals such as Carl F. H. Henry criticized younger "radicals" for vilifying capitalism and rejecting patriotism. African Americans and women complained that white male leaders failed to prioritize the respective injustices of racism and sexism. And Reformed evangelicals, who wanted to work through existing political structures and legislative changes, clashed with the leadership of the *Post-American*, *The Other Side*, and the newly formed ESA, who often emphasized the Anabaptist ideal of working through Christian communities. To be sure, these factions all endorsed the ideal of social justice. But disagreements regarding political priorities and strategies fragmented the progressive evangelical coalition. Some black, female, and Reformed evangelicals began to work through their own respective organizations, thus draining the momentum that appeared immediately after the 1973 workshop.[44]

Second, and most important, the Religious Right and groups like Jerry Falwell's Moral Majority soon stole progressive evangelicals' thunder. By the end of the decade, millions of evangelicals did become politicized—but not as progressive evangelicals had hoped. "We wanted to get evangelicals politically engaged," Sider later lamented. "We never expected that the

Moral Majority would be the result." As the Religious Right aligned itself with the Republican Party, conservative leaders successfully mobilized voters and used their superior media networks to establish themselves as the primary public voices of evangelicalism. As a result, evangelical progressives found themselves overshadowed and struggling to challenge the popular association of evangelicalism with conservative social and political positions. Nevertheless, the *Post-American* (soon renamed *Sojourners*), *The Other Side*, and ESA continued to lead a small but vigorous movement of progressive evangelicals whose public engagement built upon the Chicago Declaration of Evangelical Social Concern.[45]

Well into the twenty-first century, progressive evangelical leaders consistently supported public policies intended to address injustices outlined in the Chicago Declaration: the effects of racism, the inequality of women, the lack of economic resources among the poor and oppressed, and the consequences of American nationalism and militarism. It is notable that the 1973 Chicago Declaration made no mention of two primary issues that soon animated the Religious Right: legalized abortion and gay rights. Contemporary progressive evangelicals politicized in response to injustices, not in response to perceived assaults on "family values" as did evangelical conservatives.[46] Although most in the evangelical left eventually adopted pro-life stances and endorsed heterosexual marriage as God's ideal, they decried the ways in which the Religious Right interpreted and exaggerated these issues above others in their political platforms and evaluation of candidates. Leaders also rebuked Christian conservatives for aligning themselves with Republican politicians, for they continued to insist—as in the Chicago Declaration—that they endorsed "no political ideology or party." Progressive evangelicals' politically liberal focus on social justice distinguished them from the religious and political right, while their explicitly religious motivations and stances on abortion and homosexuality made them unwelcome allies among political liberals.

Subsequent chapters trace progressive evangelicals' evolving responses to racism, feminism, abortion, homosexuality, economic justice, and militaristic nationalism from the 1970s into the twenty-first century. First, however, chapter 2 outlines the public theology—a set of theological interpretations regarding Christians' political responsibilities—that leaders embraced over the course of their activism. This public theology underlay and united the unusual combination of political positions that marginalized progressive evangelicals in American partisan politics.

2. A Public Theology of Community

I n the early 1990s, Sojourners' Jim Wallis described the state
of his adopted hometown of Washington, D.C., in Dickensian
terms. In his own "tale of two cities," Wallis emphasized the
dissonant realities within the nation's capital. Affluent white politicians
fought for power as black residents of the city fought poverty. Political lob-
byists hosted dinners of caviar and champagne while homeless people dug
through trash for food. Commuters from the comfortable suburbs worked
in the stately city center as low-income families lived in the surrounding
dilapidated neighborhoods. America's power elites governed from impos-
ing offices, but residents of the impoverished District of Columbia lacked
voting representation in Congress. "Everyone knows 'official Washington'
with its marble, monuments, and malls," Wallis wrote. "But the 'other
Washington' has been off-limits to the blue-and-white tour buses and to
the consciousness of the rest of America."[1]

Wallis regarded these divisions and inequalities within Washington
as symptomatic of the principal disease afflicting American public life:
"broken community." "Today the fundamental covenant that holds life
together has been profoundly damaged," he argued. "We have little sense
of community." Widespread patterns of racism, sexism, disintegration of
family life, economic injustice, and destructive militarism all testified to
this fracture of community. Political practices exacerbated rather than
resolved the problem, Wallis lamented, for "politics has been reduced to
the selfish struggle for power among competing interests and groups." In
response, Wallis proposed that a "politics of community" dedicated to "a
process of searching for the common good" should replace the "politics

of power." "The moral requirements of relationship and community serve to correct our human tendencies toward individual selfishness and exploitation of our neighbors," he proclaimed. For Wallis and other progressive evangelical leaders, the connotations of community and care for one's neighbors offered the prescription for building just and peaceful societies.[2]

Through the course of their activism that stretched from the 1970s into the twenty-first century, leaders of the progressive evangelical movement constructed what I label an implicit "public theology of community" as their operative political philosophy. That is, based upon perceived rights and responsibilities that flow out of humans' communal nature, they developed a set of theological convictions about public affairs and politics that shaped their efforts to promote a just society. God's creation of each individual gives all people essential sanctity and equality, leaders believed, and thus social conditions and public policies must ensure individual rights and liberties. But God also creates people as interdependent communal beings, linked as neighbors with reciprocal responsibilities for each other's welfare and the common good. Evangelical progressives argued that such responsibilities extend beyond the personal to the public sphere, as political policies codify these obligations and coordinate collective social programs. Because social justice provides the vital framework for balancing individual rights and the common good, leaders regarded it as the highest ideal of public life. They insisted that the biblical vision for social justice requires substantively equal opportunities that depend upon the equitable distribution of socioeconomic resources. Because the state acts as the organized political community, progressive evangelical leaders concluded, the government should foster social justice by promoting policies of distributive justice.

Progressive evangelicals' public theology of community placed them in dialogue with competing political philosophies and their practical applications. In particular, they contested two important aspects of liberalism, the broad political tradition defended by philosophers ranging from John Locke to John Rawls. First, progressive evangelical leaders rejected liberal theorists' political prioritization of individual liberties and rights that seemingly failed to affirm the equal importance of communal responsibilities and the common good. Second, they disputed the claim of liberal philosophers who argued that a just political order requires the limitation or privatization of religion in order to reach consensus among religiously diverse citizens. Evangelical progressives regarded these expectations as an unjustified bias for secularism, and they maintained that the principle

of the separation of church and state does not mandate relegation of religion to private spheres. By promoting the inclusion of all perspectives—
religious or otherwise—in democratic debates about moral issues of political significance, progressive evangelicals aligned themselves with their
usual sparring partners in the Religious Right while alienating many potential allies in the political left.

As activists, progressive evangelical leaders devoted more time and energy to combating perceived injustices than to producing detailed political
philosophies. Systematic theories and theologies for public engagement
did not precede their practical efforts to address pressing problems. Evangelicals for Social Action president Ron Sider admitted in his 2008 book
The Scandal of Evangelical Politics that evangelicals had largely "failed to
develop a biblically grounded, systematic approach to the complicated
task of politics. Our approach was 'ready, fire, aim,'" he wrote. Nevertheless, from the earliest stages of their movement, contemporary progressive evangelicals operated under a tacit set of theological interpretations
regarding Christians' responsibilities for social justice and political participation. Beginning in the mid-1990s, the two most prominent leaders—
Wallis and Sider—published books containing more sustained, systematic analyses of the biblical principles and paradigms that they believed
should guide Christians' public engagement. For Wallis, this represented
an evolution in emphasis. His first book, *Agenda for Biblical People*, published in 1976, reflected an Anabaptist focus on the internal life of Christian communities. Wallis outlined how the church should manifest the
kingdom of God and thus offer a prophetic political alternative to sinful
worldly states, yet he also insisted that this ideal was not a call for apolitical withdrawal. In the early 1980s Wallis responded to the rise of the
Religious Right by increasingly emphasizing Christians' *public* responsibilities for approximating social justice through *political* means. By the
early twenty-first century Wallis embraced the label of "public theologian" for himself. He also heralded Sider as "one of our most important
public theologians." Unlike Wallis, Sider was also an academic—he had
earned a Ph.D. in history from Yale University and long served as a professor at Palmer (née Eastern Baptist) Theological Seminary. *The Scandal
of Evangelical Politics* culminated Sider's decades-long efforts to develop
a public theology, for he saw the need for a "biblically grounded, sophisticated evangelical political philosophy" that "could guide hundreds of
millions of evangelicals all around the world to love their neighbors more
effectively through wise political engagement." This chapter draws upon

key articles and popular books, particularly those published by Sider and Wallis, in order to outline the underlying public theology of community that shaped progressive evangelicals' political praxis from the 1970s into the twenty-first century.[3]

AN EVANGELICAL PUBLIC THEOLOGY

Because progressive evangelical leaders based their moral vision for public life upon biblical interpretations, their framework for political engagement represented an evangelical public theology. As Victor Anderson has defined it, "public theology is the deliberate use of distinctively theological commitments to influence substantive public debate and policy." Some advocates, such as David Tracy and Max Stackhouse, have argued that public theologians must make use of evidence and arguments that are theoretically open to all people, regardless of religious tradition—that is, they should avoid appealing only to premises and warrants that are "explicitly religious and specific to the religious tradition in which the public theology develops and from which it speaks." Yet progressive evangelical leaders rejected this restriction. They agreed with Ronald Thiemann's argument that such a requirement "undercuts the ability of Christians to employ the specific resources of their traditions to engage in public conversation" and therefore "threatens to render the distinctive content of Christian belief inapplicable to the public sphere." Indeed, Sider explicitly claimed, "My proposal rejects any suggestion that public theology must use only arguments that are independent of a particular faith." Instead, he wrote, Christians should "work within the Christian community to develop a framework for political engagement that is thoroughly grounded both in a biblical worldview and in systematic analysis of society." After constructing their distinctive theology for public life and using it to reach specific political positions, progressive evangelicals accepted that they must then participate in the pluralistic public sphere and seek to persuade others who do not share their particular religious convictions.[4]

As evangelicals, leaders looked first and foremost to interpretations of the Bible in order to construct their public theology. They believed that scripture reveals God's intended ideals for all human societies, and from the beginning of their movement they argued that, as Sider stated, "American public life needs to be shaped by biblical principles." Wallis claimed that his political proposals reflected biblical blueprints. "The 'vision' we will put forward in this book for our contemporary society is simply the content of what the Old Testament prophets, Jesus, and the New Testament writers had to say—about our public commitments, our common life, and the social bonds we share in community," he wrote in his 2005 best-selling *God's Politics*. In his follow-up book, *The Great Awakening*, Wallis outlined more systematically the "biblical narratives, themes, and stories" that yielded "the theological foundations and the moral principles" that guided progressive evangelicals' public engagement. Likewise, Sider insisted that evangelicals must derive their political philosophies from "biblical revelation." To be sure, he appreciated insights from other sources such as the natural law tradition, philosophical reflections, and socioeconomic, political, and historical analyses. Yet, Sider argued, the obscuring effects of sin upon human reasoning "means that we should turn primarily to the Bible" to establish "our fundamental normative principles for politics." Both Wallis and Sider claimed to avoid simplistic biblical proof-texting and ideologically driven interpretations that distort the Bible's full testimony. "To develop a normative biblical framework," Sider explained, "we must in principle examine all relevant biblical passages, understand each text according to proper principles of exegesis, and then formulate a comprehensive summary of all relevant canonical material." For progressive evangelical leaders, biblical paradigms concerning human identity, communal responsibilities, substantive equality, socioeconomic rights, distributive justice, and the role of the state all became important planks in the evangelical public theology that they developed.[5]

THE CENTRALITY OF COMMUNITY AND THE COMMON GOOD

Progressive evangelicals began their public theology with the affirmation that humans bear the *imago Dei*, and therefore God endows each individual person with sacred value and metaphysical equality. "Every human being—and only human beings—is made in the image of God," wrote Sider, and the "special dignity and sanctity of every human being" should serve as the cardinal biblical principle in Christians' political engagement. As unique creations of God, individuals possess inherent worth and rights. "Every person's human right to life, freedom, and all the other things the Creator reveals as human rights flows from God's creative design," Sider claimed. Thus neither governments nor societies establish human rights, progressive evangelicals believed, but rather only provide contexts for their full recognition. Wallis suggested that rooting universal human rights in the theological conception of "the image of God in every human being" rather than in abstract political ideals offered an objective, moral buttress against human rights abuses. Progressive evangelicals additionally maintained that people's common reflection of the *imago Dei* confirms the essential equality of all people. Leaders appealed to biblical interpretations of human worth and equality, but Wallis also asserted that this principle transcends religious boundaries. "Most of the world's great religions teach that humankind and every human being is created in the divine image," he wrote. "That most foundational premise gives each person an equal and sacred value." In practice, progressive evangelicals held, this sacrosanct egalitarianism establishes an inviolable basis for the formal equality of all people in all human societies. Formal equality denotes that each person should possess equal rights under the law and receive equal treatment without regard to differences of race, sex, class, or other personal characteristics.[6]

Although the commitments of evangelical progressives to the sacred worth, essential rights, and formal equality of each individual represented conventional religious and political convictions, leaders believed that additional biblical paradigms should direct the interpretation and application of these basic principles. In particular, they concluded that the latitude of human rights and the scope of citizens' political responsibilities flow from God's design for humans to live in community—a design based upon both God's creation of humans with a communal nature and God's command to love one's neighbors as oneself. Therefore the image and implications of community became central in progressive evangelicals' public theology.

Leaders claimed that proper interpretations of human identity recognize both its personal and social aspects, and therefore an immutable connection exists between individuals and communities. The *imago Dei* marks people not only as sacred individuals but commensurately as communal beings. "An isolated individual cannot adequately image the God who is triune, a loving community who is three persons in the one God," Sider wrote. As a result, the Bible balances an "affirmation of the dignity of the individual person with an equal emphasis on the communal nature of persons." This theologically informed anthropology led Sider and evangelical social ethicist Stephen Mott to declare that God creates people "both for personal freedom and communal solidarity." While individual humans possess innate worth, they cannot achieve fulfillment independently. "The Creator made us individual persons so completely designed for community that we cannot be whole unless we enjoy mutual interdependence with others," Sider explained. Thus the principle of humans' inherent interdependence became another cardinal tenet in progressive evangelicals' public theology. "The moral and political foundation for community is that, fundamentally, *we need each other,*" Wallis wrote. He proposed that rejecting the unbiblical view of individuals as autonomous beings, free from all but voluntary social associations, would deepen awareness of humanity's shared identity and obligations. Within their public theology, progressive evangelicals emphasized interdependent responsibilities within communities as much as individual rights.[7]

Leaders adopted the metaphor and rhetoric of "neighbors" in order to describe these divinely designed communal relationships and mutual responsibilities. In their political proposals, evangelical progressives regularly invoked Jesus's command to love one's neighbor as oneself and the ensuing parable of the Good Samaritan that offered his expansive answer to the question of "Who is my neighbor?" (Luke 10:25-37). Indeed, Sider summarized the purpose of progressive evangelicals' public theology as "loving one's neighbor through faithful political engagement." From the beginnings of their movement, leaders interpreted the scale of their neighborly relationships broadly. Endorsers of the 1973 Chicago Declaration of Evangelical Social Concern acknowledged their obligations to "a billion hungry neighbors" throughout the world. These relationships transcend differences in race, sex, class, or national identity. As a result, local, national, and international communities link *all* people as de facto neighbors in an increasingly globalized world. "Christ makes our in-group not just the church but the whole family of humanity, refusing to let ethnicity, ancestry, geography, ideology or even theology limit our responsibility to our neighbor," wrote former ESA president Vernon Grounds. "Nobody is excluded from neighbor love." As the context for identifying neighbors and how to treat them, an imagined community represented the heart of progressive evangelicals' public theology.[8]

To fulfill what Sider and Mott labeled the "inherent duties of care and responsibility for each other," progressive evangelical leaders promoted the ideal of the common good. The common good represents a comprehensive vision for the shared welfare of all members of a community. It consists of "the sum total of all the conditions of our social life—economic, cultural, spiritual, and political," Wallis stated. "Those conditions must make it possible for men, women, and children to be protected and fulfilled in their basic human dignity." In addition to identifying the biblical bases for the concept of the common good, leaders buttressed their arguments with references to Roman Catholic theology beginning in the mid-1990s. "I am an evangelical Christian, but I am also a convert to Catholic social teaching with its long and rich history," Wallis wrote. "It suggests that the good of each individual is necessarily and vitally connected to the common good." Progressive evangelicals believed that the dominant but distorted view of people as mostly autonomous beings led to the exaltation of individual freedoms in American culture at the expense of the common good—an imbalance that inevitably produced fractured communities, inequalities, and injustices. "In our self-centered, individualistic actions," Sider lamented, "we violate communal obligations and trample upon the common good of our neighbors." Yet, Wallis proposed, replacing "the politics of individual gain and special interests" with "a common-good politics" offers both "a direct challenge to the rampant individualism that shapes our society" and "the moral ground on which a new political consensus can be built." As part of their public theology, evangelical progressives viewed the common good as the benchmark for all political and socioeconomic practices. Because "community—the common good—is one of the ultimate moral values," *Sojourners'* Duane Shank argued, it offers a clear guiding principle—independent of specific, complex political issues—for Christians committed to "grounding our political work in our biblical faith."[9]

Progressive evangelicals claimed that reciprocal responsibilities for the common good both constrain individual liberties and best safeguard the rights of all community members. Leaders challenged widespread assumptions about the unrestricted nature of certain political rights. "Because our communal nature demands attention to the common good, individual rights, whether of freedom of speech or private property, cannot be absolute" and "dare not undermine the general welfare," Sider and Mott wrote. In fact, Wallis declared, God expects individuals to exercise their rights on behalf of creating communal conditions that affirm the sanctity and worth of all people. "Individual rights are always seen in the context of promoting the spirit of community," he stated. "Human dignity will only be recognized and protected in relationship with others." Thus in practice, the mutual commitment of community members to the common good does not undermine individual rights—it protects and promotes them. "God demands that within the limits of our finite, historical setting, we treat our neighbors in such a way that they can reach full human dignity and flourish in the way the Creator intended," Sider argued. "My obligation to treat my neighbors that way is the foundation of my neighbor's human rights. And their obligation to treat me that way is the foundation of mine." In their public theology, progressive evangelicals advocated a communitarian ethic that called upon members to advance the common good by associating their self-interests with the welfare of others. In order to define the balance between individual rights and communal responsibilities, leaders appealed to what they regarded as biblical standards for social justice.[10]

SOCIAL JUSTICE: SUBSTANTIVE EQUALITY, SOCIOECONOMIC RIGHTS, AND THE STATE

Social justice represented the centerpiece of progressive evangelicals' public theology of community and consequent goal of their political engagement. While love and compassion should characterize private actions, leaders argued, social justice should serve as the "public expression" of Christian discipleship. "We must challenge the church to realize that our social responsibility does not come out of the political or economic times but out of scripture—the mandate we have to do justice," claimed ESA executive director Bill Kallio. "We do justice because we are followers of Jesus Christ." Progressive evangelical leaders consistently proclaimed that the ambition to achieve justice for all motivated their public activism. "It is out of a holy concern for all God's children and the biblical demands for doing justice that Christians enter the political arena," wrote political scientist Stephen Monsma in ESA's newsletter. Wallis identified the fact that "God hates injustice" as the first of the "basic principles for Christian political involvement in the world," for "fighting for justice, not partisan political goals, is the core of biblical politics." Progressive evangelical leaders viewed biblical descriptions of justice as guidelines for ordering social life. "Justice identifies what is essential for life together in community and specifies the rights and responsibilities of individuals and institutions in society," claimed Sider and Mott. In other words, Sider wrote separately, "justice from a biblical perspective must pay equal attention to the rights of individuals and the common good of all." Evangelical progressives viewed social justice as present when persons, groups, and institutions fulfilled their respective responsibilities for ensuring the equal rights of all community members.[11]

Expectations for each individual's dignified community participation shaped how leaders defined human rights and equality. "Since persons are created for community, the Scriptures understand the good life as sharing in the essential aspects of social life," Sider stated. "Rights are the privileges of membership in the communities to which we belong" and guarantee "the ability to share fully within one's capacity and potential in each essential aspect of community." Yet without "the material resources necessary for a decent life," evangelical progressives argued, individuals are unable to participate fully in the "multiple dimensions" of community life such as "decision-making, social life, economic production, education, culture, and religion." Therefore, leaders declared that universal human rights entail more than civil and political rights—they also comprise "socioeconomic benefits crucial to participation in community." Sider identified "a right to food, productive assets, private property, health care, education, and work" as "basic socioeconomic rights." Drawing upon both biblical principles and Catholic social teaching, Wallis similarly affirmed that "all people have a right to life and to secure the basic necessities of life (e.g. food, clothing, shelter, education, health care, safe environment, economic security)."[12]

By affirming access to "the benefit rights necessary for dignified participation in community" as an essential human right, leaders suggested that social justice requires not only formal equality but also substantive equality. While formal equality ensures equal treatment under the rule of law, substantive equality additionally seeks to recognize differences and to redress disadvantages in order to promote genuinely equal opportunities and more equivalent outcomes. Thus formal equality represents a necessary but not sufficient condition for substantive equality. For example, antidiscrimination laws that grant the equal right of all people to own means of production do not take into account the capacity to exercise this right, such as one's access to financial resources. Without such access, a person would have the formal right but lack the substantive opportunity to produce wealth. Therefore, progressive evangelicals declared that societies must correct disadvantages and promote substantive equality by guaranteeing the right to socioeconomic benefits. "Justice demands that every person or family has access to the productive resources (land, money, knowledge) so they have the opportunity to earn a generous sufficiency of material necessities and be dignified participating members of their community," Sider concluded.[13]

Since individuals have a right to basic socioeconomic resources, leaders argued, just distribution of these benefits becomes "the responsibility of the community to guarantee." In their public theology, therefore, progressive evangelicals championed distributive justice as vital. "The fact that justice in the Scriptures includes socioeconomic benefits means that we must reject the notion that biblical justice is merely procedural, merely the protection of property, person, and equal access to the procedures of the community," stated Sider. "Fair distribution is also central to the biblical understanding of justice." Because lack of education, financial resources, and social capital prevent some community members from having genuinely equal opportunities, progressive evangelical leaders regarded distributive justice as essential to achieving substantive equality for all. "To treat people equally . . . justice looks for barriers that interfere with a person's access to the productive resources needed for them to acquire the basic goods of society or to be dignified, participating members of the community," Sider claimed. "Distributive justice gives special consideration to disadvantaged groups by providing basic social and economic opportunities and resources." As a result, underprivileged community members deserve disproportionate benefits. "Because of unequal needs," Sider concluded, "equal provision of basic rights requires justice to be partial in order to be impartial." Wallis argued that societies "must ensure that all people who are able to work have jobs where they do not labor in vain, but have access to quality health care, decent housing, and a living income to support their families." For those unable to provide for themselves, leaders insisted that biblical models and mandates for social justice require communities to distribute "a generous sufficiency" to them. Ultimately, Sider stated, the provision of needed socioeconomic goods should help "people return to the kind of life in community that God intends for them."[14]

In assessing which community members and institutions have responsibilities for distributing these benefits, progressive evangelicals determined that God intends the state to play a critical role in establishing social justice. They viewed governmental structures, powers, and policies as appropriately coordinating many aspects of humans' cooperative social life. "The state is an instrument of the community and is an expression of our created social nature," Sider explained. Leaders concluded, as Wallis wrote, that "Scripture suggests a clear role for government in ensuring the common good" in three respects. First, the state should restrain evil by discouraging and punishing the injurious acts of individuals. Second, the state must also address social sins and use its power to correct unjust social structures. "The restraining hand of government can reduce the ways sin becomes embedded in socio-economic systems" by enforcing "policies that promote liberty, justice, and peace," ESA explained in an early statement of its political philosophy. Third, the state should nurture social justice by ensuring a just distribution of socioeconomic benefits. "When selfish, powerful people deprive others of their rightful access to productive resources, the state rightly steps in with intervening power to correct the injustice," Sider declared. "When other individuals and institutions in the community do not or cannot provide basic necessities for the needy, the state rightly helps." Thus progressive evangelicals' public theology pushed for communities to expand their definition of political rights to include socioeconomic benefits.[15]

Interpreting the government's role as limited but vital, leaders repudiated the twin errors of totalitarianism and libertarianism. They viewed the evils of twentieth-century communism as clearly demonstrating that a government should not have sole responsibility for social justice. Wallis criticized "the idolatries of state totalitarianism," for the communist promise of "a controlled society that would lead to a workers' paradise never moved beyond control" and produced only "a stifling and murderous bureaucracy." In addition, progressive evangelicals emphasized that the government represented only one of many vital social institutions. Families, churches, businesses, schools, and other cultural and civic institutions all offer crucial contributions and have partial responsibilities for social justice. In concert with the Catholic concept of subsidiarity, in which "social problems should be dealt with at as local a level as possible," both Sider and Wallis called for these nongovernmental organizations to address social problems and to distribute socioeconomic goods when able. Yet, they argued, these institutions cannot provide sufficient access to benefits such as education, health care, food programs, or even financial resources. When "the depth of social need exceeds the capacity of non-state institutions," Sider claimed, "the state must act directly to demand patterns of justice and provide vital services." Thus progressive evangelicals criticized Christian conservatives who championed libertarianism. "It is simply unbiblical to claim that government has no responsibility to seek justice for the poor," Sider and ESA editor Fred Clark wrote. "Government is God's servant for good. Part of its God-given task is to make sure that the poorest have the resources to earn their own living." In their political engagement, therefore, progressive evangelical leaders sought to hold the state "accountable for upholding justice" by promoting policies consistent with their theological interpretations of social justice.[16]

As a whole, this public theology of community represented the underlying political philosophy that inspired progressive evangelicals' practical activism from the 1970s into the twenty-first century. Sider best summarized this theological vision for public engagement: "All Christians," he wrote, "should recognize their civic responsibilities to love their neighbor and promote the common good through wise political engagement that nurtures justice through the state." Indeed, Wallis's most recent book—*On God's Side: What Religion Forgets and Politics Hasn't Learned about Serving the Common Good*—drew upon this public theology of community anew to outline how to "put the faith community's influence at the service of this radical neighbor-love ethic that is both faithful to God and to the common good." Thus as the progressive evangelical movement evolved, leaders such as Wallis and Sider became increasingly articulate about the fundamental biblical interpretations and theological convictions that shaped their political engagement. In the process, they sought to define over against conservative evangelicals—especially those associated with the Religious Right—the principles, priorities, and practices of faithful Christian citizenship.[17]

THE LIMITS OF LIBERALISM

In constructing their public theology of community, progressive evangelical leaders entered philosophical debates about the foundations for a just political order. In the political culture of the United States, different interpretations of liberalism have had the most formative and enduring effects. Liberalism here refers neither to the opposite of conservatism nor to the platforms of the contemporary Democratic Party. Rather, as promoted by divergent theorists ranging from John Locke to John Stuart Mill to John Rawls in recent years, liberalism as a broad political tradition emerged from the Enlightenment and influenced the development of constitutional democracy and subsequent political debates in the United States and beyond. Despite the predominant status of liberalism in its different forms, however, progressive evangelical leaders challenged both its individualistic foundations and its restrictive expectations for religion in the public sphere.

At their core, all liberal political philosophies place supreme value on individual freedoms and rights. Because liberals view humans as equal, rational, and autonomous agents, they insist that all limitations on personal liberties must have adequate justification. However, as Isaiah Berlin described, liberal philosophers disagree in their interpretations of both the nature of liberty and justified restrictions. Classical political liberals in the tradition of Locke, Adam Smith, and Friedrich Hayek define liberty primarily in negative terms—the absence of interference or coercion—and thus champion free markets and limited governmental constraints on individuals' private property rights, other freedoms, and idiosyncratic pursuits of happiness. In contemporary America, libertarians and (to a lesser extent) political conservatives are the heirs of classical liberalism. But modern political liberals most associated with the Democratic Party also stand within the broad tradition of liberalism. They likewise prioritize civil and personal freedoms but differ by emphasizing how social and economic inequalities can obstruct a person's liberties. As a result, modern liberals define liberty in more positive terms—the actual capability to exercise one's liberty in pursuit of personal fulfillment. In line with the "new liberalism" of British thinkers such as T. H. Green and L. T. Hobhouse, the economic theories of John Maynard Keynes, and recent philosophers such as John Rawls, they accept a greater role for the state in redistributing socioeconomic goods in order to ensure individuals' substantively equal capabilities to exercise their personal liberties. Nevertheless, the goal of such governmental actions remains enabling all people to develop their individualistic pursuits of happiness without external constraints.[18]

By promoting a public theology of *community* and emphasizing the *common* good, progressive evangelical leaders offered an alternative to the cultural dominance of liberal individualism and its perceived consequences. As the authors of an influential sociological study concluded, "Individualism lies at the very core of American culture." Most Americans believe that "anything that would violate our right to think for ourselves, judge for ourselves, make our own decisions, live our lives as we see fit, is not only morally wrong, it is sacrilegious." Yet progressive evangelical leaders rejected this apparent idolization of personal liberty and fulfillment. "Here in the United States, freedom has become an obsession. It's become not only our goal but our god," stated *The Other Side*'s Mark Olson. As a result, "we think it's our right to do what we want—and the notion that freedom is to be exercised, in consideration of others, has gone out the window." He stressed that the common good must take precedence. "In freedom, we are to love our neighbor as ourselves" and "put the needs of others first," Olson claimed. Progressive evangelicals argued that liberalism fails to balance individual rights and communal responsibilities. "Western liberalism in the tradition of John Locke over-emphasizes the individual and ends up with radical individualism," Ron Sider claimed. In turn, Western societies "have trouble affirming persons' responsibilities and obligations to promote the common good." Jim Wallis proclaimed that a "politics of community" offers a "more profound understanding of the meaning of justice" than liberalism's "individualistic idea of justice." He proposed the "biblical vision of *shalom*"—a holistic concept of peace and "right relationships"—as "the best definition of justice," for "restoring right relationships takes us further than respecting individual rights. It pushes us to see ourselves as part of a community, even as members of an extended but deeply interconnected global family." While Sider and other leaders affirmed "the profoundly important truth about the dignity, worth, and freedom of each individual," progressive evangelicals rejected liberal "individualism and its inadequate affirmation of obligations, duties, the common good, and our creation as communal beings."[19]

With respect to religion, liberal political philosophies promote the ideals of government neutrality and toleration, the institutional separation of church and state, and maximum individual freedom in private contexts. In the public sphere, however, a range of contemporary theorists such as John Rawls and Robert Audi—despite differences in arguments and nuanced qualifications—have claimed that citizens should practice restraint and not introduce personal religious views as the primary rationale for political decisions. In a religiously pluralistic society, they have contended, justification for theories of justice, political authority, and coercive laws should depend upon commonly affirmed or universally accessible political values rather than on particular religious principles. Appeals to religion as the rationale for coercive state actions undermine political consensus, these theorists have claimed, for such appeals fail to respect and cannot logically persuade compatriots who do not share the religious presuppositions. Therefore, they have argued that theories of justice and consequent laws and policies must be justified by ostensibly neutral, rational, secular evidence and arguments—what Rawls identified as "public reason"—that can transcend religious differences and prove acceptable to all rational citizens. "One has a prima facie obligation not to advocate or support any law or public policy that restricts human conduct, unless one has, and is willing to offer, adequate secular reason for this advocacy or support" and "unless one is sufficiently *motivated* by (normatively) adequate secular reason," Audi wrote. While some liberal philosophers have argued that the history of religious warfare and the problems caused by religious divisiveness demand a completely secular public square through the privatization of religion, Audi, Rawls, and other theorists have allowed religion a limited role: citizens may offer religious rationales in public deliberations, but *only if* they can also offer sufficient corroborating secular justification for their preferred political positions. In both cases, these advocates have given privilege to secularism in liberal democracies by endorsing public restraints or restrictions on religion.[20]

In contrast, progressive evangelicals' *public theology* of community reflected their foundational commitment to a robust role for religion in public discourse and political debates. "God is personal but never private," Wallis repeatedly proclaimed, for the Bible reveals "a God who speaks about 'politics' all the time ... about faith and 'public life' (not just private piety), about our responsibilities for the common good (not just for our own religious experience)." Leaders argued that Christians' fundamental profession of faith—"Jesus is Lord"—should inspire both their personal pursuit of holiness and their public pursuit of justice. "Christians must embrace and live out Christ's lordship not just in their personal lives and in church but also in every area of life," Sider argued. "The very essence of Christian faith requires that it find expression in public in many different ways." Both Sider (a lifelong Anabaptist) and Wallis were deeply influenced by Mennonite theologian John Howard Yoder, and they endorsed his Anabaptist view of the church as a countercultural, alternative community—a visible witness to God's just kingdom. Yet they did not believe that Christians should withdraw into separatist communities such as the Amish. Instead, they must work to "transform the kingdoms of this world" by identifying injustices and addressing them through public and political participation. By arguing that the church should act in *both* "countercultural" and "transformational" roles, progressive evangelical leaders challenged the classic typology developed by H. Richard Niebuhr in his book *Christ and Culture* regarding how Christians relate to their cultural contexts. "Niebuhr suggests that we must choose between the two, but we do not," Wallis declared. "Christ is both 'against culture' and the 'transformer of culture.'" Although progressive evangelical leaders spent the initial phase of their movement trying to convince evangelical audiences of Christianity's public implications, by the 1980s evangelicals across the ideological spectrum became eager political participants. "Relating faith to public life and to society is now assumed to be both important and necessary, and the debate is only about *how* faith should publically express itself," Wallis wrote on *Sojourners'* fortieth anniversary.[21]

Yet if progressive leaders felt little remaining need to persuade other evangelicals, they did address liberal philosophers and activists who believed that religion should be either minimized or barred in public debates in order to ensure a just, tolerant society. Sider rejected John Rawls's insistence upon "public reason" rather than religious justifications for laws and policies. Despite Rawls's attempts to identify a "perfectly neutral starting point free of any specific [for example, religious] definition of disputed claims about the good," Sider criticized Rawls's appeal to the "overlapping consensus" of "reasonable" worldviews as far from unbiased or universal. Rawls's criterion has no more objective basis than a religious one, he argued, and thus represents merely a different particular, prejudiced, and artificially privileged standard for determining a just political order. Unlike Rawls and other liberals, Sider stated, "We will nurture not a naked public square free of all religious reasons for political proposals, but rather an open, pluralistic, and civil public square open to all the different religiously and philosophically grounded arguments and proposals that every citizen and every particular community wish to advance." The most prominent progressive evangelical interlocutor in philosophical conversations regarding the role of religion in politics was Nicholas Wolterstorff. A renowned philosopher who taught for three decades at the Christian Reformed Calvin College before moving to Yale University, Wolterstorff engaged in direct debates with Robert Audi and others who advocated public restraints or restrictions on religion in liberal democracies. Not only did Wolterstorff doubt that a pluralist society could reach consensus regarding justice based upon purportedly neutral and rational secular principles, but he also viewed the exclusion of religious discourse as an ironic restriction of liberty. "Given that it is of the very essence of liberal democracy that citizens enjoy equal freedom in law to live out their lives as they see fit, how can it be compatible with liberal democracy for its citizens to be *morally restrained* from deciding and discussing political issues as they see fit?" he asked.[22]

Wallis proved more interested in practical than in philosophical debates. "The real question is not *whether* religious faith should influence a society and its politics, but *how*," he reiterated. Indeed, Wallis identified those who "want to banish faith from public life" as "new fundamentalists in the land." These "secular fundamentalists"—ranging "from the Anti-Defamation League, to Americans United for the Separation of Church and State, to the ACLU and some of the political Left's most religion-fearing publications"—would "deprive the public square of needed moral and spiritual values often shaped by faith." By neglecting or explicitly rejecting religion, Wallis argued, secular liberalism proves "unable to articulate or demonstrate the kind of moral values that must undergird any serious movement of social transformation." Progressive evangelical leaders were not alone in voicing these concerns. Among other Christian public intellectuals, two especially popularized such arguments: neoconservative theologian Richard John Neuhaus in *The Naked Public Square: Religion and Democracy in America* and Yale Law School professor Stephen L. Carter in *The Culture of Disbelief: How American Law and Politics Trivialize Religious Devotion.* All of these Christians regarded the liberal demands for religion's minimization or privatization as dogmatic decrees that would produce a morally impoverished public sphere.[23]

In fact, because progressive evangelicals shared the antiliberal commitment to religiously motivated public engagement with Christian conservatives, their movement represented a mirror image of the Religious Right. Both groups unapologetically promoted theological visions for American society. Even as he pilloried the political agendas of Religious Right leaders, Wallis often acknowledged their shared impulse. During the 1988 presidential primaries, for example, he defended televangelist Pat Robertson's appeals to religion and agreed that "'liberal secular humanism' cannot provide an adequate moral basis and framework for social life." After Moral Majority leader Jerry Falwell died in 2007, Wallis expressed appreciation that "Falwell, in his own way, did help teach Christians that their faith should express itself in the public sphere, and I am grateful for that, even if the positions he took were often at great variance with my own." The Religious Right did not err by promoting its theology in public, progressive evangelicals insisted; it erred by getting "the public meaning of religion mostly wrong—preferring to focus only on sexual and cultural issues while ignoring the weightier matters of justice." Wallis therefore tried to persuade liberals that "the answer to bad theology is not secularism; it is, rather, good theology. It is not always wrong to invoke the name of God and the claims of religion in the public life of a nation." On occasion, Wallis did caricature conservative evangelical leaders in an apparent effort to win support among liberals who feared the Religious Right. "Al Qaeda, the Taliban, and American fundamentalists like my old debate partners Jerry Falwell and Pat Robertson are, indeed, all theocrats who desire their religious agenda to be enforced through the power of the state," he exclaimed in *God's Politics.* Not only did this comparison fail to do justice to the democratic commitments of the Religious Right, but also one could charge Wallis equally guilty of "theocracy" by this definition. Progressive evangelicals too hoped that their own "religious agenda" would become public policy—enacted through democratic procedures and enforced by the state. On the whole, however, leaders sparred with the Religious Right not over the proper role of religion in the public square but over biblical interpretations and political priorities.[24]

This parallel dedication of progressive evangelicals and the Religious Right to religiously inspired politics was not lost on a variety of critics. For example, in a provocative 2001 essay in *The Nation* titled "Freedom from Religion," left-wing social critic Ellen Willis castigated religious progressives such as Wallis for joining the Religious Right's "attacks on secularism." Insisting that "a genuinely democratic society requires a secular ethos," White accused progressive evangelicals as well as the Catholic left of doing the Religious Right's "dirty work" and furthering "efforts to dilute the separation of church and state and increase the power and influence of religion in American life." In similar fashion, Americans United for the Separation of Church and State simultaneously rebuked the political engagement of Wallis and James Dobson, president of the conservative Focus on the Family organization. While Dobson was demanding that Republicans "start passing laws that advance the Religious Right agenda," Americans United announced in 2005, "Wallis is pressuring Democratic Party leaders to couch their positions in religious language." Americans United director Barry Lynn judged Wallis's and Dobson's actions equally illiberal. "Despite the threats from Dobson and the preachments from Wallis, elected officials should make decisions based on the public good, not private religious belief," he declared. "Our nation's laws must be rooted in constitutional values and reasoned analysis, not someone's personal take on scripture." In his recent book *To Change the World,* James Davison Hunter offered a theological and sociological critique of Christians' public engagement in which he concluded that the evangelical left simply "imitates the Christian Right." Because both groups seek to use political power to achieve their theological goals, Hunter lamented, both allow Christianity to become "instrumentalized (or used as a means to an end)" by political parties in their quests for power. To many observers, the political activism of progressive evangelicals and the Religious Right differed in content but not in kind.[25]

In response, progressive evangelicals insisted that their public theology and political engagement were faithful to democratic principles. Leaders claimed that they were merely exercising their political rights. "Religious people shouldn't be told just to be quiet," Wallis argued. "They should be invited to participate as *citizens* who have the right and the obligation to bring their deepest moral convictions to the public square for the democratic discourse on the most important values and directions that will shape our society." At the same time, progressive evangelicals acknowledged the pluralism of American society and accepted the pragmatic need to translate their biblical rationales into broader, more inclusive terms. "'The Bible says' is not the most effective way to persuade non-Christians—whether Jews, Muslims, or 'secular humanists'—to adopt our specific proposals," Sider wrote. "We must be ready to search for language and arguments that others can understand." Likewise, Wallis stated, "To influence a democratic society, you must win the public debate about why the policies you advocate are better for the *common good*." Leaders believed that this commitment to the democratic process exonerated them from any charge of theocracy. Because of "our respect for human freedom and our recognition of the reality of widespread pluralism, we will distinguish between what biblical norms should be legislated and what should not," Sider proclaimed. "We will also refuse to seek to impose our good legislative proposals on society until a majority in our democratic society freely embraces our proposals."[26]

Although rejecting the separation of religion and politics, leaders repeatedly affirmed the institutional separation of church and state. "We can demonstrate our commitment to pluralist democracy and support the rightful separation of church and state without segregating moral and spiritual values from our political life," Wallis assured audiences. In progressive evangelicals' interpretation of the religion clauses of the First Amendment—"Congress shall make no law respecting an establishment of religion, or prohibiting the free exercise thereof"—such separation entails institutional differentiation and independence. It prohibits "a state-controlled religion" and governmental interference with both "the independent functioning of religious institutions" and individual religious liberties. But, Sider maintained, the separation of church and state "does not mean that we should try to separate ethical or religious values from the political process nor that religious leaders should 'stay out of politics.'" In fact, Wallis argued, the original intent of the First Amendment was to allow religion to affect public deliberations. "In choosing not to establish any religion in American public life, the founders of our country were not seeking to diminish the influence of faith and its moral values, but rather to increase their influence on the social fabric and political morality—precisely by setting religion free from the shackles of the state," he wrote. "The attempt to strip the public square of religious values undermines the moral health of the nation, just as any attempt to impose theocratic visions of morality is a threat to democratic politics." Thus progressive evangelicals rejected liberal political philosophers' "strict separationist" interpretation of the First Amendment in which religion should play no role in public life. With confidence in their right to promote their evangelical public theology, leaders built and sustained a vigorous movement dedicated to social justice and the common good.[27]

PUBLIC THEOLOGY IN PRACTICE

The progressive evangelical movement's political priorities and anomalous combination of positions represented the application of their underlying public theology of community. Based upon their interpretation of social justice, leaders championed issues and promoted public policies designed to ensure the substantive equality, socioeconomic rights, and peaceful welfare of their neighbors both in the United States and beyond.

Because both racism and sexism deny the equal worth and dignity of minorities and women, each form of discrimination became a natural target of progressive evangelical activism. Leaders identified social patterns, practices, and policies that placed racial minorities and women at a disadvantage, and they promoted both antidiscrimination laws and distributive justice programs intended to advance their substantive equality. With respect to abortion, most progressive evangelical leaders concluded that unborn children deserve the same protection and rights as other community members. As a result, pro-life progressive evangelicals gave preference to the community's responsibility for the welfare of fetal life over the individual rights of women to choose whether or not to terminate a pregnancy. At the same time, however, they refused to prioritize opposition to abortion over other assaults on human life, dignity, and substantive equality. Leaders' commitment to social justice also inspired their defense of the full civil rights of gays and lesbians. Yet the majority remained convinced that biblical teachings concerning sexual morality prohibited same-sex behavior. Therefore these progressive evangelicals refused to endorse gay and lesbian relationships as a matter of personal Christian ethics, and they came to promote civil unions for same-sex couples as a compromise that simultaneously upheld heterosexual marriage as best for the common good and protected the civil rights of gays and lesbians. In economic issues, leaders argued that a community must show especial concern for its impoverished members. Condemning the grossly unequal distribution of resources that they regarded as the root of much poverty, they called for redistributive public policies and governmental programs intended to empower the poor and to diminish substantive inequalities. Finally, progressive evangelicals rejected militarism and American nationalism as attacks on the sacred worth and equality of all humans. Most leaders promoted nonviolence and an internationalist perspective that valued the common good of all global "neighbors." As the following chapters detail, each of these political convictions reflected the comprehensive commitment to social justice that stood at the heart of progressive evangelicals' public theology of community.

3. Racism

"AMERICA'S ORIGINAL SIN"

On the fiftieth anniversary of the Supreme Court's 1954 ruling in *Brown v. Board of Education, Sojourners* published a commentary titled "Still Separate, Still Unequal." The promise of racial equality remained unfulfilled, *Sojourners* believed. In fact, "racism embedded in our society" resulted in "structural violence" that kept poor African Americans just as segregated and even more endangered than fifty years before. Discriminatory zoning laws, lack of affordable housing, and underfunded schools institutionalized patterns of segregation and poverty. "Most of us who don't suffer from the violence of our structures don't see it," the author, David Hilfiker, claimed. "We live the myth of equal opportunity and don't see our opportunities for the privileges they are." Until privileged Americans recognized how social structures sustain racial inequalities, Hilfiker wrote, they would likely continue to oppose vital solutions such as government antipoverty programs, access to affordable housing, more equitable funding of schools, and community development projects. "Fifty years later, we are not only still segregated but cannot even pretend that the separate are equal," the author concluded.[1]

This *Sojourners* article epitomized how evangelical progressives analyzed racism as an institutionalized injustice that required corrective public policies and programs. Beginning in the late 1960s, leaders identified persistent racial inequalities as one of the most egregious social problems that Christians must address. Indeed, growing recognition of inequities faced by African Americans inspired many progressive evangelicals' early activism and became a central concern within their emerging movement. Indignation at minorities' consistent lack of socioeconomic resources became a recurrent theme in *Sojourners*, *The Other Side*, and the publications of Evangelicals for Social Action (ESA), and leaders condemned fiscal policies that exacerbated their already disproportionate poverty. In the 1980s Ronald Reagan's administration particularly vexed evangelical progressives. They regarded his opposition to social welfare programs and civil rights regulations as undermining racial progress. In addition, Reagan's support for the apartheid regime in South Africa outraged progressive evangelicals and galvanized their campaign against that country's legalized segregation and oppression. Although overt racism in America seemed on the decline by the end of the twentieth century, leaders argued that improved personal relations obscured the persistence of minorities' relative lack of wealth, employment, education, and equal opportunities. Therefore throughout the 1990s and into the twenty-first century, they continued to draw attention to racial problems through both periodic analyses and coverage of prominent public events ranging from the Los Angeles riots in 1992 to Barack Obama's presidential campaign in 2008. Although progressive evangelicals viewed Obama's victory as an auspicious opportunity to advance racial justice, leaders insisted that more work remained to overcome the inequalities perpetuated by institutional racism.

Despite their unequivocal commitment to racial equality, *Sojourners*, *The Other Side*, and ESA attracted almost exclusively white audiences. Black Christians' distinct religious heritage and progressive evangelicals' broad social justice agenda limited their movement's appeal for many African Americans. Nevertheless, the leading progressive evangelical journals published didactic articles and commentaries by minority authors in order to increase their white constituencies' awareness of racial injustice and its causes. Most evangelicals in the late twentieth century interpreted racial problems almost exclusively in terms of discriminatory attitudes and actions of individuals. In contrast, evangelical progressives believed that racial injustice resulted primarily from established social and political institutions (such as educational, economic, and legal structures) that systematically discriminated against minorities. This understanding of institutional racism reflected progressive evangelicals' comprehensive interpretation of sin as both personal immorality and social injustice. Therefore, they argued, combating racism required more than personal changes and private initiatives. Leaders supported both political efforts to redress minorities' unequal access to socioeconomic resources and affirmative action programs designed to compensate for the consequences of past discrimination. Because working for the substantive equality of all community members stood at the heart of progressive evangelicals' public theology, promoting public policies and programs designed to enhance racial justice became one of their political priorities.

RACISM AND THE RISE OF CONTEMPORARY EVANGELICAL PROGRESSIVISM

A sense of Christian responsibility to oppose racism and to reverse its unjust social effects helped to propel the rise of contemporary evangelical progressivism. While significant numbers of mainline Protestants, Catholics, and Jews supported the civil rights movement, most evangelicals distanced themselves from public and political efforts to advance racial equality. Some evangelicals, especially in the south, defended segregation. Many others viewed social activism as a distraction. Even those committed to racial equality typically preferred a gradualist approach toward civil rights and focused on opposing personal prejudices and discrimination— a position exemplified by Billy Graham, the most prominent evangelical leader.[2] In response to evangelicals' meager support for the civil rights movement, Fred, Anne, and John Alexander began the publication of *Freedom Now* in 1965 in order to convince fellow conservative Christians to support blacks' equality and integration. Their motivation came not from simply reading their Bibles but rather from witnessing firsthand the injustices and inequalities faced by African Americans. "Our concerns were biblically based and motivated, but to be truthful, that wasn't their origin," remembered John Alexander. "Their origin was in what was happening in society." In its early years the magazine highlighted racial inequalities, challenged readers to recognize how blacks "have been oppressed by those of us who are white," and insisted that evangelicals adopt both personal and political strategies for fighting racial injustice. By 1970 the Alexanders had changed the magazine's name to *The Other Side* and expanded its attention to forms of social injustice beyond racism. Even after *The Other Side* broadened its focus, however, editorials by John Alexander and regular articles by black authors such as John Perkins, Bill Pannell, William Bentley, and Tom Skinner called attention to racial inequalities and exhorted white evangelicals to work for racial justice.[3]

The Post-Americans (who later renamed their group Sojourners) likewise identified racism as a pressing injustice. Like the Alexanders, Jim

Wallis's personal exposure to the plight of African Americans in Detroit helped inspire his zeal for social justice. With fellow seminarians at Trinity Evangelical Divinity School, he formed the People's Christian Coalition to promote "the biblical demands for public justice." In the initial 1971 issue of the *Post-American*, Wallis condemned what he regarded as a "society cancerous with racism," and Glen Melnik identified "Black liberation" along with the Vietnam War as one of the two paramount issues Christians must face. Unlike *Freedom Now* and its successor, *The Other Side*, however, the *Post-American* in its early years rarely included articles explicitly devoted to defending black equality or to exploring proposals for combating racism. Its preoccupation with American militarism reflected the genesis of the magazine at the apex of opposition to the Vietnam War rather than in the midst of the civil rights movement. Nevertheless, as part of their insistence that "Christians must be active in rejecting the corrupt values of our culture," the Post-Americans called readers to become "prophetic in our resistance and activism against the injustice of a racist society." Along with *The Other Side* in the early 1970s, the *Post-American* ensured that the emerging progressive evangelical network would make the substantive equality of racial minorities a prominent objective within its public engagement.[4]

The 1973 Chicago Declaration of Evangelical Social Concern made this intention clear. The workshop that issued the declaration was organized by Ron Sider, who also had formative experiences with African Americans that shaped his interpretation of Christians' social responsibility. In the mid-1960s Sider and his wife had lived in a predominantly black neighborhood while he studied for his doctorate at Yale University. Witnessing events through the eyes of the African American couple from whom they rented proved particularly influential. "We actually sat with them the night that Martin Luther King was killed, [and] we felt their pain," he remembered. "We got to know their son, who was an angry young man open enough to talk to a white person." Sider attributed much of his sensitivity to injustice to such relationships. "Most of what I know about oppression I've learned from black Americans," he declared. Sider and other organizers invited several leading black evangelicals to the workshop that produced the Chicago Declaration. Prodded by these black participants, the statement included a strong repudiation of evangelicals' culpability for racial inequalities and estrangement: "We deplore the historic involvement of the church in America with racism and the conspicuous responsibility of the evangelical community for perpetuating the personal attitudes and institutional structures that have divided the body of Christ along color lines." The document then emphasized the financial consequences of such attitudes and actions. "Further, we have failed to condemn the exploitation of racism at home and abroad by our economic system." For evangelical progressives, equitable access to socioeconomic resources would become a litmus test for determining the state of racial justice.[5]

The first issue of *The Other Side* in 1974 featured several paradigmatic articles. Despite the passage of civil rights legislation, Fred and John Alexander argued that attempts at integration had failed to achieve the supreme goal: "justice and human development." In response, the Alexanders suggested that financial redistribution from wealthy white Christians to black Christians would enable more equal opportunities for development than forced integration efforts. Two black authors reached similar conclusions. "Integration isn't the answer," argued John Perkins. Instead, African Americans needed "an equal economic base" that allowed for "self-determination" and "human development." Ron Potter insisted that "equal footing" was in fact a prerequisite to equitable integration and racial reconciliation. "Before reconciliation takes place there must be an equal distribution of power across the board," he wrote. As progressive evangelicals increasingly emphasized, power proved inextricably tied to money. At a 1974 conference on politics that gathered many leaders of the nascent evangelical left, Jim Wallis reported that "the strong presence of black evangelical Christians forced white evangelicals to begin to come to grips with the ugly history of racism." In discussions at the conference, Wallis noted, "the question of economic justice surfaced again and again." Black participants in the progressive evangelical movement continued to highlight economic inequalities as evidence of systemic barriers to their substantive equality.[6]

As the 1970s progressed, a severe recession led progressive evangelical leaders to frame discussions of racial inequality within analyses of economic injustice. Budget deficits grew as the government financed both the social programs of President Lyndon Johnson's "Great Society" and America's military involvement in Vietnam. The 1973 oil embargo by the Organization of Petroleum Exporting Countries (OPEC) precipitated soaring energy and gas costs. Sluggish business, dramatic increases in unemployment, and historically high inflation produced the economic quagmire of "stagflation"—rising prices and low growth. This economic uncertainty reinforced progressive evangelicals' sensitivity to issues of poverty and unequal distribution of wealth. In many ways these economic crises seemed more urgent than racial prejudice. An end to legalized seg-regation, a reduction in overt racism, and affirmative action policies had created greater economic and educational opportunities for a large number of African Americans. As the black middle class expanded, however, many inner-city blacks without access to the same socioeconomic resources and opportunities remained trapped in poverty. William Julius Wilson, an influential black sociologist at the University of Chicago, suggested in *The Declining Significance of Race* that class affected African Americans' welfare more than race. Thus racial injustice seemed intimately linked to the disproportionate economic and social inequalities faced by racial minorities.[7]

Articles in *Sojourners* and *The Other Side* from the late 1970s demon-strate how arguments regarding economics served as vehicles for expec-tations of racial equality. For example, in a 1978 editorial highlighting "the plight of the urban poor," Jim Wallis emphasized that poverty-stricken inner cities "need almost every kind of basic community development: employment, housing, education, health care, sanitation, nutrition, rec-reation, and police protection." He emphasized that the lack of such resources had its most debilitating effects on racial minorities. "Most blacks have yet to benefit substantially from the gains of the civil rights movement," Wallis declared, and "a whole class of mostly young and non-white urban dwellers have been left behind, stuck in permanent cycles of poverty, racism, and crime." In the same *Sojourners* issue, John Per-kins described the hostility of white evangelicals toward black evangeli-cal leaders not when they denounced racism but rather when they chal-lenged economic inequalities. "As soon as I question the economic order that has made America unfairly rich and is creating massive poverty," he wrote, "I find myself in very, very hot water." He accused the white leadership of evangelicalism of defending a system that prevented sub-stantive equality for African Americans by unfairly distributing wealth and perpetuating poverty. When blacks such as Tom Skinner, Bill Pan-nell, and William Bentley emphasized the association between economic and racial inequalities, they had been called communists and barred from white evangelical institutions. Perkins identified this treatment as the "institutional assassination of prophetic black leaders," and he pleaded for white evangelicals to "stop stoning our black prophets." In 1979 *The Other Side*'s Mark Olson cited statistics showing the ongoing economic, social, and educational inequalities faced by African Americans. Despite "the myth of black progress," he claimed, "racism is not over." Olson described President Jimmy Carter as a "huge disappointment" for African Americans and accused him of "establishing an economic philosophy that ignores the plight of ghetto-dwelling blacks." The slow advance toward racial minorities' substantive equality caused Olson to anticipate that "the 1980s may see a resurgence of black activism." The policies of President Ronald Reagan made Olson's prediction come true.[8]

"RONALD REAGAN IS NOT THEIR FRIEND"

The Republican Party's platform in 1980 signaled how the Reagan administration would interpret racial equality. Although affirming that "no individual should be victimized by unfair discrimination because of race" or other personal characteristics, Republicans insisted that "equal opportunity should not be jeopardized by bureaucratic regulations and decisions which rely on quotas, ratios, and numerical requirements to exclude some individuals in favor of others, thereby rendering such regulations and decisions inherently discriminatory." In other words, political conservatives repudiated affirmative action. Enforced by the Equal Employment Opportunity Commission and the Office of Federal Contract Compliance, affirmative action programs grew out of the civil rights legislation of the 1960s in order to prevent discrimination and to increase opportunities for minorities. To meet affirmative action goals, many businesses and institutions gave special preferences to nonwhites in order to overcome the effects of historical inequalities. By the late 1970s, however, white conservatives became increasingly frustrated by liberals' support for compensatory treatment for past racial oppression and discrimination. Many Americans believed, in fact, that affirmative action programs represented "reverse racism" and subverted the ideal of equal opportunity by giving advantages to certain groups. During the 1980 presidential election, Ronald Reagan and other Republicans appealed to this backlash against affirmative action. Political conservatives objected to both federal intervention and legal efforts to promote racial equality. Reagan's promises to end the intrusion of "big government" tied together his opposition to affirmative action, civil rights regulations, and social welfare—positions that appealed to newly politicized members of the Religious Right.[9]

Almost immediately following Reagan's election, progressive evangelical leaders began worrying about the consequences of his proposals. Although *Sojourners* and *The Other Side* had preferred Carter, disillusionment with electoral politics led them largely to treat the 1980 presidential election with indifference. But the effects of Reagan's policies on the poor and racial minorities not only deepened progressive evangelicals' commitment to support more actively the best among flawed candidates in future elections but also inspired them to address racial inequalities with renewed urgency. Explicit racial issues had been neglected recently, Wallis conceded early in 1981, but the new administration was already undermining the precarious hopes of African Americans for equality. He therefore called for renewed attention to "white racism" as "this country's oldest and deepest sin." In particular, Wallis decried "the vulnerability of black children and of all black people" who "are forced to live on the margins of a society that still refuses to grant them the most basic requirements of human dignity and justice." He accused Reagan of justifying the "official neglect of the poor" in "the name of sound fiscal policy," claiming that the disproportionate poverty of racial minorities represented the persistence of racial injustice. Progressive evangelicals' anxiety over prospects for racial equality soon turned to disgust with the Reagan administration.[10]

While the president justified his desire to slash programs that benefited the poor and minorities by appealing to his philosophical commitment to limited government, progressive evangelicals regarded his political agenda as thinly disguised assaults on black communities. "Instead of protecting civil rights and eliminating the demonic effects of racism," wrote Bill Kallio, the executive director of ESA, "our government only talks about reverse discrimination and getting rid of affirmative action." *Sojourners* editor Danny Collum believed that Reagan had revealed himself "personally and officially" against the needs of blacks. "The signal [his] policies are sending to black people is that Ronald Reagan is not their friend," Collum declared. "The small gains toward racial equality made in the last twenty years are being eaten away by an administration whose officials have made it clear that racial discrimination is a tolerable evil." Evangelical progressives interpreted the combination of Reagan's opposition to affirmative action and domestic spending cuts that most affected racial minorities as reversing the modest gains of the civil rights movement.[11]

Throughout Reagan's tenure, progressive evangelicals repeatedly denounced the apparent active and passive enforcement of racial inequalities over which the president presided. In its twentieth anniversary issue in 1985, for example, *The Other Side* carried articles by John Perkins, Bill Pannell, Coretta Scott King, and civil rights veterans Vincent and Rosemarie Harding that addressed the ongoing challenges faced by African Americans. Pannell especially lashed out at the Reagan administration and the Republican Party, calling the president's professed commitment to civil rights "baloney" in light of Republicans' message that "this country is better off in the hands of a few white folks with plenty of money." *Sojourners* devoted its January 1986 issue to honoring the first celebration of Martin Luther King Jr.'s birthday as a national holiday. While lauding the inauguration of an annual tribute to "a great prophet of God," Wallis also insisted that King's vision of justice should inspire ongoing efforts to achieve racial equality. Prominent black theologian James Cone asserted that Reagan willingly ignored the existence of poverty and racial discrimination in his proclamations that the American dream had already been realized. He therefore challenged readers to remember that King's dream of racial equality in America must not obscure Malcolm X's message of the nightmare of racial oppression. "No promise of equality, no beautiful word about freedom and justice, can serve as a substitute for the bestowal of basic human rights for all people," Cone wrote.[12]

At the end of 1987, *Sojourners* published its most sustained rebuke of racial inequality. On the cover, a white figure stood triumphantly on the back of a kneeling black silhouette next to a title blaring "White Racism: America's Original Sin." Once more, Wallis tried to direct attention to a matter that no longer seemed a "hot topic." He confessed that improvements in personal attitudes and increased opportunities for some black citizens had caused most Americans and even activists like himself to prioritize other concerns. Indeed, racism had received less attention from evangelical progressives over the previous decade than protests against nuclear arms, America's militarism in Central America, and persistent poverty. Yet Wallis argued that racism endured, and he again used financial statistics as the prime evidence of intensifying inequalities faced by African Americans. "The heart of racism was and is economic, though its roots and results are also deeply cultural, psychological, sexual, even religious, and, of course, political," he wrote. "That blacks are disproportionately consigned to the lowest economic tier is an indisputable proof of racism. The existence of a vast black underclass, inhabiting the inner cities of our nation, is a testimony to the versatility of white racism twenty years after legal segregation was officially outlawed." Subsequent articles recounted the history of racism in America, gave examples of recent racial violence, and urged white Christians to work for equal educational, economic, and social opportunities. The detrimental effects of Reagan's political agenda upon African Americans had provoked renewed concern among evangelical progressives for racial equality in the United States.

Meanwhile, the president's policies toward South Africa had intensified their protests against racism abroad as well.[13]

In the late 1970s progressive evangelicals joined the growing international opposition to apartheid in South Africa. Beginning in 1948 the system of apartheid (Afrikaans for "separateness") extended and institutionalized racial segregation that allowed the minority of white South Africans to dominate the majority nonwhite population. Countries throughout the world opposed this oppression, and in 1962 the United Nations General Assembly urged member nations to end diplomatic and economic relationships with the South African government. Within South Africa, groups such as the predominantly black African National Congress led protests that often ended in arrests and violent suppression. Following the 1977 death of black opposition leader Steve Biko, progressive evangelical publications began exhorting readers to join anti-apartheid campaigns. "As Americans we have a personal responsibility to end our corporate and governmental alliances with the racist South African regime," wrote Perry Perkins in *Sojourners*. "We must muster all the energy of nonviolent struggle and end our country's participation in a deeply oppressive system." *Sojourners* began profiling both South African and American Christians working to end apartheid. Writing in *The Other Side*, ESA president Ron Sider urged Christians to pray and to lobby on behalf of South Africans. Another contributor claimed that "our unity with suffering South African humanity" required American Christians to "disrupt the political, economic, and moral alliance that exists between the United States of America and the fascist Union of South Africa." As with domestic issues of racial inequality, the Reagan administration's policies heightened progressive evangelicals' protests.[14]

In light of Reagan's unwillingness to distance the United States from South Africa, leaders increased their publication of articles that highlighted the injustices of apartheid. Rather than racism, Reagan understood the primary problem in South Africa as the threat of communism gaining a foothold in the region. The Cold War with the Soviet Union dominated his thinking, and he declared that concern for human rights in South Africa drew attention away from the Soviet threat to the Western world. Jeane Kirkpatrick, Reagan's ambassador to the United Nations, claimed that "racist dictatorship is not as bad as Marxist dictatorship."

Many leaders of the Religious Right supported South Africa for similar reasons. For example, Jerry Falwell visited the country in 1985 and met with President Pieter Botha. Afterward, Falwell downplayed the government's enforcement of apartheid, called Bishop Desmond Tutu "a phony" for claiming to represent oppressed blacks, and pledged that his Moral Majority coalition would oppose any economic sanctions against South Africa. In contrast, progressive evangelical leaders repeatedly decried how the American government and industries not only sanctioned but also empowered the repressive system of apartheid. For example, a *Sojourners* article titled "Greasing the Wheels of Apartheid: How the Reagan Administration and the U.S. Corporations Bolster the South African Regime" detailed the extent to which American diplomatic and economic support for the country had increased since Reagan took office. "In the face of the most racist and totalitarian government on earth today," Jim Wallis concluded in 1986, "Ronald Reagan is trying to do as little as possible."[15]

For the rest of the decade, progressive evangelical publications urged readers to join efforts to end apartheid. *Sojourners* especially promoted Christian opposition to apartheid by publishing over forty relevant articles between 1986 and 1991. In addition, Wallis and associate editor Joyce Hollyday visited South Africa in 1988 and edited a book titled *Crucible of Fire: The Church Confronts Apartheid*. ESA also carried regular updates in its newsletters, advocated sanctions against South Africa, and sponsored a tour of evangelical colleges by a black South African evangelical, Moss Ntlha. Progressive evangelical leaders such as Ron Sider, Joyce Hollyday, Tony Campolo, Mark Hatfield, and John Perkins joined together to promote the "Kabare Declaration," a statement calling upon "all evangelicals to rigorously oppose the apartheid regime that is oppressing black Christian brothers and sisters in South Africa." When a democratic election with full black participation finally occurred in 1994, evangelical progressives heralded it as a landmark victory in the nonviolent struggle for justice.[16]

Yet even as anti-apartheid efforts played a significant role in the progressive evangelical movement in the 1980s, participants did not lose focus upon domestic issues. "As we are appalled by the institutionalized racism imposed in South Africa," ESA's Sharon Temple wrote in 1988, "let us not forget our own shamefully recent history of a similar apartheid that denied full rights of citizenship and humanity to our black neighbors—and which continues in many ways today." *Sojourners* focused its 1988 Peace Pentecost campaign upon "the pervasive and persistent character of white racism in the United States." A year later, an article in *The Other Side* argued that high-stakes testing practices in American education discriminated against minorities who languished in underfunded schools. "Testing has become the new political instrument for disenfranchising minority students, particularly black students, and denying them opportunities that are their natural birthright as American citizens," the author wrote. Evangelical progressives remained resolved to redress all forms of racial injustice.[17]

THE PERSISTENT PROBLEM

From the 1990s into the twenty-first century, progressive evangelicals developed two strategies to demonstrate that racism remained a persistent problem. First, leaders continued to publish periodic analyses of racialized inequalities. At the beginning of the decade, for example, *Sojourners* devoted an issue to reexamining race relations since the civil rights movement. Authors insisted that efforts to achieve an integrated society had failed to produce any semblance of substantive racial equality. "In the critical areas of income and employment, education, housing, and health," wrote Jim Wallis, "life for most black Americans is still separate and very unequal." An ostensible commitment to integration had allowed whites to assimilate blacks selectively into social structures that they still controlled. "White society has preferred integration to equality," he argued, and continued to "cover up the fundamental questions of justice." Contributors called for the goal of social transformation to replace that of integration in order to create "a multicultural partnership of equals."[18]

As a second strategy, progressive evangelicals regularly took advantage of prominent public events that sparked national conversations regarding racial issues to educate their audiences. For example, the impending 500th anniversary of Christopher Columbus's arrival in the Americas allowed leaders to remind audiences that blacks were not the only victims of racism. *The Other Side* and *Sojourners* first highlighted injustices faced by Native Americans in the late 1970s. The American Indian Movement (AIM) organized a walk across the United States in 1977 to protest legislation that would abrogate treaties between the American government and Native American tribes. AIM's activities successfully grabbed progressive evangelicals' attention, and didactic articles in *The Other Side* and *Sojourners* described threats to "Indian self-preservation" and efforts to "survive the onslaught of anti-Indian legislation being proposed in the U.S. Congress." In the mid-1980s *The Other Side* published several more articles that accused the FBI of conducting a "secret war" against AIM and framing American Indian activist Leonard Peltier for the murder of FBI agents during a siege of Pine Ridge Indian Reservation in 1975. To progressive evangelicals, these events served as reminders of persecution suffered by Native Americans that called not only for repentance but also for "restitution of stolen land" and "reparation for three hundred years of injustice." In 1987 a coalition of progressive evangelicals including Jim Wallis, John Alexander, and Ron Sider endorsed a petition urging a "stand for justice" that demanded Congress investigate the 1975 siege of the Pine Ridge Reservation.[19]

As 1992 approached, the opportunity to thrust Native Americans into the public eye alongside Columbus offered a promising strategy to increase awareness of their plight. Plans to commemorate Columbus's "discovery" represented a fitting symbol to progressive evangelicals of how celebrations of American history often masked racial oppression. White Americans should realize that "1992 actually marks the 500th anniversary of an invasion and the heinous consequences that resulted for America's indigenous people," wrote Bob Hulteen in *Sojourners*. Additional articles in *Sojourners*, *The Other Side*, and ESA's newsletter all described the persistence of anti-Indian prejudice and the devastating rates of poverty among contemporary Native Americans. Authors called for both symbolic apologies and substantive reparations. "It is past time that the United States took its responsibilities toward Native Americans seriously and empowered them to earn an [adequate] standard of living," ESA asserted. "White America has at least one thing left to discover," Hulteen concluded: "justice for American Indians." Even as they focused primarily on African Americans, progressive evangelicals defended other minorities who suffered discrimination and injustice.[20]

Two prominent trials in the 1990s offered additional occasions for progressive evangelicals to stress that racial equality remained unrealized. In 1992 a jury acquitted Los Angeles police officers of using excessive force in the arrest of a black motorist, Rodney King, despite well-publicized video evidence of the officers beating and kicking him. Several days of violence and vandalism in Los Angeles ensued. Progressive evangelicals interpreted the decision as yet another example of racial injustice. "There was no question that Rodney King was brutalized; the issue was whether it mattered," Wallis wrote. "The verdict, in effect, told every black American that it did not." While condemning the riots, Wallis maintained that blacks had just grievances against ongoing discrimination and inequalities that "demonstrate the absolute and persistent reality of racism on every level of American life." In 1995, after the lengthy televised murder trial of African American football star and actor O. J. Simpson, many blacks celebrated the not guilty verdict while most whites watched in disbelief. In response, Wallis explained how experiences with racism contributed to blacks' reactions. "Black jubilation over the acquittal reflected a belief that this case hadn't been proven beyond a reasonable doubt," he claimed, "that it had been tainted by police sloppiness and racial corruption, and that a black man finally had the resources to beat the system, as whites have done for years." ESA's Rodney Clapp interpreted "the extraordinary attention devoted to the O. J. Simpson trial" as a reflection of "the passions and fears race engenders in a country with a history of such tortured racial relations." Wallis used the Simpson case to illustrate the ongoing racial polarization in American culture that demanded "a new national *conversation* on race" led by religious communities. "It is absolutely clear," Wallis concluded, "that continuing efforts are still vitally needed to open up opportunities for people of color."[21]

Yet such efforts required an acknowledgment that racism and its consequences persisted, and thus progressive evangelical leaders continued to challenge their white audiences to recognize racial injustice. "The white community needs to move beyond denial to the facing of racism, the naming of racism, and the commitment to do everything in its power to change racist behavior and systems of injustice," wrote *Sojourners* contributing editor Yvonne Delk. Several authors hoped that a historical account of how whites had gained privileges and power would help readers understand contemporary injustices. The ideological concept of "white identity" arose in order to justify enslavement and oppression, explained Eugene Rivers, an African American pastor and another *Sojourners* contributing editor. He argued that the bifurcation of people into white and nonwhite identities empowered "the demonic ideology of white supremacy" that remained "the dominant principle governing American culture." In separate articles, Rivers and Bob Hulteen each entreated white Christians no longer to think of themselves as white, for accentuating racial distinctions undermined the equality of *all* people. In 1998 both *Sojourners* and ESA's *Prism* marked the thirtieth anniversary of Martin Luther King Jr.'s assassination by again highlighting widespread discrimination, racial estrangement, and African Americans' disproportionate poverty. "The hopes and dreams that followed the 1960s civil rights and voting rights legislation have yet to be fulfilled," Wallis reiterated. "America is still a racially divided society, where diversity is widely perceived as a greater cause for concern than for celebration." Delk outlined a strategy to dismantle racism that included acknowledging racism's existence and challenging organizational structures and cultural patterns that reinforced racial inequalities. In *Prism*, editorial board member Harold Dean Trulear pointed to King's vision for social transformation, not superficial integration, as vital to achieving equality for minorities. Americans must change "the quality of inter-racial interaction," he proposed, "so that the gifts of all persons in society come to form what he called 'the beloved community.'"[22]

To be sure, leaders recognized signs of progress at the close of the twentieth century. During Bill Clinton's presidency, African Americans benefited from benign public policies and a robust economy. The growth of the median income for black households exceeded that of whites, while poverty among blacks decreased dramatically. Among their more politically conservative peers, progressive evangelicals noted several encouraging developments. In 1996 National Association of Evangelicals president Don Argue publicly confessed his group's past sins of racism and committed it to addressing patterns of racial inequality. The conservative evangelical men's organization Promise Keepers likewise embraced the goal of racial reconciliation as a prominent part of its agenda. Even as progressive evangelical leaders expressed cautious appreciation, they warned that no one should mistake these advances and events for the achievement of racial equality. Poverty and unemployment rates still stood over twice as high for blacks as compared to whites. African Americans had significantly less access to quality education and a lower life expectancy than whites by six years. Although heartened by conservatives' rhetoric of racial reconciliation, progressive evangelicals insisted that justice must *precede* authentic reconciliation, not merely stand as its potential result. "Outside the church meeting rooms and stadium rallies where white and black Christians are hugging each other is a nation where racial polarization is on the rise," Jim Wallis observed, "where the legacy of slavery and discrimination is still brutally present, and where the majority white population is signaling its tiredness with the 'issue' of race by voting down long-standing affirmative action policies." As *Sojourners'* Bill Wylie-Kellermann stated in 1998, progressive evangelicals believed that "no force in U.S. history has proven more relentless or devastatingly resilient than white racism."[23]

Therefore leaders remained vigilant in the first decade of the twenty-first century. ESA published a forum on racial reconciliation that urged readers not only to acknowledge the "historical sins of white people" but also to work for "the economic and political empowerment" of minorities. Numerous articles in *Sojourners* reemphasized the crippling consequences of blacks' unequal socioeconomic resources, and authors endorsed both governmental and community development programs that facilitated access to education, employment, and home ownership. *Sojourners* assistant editor Elizabeth Palmberg highlighted how "systemic and individual racism" and whites' greater financial abilities to hire lawyers produced "racial disparities in our penal system": a black person was seven times as likely as a white to be imprisoned, and minorities received much harsher sentences for similar crimes. In 2007 evangelical progressives pointed to the highly publicized case of the "Jena 6"—six black teenagers from Jena, Louisiana, arrested in the beating of a white classmate—as prime evidence of the "racial injustice in our legal system." Critics charged that authorities had ignored underlying racial tensions, treated whites leniently, and excessively charged the black students with attempted murder. "If we feel that racial justice has already been achieved," ESA's Harold Dean Trulear wrote in response, "we are merely engaging in head-burying and will be impotent to work toward any justice, for any cause." All the while, leaders lamented that racial issues still seemed politically insignificant. For example, during the 2004 presidential election, Danny Duncan Collum complained that concerns over racial inequality played less of a role than it had in sixty years. "The de-racializing of this election is bad news for anyone who cares about social justice in this country," he declared in *Sojourners*. Four years later, however, Barack Obama's presidential candidacy ensured that race moved back into the political spotlight.[24]

Progressive evangelicals viewed Obama's campaign as a pivotal moment in the struggle for racial justice. Wallis had built a friendship with the future president in the 1990s, and in 2006 Obama spoke at a conference hosted by Sojourners at which he described his conversion to Christianity. Yet Obama was plagued during his campaign (and well into his presidency) by rumors that he was secretly a Muslim—a charge that Wallis, Ron Sider, Tony Campolo, and other progressive evangelicals sought to discredit. In addition, controversy erupted when media outlets began showing incendiary excerpts from sermons of Obama's longtime pastor, Jeremiah Wright of Chicago's Trinity United Church of Christ, in which he preached that God would "damn America" for its history of violence and racial oppression. While these sermons reflected well-established themes within black liberation theology, conservative critics not only denounced Wright for promoting black racism and anti-Americanism but also questioned Obama's own racial views and patriotism. Obama eventually ended his association with Wright and condemned his racially divisive statements. Yet both Sider and Wallis hoped that a few "silly" and "irresponsible" accusations—for example, the charge that "the US government invented AIDS to destroy the black community"—would not obscure "the truth behind Wright's exaggerated words." Wallis declared it "hard to disagree with many of the facts" presented by Wright, while Sider affirmed Wright's claims that "white Americans took the country by terror from Native Americans" and "our seizure of Africans from their homeland was terrorism." To evangelical progressives, the astonishment and outrage over Wright's provocative sermons demonstrated whites' ongoing ignorance of the "real oppression, discrimination, and blocked opportunities" that African Americans experienced. "In 2008, to still not comprehend the reality of black frustration and anger is to be in a state of white denial," Wallis claimed. Leaders warned against political attacks on Obama that used the controversy to stir whites' fear. "That will deepen racial division, strengthen white racism, . . . intensify black anger," and "torpedo any chance of seizing upon our present opportunity to reach another plateau of racial understanding," Sider wrote.[25]

Indeed, progressive evangelicals were optimistic that Obama's campaign offered a "genuine possibility" to inspire "greater racial justice" and "racial reconciliation." Both Sider and Wallis praised a nationally televised address in which Obama discussed the controversy over Wright. Titled "A More Perfect Union," this speech acknowledged the bitter legacy of racism that produced black anger and white resentment. But Obama concluded by calling Americans to transcend the "racial stalemate we've been stuck in for years" in pursuit of justice for all people. Wallis called it "the most honest and compelling speech about race in decades," for it "offered new hope for opportunity and equality and the beginning of the kind of racial reconciliation that few have dared to speak of since the civil rights movement." For longtime progressive evangelical activists, Obama's nomination as the Democratic presidential candidate marked a milestone in the drive for racial equality. "This is a transformational moment, one we didn't think would happen in our lifetime," Wallis declared. Sider told *Christianity Today* that Obama's election would represent "a huge step toward racial reconciliation in this country" and signal "that the majority of white people have moved beyond racism." Yet evangelical progressives cautioned that the election of a black president itself would neither end racism nor fulfill racial justice. An Obama victory would demonstrate only "that we have made (some) progress in overcoming our tragic, wrenching racist history," Sider predicted. After Obama's election, Wallis celebrated the "watershed moment" but maintained that the country still had to take advantage of "this profound opportunity for deeper racial reconciliation and social justice." Likewise, Sojourners board member Mary Nelson rejected claims that America had entered a post-racial era. "Post-racial? No, not yet; racism and bigotry are still alive," she wrote. "But we now have opportunity to move beyond bigotry, with the younger generation leading the way." Despite racism's persistence, Obama's presidency offered progressive evangelicals new hope for racial justice.[26]

CONFRONTING WHITE AUDIENCES

Although progressive evangelicals' public theology fueled leaders' commitment to the substantive equality of racial minorities, self-reported statistics from *The Other Side, Sojourners,* and ESA reveal that white supporters overwhelmingly formed the movement's constituency. In 1978 and 1982 *The Other Side* reported that 96 percent and then 98 percent of respondents to respective reader surveys identified as "European American (white)." Similarly, 95 percent of respondents to a 1980 questionnaire distributed to *Sojourners* subscribers were white. Membership surveys by ESA produced remarkably comparable data, as 95 percent of members in 1984 and 96 percent in 1988 identified as white. Despite emphatic commitments to racial justice, therefore, the leading progressive evangelical groups did not attract appreciable numbers of nonwhite supporters. Two important factors contributed to this lack of racial diversity.[27]

First, though most black Christians shared the conservative theology of white evangelicals, they had distinct religious and cultural identities. In response to slavery and segregation in the nineteenth and early twentieth century, African Americans developed their own independent churches, denominations, and institutions. As a result, few black Christians participated in the fundamentalist-modernist controversy that divided white Protestantism in the 1920s and led to the modern evangelical movement. Fundamentalism arose as a separatist movement to defend traditional interpretations of Christian doctrines against the spread of theological liberalism, or modernism. Beginning in the 1940s, however, a group of fundamentalists rejected this separatism and sought to reengage with the broader American culture. Concerned primarily with intellectual and cultural respectability, leaders such as Billy Graham and Carl F. H. Henry adopted the name "evangelicals" to describe themselves. Although attracting some African Americans, modern evangelicalism as a self-conscious religious and social movement almost exclusively comprised predominantly white denominations, institutions, and participants. As a result, many black Christians who participated in the evangelical movement expressed ambivalence about calling themselves "evangelicals." "One reason blacks aren't comfortable with the word is that it grows out of the fundamentalist-liberal controversy, and in the black church we've never had that controversy," William Bentley, president of the National Black Evangelical Association, told *The Other Side* in 1975. In addition, the dominant political, social, and economic conservatism within white evangelicalism only reinforced this discomfort among more politically liberal black Christians. Even as progressive evangelicals began to challenge this reflexive conservatism in the early 1970s, they drew upon the institutional and social networks of white evangelicalism. Leaders often defined their goal as the reformation of the white evangelical subculture and subsequently promoted their agenda as an alternative to the Religious Right. Thus the story of contemporary evangelical progressivism stands primarily as part of the larger narrative of theologically conservative white Protestantism in the twentieth and early twenty-first century. In spite of black Christians' theological and political affinities with the progressive evangelical movement, separate sociological and ecclesiological histories curtailed the participation of minorities.[28]

Second, the ways in which progressive evangelical leaders prioritized and articulated issues of race reaffirmed that white Christians represented their primary audience. As the 1973 Chicago Declaration of Evangelical Social Concern symbolized, the movement's commitment to a broad social justice agenda did not stress racism to the extent that some black evangelicals wished. In fact, the force of the declaration's condemnation of racism resulted only after the insistence of the participating black minority. "Blacks especially had to press aggressively for a strong statement on the complicity of white evangelicalism in the individual manifestations and group mechanisms that originated and perpetuate racial oppression in America," Bentley wrote afterward. While other issues of justice preoccupied the white majority, African Americans understandably considered racism the most urgent. "We felt that while racial prejudice and discrimination are not the only social issues that plague America and her churches," Bentley claimed, "it is the one above all others that colors all others." Wyn Wright Potter, a black activist from Chicago, described the difference in perspective in even stronger terms. "I felt an insensitivity to the criticalness of the racial crisis," she remembered concerning early gatherings of the evangelical left. In her opinion, white evangelical progressives believed that "we have all these problems" and "racism is just one of them." "That sickens me," Potter vented in an interview with *The Other Side*. "Granted that other things are important, but there's nothing like racial oppression." To many African Americans associated with the early progressive evangelical movement, racial equality remained the sine qua non of social justice.[29]

Nevertheless, the issue of racism would never dominate the agenda of the progressive evangelical movement. It continued to represent only one form of injustice that leaders protested. For example, as ESA defined the scope of its public policy analyses, racism and minority issues represented just one of eleven categories on which they pledged to report. In *Sojourners* and *The Other Side*, explicit articles addressing racial equality became overshadowed at times by other pressing concerns such as economic justice, the influence of the Religious Right, or American militarism in the Cold War, Central America, and the Middle East. To be sure, evangelical progressives never wavered in their commitment to equality and justice for racial minorities. Yet they remained what Ron Sider described as "stubbornly multi-issue." "If the Bible is any clue, God seems to be very concerned both with peacemaking and with the family, both with justice and life," wrote Sider. "Violating the integrity of persons through racism, sexism, and economic oppression all displease God." As a result of this commitment to a broad range of social justice issues, progressive evangelical publications carried irregular coverage of racial problems. Minorities who sought consistent and primary analyses of racial justice likely joined alternative social and religious movements. Indeed, several prominent black evangelicals who participated in the earliest progressive evangelical gatherings in the 1970s grew disgruntled with white leaders and poured their energies into separate black organizations such as the National Black Evangelical Association. By placing issues of race within the broader framework of social justice, *The Other Side*, *Sojourners*, and ESA would continue to attract an overwhelmingly white constituency.[30]

Even when demands for racial justice did move into the spotlight, the repetitious insistence upon racism's persistence and consequences appeared most fitting for white audiences. As with many subsequent progressive evangelical articles on race, the Chicago Declaration assumed that its audience needed to acknowledge the existence of racial inequality. Both the specific contrition for racism within the declaration and the broader appeals for social action clearly targeted white evangelicals, thus limiting the statement's relevance for racial minorities. Bentley appreciated the significance of the statement for white evangelicalism yet acknowledged that "the declaration would not be adequate for a purely black constituency." The focus of the movement's leaders would remain upon urging whites to recognize racism and to advance racial equality. "White people are long overdue to begin a prophetic interrogation of our personal attitudes, social structures, and cultural and religious institutions in order to reveal and remove the racism we have long accepted or ignored," Jim Wallis claimed. As a result, progressive evangelical publications contained didactic articles on racism, attempting to persuade readers that, in Wallis's words, "we have yet to come to terms with it and the way it has poisoned our national life and corrupted the American spirit." Over and over, authors explicitly challenged white readers. "Whites in America must admit the reality and begin to operate on the assumption that ours is a racist society," Wallis declared. Because "all white people have benefited from the structure of racism," he argued, "whites must try to change it." Ultimately, "racism has to do with the power to dominate and enforce oppression, and that power in America is in white hands," Wallis concluded. "There is no such thing as black racism. Black people in America do not have the power to enforce that prejudice." Progressive evangelical leaders largely directed their messages to white audiences in order to deepen their awareness of racial injustice.[31]

At the same time, they strategically decided that these messages should frequently come from racial minorities themselves. Contributors to *Sojourners*, *The Other Side*, and ESA's publications displayed decidedly more racial diversity than their readerships. By publishing accounts and analyses of racism from the perspectives of minorities, especially blacks, progressive evangelical leaders confronted readers with lived experiences of racial injustice. In the early stages of the movement, the prominence given by *The Other Side* to black authors stood out within the overwhelmingly white circles of evangelicalism. "It was in the pages of this vital organ that many of us [black evangelicals] were given the opportunity which no other magazine would even consider," William Bentley recalled. "There can be no mistake that it was first *Freedom Now*, and then *The Other Side* which gave our viewpoints a chance at unedited expression."

Sojourners and ESA also began to carry regular articles by African Americans and added minority representatives to their editorial and advisory boards. In October 1984, for example, *Sojourners* published lead articles by James Cone, the foremost black liberation theologian who was anathema to conservative evangelicals, and Vincent Harding, a civil rights activist and historian. The articles originated as addresses to black Christians, and associate editor Danny Collum admitted that "our staff discussed whether this magazine, with a majority-white readership, was an appropriate forum" for them. However, the editors concluded, "God's desire for people of faith is often seen most clearly from the perspective of the oppressed," and therefore white Christians must "listen closely to prophetic voices from the black church." Likewise, ESA invited African American minister Michael McKinley in 2000 to offer "some frank views from within the black church" for "the white evangelical church to be aware of and to act on." Over the years, progressive evangelical publications also featured profiles of nonwhite activists, theologians, and academics addressing racial injustices and inequalities. Through promoting these minority perspectives, evangelical progressives attempted to ensure that white audiences remained neither isolated from nor ignorant of racial problems.[32]

A SOCIAL AND STRUCTURAL SIN

Progressive evangelical leaders hoped that their coverage of racism and calls for both social transformation and corrective public policies would revolutionize how the majority of white evangelicals interpreted racial issues. As with most social problems, racism appeared to mainstream evangelicals as the aggregate of magnified personal failures. They viewed humans as free and independent actors, in control of and fully responsible for their decisions; therefore social problems such as racism and poverty resulted almost exclusively from the poor decisions and sinfulness of individuals. This interpretation showed little appreciation, however, for the ways in which historical factors, social structures, and cultural patterns affect a person's beliefs and behaviors. At the end of the twentieth century, an influential study of evangelicals' racial attitudes by sociologists Michael Emerson and Christian Smith demonstrated how the individualistic ethos of most evangelicals limited their understanding of racism. Evangelicals largely believed that the only racial problems that existed were the prejudice and discrimination of individuals that damaged interpersonal relationships. Yet, as Emerson and Smith noted, "this perspective misses the racialized patterns that transcend and encompass individuals, and are therefore often institutional and systemic." In addition, very few white evangelicals believed that racial problems included economic inequalities—one of the dominant themes within progressive evangelicals' analysis of racial injustice. Instead, most assumed that equal opportunities existed for all Americans, and thus any inequalities resulted from personal deficiencies. White evangelicals overwhelmingly disregarded relevant social structures that influence individuals such as "unequal access to quality education, segregated neighborhoods that concentrate the already higher black poverty rate and lead to further social problems, and other forms of discrimination." Emerson and Smith concluded that, despite their intentions, these evangelicals reinforced racial inequality by minimizing its reality and by proposing inadequate solutions based upon personal rather than social transformation.[33]

In contrast, the most striking aspect of progressive evangelical leaders' opposition to racism was their insistence on its institutionalized and structural nature. "Racism goes beyond mere prejudice and personal attitudes, but is rooted in institutional patterns and structural injustices," Jim Wallis declared in a typical statement. Institutional racism reflects "established laws, customs, and practices which systematically reflect and produce racial inequities in American society." That is, regardless of any particular person's intentions, prevailing legal and social structures systematically disadvantage racial minorities. As early as 1970, *The Other Side* began decrying "institutional racism" and advocating changes in social and economic patterns. Signers of the 1973 Chicago Declaration of Evangelical Social Concern acknowledged not only the "personal attitudes" but also the "institutional structures" that segregated Christians and fed racial injustice. As President Reagan aligned his policies with individualized interpretations of racial problems in the 1980s, evangelical progressives condemned views that discounted structural causes of racial inequalities. "Reagan's approach in matters of racial justice, as in economics, is to reduce everything to isolated transactions between individuals," wrote Danny Collum in *Sojourners*. "This is essentially an attempt to escape from history, to abdicate human responsibility for the powerful economic, political, cultural, and spiritual forces that form and feed the racist impulse in people and societies." Wallis argued that the appearance of improved personal attitudes belied the pervasive institutional nature of racism. American economic, education, and judicial systems remained biased toward the benefits of whites and thus perpetuated African Americans' inequality. "Merely to keep personally free of the taint of racial attitudes is both illusory and inadequate," he argued. "Just to go along with a racist social structure, to accept the economic order as it is, just to do one's job within impersonal institutions is to participate in racism." Unlike most evangelicals, therefore, evangelical progressives believed that the primary obstacles to racial equality lay not in personal prejudices but in social patterns and structural injustices.[34]

These convictions regarding institutional racism stemmed from progressive evangelicals' broad understanding of sin. From the early stages of their movement, leaders criticized the ways in which most evangelicals tended to restrict their interpretations of sin to only "consciously-willed individual acts." On the contrary, evangelical progressives insisted that "humanity's proud rebellion against God expresses itself in both personal *and* social sin." These social sins become manifested in unjust laws, inequitable social structures, and oppressive political and economic systems. Ron Sider identified "neglect of the biblical teaching on structural injustice, what we might call institutionalized evil," as "one of the most deadly omissions in evangelicalism today." As a result, when "Christians frequently restrict the scope of ethics to a narrow class of 'personal' sins," he argued, "they fail to preach about the sins of institutionalized racism, unjust economic structures and militaristic institutions which destroy people just as much as do alcohol and drugs." ESA contributor Craig Wong criticized evangelical "theology that largely addresses sin at the personal, but not systemic, level," for such "shallow theology" reduces racial reconciliation to a "personal discipleship project, solvable by 'befriending people of color.'" Their theology of social and structural sin primed progressive evangelicals to recognize racism as both individual discrimination and social injustice.[35]

Since they acknowledged the power of institutional racism, progressive evangelical leaders rejected strategies for improvement based merely upon the transformation of individuals, including spiritual regeneration. Instead, their commitment to distributive justice led them to promote public policies designed to compensate for racial minorities' unequal access to socioeconomic resources that led to their disproportionate poverty. In addition, evangelical progressives supported a controversial method—one abhorred by political and Christian conservatives— to counter the legacy of racial discrimination and to offer minorities substantively equal opportunities: affirmative action. In response to the

Supreme Court's ruling in the landmark 1978 case of *Regents of the University of California v. Bakke*, both *The Other Side* and *Sojourners* endorsed affirmative action programs. John Alexander provocatively defended "reverse racism." To be sure, he admitted in *The Other Side*, "choosing people on the basis of merit without regard to color sounds fair." Yet in practice, blind meritocracy preserves white privilege and power, Alexander argued, for "it ignores history" and "the long legacy of discrimination in America." He concluded, "Something must be done to correct past crimes." Jim Wallis similarly argued that affirmative action remained necessary to create substantive equality for disadvantaged racial minorities. "To legally enforce equality in a society of inequities is to perpetuate those inequities," he wrote. "The Blind Lady of Justice has peeked through her blindfold just enough to see race and class and adjust her decisions accordingly."[36]

In the coming decades, progressive evangelical leaders employed similar arguments to oppose periodic attempts to dismantle affirmative action programs. Backed by the Religious Right, Republicans campaigned against affirmative action on the grounds that it provided preferential treatment (and therefore *une*qual opportunities) for some based upon race, gender, or other factors. Yet evangelical progressives rejected this argument. Certain preferential policies do not deprive white males of opportunity, ESA's Van Temple wrote, but only chip away at unfair advantages that those in power have possessed. Wallis highlighted the reality of these advantages. "Affirmative action has always existed in America—for white men from affluent classes, in particular," he wrote. "It is not whether anyone should get affirmative action, but rather whether anyone other than white men should get it." *Sojourners* contributor Barbara Reynolds encouraged readers to think of affirmative action not as "preferences" but as a "remedy." "Affirmative action done correctly lifts up, rather than tears down," she declared. "It makes up for past wrongs, while not unjustly creating new wrongs." For progressive evangelical leaders, the legitimacy of affirmative action stemmed from their interpretations of sins such as racism as not only personal but also social and structural. "Can we acknowledge that God exercises impartial justice, but at the same time shows special consideration for victims of structural sin?" asked Timothy Tseng in ESA's *Prism*. "Affirmative action is an important mechanism for compensatory racial justice—perhaps the only mechanism," he insisted. "It deserves the support of evangelicals." Nevertheless, most white evangelicals failed to recognize institutional and systemic forms of racism. Thus wider support for affirmative action remained wishful thinking for progressive evangelicals.[37]

✤ Progressive evangelicals' campaigns against racism represented an important expression of their public theology of community. Regardless of skin color, they insisted, all people equally bear God's image and thus have inalienable, sacred worth. Leaders viewed racist attitudes and acts as dehumanizing assaults on the dignity of minorities. "To treat any bearer of God's image as sub-human is to contradict the gospel," ESA president Vernon Grounds wrote. "To permit blacks to be treated as sub-human is heresy in act. It is not just heresy. It is sin." But they also condemned the dehumanization and substantive inequality caused by institutional racism. *Sojourners* argued that minorities were often forced "to overcome numerous obstacles to obtain the basic necessities of life and the basic human dignity deserved by all children of God." Not least, progressive evangelicals lamented that artificial racial distinctions undermined God's intentions for human communities. "There is no such thing as 'race' in the eyes of God—in whose image we are all created as equal," Jim Wallis maintained. "Race is a social construct created by human beings for the purpose of justifying oppression." In response, leaders believed that God called Christians to combat *all* forms of racism and "to build community across racial lines in this troubled nation." "Racial justice and reconciliation," Wallis wrote, "are required of us by a God who loves all the little children, and a Christ who gave his life to break down the barriers between us." Progressive evangelicals insisted that this justice and reconciliation required not only personal but also political action. Their interpretations of institutionalized injustice led them to promote public policies and programs designed to enhance minorities' substantive equality. Thus the drive to combat racism played a pivotal and persistent role in the public activism of contemporary progressive evangelicalism. As the next chapter demonstrates, efforts to achieve justice and equality for women became a similar core commitment of the movement.[38]

4. Trials and Triumphs of Biblical Feminism

F ew statements would have shocked evangelicals more in the early 1970s than the *Post-American*'s bold claim. "Jesus was a feminist, and a very radical one," the new progressive evangelical magazine declared in 1972. "Can his followers attempt to be anything less?" Behind the leadership of Jim Wallis, the Post-Americans were seeking to convince fellow evangelicals that those "who live by the values and ethical priorities of Jesus Christ and His Kingdom" must "be active in rejecting the corrupt values of our culture." Based upon the example of Jesus, they argued, such corrupt values included patriarchal attitudes and actions. Because "it is clear from the Gospels that Jesus vigorously promoted the dignity and equality of women in the midst of a very male-dominated society," the Post-Americans asserted, Christians should support the feminist movement's goals of women's full equality and freedom from patriarchal injustices. Yet to nearly all evangelicals in the early 1970s, identifying Jesus as a feminist would have seemed absurd if not blasphemous. Although a significant number of nineteenth-century evangelical revivalists and reformers pushed for women's equal rights during the first wave of feminist activism, most modern evangelicals regarded calls from contemporary feminists to support women's equality and liberation as siren songs that would wreck God's designated social order. They believed that the Bible unambiguously affirmed a gender hierarchy in which men should exercise unique leadership in domestic, public, and religious life. As the *Post-American* article indicated, however, the emerging progressive evangelical movement viewed feminism more sympathetically.[1]

Based upon the combination of their public theology and biblical interpretations of God's design for gender egalitarianism, support for "biblical feminism" became a distinguishing mark of contemporary progressive evangelicals. Their comprehensive commitment to women's substantive equality inspired leaders to promote feminist reforms in both the church and the broader culture. Beginning in the early 1970s, pioneering evangelical feminists participated in and received crucial support from the initial network of progressive evangelical leaders. Indeed, the progressive evangelical movement helped to launch and to nurture the growth of biblical feminism. The 1973 Chicago Declaration of Evangelical Social Concern included a brief confession of evangelicals' patriarchal past, and the most prominent biblical feminist organization—the Evangelical Women's Caucus—grew out of the 1974 Thanksgiving workshop of the newly formed Evangelicals for Social Action (ESA). The leading progressive evangelical journals, the *Post-American* (soon renamed *Sojourners*) and *The Other Side*, embraced biblical feminism and exposed wider audiences to its central argument: scriptural passages suggesting men's exclusive leadership in the home, church, and society reflected ancient cultural traditions rather than the eternal truth of gender egalitarianism. Yet Christian conservatives condemned biblical feminism as a heretical mistake and opposed the broader feminist movement as a social disaster. Throughout the 1970s and early 1980s, conservative evangelicals solidified their theological hostility to feminism in the church, while leaders of the growing Religious Right crusaded against feminists' political goals. In the face of this opposition, progressive evangelical leaders defended the orthodoxy of biblical feminism. They also joined the broader feminist movement in denouncing women's inequalities as injustices, supporting legislative remedies such as the Equal Rights Amendment (ERA), and criticizing patriarchal traditions.

Even as women's relative status improved by the end of the century, progressive evangelicals continued their political and religious campaigns against persistent injustices faced by women. Leaders highlighted ongoing economic imbalances and sexist cultural patterns that disproportionately impoverished women. They denounced violence against women and patriarchal attitudes that fostered rape and domestic abuse. Evangelical progressives also lobbied for and celebrated women's empowerment in developing nations. Above all, contributors to *Sojourners*, *The Other Side*, and ESA's publications criticized sexist discrimination in the church and obstacles to women's religious leadership. They sought to encourage the growth of biblical feminism by publishing firsthand accounts and practical analyses of women in ministry. *Sojourners* and *The Other Side* also supported Christian feminists in their attempts to reinterpret patriarchal imagery, theology, and traditions. While the commitment to social justice at the heart of their public theology led evangelical progressives to champion the feminist goals of equality and liberation from patriarchy in the public sphere, their theological understanding of gender egalitarianism rather than hierarchy inspired their support of women's substantive equality in the church as well.

THE EMERGENCE OF CONTEMPORARY BIBLICAL FEMINISM

Although most modern evangelicals firmly embraced antifeminism, notable groups of evangelicals in the nineteenth century promoted women's rights within both the church and society. Popular evangelical revivals often undercut gender hierarchies and other forms of social order by emphasizing the spiritual equality of all people and the authority of one's religious experiences. This egalitarian impulse opened the door for some women to claim the right to obey God's call for them to share their testimonies and even to preach. While most early cases were isolated, women became especially encouraged to speak publicly by revivalist Charles Grandison Finney and within the holiness movement that spread among Methodists and other Wesleyan groups. Advocates for women's equality began contesting traditional biblical interpretations of women's subordinate and domestic roles. In works such as Sarah Grimké's *Letters on the Equality of the Sexes*, Phoebe Palmer's *The Promise of the Father*, and Frances Willard's *Woman in the Pulpit*, they foreshadowed the arguments of contemporary biblical feminists by pointing to scriptural examples of women's leadership, alternative interpretations of passages used to support patriarchy, and the overarching egalitarian ethos of Christianity expressed in passages such Galatians 3:28. The experience of many of these women in abolitionist, temperance, and other reform movements inspired and trained them to campaign for women's suffrage, additional political rights, and public roles. Thus evangelical revivalists and reformers made significant contributions to the development of nineteenth-century feminism.[2]

But these advocates failed to carry the day, for most evangelicals came to accept a more rigid set of gender ideals that developed during the Victorian era and reinforced traditional biblical interpretations of gender hierarchy. As cultural and economic changes increasingly placed men outside of the home, a "cult of domesticity" arose that associated piety especially with women and their spiritual duties in the home. Masculinity became defined by economic provision and less association with religion, while femininity became identified with domesticity, submission, purity, and piety. In the years surrounding the beginning of the twentieth century, however, challenges to this model arose. Women increasingly entered the public sphere, and traditional roles for women as wives and mothers were being delayed or even rejected by "the New Woman." Simultaneously, rapid urbanization and industrialization challenged the foundations for masculinity as men found fewer options for self-employment. Evangelicals joined other critics in blaming the sense of social unrest upon the loss of traditional gender roles and changes in family life. Yet most of their attention was directed to the theological crises occurring in the same period, and thus their concerns for gender were inextricably tied to this controversy. Fundamentalist evangelicals defended the notions of an inerrant Bible against more liberal Protestants' acceptance of Darwinian science and biblical criticism. As a result, their commitment to traditional views of the Bible—including conventional interpretations of gender hierarchy—took on new importance. To be sure, from the late nineteenth through the mid-twentieth century, fundamentalist evangelicals in practice depended upon women's work in church ministries and missions. Nevertheless, leaders such as John Rice perpetuated ideals of male leadership and women's submissiveness through works such as his popular 1941 book *Bobbed Hair, Bossy Wives, and Women Preachers.* In the mid-1940s a group of "new evangelical" leaders broke with the defensive and separatist stance of the fundamentalist movement. Yet even as their desire to reengage with American intellectual and social culture formed the basis for modern evangelicalism, they continued to accept gender hierarchy in churches, homes, and society.[3]

As a result, evangelicals overwhelmingly resisted the modern feminist movement. Beginning in the 1960s, contemporary feminist leaders launched a campaign to identify and to protest social, political, and economic inequalities faced by women. Representatives such as Betty Friedan, Gloria Steinem, and Mary Daly particularly denounced expectations of women's submissiveness and domesticity. But, in the words of a 1969 *Christianity Today* article, conservative Christians regarded these very qualities as "timeless spiritual principles." Evangelical polemicists believed that women experienced authentic freedom only by fulfilling the roles to which God had called them. "The truly liberating option for modern mothers lies in a broadened sense of homemaking," Mary Bouma assured *Christianity Today*'s readers in 1971. Thus most evangelicals responded to the feminist movement by reaffirming biblical interpretations that emphasized a gender hierarchy. God had established a patriarchal order, they argued, in which men and women possess inherently different social roles and responsibilities despite their equal sacred worth.[4]

Yet not all evangelicals rejected the feminist impulse out of hand as they wrestled with its implications. Despite widespread assumptions of gender hierarchy, mainstream evangelical journals carried several early articles that explored support for women's equality. In 1966 Letha Scanzoni wrote an essay in the magazine *Eternity* that questioned the consistency of conservative Christians who allowed women to lead evangelistic activities but prohibited them from teaching a mixed Sunday school class. Two years later *Eternity* carried another feature by Scanzoni in which she defended marriage as a "partnership" rather than a hierarchical relationship. Attempting to temper the threat of these respective articles, Scanzoni included disclaimers that she was neither calling for female ordination nor rejecting "loving direction by a husband" in marriage. In the early 1970s several authors questioned conventional views of gender even more boldly. For example, Ruth Schmidt criticized the ways in which Christians replicated cultural discrimination against women. "I'm tired of being considered a second-class citizen in the Kingdom of God," she wrote in *Christianity Today*. She lamented that "the Christian Church has not been a leader in the struggle for *full* equality for women in society, nor has it allowed women to experience freedom from society's prejudices within the Church." In *Eternity*, assistant editor Nancy Hardesty published an article titled "Women: Second Class Citizens" in which she developed similar arguments. In comparison to more contentious feminists, calls for greater ministry opportunities and mutual submission in marriage represented modest reforms. Yet suggestions of gender egalitarianism proved far too threatening for most evangelicals.[5]

Rebuttals in defense of traditional gender hierarchy overwhelmed these early attempts to identify biblical support for Christian forms of feminism. A steady stream of editorials, articles, and letters within *Eternity*, *Christianity Today*, and other evangelical circles acknowledged abuses of male authority but reaffirmed its necessity in society and the family. "In the beginning, Eve bit into forbidden fruit and fell into subjection to Adam," *Christianity Today*'s editors wrote. "Her descendents face a lesser temptation—equality with man instead of with God—but they are biting no less eagerly into their forbidden fruit." Billy Graham, the most influential evangelical leader, made clear his support of traditional feminine roles. "Wife, mother, homemaker," he told *Ladies' Home Journal*, "this is the appointed destiny of true womanhood." Popular literature and teaching on family life, such as Larry Christenson's *The Christian Family* and Bill Gothard's parenting and marital seminars, also reaffirmed men's leadership and women's submission in the home and culture at large. As the feminist movement gained strength and visibility—in 1972, for example, Congress passed the Equal Rights Amendment and *Ms.* magazine debuted—the conservative majority of evangelicals increasingly asserted the incompatibility of Christian orthodoxy and feminism. Pushed away from the mainstream, emerging biblical feminists soon found support within the growing progressive evangelical movement.[6]

Concern for gender equality contributed little to the rise of contemporary progressive evangelicalism. Only after eight years of publication did *The Other Side* address sexism, and even then its 1973 issue on the subject reflected ambivalence about feminist claims. The editors included articles from several women who had challenged traditional views of women in mainstream evangelical magazines. Authors such as Letha Scanzoni and Nancy Hardesty highlighted biblical support for women's equality, historical precedents for women's ministry, and the ways in which Christians wrongly accepted cultural sex-role stereotypes. In separate editorials, John Alexander and his wife, Judy, agreed that the feminist movement rightly identified unjust inequalities and false assumptions of gender roles. But, they each maintained, the Bible *did* teach some binding form of male authority and female submission. As a result, John Alexander concluded, evangelical progressives should admit ambiguity on how to apply biblical teachings, challenge clear social discrimination against women, and follow Jesus's model of siding with the oppressed (in this case, women). In its early years, the *Post-American* published less tentative yet still isolated support of feminist convictions. The magazine revealed its sympathy in the brief description in 1972 of Jesus as a feminist—"that is, a person who promotes the equality of women with men, who treats women primarily as human persons and willingly contravenes social customs in so acting." Another article urged readers both to reassess domestic expectations for women and to combat the "economic exploitation" of those who did work outside the home. In early 1973 the *Post-American* also carried a supportive report regarding the first convention of the National Women's

Political Caucus. Yet the magazine's preoccupations with the Vietnam War, economic injustice, and theological justification for social action marginalized attention to feminist concerns. Nevertheless, the foundational commitments to social justice and substantive equality of both the *Post-American* and *The Other Side* offered fertile soil in which biblical feminism soon flourished.[7]

The 1973 workshop that issued the Chicago Declaration of Evangelical Social Concern catalyzed the growth of evangelical feminism. The original draft submitted by the all-male planning committee made no mention of women's issues—a fact protested by the few female participants. Although a second committee charged with preparing a more succinct statement again comprised all men, Stephen Mott asked Nancy Hardesty to compose a line on women's issues that he might include. Her suggestion formed the basis for a confession and call within the Chicago Declaration: "We acknowledge that we have encouraged men to prideful domination and women to irresponsible passivity. So we call both men and women to mutual submission and active discipleship." Despite the brevity and political restraint of this affirmation, it seemed threatening to many evangelicals. Indeed, Hardesty later reported that Billy Graham refused to endorse the declaration because of these sentences. Among progressive evangelicals, however, this statement led to more sustained attention to feminist concerns at a second conference the following year. Meeting under the auspices of the newly organized Evangelicals for Social Action, the 1974 conference divided into six groups, or caucuses, devoted to various forms of injustice. Hardesty led a caucus analyzing women's issues, and it developed recommendations that included encouraging expanded opportunities for women within evangelical institutions, opposing sexist stereotypes in Christian educational literature, endorsing the ERA, and using a newly formed newsletter—*Daughters of Sarah*—to publicize Christian feminism. Most important, the group decided to organize separately as the Evangelical Women's Caucus. With a national meeting scheduled for late 1975 and use of *Daughters of Sarah* as an organ, the organized emergence of biblical feminism from within progressive evangelical circles became official.[8]

By the mid-1970s, support for biblical feminism became a marker of progressive evangelical identity. As early evangelical feminists disseminated their biblical defenses of gender egalitarianism, the most prominent progressive evangelical journals endorsed their theological arguments and political agenda. Just prior to the 1974 ESA conference, the *Post-American* devoted an issue to "evangelical feminism." Jim Wallis confessed that male activists had initially failed to translate lessons they learned about oppression from protests against racism and the Vietnam War into support for women's equality. But by equating "women's liberation" with other "freedom movements," Wallis framed support for gender equality within the larger commitment to social justice. Beginning with this issue, the *Post-American* and its successor *Sojourners* regularly carried supportive apologetic articles, theological analyses, and news items. In addition, the magazine promoted *Daughters of Sarah*, which quickly became the fount of evangelical feminism, and published an enthusiastic review of the inaugural conference of the Evangelical Women's Caucus. *The Other Side* also assumed unqualified women's equality as a matter of principle. Despite his previous hesitancy, John Alexander came to agree with evangelical feminists that proper biblical interpretations taught gender egalitarianism rather than hierarchy. The magazine added as associate editors leading figures within the Evangelical Women's Caucus, including Nancy Hardesty, Letha Scanzoni, and Virginia Mollenkott. These women contributed articles that detailed sexist exploitation and defended feminist biblical hermeneutics. Like Wallis, the editors of *The Other Side* also connected women's substantive inequality with other forms of injustice. "Until the biblical standard of *mutuality and partnership* is practiced in Christian homes, there is little hope for the Christian community to bring a prophetic challenge to bear on the carnal concept of dominance and submission which leads to racial, economic, and military oppression," the journal quoted Mollenkott. "Sexism, rooted in home and family, must be defeated as a foundation for lasting solutions to other forms of oppression." For progressive evangelicals, support for the feminist goal of women's equal rights flowed naturally from their resistance to perceived injustice.[9]

THEOLOGICAL AND POLITICAL BATTLES

Progressive evangelical leaders' support for biblical feminism proved crucial as it faced assaults from conservative evangelicals from the mid-1970s into the 1980s. Traditionalists rejected the orthodoxy of evangelical feminism as part of their defense of a strict definition of biblical inerrancy. Throughout the 1970s, intense debates swirled within evangelicalism regarding interpretations of the Bible's inspiration. Conservatives insisted that orthodox Christians had always regarded the Bible as "inerrant"—that is, free from *all* errors through the divine inspiration of its human authors. Other evangelicals, however, defined the scriptures as "infallible" in matters of faith and practice but adopted a more limited view of the Bible's authority. They conceded minor historical or scientific inaccuracies in biblical accounts and willingly used the methods of higher criticism to show how authors' cultural and historical contexts shaped their texts. To proponents of strict inerrancy, any qualification undercut biblical authority. "The authority of Scripture is inescapably impaired if this total divine inerrancy is in any way limited or disregarded, or made relative to a view of truth contrary to the Bible's own," declared the authors of the 1978 Chicago Statement on Biblical Inerrancy. Because straightforward readings of passages such as 1 Corinthians 11:3 and 14:34-35, Ephesians 5:22-24, and 1 Peter 3:1 suggest unique male authority, conservative evangelicals regarded gender hierarchy as part of the Bible's authoritative "view of truth." In other words, they believed, to reject male leadership was to reject biblical authority. As a result, strict inerrantists turned affirmation of gender hierarchy into a litmus test for evangelical orthodoxy.[10]

Evangelical feminists refused to conflate biblical authority and gender hierarchy. They upheld the Bible as authoritative but insisted that gender egalitarianism represented its true message. Beginning in earnest with the pioneering work of biblical feminism, Letha Scanzoni and Nancy Hardesty's *All We're Meant to Be: A Biblical Approach to Women's Liberation* published in 1974, numerous authors employed historical and cultural criticism to debunk patriarchal interpretations and to recast the Christian ethos as feminist. They emphasized, for example, that Paul's command for his readers to practice mutual submission (Ephesians 5:21) precedes and thus tempers his derivative instruction regarding wifely submission (Ephesians 5:22). Proponents also regarded restrictions placed upon women in passages such as 1 Timothy 2:11-12 and 1 Corinthians 14:34 as specific instructions to local and cultural situations of the first century and no longer applicable in modern society. Most important, evangelical feminists stressed the egalitarian principle of Galatians 3:28: "There is neither Jew nor Greek, slave nor free, male nor female, for you are all one in Christ Jesus." "Passages which are theological and doctrinal in content are used to interpret those where the writer is dealing with practical local cultural problems," Scanzoni and Hardesty argued. "Except Galatians 3:28, all of the references to women in the New Testament are contained in passages dealing with practical concerns about personal relationships or behavior in worship services."[11]

The leading biblical feminists claimed to embrace gender egalitarianism not in spite of but rather because of their loyalty to the Bible. "We did not become feminists and then try to fit our Christianity into feminist ideology," insisted Scanzoni. "We became feminists because we were Christians" and "were convinced that the church had strayed from a correct understanding of God's will for women." Likewise, author Patricia Gundry clarified that evangelical feminists challenged explanations of the Bible and not its authority. "We must not be confused by the words *inspiration* and *interpretation*," she explained. "To claim the *inspiration* of the Scriptures is to believe that what the Bible says is true—that it is God's written Word to us. *Interpretation* involves explaining what this Word means to us on a human level." Gundry argued that "human error" may skew interpretations, and advocates of hierarchy "are not infallible in their interpretation of Scripture." Thus, she concluded, evangelical feminists did not abandon biblical authority when they rebutted advocates of gender hierarchy. To have credibility within evangelical circles, biblical feminists knew they must persuade audiences that they remained faithful to the evangelical absolute of biblical authority.[12]

Defenders of strict biblical inerrancy remained unmoved. They regarded evangelical feminism as a subtle but serious threat. "At stake here is not the matter of women's liberation," wrote Harold Lindsell, editor of *Christianity Today* and author of the polemical *The Battle for the Bible*. "What is the issue for the evangelical is the fact that some of the most ardent advocates of egalitarianism in marriage over against hierarchy reach their conclusion by directly and deliberately denying that the Bible is the infallible rule of faith and practice." For conservative evangelicals like Lindsell, biblical feminism was an oxymoron. He bluntly accused Scanzoni, Hardesty, Mollenkott, and other evangelical feminists of sliding down the slippery slope to heresy. Author Richard Quebedeaux likewise maligned biblical feminists by writing that they adopted "traditionally liberal methodology" in their biblical interpretations. Although he had previously written an appreciative survey of early progressive evangelicalism, by 1978 Quebedeaux accused the movement of subordinating biblical teaching to political interests rather than vice versa. Thus opponents sought to discredit biblical feminism by associating it with theological liberalism. Indeed, Patricia Gundry complained, the frequent accusation that evangelical feminists denied the inspiration of scripture served as "an all-purpose silencer."[13]

Yet biblical feminists remained outspoken, and the leading progressive evangelical organs amplified their message. By opening their pages and editorial boards to prominent evangelical feminists, they popularized biblical feminism for audiences far beyond the dedicated but small number of readers of *Daughters of Sarah*. In the initial *Post-American* issue devoted to evangelical feminism, for example, Jim Wallis summarized and commended the movement's central biblical arguments. A subsequent article by Lucille Sider Dayton provided a detailed explanation of the "hermeneutical principles" that produced interpretations of women's equality in church, home, and society. In a review essay, Boyd Reese also praised the "richness of the Biblical research" in Scanzoni and Hardesty's *All We're Meant to Be*. A year later, the *Post-American* published the article "Dialogue on Women, Hierarchy and Equality" featuring Donald Dayton, one of its contributing editors, and Thomas Howard, the brother of evangelical antifeminist Elisabeth Elliot. Like his sister, Howard rejected the "modern, unbiblical dogmas of egalitarianism" and defended a hierarchical view of the universe in which women fall under male authority. In contrast, Dayton outlined the view of progressive evangelicals that egalitarianism served as the Bible's overriding theme. *The Other Side* also carried exegetical articles by biblical feminists and sold their publications through its book service. Thus the leading progressive evangelical journals confronted readers with arguments that claimed to reject fallible interpretations without sacrificing biblical authority. "One does not deny the inspiration of scripture," Hardesty wrote reassuringly in *Sojourners*, "when one either disputes a traditional interpretation of a passage or declares a passage less than relevant to one's own cultural situation." Likewise, in a feature interview in *The Other Side*, Mollenkott argued that Christians "must de-absolutize the biblical culture as we have already done for slavery and monarchy" and instead give interpretive precedence to the biblical ideal of equality that transcends specific cultures. Both *Sojourners* and *The Other Side* touted the orthodoxy of biblical feminists as theologically conservative opponents attempted to discredit their evangelical credentials.[14]

More politicized Christian conservatives viewed evangelical feminism as not merely a religious mistake but also a social menace. Beginning in the mid-1970s, leaders of the emerging Religious Right attacked the feminist movement for denigrating the "family values" of marriage, motherhood, and monogamy. These conservatives blamed "women's liberation" and feminist groups such as the National Organization of Women (NOW) for what they perceived as alarming increases in divorce rates, illegitimate births, and sexual promiscuity. The ERA became the tangible target for critics' fears of feminism. Intended by supporters as a legal guarantee of women's equality, the ERA passed Congress in 1972 and initially appeared destined for success. Thirty-four of the necessary thirty-eight states ratified the amendment by 1975, well before the 1979 deadline. Evangelical feminists joined secular women's organizations in celebrating the ERA as a step toward justice and campaigning for its final approval. Yet, galvanized by the leadership of political activist Phyllis Schlafly and her Stop ERA campaign, Christian conservatives rallied to prevent final ratification. They believed that the ERA's ostensibly innocuous language—"Equality of rights under the law shall not be denied or abridged by the United States, or any State, on account of sex"—masked feminists' subversive agenda.[15]

Schlafly, Jerry Falwell, and other leaders of the burgeoning Religious Right condemned the ERA as a feminist ploy to annul divinely established gender distinctions. Feminists "believe that we should use the Constitution and legislation to eliminate the eternal differences and the roles that God has ordained between men and women," Schlafly declared. The Religious Right maintained that proper gender conventions ensured stability in both personal relationships and the public order. Falwell explicitly tied the feminist movement's rejection of traditional gender roles to social disintegration. By implementing a "godless philosophy" that denied women's "God-given roles" as mothers and housewives, he argued, "the Equal Rights Amendment strikes at the foundation of our entire social structure." These opponents motivated audiences by warning that the ERA would abrogate laws and customs that delineated sex roles and thus have dramatic consequences: unisex bathrooms, women forced into military combat, same-sex marriages, men abandoning families with impunity, and the loss of "the marvelous legal rights of a woman to be a full-time wife and mother in the home supported by her husband." Though such claims rested upon dubious interpretations of the ERA, these arguments inspired many evangelicals to oppose the "anti-family" agenda of feminists and the ERA's "definite violation of holy Scripture." Conservative Christians mounted successful grassroots campaigns against the ERA's final ratification. When Congress extended the deadline from 1979 until 1982, leaders of the Religious Right elevated their opposition to a national scope. They also asserted their influence in partisan politics, as the Republican Party dropped its previous support of the ERA in 1980. By pitting feminism and "family values" as mutually exclusive, leaders of the Religious Right stigmatized feminism as a political threat to the very fabric of Christian civilization.[16]

In the midst of this political antagonism toward feminism, progressive evangelicals defended the legitimacy of feminist concerns in general and the ERA in particular. Their refusal to vilify feminism placed them directly at odds with the Religious Right and political conservatives. Evangelical progressives disputed accusations from these critics that belief in gender egalitarianism abetted familial and social disorder. In 1977, for example, *Sojourners* contributing editor Sharon Gallagher wrote an article in response to a *Time* magazine cover story on "the new housewife blues." The *Time* article alleged that the feminist movement created insecurity among wives and mothers by devaluing these traditional roles. As a contrast, *Time* featured Marabel Morgan and her "Total Woman" philosophy. Morgan had become wildly popular among conservative Christians—her 1973 *Total Woman* book had sold over 3 million copies. She taught that "every housewife can find happiness by pampering and submitting to her husband" and catering "to her man's special quirks, whether it be in salads, sex or sports." But Gallagher rejected the portrayal of feminists as "villains who make housewives feel insignificant." She complained that the *Time* article insinuated that the ideal "woman should return to the bedroom and kitchen" while the ideal "man should return to his historical prerogative to dominion." Gallagher characterized this "mentality of the 1950s" as a recipe rather than remedy for social problems. "The breakdown of American family life which *Time* blames on the women's movement might just as easily be blamed on what the movement is reacting to—a paucity of shared experience in the fifties-style marriage," Gallagher wrote in *Sojourners*. Progressive evangelical leaders recognized that support for feminism required not only a new mentality but also new practices. *The Other Side* published a regular column in the late 1970s by Letha Scanzoni and her husband, John, that addressed practical issues of gender egalitarianism in marriages and family life. Ultimately, progressive evangelicals defended the feminist emphasis on women's full equality as more healthy for families and society at large than traditional gender hierarchy and stereotypical sex roles.[17]

The 1980 presidential election and final efforts to support the ERA allied progressive evangelicals with other women's rights advocates against politically conservative Christians. *Sojourners'* associate editor Joyce Hollyday rejected the Religious Right's attacks on feminism as simplistic. "It is too easy to blame the disintegration of the family and moral values on the changing role of women while ignoring mobility, technology, materialism, alienation from authority structures, and other factors that have set the tone of the times," she argued. Within six months of Reagan's inauguration, Hollyday grew exasperated with the president's stance on women's and family issues. Reagan not only opposed the ERA but also proposed budget cuts in programs such as Women, Infants, and Children (WIC) that disproportionately benefited poor women. There exists "a calculated effort by the Reagan administration to undermine the progress of the recent past toward equality for women," Hollyday charged. "It is ironic and tragic that a so-called 'pro-family' president is doing so much to destroy the families of the poor, and placing the greatest hardship on women." As the 1982 deadline for the ERA's ratification approached, progressive evangelical groups joined the unsuccessful efforts of groups such as NOW, the Democratic National Convention, and the AFL-CIO to overcome the opposition of political and Christian conservatives.[18]

At the same time, progressive evangelical leaders did qualify their political support for the broader feminist movement. Advocates of biblical feminism occasionally criticized other feminists for goals and rhetoric they found objectionable. They contested, for example, the growing insistence that women must seek power historically denied them. Writing in *Sojourners*, Virginia Mollenkott reproached the well-known feminist intellectual Susan Sontag for stating that "liberation is not just about equality. . . . It is about *power*. Women cannot be liberated without reducing the power of men." Mollenkott accused feminists like Sontag of betraying the "ultimate goal" of women's liberation by perpetuating a society based on "machismo" rather than on "mutuality." She insisted that Jesus's own renunciation of power and exploitation in the name of reciprocal servanthood should guide feminists. "It is this feminist drive toward human justice and mutuality that should properly call forth cooperation from the whole Christian community," Mollenkott argued. Similarly, *Sojourners*' Joyce Hollyday pointed out how progressive evangelicals' theological orientation restricted their identification with other feminists. "There is much that we can benefit from in the secular feminist movement," she wrote. "Our Christian faith, however, will temper many feminist expressions of power." In the judgment of progressive evangelicals, the stress on power by secular feminists conflicted with the biblical themes of "mutual submission" and "male-female equality" by which they defined their feminist convictions.[19]

A particular expression of power demanded by most feminists made progressive evangelicals especially wary. Prominent feminist leaders asserted that women's liberation from patriarchy required their ability to control their bodies and sexuality. The legal right to terminate a pregnancy by abortion epitomized this power, they believed, and thus the feminist movement in the late 1960s and early 1970s pressed for abortion rights. After the Supreme Court established the legality of abortion in 1973, Christian conservatives began to wage campaigns at the end of the decade to overturn the ruling. They regarded support for abortion as feminists' most egregious sin. In response, most feminists and religious liberals devoted equal energy to defending "reproductive rights." As the debate over abortion became the critical fault line in American politics in the late 1970s, evangelical progressives faced a dilemma: did their support for women's equality require their endorsement of legalized abortion? As chapter 5 details, most progressive evangelical leaders ultimately chose to oppose abortion. Despite this key reservation, they refused to relinquish their commitment to feminism itself. Progressive evangelicals continued to challenge Christian conservatives' blanket vilification of the feminist movement.

"KEEP PUSHING THE DOOR OPEN"

By the early twenty-first century, the feminist movement had helped to narrow many aspects of women's inequality and to transform countless features of American culture. Educational and career opportunities for women dramatically expanded. Some 55 percent of college undergraduates and nearly half of those entering business, medical, and law schools were females. Women increasingly entered the workforce, and many families depended upon dual incomes. Average wages for women working full-time rose from 62.5 percent of similarly employed men in 1979 to 81 percent in 2006. For younger women, the trends appeared even more encouraging: the median salaries of women aged twenty-five to thirty-four reached 88 percent of their male peers. Women also had gradual success in electoral politics. Between 1977 and 2008 the number of female senators increased from two to sixteen; women in the House of Representatives rose from eighteen to seventy-two. Feminist organizations pushed into the public consciousness issues such as breast cancer, maternity leave, sexual harassment, and domestic violence and rape. As one historian observed, contemporary Americans take for granted "many aspects of feminism that have become so much part of the mainstream (language, laws, labor force, and access to professional education)." By almost any standard, modern feminism proved one of the most successful social movements in American history.[20]

Despite these advances, feminists continually felt beleaguered in the final decades of the twentieth century. The ERA's defeat in 1982 proved symptomatic of the powerful opposition of social, political, and religious conservatives who had swept Ronald Reagan into office. Under the presidential administrations of both Reagan and George H. W. Bush, feminists scrambled to defend programs and anti-discrimination statutes they initially thought secure. As a new generation of young women came of age in the 1980s and 1990s, they often failed to appreciate the benefits produced by the pioneers of contemporary feminism. "Feminism is a victim of its own resounding achievements," an article in *Time* asserted. "Its triumphs—in getting women into the workplace, in elevating their status in society and in shattering the 'feminine mystique' that defined female success only in terms of being a wife and a mother—have rendered it obsolete, at least in its original form and rhetoric." In addition, the multitude of single-issue feminist organizations that proliferated after the ERA's failure masked the strength of the movement. Observers misinterpreted its lack of coherence as a lack of resilience, and the popular media began to discuss "the death of feminism" and rise of a "post-feminist generation." As Susan Faludi documented in *Backlash: The Undeclared War against American Women*, many journalists emphasized the ostensible dissatisfaction and anxieties experienced by "liberated" women who either delayed marriage and family life or struggled to balance vocational and domestic responsibilities. In the 1990s radio talk-show host Rush Limbaugh popularized the term "feminazis" and helped to sustain conservatives' visceral opposition to feminism and its "political correctness." Leaders of the Religious Right continued to demonize feminists as undermining "family values." "The feminist agenda is not about equal rights for women," Christian Coalition leader Pat Robertson claimed in 1992. "It is about a socialist, anti-family political movement that encourages women to leave their husbands, kill their children, practice witchcraft, destroy capitalism and become lesbians." While feminists celebrated gradual improvements for women, a sense of embattlement and desire to address ongoing inequalities continued to fuel their movement.[21]

Sojourners associate editor Joyce Hollyday described this combination of problems and progress as the "trials and triumphs for feminism." Just in the past year, she wrote in 1992, notable events had opened a door for "the nation to look at itself once more in light of gender issues": Anita Hill's charges of sexual harassment against Supreme Court nominee Clarence Thomas; the conviction of former boxing champion Mike Tyson for raping a Miss Black America contestant; Carol Moseley Braun's campaign to become the first black female senator; Hillary Clinton's prominent role in her husband's presidential campaign; and a report that working women earned only 71 percent of men's salaries. Hollyday appreciated signs of improvement but called for continued dedication to women's issues. While "real progress has been made," she claimed, "we must keep pushing the door open—until the nation can look at itself and see a society in which women are equal." Hollyday's editorial exemplified progressive evangelicals' ongoing commitment to feminism from the mid-1980s through the early twenty-first century. As they countered the Religious Right's attacks on feminism, contributors to *Sojourners, The Other Side*, and ESA's publications criticized women's economic inequality, condemned violence against women, and promoted the development of global feminism. In addition to these overlapping political concerns with the feminist movement, evangelical progressives also remained determined advocates for biblical feminism. Leaders pushed for equal ministerial opportunities for women and defended the legitimacy of feminist theology.[22]

Economic inequality represented one of the most glaring forms of injustice that progressive evangelicals highlighted. For example, *Sojourners* dedicated its March 1986 issue to the theme "Women in Poverty: Left Out and Left Behind," and a series of articles analyzed the persistent gap between women's and men's wages. Vicki Kemper described the disproportionate number of poor women as "the feminization of poverty," outlining how "women's unequal position in the labor market and women's child care responsibilities" increased their susceptibility to impoverishment. A year later, Joyce Hollyday followed up with editorials in which she called for political efforts to redress "the gender gap at work." In the late 1980s and early 1990s, ESA encouraged its members to petition congressional representatives to support legislation that included a pay equity bill, the Family and Medical Leave Act, and a bill eliminating caps on damages awarded to victims of sex discrimination. However, with the gradual improvement in women's relative financial fortunes and the success of statutes such as the Family and Medical Leave Act of 1993, economic inequality lost much of its urgency by the mid-1990s. While occasional articles in progressive evangelical forums still addressed women's more limited job opportunities and unpaid domestic work, leaders devoted greater attention to issues that appeared more pressing.[23]

As in other feminist circles, condemnations of violence against women became a recurrent theme among progressive evangelicals. Articles in *Sojourners, The Other Side,* and ESA publications asserted the connections between women's inequality and violence against them. As early as 1981, *Sojourners* brought the issue to its readers' attention. In a lengthy article, Donna Schaper outlined the pervasiveness of sexual violence and attributed it to "sexism in our Western culture" that reflected "the unequal distribution of power on the basis of sex." She called upon churches to lead society in redressing this imbalance of power by replacing ideals of male dominance with those of mutuality. Throughout the decade, *Sojourners* highlighted the prevalence of violence against women, explored its cultural and religious roots, and shared victims' stories of anguish and hope. By 1990 editors proclaimed that the "staggering" statistics of violence against women constituted an "epidemic." A rape or attempted rape occurred every three and a half minutes, and an estimated six million husbands abused their wives each year. "There is literally a war going on in this country—a war against women" that "is fueled by sexism and misogyny" and "kept alive by a refusal to accept the equality and humanity of women," *Sojourners* declared. The organization dedicated its Peace Pentecost gathering in Washington, D.C., to the theme "Breaking the Silence: A Call to End Violence against Women." In subsequent years *Sojourners* coupled condemnations of rape and domestic abuse with stories of women's healing and recovery from physical violence. While less frequent, articles in *The Other Side* and ESA's publications also condemned sexism as the source of violence against women throughout the 1990s. Authors blamed "continued patriarchy" for domestic violence and encouraged readers "to reject attitudes and cultural practices" that demean women and thus "allow rape and other types of abuse to be tolerated in society." "At the end of the century," Catherine Clark Kroeger claimed in ESA's *Prism* magazine, the "prevention of domestic violence and abuse" represents "the most pressing item on the agenda for biblical feminists."[24]

Progressive evangelical leaders continued to consider violence against women an acute injustice into the twenty-first century, and they published more stories and statistics designed to animate readers' activism. "Scan the pews on a typical Sunday morning, and it's likely that several women within eyeshot have been hit, verbally abused, stalked, or raped by the men in their lives," *Sojourners* associate editor Molly Marsh wrote in

2008. "In the United States and worldwide, gender-based violence affects one in three women, regardless of how much money she makes, her level of education, or where she lives." Specific topics included support groups for victims, preventive public policies, the prevalence of domestic violence within churches, wartime rape in foreign conflicts, and the growth of sex trafficking. Writing in ESA's *Prism*, Al Miles insisted that Christians must "speak out at every level—both inside and outside the church—against patriarchal beliefs, teachings, and traditions which help male perpetrators feel justified in their abuse of women." The recurrent focus of progressive evangelical leaders on violence against women marked an important expression of their feminist commitment to women's inviolate dignity and equality.[25]

Sojourners, The Other Side, and ESA also repeatedly heralded the growth of global feminism, particularly in developing nations. Since their earliest activism, progressive evangelical leaders had promoted human rights worldwide. Beginning in the 1980s, articles exploring the status of women in foreign societies appeared regularly as one aspect of their support for universal justice. In 1983, for example, *The Other Side* published an article identifying "signs of hope for women in the third world." Author Mary Burke highlighted the ways in which women in developing nations were "finding ways to claim their personhood" in the face of sexist patterns and social turmoil. *The Other Side* carried subsequent articles on women in areas ranging from Palestine to Latin American countries. Likewise, *Sojourners* published features on women's progress in countries such as South Africa, El Salvador, Haiti, and Nicaragua. Articles lauded women's peacemaking efforts, identified women as "key to fighting global poverty," advocated foreign aid programs that empowered women, and highlighted Muslim women pushing for greater equality. In its own treatment of "women's rights as human rights," ESA also outlined the barriers faced by women around the world who confronted entrenched social and political injustice. James Moore favorably quoted a United Nations document regarding women's discrimination: "The full and complete development of a country, the welfare of the world and the cause of peace require the maximum participation of women on equal terms with men in all fields." In 2006 Ron Sider outlined global examples of "blatant injustice against women" that Christians must combat: the abortion of female fetuses in light of cultural preferences for males; women's unequal access to education, healthcare, and wealth; and the high rates of violence and sex trafficking. Progressive evangelical leaders refused to let advances in the substantive equality of American women obscure the suffering of other women throughout the world.[26]

While evangelical progressives gave considerable attention to women's economic and social standing, the effects of sexist discrimination in religious settings predominated over other issues. From the 1980s into the new millennium, no issue of women's equality appeared in progressive evangelical publications as frequently as women's roles within the church. Although most mainline Protestants had endorsed women's ordination by the late 1970s, conservative evangelicals remained belligerent opponents. Organizations such as the Council on Biblical Manhood and Womanhood, Promise Keepers, and the Southern Baptist Convention explicitly attacked biblical feminists and continued to insist upon women's subordinated religious roles. Indeed, for conservative evangelicals, belief in men's unique leadership within the church served as an important subcultural religious boundary that they used to distinguish themselves from more liberal Protestants. While they still affirmed gender hierarchy, most evangelicals by the late twentieth century had adopted pragmatic partnerships in marriage and embraced women's employment outside the home. As a result, their opposition to women's leadership in *religious* contexts became even more symbolically important. Thus evangelical feminists continued to feel embattled and compelled to justify their convictions, even as their own movement fractured. At a contentious 1986 meeting, the Evangelical Women's Caucus (EWC) affirmed a resolution that recognized "the lesbian minority" among its members and thus affirmed "civil-rights protection for homosexual persons." Dissenters, wanting to avoid the appearance that support for feminism led to affirmation of homosexuality, broke away and formed a more conservative biblical feminist group, Christians for Biblical Equality (CBE). Several years later, EWC renamed itself the Evangelical and Ecumenical Women's Caucus (EEWC) in recognition that its membership extended beyond evangelical circles. Despite this division, CBE and EEWC remained committed to promoting Christian feminism, and progressive evangelical leaders continued to publicize their cause. *Sojourners, The Other Side,* and ESA's publications regularly carried articles that defended women's religious leadership and analyzed the unique challenges facing women in ministry. In addition, *Sojourners* and *The Other Side* joined *Daughters of Sarah* in publishing feminist theologians and questioning patriarchal imagery and language regarding God.[27]

Because of their theological interpretations of gender egalitarianism, advocates of biblical feminism expected no less for women in religious contexts than in secular affairs. They demanded that women have equal opportunities to lead and to participate unconditionally in churches and ministries. As a result, progressive evangelicals regarded conservative Christian dogma restricting women's religious leadership as sexist discrimination. "The ordination of women has been seen primarily as a justice issue," for women have "every right to exercise all levels of leadership in the churches," Barbara Hargrove summarized in a 1987 *Sojourners* review of women's struggle for religious equality. Likewise, ESA board member Gretchen Gaebelein Hull rejected claims that Christians could legitimately discriminate within their own institutions. "Just as there is not scriptural support for treating women inequitably in society," Hull concluded in an extensive biblical defense of women in ministry, "so there is no biblical basis for treating women as second-class members of the church." Progressive evangelicals often resorted to analogies in these arguments. *Sojourners* contributor Kari Jo Verhulst compared protests against the Christian Reformed Church's 1994 decision to deny women's ordination with "the struggles against slavery, abuse, war, and apartheid, which all were once sanctioned by the church." A year later, Hull made similar charges in ESA's *Prism* magazine. "In many ways, we as a church have treated women as we once treated people of color," she argued. "While affirming gender equality theoretically, the church has continued to limit the roles and self-determination of women." By equating sexism with racism, leaders framed conservative evangelicals' opposition to women's religious leadership as an injustice that they would eventually regret.[28]

Progressive evangelicals' periodic coverage of personal stories and practical analyses of women in ministry represented strategic means for encouraging women's religious leadership. Such articles sought to arouse readers' support by sympathetically portraying women's religious callings and unique challenges. *The Other Side* initiated this trend in 1979 with a cover article titled "Women in Pulpits: How Are They Faring?" That year *Sojourners* highlighted the importance of female ministers' experiences through a positive book review of *Our Struggle to Serve: The Stories of 15 Evangelical Women*. Soon thereafter ESA also focused attention on barriers to women's ministry by publishing a dialogue in which leaders discussed how they were exercising their gifts within churches. In the mid-1980s *Sojourners* seemed particularly eager to defend women's ministry within its pages. Roberta Hestenes, a leading evangelical feminist, wrote an article in *Christianity Today* that praised *Daughters of Sarah* and *The Other Side* for "calling the church to seek new directions in their attitudes toward women." Disappointed by the omission of *Sojourners*, Jim Wallis sought Hestenes's advice and endorsement. "Is there any reason why you didn't mention us?" he wrote to her privately. "My concern here is not for publicity," Wallis claimed, "but whether you have any concerns or feelings about *Sojourners* that I'm not aware of." He invited Hestenes to submit an article to the magazine, and she did in fact contribute a piece a year later to a thematic issue on female religious leadership that offered first-person accounts of ordained female pastors. Continuing this pattern in 1988, *Sojourners* celebrated the election of Barbara Clementine Harris as the first female bishop in the Episcopal Church and published an interview with Nancy Hastings Sehested, a female Southern Baptist pastor fighting her denomination's increasing resistance to the ordination of women.[29]

Printing women's firsthand struggles for equality in ministry gained even greater significance in the mid-1990s when *Daughters of Sarah*, the preeminent forum for Christian feminism, ceased publication. Both *The Other Side* and *Sojourners* lamented its discontinuation and renewed their commitments to giving voice to women's experiences. In addition to publishing articles by female authors, *The Other Side* inaugurated a new forum in each issue, "At the Well," in order to feature "daughters of God conversing together" on topics regularly related to women in ministry. *Sojourners* also continued to give prominence to women's experiences. First-person accounts ranged from an interview with a female seminary professor studying women in the church to a cover article on Yvonne Delk, the first black woman ordained in the United Church of Christ. In the early twenty-first century, ESA increased the frequency of its own coverage. Its *Prism* magazine carried a forum in 2000 exploring how to advance gender egalitarianism within churches and society. Several years later, *Prism* introduced a regular column, "In Like Manner . . . the Women," by Elizabeth Rios. "Rather than join the theological debate on women in ministry, this column will tell the stories of women who themselves have put the debate on the shelf and have gone on to 'just do it,'" Rios stated in her inaugural feature. "It will also identify and tell stories about the issues that trouble women in ministry." In 2006 *Prism* profiled "seven dynamic women of the cloth" who exemplified a "soul-level conviction that God has called them into leadership within his Body." Editors hoped these stories would prove inspirational. "We are convinced," they wrote, "that a great many more women would heed God's call to do the same if it were not for the very real pressures that (at best) discourage and (at worst) explicitly exclude women from ministry." Progressive evangelical publications used these firsthand accounts to endorse the callings and to encourage the ministries of women.[30]

Sojourners and The Other Side did not limit support for women in Christian ministry to Protestant contexts. Catholic peace activists had long contributed to Sojourners, and thus its leaders also promoted Roman Catholic feminists. In 1985 the journal carried a cover article featuring a dialogue among five Catholic women regarding "new roles and new leadership [that] appear to be emerging among religious women." One of these participants, the Benedictine nun Joan Chittister, became a contributing editor of Sojourners, and the magazine published several articles by her that challenged patriarchal traditions of the Catholic Church—especially its ban on women's ordination. "It is inevitable," Chittister wrote in 1987, "that one day [the church] will also confess and repent of the sin of sexism." The Other Side also published an interview with Chittister—"a model for Christian feminism," according to the editors—in which she argued for women's ordination. In the 1990s and early twenty-first century, Sojourners continued to label women's exclusion from the Catholic priesthood an injustice. Joe Nangle, a Franciscan priest on the magazine's staff, described "the church's exclusionary policies toward women" as "a system of apartheid within its own ranks" and expressed anguish after Pope John Paul's 1994 letter reaffirming the ban on women's ordination. In 2002 Sojourners published another article by Chittister that challenged readers to work within the church to open all ministries to women. Catholic associate editor Rose Marie Berger went even further several years later by approving the "ecclesial disobedience" of the international organization Roman Catholic Womenpriests when it conducted its first ordination ceremony for American women. Leaders encouraged forms of "faithful dissent" among their Catholic constituency in order to promote gender equality in all Christian traditions.[31]

As with Daughters of Sarah, the primary progressive evangelical publications endorsed not only women's practical ministry but also their pursuit of feminist theology. Articles and supportive book reviews in The Other Side challenged patriarchal symbols, interpretations, and traditions within Christianity. As early as 1977, for example, Nancy Hardesty argued that "to use masculine language exclusively [for God] is to violate the central message of Scripture and theology." In the 1980s The Other Side published articles by Virginia Mollenkott that pointed to feminine images of God and linked the issue to women's religious and social roles. "It's important to reclaim the biblical images of God as female," she wrote, "so that we won't continue to unjustly cut off women from full participation in spiritual and public leadership." *The Other Side* distinguished between Christian feminism and other forms of feminist theology. In the late 1980s two cover articles acknowledged that some feminists had rejected Christianity as irredeemably patriarchal and turned to forms of goddess worship or pantheism. Yet contributors proposed theological principles by which they sought to remain equally faithful to both "the traditional categories of Christian orthodoxy" and feminist ideals. Karen Torjesen and Leif Torjesen argued that an "orthodox feminist theology" rightly repudiated the "conceptual imaging of God as male" but must avoid committing the equivalent error of imaging God as female. Therefore they advocated an "inclusive orthodoxy" based upon the biblical revelation of "the God who encompasses male and female" and Christ as "gender-inclusive." In another lengthy article, Reta Halteman Finger, the editor of *Daughters of Sarah*, also assessed feminist theology from the perspective of Christian feminism. She promoted "guidelines for an evangelical feminist hermeneutic" that regarded "the whole of Scripture as authoritative" even as women challenged "patriarchal texts and sexist assumptions" within the Christian tradition. Until ceasing publication in 2004, *The Other Side* continued to regularly highlight women's theological efforts to experience "liberation from patriarchal religion."[32]

Sojourners similarly encouraged feminist theology. Contributors periodically commended the insights of pioneering feminist theologians outside of evangelicalism such as Elisabeth Schüssler Fiorenza and Rosemary Radford Ruether and defended feminist explorations grounded in Christian theology. In 1993, for example, contributing editor Sharon Gallagher criticized a *Christianity Today* cover article, "Why God Is Not Mother," for rejecting inclusive and feminine language for God. Using feminine language for God does not reflect "a withdrawal from worshipping the Creator God—the God of the Bible," she protested, but rather a commitment to "be faithful to the whole biblical message about who God is." In a subsequent article on diverse forms of feminist theology, associate editor Julie Polter made it clear that "*Sojourners* has maintained a feminist position that is deeply rooted in the central authority of scripture." Although articles addressing feminist theology peaked in the early 1990s, *Sojourners* remained supportive of women's efforts to reinterpret male-centered Christian theology.[33]

Unlike the leading progressive evangelical journals, ESA's publications rarely addressed feminist theology beyond biblical arguments for women's unconditional equality in the church. Nevertheless, Ron Sider admitted the legitimacy of its explorations. God is no more male than female, he told an interviewer, and thus "it seems right to me that you have to talk about Father and Mother" in reference to God. Yet he confessed that this practice as well as other "aspects of radical Christian feminism" made him uncomfortable. Sider demonstrated this discomfort when he attempted to employ inclusive language in a letter to God outlining his 1989 Christmas hopes for a more just world. "Dear Heavenly Father," he began—but then he immediately added, "Well, yes, and dearly Heavenly Mother, too, although that doesn't feel quite so natural." As a rule, however, ESA avoided feminist theology. A 2004 *Prism* article exemplified how ESA sidestepped the issue in pursuit of other goals. In "Using the 'F' Word: The Pursuit of Gender Equality in the Church," author Laura Coulter stated that she purposely avoided debates concerning whether or not "the church should make a shift toward worshipping what is generally called 'the divine feminine.'" Instead, she pragmatically sought to promote feminism in the church by highlighting biblical and historical examples of women in ministry and the benefits of allowing women equal "opportunities to use their God-given gifts and abilities." ESA's commitment to biblical feminism remained focused on more practical discussions of women's equality in churches and ministries.[34]

FEMINISM AS SOCIAL JUSTICE

From its inception in the 1960s, the modern feminist movement promoted two related themes: equality and liberation. Early feminist leaders drew upon the discourse of the political tradition of liberalism—emphasizing the sovereignty of the individual, natural rights, and the protection of civil liberties—in order to campaign for women's equality in public life. This liberal strand of feminism viewed the primary barriers to such equality as discriminatory customs and legal constraints. As a result, leaders promoted public and political reforms to secure women's full civil rights and equal opportunities. In 1966 the founders of NOW reflected this agenda by pledging "to take action to bring women into full participation in the mainstream of American society now, assuming all the privileges and responsibilities thereof in truly equal partnership with men." As anti-discrimination legislation, the ERA embodied the liberal feminist goal of gender egalitarianism. Yet women needed more than just formal equality in the public sphere, more radical feminists insisted, and thus they championed women's liberation from repressive cultural definitions of womanhood and femininity. Radical feminists denounced patriarchal systems and the confines of traditional sex roles as the primary roots of women's oppression—oppression that occurred as much in women's private lives as in their public activities. These feminists campaigned for freedom from cultural institutions and practices that allowed men to control their opportunities and even bodies. Men subjugated women not only through domestic violence and rape, radical feminists argued, but also through the oppressive expectations of motherhood and men's sexual fulfillment. Supporters promoted consciousness-raising groups in which women shared personal experiences of oppression and connected them to larger patterns of social and political patriarchy. "The personal *is* political" became the mantra of women's liberation. By the early 1970s the lines had blurred within the feminist movement between liberal feminism's expectations of equality and radical feminists' demands for liberation from patriarchy.[35]

Progressive evangelicals' public theology led them to endorse feminism as a "movement for social justice." Their dedication to the liberal feminist goal of securing women's substantive equality stemmed from their biblical interpretations of gender egalitarianism—an equality not only in status before God but also in rights, responsibilities, and roles. Ron Sider declared that all inequalities and discrimination against women stand "in blatant defiance of the biblical teaching that every person, both male and female, is made in the very image of God and is therefore inestimably precious in the eyes of God." Since women share this sacred worth, leaders resolved to combat attitudes and actions that "devalue or rob females of the equality to which all humans are intrinsically entitled." Progressive evangelicals believed such entitlements included equal treatment and opportunities in public, homes, and churches. In the public sphere, they joined liberal feminists in promoting formal equality for women through policies and legislation that prohibited discrimination based upon sex. Although women's rights and responsibilities in domestic and religious settings were not matters of public theology, evangelical progressives insisted that biblical expectations for gender egalitarianism applied in these private contexts as well. Thus leaders clashed with Christian conservatives who promoted God's design for gender hierarchy and distinct roles for men and women. Instead, as Christian feminists, they called for mutuality in marriages and the equal rights of women to exercise leadership in the church.[36]

Yet in order to advance their substantive equality, progressive evangelicals also agreed that women needed liberation from many patriarchal structures and restrictive gender roles. "The problem with the platform of liberal feminism is that it is not critical enough of our society" and "does not begin with a critique of patriarchy," claimed *Sojourners* contributor Ginny Earnest. Jim Wallis defined patriarchy as the systematic "subordination of women to men" that creates "a structure of domination." He and other leaders compared the "institutional character" of patriarchy with that of racism. "Women are subject to the structures of male power," Wallis wrote, and "the desire for control is expressed not only individually and culturally, but also institutionally—just as in racism." Therefore, justice for women required not only formal equality but also activism that addressed forms of patriarchy "embedded in social and political institutions." As a result, progressive evangelicals denounced economic patterns that trapped women in low-paying jobs and devalued domestic and child-rearing labor. Leaders opposed the "oppressive burden of sex-role stereotyping," promoted egalitarian rather than hierarchical marriages, and called for "work on the political level" that included "restructuring institutions and living patterns" to enable men and women to share vocational and family responsibilities. Evangelical progressives also condemned patriarchal attitudes and actions that contributed to violence against women. Finally, leaders sought to confront "the weight of centuries of patriarchy in the church" and urged readers to "recapture the radical nature of our evangelical heritage on the issue of feminism." Because "feminism holds that women are, in contrast to the implications of patriarchy, fully human and fully equal," claimed *Sojourners* associate editor Julie Polter, progressive evangelicals championed the feminist goals of women's substantive equality and liberation from patriarchy as integral to social justice.[37]

Even as they identified as feminists, progressive evangelicals never unreservedly endorsed the broader feminist movement. Most other feminists concluded that women could not achieve true equality and liberation from patriarchy without access to legalized abortion. They viewed abortion rights as a guarantee of their freedom to control their bodies and decisions regarding motherhood. "For feminists," one historian observed, "abortion was the biological bedrock on which their demands were based." But the majority of progressive evangelical leaders disputed this claim, challenging those who made support for abortion a shibboleth of authentic feminist identity. As the next chapter indicates, their anomalous attempts to affirm feminism but oppose abortion created unique challenges in America's political landscape.[38]

5. The Agony of Abortion

Joyce Hollyday articulated the frustration that many progressive evangelicals felt in the early 1980s. "Unfortunately, the secular feminist movement has used abortion as a test of commitment to women's equality," the associate editor of *Sojourners* complained. "Access to abortion is considered part of 'reproductive rights.'" As self-identified pro-life feminists, however, most leaders of the progressive evangelical movement disputed these premises. Yet they faced a daunting task, for almost all defenders and detractors of feminism regarded the feminist movement as the guardian of abortion rights. In 1973 the Supreme Court had ruled in *Roe v. Wade* that women have a constitutionally protected right to abortion in the first six months of pregnancy. Feminist organizations that had fueled abortion rights activism celebrated the decision as a key victory for women's rights and freedom, and support for legalized abortion became a hallmark of feminist identity and nonnegotiable for the political left. By the late 1970s Christian conservatives considered such support the most damning of feminism's many sins, and Religious Right leaders gradually made efforts to reverse *Roe v. Wade* their movement's principal political goal. Thus not only feminist leaders but also their conservative opponents assumed the inextricable link between feminism and abortion. To the majority of progressive evangelicals, however, this assumption appeared too facile.[1]

Frustrated by the polarized positions of both the political left and Religious Right, most progressive evangelical leaders embraced a "completely pro-life" agenda that combined opposition to abortion with support for feminism and other issues of social justice. After prolonged initial uncertainty about abortion, in 1980 the leading progressive evangelical representatives began to define their respective positions. *The Other Side* declared that abortion appeared both biblically and morally ambiguous. Refusing to offer a generalized condemnation or endorsement of the practice, its editors adopted ambivalence as the journal's stated position. In contrast, both *Sojourners* and Evangelicals for Social Action (ESA) took a stand against abortion. Each organization ultimately interpreted abortion as an issue of violence against unborn life that trumped debates about women's choices. They believed, therefore, that feminism and a pro-life position were not merely compatible but even necessarily consistent campaigns against injustice.

Despite their objections to abortion, *Sojourners* and ESA distanced themselves from the politically conservative pro-life movement. Progressive evangelical leaders framed their anti-abortion stance as part of a "completely pro-life" agenda that also included opposition to war, the death penalty, economic injustice, and other affronts to human dignity such as racism and sexism. Christians must defend the sanctity of life, they insisted, not merely in the womb but wherever threats occurred. As a result, *Sojourners* and ESA criticized the Religious Right for seeming to ignore additional—and often more immediate—injustices that endangered or dehumanized people. *The Other Side*, while neither supporting nor opposing legalized abortion, joined *Sojourners* and ESA in highlighting this apparent inconsistency. As a whole, the progressive evangelical movement united in advocating expanded programs that would reduce the number of abortions. Leaders urged increased efforts to prevent unplanned pregnancies and to offer women resources and alternatives that would decrease abortion's appeal.

From the late 1980s into the twenty-first century, differences emerged among pro-life progressive evangelicals regarding anti-abortion legislation. Hesitant about the effects of restrictive measures, *Sojourners* instead focused on the less ambitious goal of reducing abortions. The magazine encouraged dialogue and pragmatic cooperation between pro-life and pro-choice proponents around the common goal of making abortions rare. Although also endorsing campaigns to reduce abortion, ESA's leaders supported legislative efforts to make most abortions illegal. While ESA and *Sojourners* led the progressive evangelical movement's opposition to abortion, *The Other Side* quietly abandoned direct attention to the issue in the early 1990s. In the midst of polarized abortion debates, its goal to present neutral coverage proved too difficult to sustain.

The unwillingness of most evangelical progressives to divorce opposition to abortion from other issues of social justice provoked their sense of political homelessness. *Sojourners* and ESA lamented how the seemingly dichotomous options of pro-life or pro-choice became the primary fault line in American partisan politics. In their estimation, neither Republicans nor Democrats offered a "completely pro-life" agenda. Thus progressive evangelicals refused to make a political candidate's position on abortion a litmus test for their support. Ultimately, leaders' efforts to broaden the meaning of "pro-life" stemmed from their movement's public theology of community. As most came to regard fetuses as unborn children and thus vulnerable nascent community members, progressive evangelicals insisted that ideal political agendas must protect the life, rights, and dignity of those threatened not only by racism, sexism, poverty, and war but also by abortion.

THE ABORTION DIVIDE

From its early development, the contemporary feminist movement embraced "reproductive freedom" as one of its primary goals. At the second annual conference of the National Organization for Women (NOW) in 1967, members passed a bill of rights that identified abortion as a "civil right of every female person" and called for the repeal of anti-abortion laws. As president of NOW, Betty Friedan helped found the National Association for the Repeal of Abortion Laws (NARAL) in 1969 and declared that feminists must endorse women's reproductive autonomy. Radical groups such as the Chicago Women's Liberation Union often operated underground abortion clinics and engaged in protests against abortion restrictions. As *Roe v. Wade* reached the Supreme Court, NOW filed an amicus brief. Not only did unwanted pregnancies endanger a mother's health and welfare, the document argued, but also anti-abortion laws effectively enslaved women by forcing them to bear children. Following the Supreme Court's decision, support for abortion hardened and transcended differences within the broad feminist movement. The proceedings of the 1977 National Women's Conference, commissioned by President Jimmy Carter, seemed to epitomize feminists' dedication to abortion rights. Despite objections from social conservatives present, a convincing majority of delegates adopted a "Plan of Action" that called for access to legal abortions and government funding for those unable to afford them. Committed to defending *Roe v. Wade*, feminists adopted the language of "reproductive rights" and "pro-choice" in order to frame legal access to abortion as essential to women's freedom and equality.[2]

Where feminists saw a woman's right to choose, Christian conservatives saw an unborn child's right to life. By the early 1980s nearly all evangelicals became aggressively "pro-life." Yet this opposition to abortion evolved only gradually. Both prior to 1973 and immediately after *Roe v. Wade*, the primary religious opposition to abortion came from Roman Catholics. Few evangelical leaders publicly condemned or even commented on the Court's action; Religious Right leader Jerry Falwell, for example, did not preach against abortion until 1978. Harold O. J. Brown, an associate editor of *Christianity Today*, later suggested that both historical unwillingness to concur with Catholics and reluctance to participate in political activism contributed to evangelicals' slow response. But as leaders such as Brown and Billy Graham pushed the issue, more and more evangelicals in the late 1970s and early 1980s began to view abortion as a unique evil requiring mobilized opposition. Especially motivating were a 1979 film and book, both titled *Whatever Happened to the Human Race?*, by influential evangelical philosopher Francis Schaeffer and future surgeon general C. Everett Koop. These popular works attributed authentic life to unborn children and compared abortion to practices such as infanticide and euthanasia. *Whatever Happened to the Human Race?* inspired audiences to join the "pro-life" movement and helped galvanize the Religious Right's political efforts to reverse *Roe v. Wade*.[3]

But this hostility to abortion reflected anxiety about more than just fetal life. The opposition of Christian conservatives also stemmed from their commitment to traditional gender roles. They interpreted feminists' abortion advocacy as part of their larger antagonism to conventional families and motherhood itself. For example, in her 1977 attack upon feminism, *The Power of the Positive Woman*, conservative political activist Phyllis Schlafly described the Equal Rights Amendment as a strategy to guarantee "the major antifamily objective of the women's liberation movement," namely "abortion-on-demand." Moral Majority leader Jerry Falwell regarded the ERA and abortion as coupled threats to God's designed gender hierarchy. He quoted a NOW-ERA fund-raising letter by Betty Friedan as evidence: "I am convinced that if we lose this struggle [for the ERA]," he cited Friedan as claiming, "we will have little hope in our lifetime of saving our right to abortion." To Religious Right leaders, abortion represented the rejection of the maternal role that God ordained for women. "Simply stated, the man is to be the provider, and the woman is to be the childbearer," wrote Beverly LaHaye, who founded Concerned Women for America in 1979. "Motherhood is the highest form of femininity," she argued, but "radical feminists" spurned their maternal calling by defending abortion. The pro-life movement comprised many conservatives who viewed motherhood as women's most important role, while most pro-choice advocates regarded motherhood as only one option for women. "While on the surface it is the embryo's fate that seems to be at stake, the abortion debate is actually about the meanings of *women's* lives," one prominent study concluded in the early 1980s. Interrelated outrage at feminism and abortion inspired the pro-life activism of conservative evangelicals.[4]

FROM AMBIVALENCE TO ACTION

Like evangelical conservatives, progressive evangelicals revealed little initial consternation at the Supreme Court's ruling in *Roe v. Wade*. In fact, a few leaders at first accepted abortion as a legitimate option. Although Ron Sider would later become one of the most outspoken progressive evangelical critics of abortion, in the early 1970s he found no persuasive reason for challenging it. "I was not opposed to abortion at this time," he remembered. "I argued in class, but I never put it in print, that since the Bible does not say the fetus is a person we cannot assume that abortion is wrong." Several evangelical feminist activists agreed. In their 1974 book *All We're Meant to Be: A Biblical Approach to Women's Liberation*, Letha Scanzoni and Nancy Hardesty recognized deep disagreements between Christians on the "agonizing" questions surrounding abortion. But, they claimed, Christian morality did not necessarily preclude abortion in cases such as unplanned pregnancies or children who would have Down syndrome.[5]

In general, however, most progressive evangelical leaders displayed unusual timidity and avoided taking a public stance on abortion through the end of the 1970s. *Sojourners* and *The Other Side* had developed explicit commitments not only to women's equality but also to a fundamental respect for human life. As a result, their leaders appeared confounded by competing appeals to women's rights and to the sanctity of unborn children. *Sojourners* published only two cautious pieces on abortion. In 1976 contributor Charles Fager proposed that the government could bridge the rival values at stake—a woman's choice versus fetal life—by affirming the "legal recognition of fetal humanity" but protecting that humanity through some alternative to criminalizing abortion. Updating Fager's proposal three years later, a brief report noted that two meetings of abortion adversaries had explored middle ground. Yet *Sojourners'* own stance remained unclear, and editors acknowledged criticism of their uncertainty by printing letters from readers who challenged the magazine's lack of consistency for speaking prophetically against war and violence yet ignoring the "anti-life activity" of abortion. While *Sojourners* carried this cursory coverage, *The Other Side* avoided abortion altogether until the beginning of 1980. When editors finally acknowledged the issue by publishing letters from readers who implored the journal to confront abortion, they pleaded for more time. "The staff of *The Other Side* has been struggling for some time with the myriad facets of the abortion question," confessed Mark Olson. He pledged that *The Other Side* would soon address the issue. As restless readers of *Sojourners* and *The Other Side* indicated, progressive evangelical leaders risked their credibility by postponing responses to what was quickly becoming the most divisive political issue.[6]

The staff of *The Other Side* finally declared their stance in the June 1980 issue titled "The Agony of Abortion." Finding merit in both pro-choice and pro-life positions, however, they made the unconventional choice neither to condone nor to condemn abortion. "The most important thing to understand in the whole debate" is that "both positions can be held in integrity and decency," explained John Alexander. "Given their assumptions, both sides are responding sensibly and morally." He believed that a lack of compelling evidence made impossible any determination of whether a "fetus is or is not human." Most notable, Alexander insisted that "the biblical evidence is sparse" and "none of it is conclusive either way." Mark Olson concurred, arguing that the ambiguity of scripture precluded evangelicals' normal reliance upon biblical certainty. Thus rather than defending "conclusions about the morality of abortion," *The Other Side* adopted an alternative goal. "We hope that what contributions we make will be to the tone of the debate," Alexander wrote. "We hope to increase respect between the camps and lower the decibel level of the argument." The editors rejected the developing tendency among evangelicals to make one's stance on abortion a litmus test of religious and political orthodoxy. Instead, they urged reconciliation between "dogmatic, self-assured factions" that would require both sides to admit ambiguity, to listen compassionately, and to rethink inflexible premises.[7]

Despite *The Other Side*'s ambivalence, its analysis foreshadowed how the progressive evangelical movement would refuse to isolate abortion from other injustices. Alexander criticized politically conservative opponents of abortion for failing to oppose unmistakable threats to life with equal vigor. "While fighting for the rights of fetuses, they have done little to support the children who will be born," he wrote. "While making movies against abortion, they have not made movies against torture or nuclear warfare. While trying to ban abortion clinics, most have supported hand-guns." Therefore, Alexander challenged those who made opposition to abortion their political priority to devote greater energy to resolving pressing social problems such as poverty, starvation, and warfare. "When millions of those who are undeniably human are suffering," he claimed, "our main effort should be for them." At the same time, Alexander supported the goal of reducing the number of abortions through improving birth control education, alternatives to unwanted pregnancies, access to decent jobs, and social services for the poor. He thus connected abortion to the inequalities, social problems, and cultural attitudes that often prompted the decision. "We should also be working for a different society," Alexander proclaimed. "Even if abortion is murder, it is only a symptom of a much deeper disorder" of an American society that believes "life is cheap, especially the life of the poor and weak." *The Other Side* did not let debates regarding abortion distract from its emphasis upon comprehensive social justice. Instead, the magazine framed its progressive social vision as a strategic means for both decreasing human suffering *and* reducing the number of abortions.[8]

Olson rightly predicted that *The Other Side*'s awaited issue on abortion would upset many readers. "No issue we've ever published has generated more mail than June's issue on abortion," Olson noted several months later. "Most of the mail has been negative, much of it *very* negative." Nevertheless, *The Other Side* reaffirmed a commitment to publishing what it regarded as the leading of God's Spirit, even if its position proved unconventional and unpopular. This resolve was tested as critical letters continued to arrive and impacted *The Other Side*'s subscription base. "A significant number of readers have now cancelled because of our issue on abortion," wrote Olson at the end of 1980. In particular, many letters accused *The Other Side* of promoting a "wishy-washy" or even "pro-abortion" position. These charges annoyed Olson, who insisted that the magazine had neither remained neutral nor endorsed abortion. "We took a firm position, calling abortion a question of moral ambiguity, requiring serious, honest, cautious struggle," he countered. "That is not the lack of a position. We wish that were more widely understood." Yet by refusing the dichotomous options of "pro-life" or "pro-choice," *The Other Side* did remain neutral between what a substantial number of readers regarded as the only two positions. The editors thus frustrated those who wanted more clarity if not explicit opposition to abortion.[9]

After its controversial issue, the magazine waited two years before addressing abortion again. Two articles in 1982 demonstrated *The Other Side's* ongoing commitment to consider both reluctant acceptance and qualified rejection of abortion. Contributor Kay Lindskoog criticized conservative pro-life advocates—especially men—for attempting to outlaw abortion without recognizing that "the right to life" in practice often meant the "right to life with an ignorant teenage mother who is incompetent, incontinent, insolvent, inconsistent, and/or indecent." Lindskoog described herself as "proabortion only in an agony of frustration" and "antiabortion as soon as people start taking care of people." Several months later, Charles Fager—who earlier had written *Sojourners'* first report on abortion—criticized the apparent inconsistency of the conservative prolife movement more directly. "Pro-lifers weep for aborted fetuses yet are ready—even anxious—to blow up millions" of indisputably human beings "in order to 'stop communism,'" he wrote. Fager favored a pro-life position and urged advocates to develop partnerships with the peace movement based upon common respect for life (or potential life). But he also criticized the methods of "the mainstream antiabortion constituency" and praised the alternative group Pro-lifers for Survival for its "persuasionist" rather than "prohibitionist" approach. The group's members refused to "coerce people into giving up abortion" through legislation but rather attempted "to convert them away from resorting to it." Published responses to the articles showed the persistent tension created by *The Other Side's* refusal to define itself as either "pro-choice" or "pro-life." While some readers urged the magazine to oppose abortion along with other manifest injustices, others pressed *The Other Side* to defend legalized abortion as part of its feminist commitment. Though the editors protested one reader's description of their stance as pro-choice, their continued insistence on abortion's ambiguity more closely aligned them with pro-choice than with pro-life advocates. This uncertainty and recognition of its position's unpopularity caused *The Other Side* to fall silent on abortion for another four years. Progressive evangelicals looking for pro-life leadership would turn instead to *Sojourners* and ESA.[10]

The November 1980 issue of *Sojourners* finally clarified the group's own position. Jim Wallis conceded in the lead editorial that a statement on abortion was overdue. Although *Sojourners* had never supported abortion, he wrote, the community had neither clearly nor publicly challenged it either. As they analyzed the issue in light of their primary concerns, however, those on the staff came to interpret abortion as inconsistent with their core ideals. "Our deepest convictions about poverty, racism, violence, and the equality of men and women are finally rooted in a radical concern for life—its absolute value and the need to protect it," Wallis explained. "It was only a matter of time before the spiritual logic of these other commitments would lead us to a 'pro-life' response to abortion as well." *Sojourners'* opposition reflected its antecedent commitment to justice, he claimed, and legal abortion allowed American society to abort children of the poor—especially minorities—instead of creating just social conditions for their welfare. "The truth is that many poor women do not regard abortion as a real solution but as a brutal substitute for social justice and even as a white society's way of controlling the population of racial minorities." Both regular *Sojourners* contributors and other politically liberal leaders—including Jesse Jackson, who at that time opposed abortion—contributed statements further defending the convergence of the feminist, social justice, peace, and pro-life movements.[11]

Defending opposition to abortion as necessarily consistent with progressive political movements represented *Sojourners'* key initiative. Authors rejected the ways in which both conservatives and liberals had framed the abortion debate. "Both Jerry Falwell and Gloria Steinem agree that to oppose abortion means to oppose equal rights for women," complained Wallis. "Both the Left and the Right have linked abortion and women's rights together and made support for abortion a crucial test of support for women's liberation." Yet the magazine placed itself in the excluded middle. *Sojourners* challenged claims by liberals that pro-life feminism was an oxymoron. "In this issue of *Sojourners* are committed feminists," Wallis wrote, "who radically dispute that twisted logic and see abortion as yet another form of violence against women." As an illustration, Sojourners community member Cathy Stentzel wrote an editorial testifying to her own conversion to a pro-life position. She initially supported *Roe v. Wade* as an integral part of the feminist agenda. Yet, Stentzel explained, she gradually came to differentiate between women's equal rights (which she still championed) and abortion (which she now opposed). Thus *Sojourners* chided the political left for equating support for feminism with support for abortion rights.[12]

Yet Wallis saved his harshest criticism for political conservatives. Declaring that abortion opponents discredited their cause by misguidedly linking their mission with social and political conservatism, he blamed conservative pro-life advocates for *Sojourners'* own evasiveness. The anti-abortion movement's "attitudes toward women and the poor, combined with its positive support for militarism and capital punishment, have been deeply offensive to us and have helped keep us away from the issue of abortion," Wallis stated. He accused leaders of the Religious Right of duplicity. The "energy and passion against abortion has been used to support a broad ideological agenda which incorporates political goals that have nothing to do with abortion and, in fact, are often directly contrary to the principles on which a genuinely pro-life position is based," Wallis asserted. "In other words, the issue of abortion is being manipulated to serve other ends," specifically a "pro-military and pro-business agenda." Wallis thus implied that a "genuinely pro-life" position entailed not merely disapproval of abortion but also opposition to sexism, militarism, the death penalty, and unjust economic conditions. He lauded some pro-life activists "whose opposition to abortion is leading them to oppose nuclear weapons and power, genetic engineering, and capital punishment," and he challenged conservatives to begin "questioning the kind of global economic system that starves children after they are born and makes expendable whole classes of human beings."[13]

Missing from Wallis's analysis, however, were any concrete proposals regarding what policies or actions abortion opponents should support. Instead, he offered the vague directive for readers to counter the pro-life movement's conservatism and thus defuse its appeal. "The unholy alliance between the anti-abortion movement and the right wing must be directly challenged by those who seriously and consistently espouse a pro-life commitment," Wallis exhorted. "The energy of the pro-life movement must be removed from the ideological agenda of the New Right." Despite this indefinite strategy, in published letters the majority of *Sojourners* readers responded positively to the journal's goal to divorce opposition to abortion from political conservatism.[14]

Sojourners may have sought to chart a new course by its distinct opposition to abortion, but it initially lacked a compass. Following its 1980 vow to defend "the sanctity of life," the magazine failed to meaningfully address the contentious issue again for four years. Wallis had called upon politically progressive abortion opponents to wrest leadership of the pro-life movement away from political conservatives. But a 1981 *Time* cover article on abortion—what it identified as "the most emotional issue of politics and morality that faces the nation today"—described the obstacles faced by pro-life progressive evangelicals. "To a large extent, the antiabortion movement has recently come under the aegis of the New Right" that incorporated "evangelical Christian groups like the Moral Majority," wrote *Time*'s reporter. "Conservative pro-life groups have formed a loose-knit alliance with organizations opposed to school busing, the Equal Rights Amendment, sex education in public schools, the ban on public school prayers, tough gun laws and foreign aid to leftist regimes." Emboldened by Ronald Reagan's own pro-life rhetoric and courting of their votes, the Religious Right came to dominate antiabortion efforts in the early 1980s through publicity campaigns and proposals for legislation. As a result, *Sojourners* became tentative and reticent regarding its own pro-life strategies. Finally, in August 1984 editors acknowledged the magazine's silence by again publishing letters from discontented readers who pushed *Sojourners* to follow up on its pro-life declaration. Since 1980, one complained, "no serious attention has been given to the Christian's responsibility to proclaim the rights of the unborn." He expressed concern that "for *Sojourners*, pro-life has become an 'aborted' issue."[15]

Sojourners' response several months later captured the frustration that had contributed to its lengthy silence and henceforth shaped its coverage. The editors acknowledged that the polarized nature of abortion debates in the 1984 elections—with Republicans proposing to outlaw all abortions and Democrats defending *Roe v. Wade* and federal funding of abortions—had created "a political and moral dilemma" to which they found "no easy answers or clear choices, only difficult questions." They tried to assure readers that *Sojourners* remained firmly pro-life. "We hold the conviction that abortion is morally wrong" and "a great social evil that must be abolished," editors wrote. As an electoral issue, however, abortion remained "especially difficult" on two accounts. Not only did conservatives' monopoly of the pro-life movement prove exasperating, but also *Sojourners*' staff remained uncertain of the best legislative approach to abortion. "We find the anti-abortion legislation currently offered," the editors explained, "to be quite offensive in its obvious biases against women and the poor." They declared that "an alternative is desperately needed," and thus *Sojourners* again called on other frustrated pro-life advocates to join them in exploring the best strategies for opposing abortion. The leadership of ESA would collaborate with *Sojourners* in this quest.[16]

Like both *The Other Side* and *Sojourners*, ESA rejected the ways in which abortion had become politicized. In 1980 ESA issued a tract titled

Can My Vote Be Biblical?—also printed in *Christianity Today*—to guide evangelicals in the upcoming elections. The organization joined *Sojourners* in connecting abortion to a broad range of social justice issues. "Political activity must reflect a biblical balance that is concerned with both poverty and abortion-on-demand, both peacemaking in a nuclear age and the family," the document read. At that time, however, the leaders of ESA had yet to explicate fully their own stance on abortion. In fact, ESA's newsletter recommended that "those wrestling with the issue of abortion" read *The Other Side*'s recent treatment of abortion as morally ambiguous. Nevertheless, the organization revealed an implied pro-life perspective. Listing "Every Human Life is Sacred" as one of its "basic biblical principles," ESA argued that "biblical people cannot remain silent" when "the value of each individual human life" is demeaned by practices such as racism, sexism, and "abortion-on-demand." ESA's pro-life identity became explicit in 1981, as its board of directors committed the organization to "articulate a consistent pro-life stance" in opposition not only to abortion but also to poverty, discrimination, and the nuclear arms race. Like *Sojourners*, the leaders of ESA came to regard abortion as incompatible with their commitment to justice and the "sacredness of human life."[17]

After several years of scattered references to abortion opposition, the leaders of ESA more fully explained their position in 1984. In his editorial "From Ambivalence to Action," executive director Bill Kallio recounted a story that resembled Wallis's own editorial four years earlier in *Sojourners*. Kallio confessed that he had "not always taken a clear stand on the issue of abortion," and he suspected that "there are many ESA members who are not sure of their position." He too blamed "the ideological captivity of the pro-life movement" and its affiliation with political conservatism for his confusion. Nevertheless, Kallio came to believe that abortion represented violence against the unborn and thus an injustice that Christians must oppose. At the same time, he reiterated a refusal to isolate the issue of abortion from other justice concerns. "Our culture needs to hear a strong Christian voice that cares for the poor and speaks for peace, for human rights, for the family and for the unborn," he wrote. "I often wonder what would happen in our society if a new coalition were to emerge that effectively linked an end to abortion with compassionate, active and well-defined concern for other peace and justice issues?" In addition to Kallio's editorial, ESA published several supporting articles: an interview with pro-life doctors, a commentary describing "abortion as a social justice issue" that discriminated against the poor and exploited women, and a profile of a pro-life organization. To be sure, ESA did not embrace an absolutist opposition to abortion. A list of resources included three pro-choice works as "alternative positions," and a survey of ESA members revealed that 87 percent believed abortion could be justified under rare circumstances. Nevertheless, ESA joined *Sojourners* in leading the progressive evangelical movement to promote a "consistent pro-life agenda" that linked opposition to abortion with other politically progressive policies.[18]

By the early 1980s, then, progressive evangelical leaders had rejected the terms that defined the prevailing political struggle over abortion. Militant parties in the debate almost exclusively described abortion in terms of a binary choice: abortion supporters' commitment to women's rights versus abortion opponents' commitment to the sanctity of life. The progressive evangelical movement protested this dichotomy. Most leaders defended women's full equality and rights while denying that these necessitated unrestricted access to legalized abortion. Despite their predominant objections to abortion, however, progressive evangelicals refused to affiliate with the conservative pro-life movement since they disdained its anti-feminism and other political positions. Instead, *Sojourners* and ESA chose to adopt the "pro-life" banner but to adapt its connotation. They argued that the defense of the sanctity of life carried moral and political obligations well beyond the womb. Even as *The Other Side* maintained its official uncertainty, *Sojourners* and ESA encouraged progressive evangelicals to support this broad "pro-life" campaign. They found kinship with Roman Catholics similarly committed to protesting a broad range of threats to human life that included not only abortion but also nuclear weapons, poverty, and the death penalty. Indeed, after Joseph Cardinal Bernardin of Chicago began to popularize calls for "a consistent ethic of life" in 1983, many progressive evangelical leaders embraced that description of their position and joined like-minded Catholics in collaborative efforts. Yet unlike Catholic bishops and many activists, pro-life evangelical progressives included support for feminism in their commitment to social justice. Thus these leaders embarked upon an idiosyncratic mission. While defending other feminist priorities, progressive evangelicals challenged conservative abortion opponents to broaden their agenda to include other peace and justice issues. Their hopes to unite Christians under a "consistent pro-life" banner soon met the realities of political estrangements.

"Of all the issues that concern Americans," Joyce Hollyday wrote in *Sojourners* in 1989, "none appears to divide us more bitterly than abortion." The "escalating pro-choice vs. pro-life battle" portended "a long and messy war ahead," she bemoaned, as "each side digs its trenches" and attacks the other side "as either 'baby killers' or 'woman haters.'" In the midst of these contentious public debates in the final decades of the twentieth century and into the new millennium, evangelical progressives continued to feel marginalized. Dissatisfied by uncompromising activists within both the pro-life Religious Right and the pro-choice political left, leaders attempted to develop mediating alternatives. In doing so, the primary progressive evangelical organizations fostered diverse approaches and agendas that built upon their initial responses in the early 1980s. *The Other Side* maintained its refusal to offer official opposition to or support for abortion, carrying occasional articles that cautiously reflected both sides of the debate. While this toleration for competing interpretations seemed to increase editors' sympathy for pro-choice arguments, after 1990 *The Other Side* avoided the controversial subject of abortion altogether. In contrast, *Sojourners* began to promote more vigorously a "consistent pro-life ethic" that framed abortion as one of numerous threats to the sanctity of life that Christians must oppose. Remaining ambivalent about legal restrictions, it focused on redressing inequalities and injustices—particularly those faced by poor women—that motivated choices to abort pregnancies. Ultimately, *Sojourners* adopted a pragmatic pro-life strategy in which pro-life and pro-choice advocates would work together to make abortion rare. Among progressive evangelicals, ESA developed the most aggressive pro-life position and supported broad legislative restrictions on abortion. Yet the organization also joined *Sojourners* in calling for expanded abortion alternatives and promoting a "completely pro-life agenda" in opposition to all dehumanizing injustices.[19]

A Retreat to Silence

The Other Side's refusal to endorse either a pro-life or a pro-choice position produced halting and awkward coverage of abortion. Between the middle of 1982 and late 1986, the magazine chose the safest method of neutrality: avoiding the subject altogether. In October 1986, however, internal disagreement regarding a new anti-abortion initiative prompted opposing articles by editors Mark Olson and Kathleen Hayes. Led by prominent pro-gressive evangelicals such as ESA's Ron Sider, a political action committee called JustLife formed in order to support candidates who championed a "consistent pro-life ethic." JustLife defined consistency as commensu-rate opposition to abortion, nuclear arms, and poverty. Olson opposed the creation of JustLife. Among other reservations, he most objected to "Just-Life's strong and unequivocal stand on abortion" and its endorsement of anti-abortion legislation. Olson remained proud of *The Other Side*'s 1980 issue on abortion, for he continued to believe that God had neither "given us a clear yes or no on abortion" nor "told us what to do in every diffi-cult situation." In contrast, Hayes joined JustLife's board of directors and supported its potential "to present society with a biblical vision for both life and justice." She argued that "mounting scientific evidence" suggests "that the fetus is alive—and genetically fully human—from the moment of conception." Hayes also proclaimed that JustLife desired not only anti-abortion legislation but also "viable alternatives for women facing the many difficulties of an unexpected pregnancy." In letters and responses to a questionnaire regarding JustLife, both pro-life and pro-choice readers of *The Other Side* defended their respective positions. This disagreement among both the editors and subscribers contributed to another prolonged silence on abortion. The journal did not address the subject in the late 1980s even as public debates about abortion intensified.[20]

When *The Other Side* did discuss abortion again in 1990, a tacit pref-erence for pro-choice arguments emerged. An article by Nancy Rockwell claimed that a crucial question—"What does a good woman do?"—lay at "the heart of the abortion controversy." She concluded that the Bible contained "a clear and consistent declaration of free choice for women." Good women were praised not for fertility but rather for overcoming vic-timization and making wise choices in difficult circumstances. Applying these lessons, Rockwell insisted that women themselves, not the state, should have power to decide the morality of abortion according to their particular situations. Thus Rockwell's article represented an unusual at-tempt to offer biblical justification for a pro-choice position. Immediately following this piece, *The Other Side* published an alternative stance in an interview with Kay Cole James, former director of public affairs for the National Right to Life Committee. As an African American, James believed that abortion represented a "civil rights issue" that had "devastating psy-chological effects on the black community." "Isn't it strange," she asked, "that poor black women have to fight for every right there is except the right to abort their unborn children?" Yet within this profile of a pro-life advocate, *The Other Side* posed questions that revealed a pro-choice bias. These questions ranged from traditional challenges ("But shouldn't those women have a right to choose?" and "How can pro-life values be placed on the heads of everyone else in our pluralistic society?") to more combative ones ("But given the grim realities of racist America, what kind of lives can unwanted, unaffordable babies hope to live?"). Combined with the preceding article, the interview suggested that the editors had developed greater sympathy for pro-choice arguments.[21]

The Other Side's next issue appeared to confirm this shift. The magazine again published an explicitly pro-choice article. To be sure, Donna Schaper criticized the individualistic focus and sexual permissiveness of many fellow abortion rights advocates. But she identified support for "right-to-life" people as "much too dangerous," for they would "make needed birth control even harder to get" and "force the creation of more life that will starve for books and square meals." Unlike the previous issue, a counterbalancing pro-life perspective was absent. Just as telling, this cluster of articles in 1990 failed to include, as previous coverage had, any editorial statements regarding *The Other Side*'s ambiguity regarding abortion. The pro-life editor Kathleen Hayes had left *The Other Side* in 1988 in order to become director of publications for the unambiguously pro-life ESA. Whether her defection signaled or produced a tacit approval of abortion, *The Other Side*'s own constituency recognized the change. Peace activist Jim Forest, a contributing editor for both *The Other Side* and *Sojourners*, criticized the magazine's recent imbalanced coverage. He acknowledged that *The Other Side* had occasionally printed pro-life articles. "But these exceptions only underline for me the magazine's usual acceptance of abortion," he wrote to the editors. Despite the "foibles" of the pro-life movement, Forest remained committed to advancing a "consistent pro-life" ethic. He therefore ended his affiliation as a contributing editor. "I am not comfortable having my name on the masthead when the magazine is one of those voices in U.S. church life dehumanizing the unborn and making it easier for them to become targets of violence." While *The Other Side* did not explicitly endorse abortion rights as its new editorial position, a preponderance of pro-choice coverage replaced the magazine's earlier balance.[22]

Whether Forest's rebuke or other concerns gave the editors pause, *The Other Side* effectively ended its coverage of abortion after 1990. The proverbial fence that divided pro-life and pro-choice proponents proved too difficult a place on which to remain seated. Rather than endorsing either side, however, *The Other Side* retreated from abortion debates by no longer running articles focused on the controversial issue. On the one hand, this silence appeared to reflect an attempt to remain faithful to *The Other Side*'s original commitment to editorial neutrality. On the other hand, silence represented a curious choice for a magazine dedicated to helping Christians discern the meaning of "justice rooted in discipleship"— *The Other Side*'s subtitle. In fact, as the next chapter details, the editors showed fortitude during this period by continuing to defend the minority position among progressive evangelicals that committed same-sex unions represented fully legitimate expressions of Christian sexuality. When it came to abortion, however, *The Other Side* chose the path of least resistance. Balanced coverage and arguments regarding abortion's moral ambiguity would likely continue to offend *both* pro-choice and pro-life advocates. Silence stirred few critics. Whether the choice reflected anxiety or confusion, *The Other Side* no longer confronted readers with competing interpretations of abortion. As a result, by the early 1990s few voices within the movement challenged the opposition to abortion that became predominant in progressive evangelical circles. The expanded pro-life advocacy of *Sojourners* and ESA contributed to this development.

Pro-Life Pragmatism

The leaders of *Sojourners* had confessed their confusion in 1984 regarding the "complicated question of abortion legislation." As a result, they pledged to advance dialogue concerning the political and legal ramifications of abortion by increasing their own attention to this issue throughout the rest of the 1980s. In the process, *Sojourners'* anti-abortion stand coalesced around three main themes.[23]

First, authors in *Sojourners* reiterated that their opposition to abortion stemmed from their comprehensive vision for social justice that entailed the flourishing of human lives in all circumstances, from womb to tomb. In a 1985 article, for example, former Planned Parenthood nurse Phyllis Taylor regretted her previous participation in abortions as "the destruction of human life" and thus incompatible with justice and nonviolence. At the same time, she challenged pro-life advocates to address other social problems—especially inadequate sex education, prenatal care, day care centers, and support for mothers releasing children for adoption— that contributed to women's tragic choices to abort pregnancies. A year later, Ginny Earnest Soley similarly acknowledged how the injustices of poverty, women's substantive inequality, insufficient health coverage, and lack of support for women with unwanted pregnancies often made abortion an attractive alternative. Yet by supporting abortion as a remedy, she argued, pro-choice advocates accepted injustice as inevitable. "Abortion is not a means of bringing about justice," Soley declared. It indicates that society refuses "to make any effort to bring about justice for women" or "to put forth any effort to guarantee a good life for children." In 1988 associate editor Vicki Kemper criticized Operation Rescue, the provocative anti-abortion group led by Randall Terry, for its aggressive demonstrations and preoccupation with a constitutional amendment against abortion. She insisted that consistent abortion opponents must also "see working for economic justice for women, better health care and social programs for the poor, and increased sex education and contraceptive availability as legitimate and necessary ways to oppose abortion." Over and over, *Sojourners* characterized its philosophy as the most thorough and the most just pro-life ideology. The magazine upheld "the sacredness of all life"—the defense of "unborn life" as well as "life threatened by nuclear weapons, on death row, and suffering under poverty and racism," associate editor Joyce Hollyday wrote.[24]

An acknowledged "lack of clarity about specific legal remedies for abortion" marked a second theme within *Sojourners'* articles. The magazine refused to endorse most efforts by conservative pro-life advocates to circumvent or to overturn *Roe v. Wade* through amending the Constitution, passing state laws restricting abortions, or supporting conservative Supreme Court nominees. Instead, *Sojourners* ran articles that considered complex questions regarding the legality of abortion. How should abortion opponents treat "extraordinary circumstances" such as fatal genetic diseases or rape? Would criminalizing abortion make desperate women turn to perilous practices and "back-alley butchers"? The Supreme Court's 1989 decision in *Webster v. Reproductive Health Services* moved *Sojourners* to address the issue at length. The Court's ruling undermined many abortion rights seemingly guaranteed by *Roe v. Wade* by upholding a state law that restricted public funding and resources for abortion. Rather than celebrating with the conservative pro-life movement, however, *Sojourners* professed to find compelling arguments for both the merit and detriment of the decision. The editors published a series of articles under the title "Abortion and the Law: How Do We Choose Life?" that featured contributors who shared opposition to abortion but differed on whether or not to legislate against it. Thus *Sojourners* further distinguished its pro-life commitment by questioning the legislative restrictions and prohibitions favored by conservatives.[25]

Finally, *Sojourners* ensured that explicit endorsements of feminism remained a theme within its analyses of abortion. Authors repeatedly countered the popular perception that feminist identity required support for abortion rights. In her 1986 article, Ginny Earnest Soley developed *Sojourners'* most thorough description of what it identified as "a Christian feminist perspective on abortion." Any discussion of the issue must account for the reality of women's oppression in a patriarchal culture and thus address how "to bring forth justice for women and their children," Soley maintained. While "liberal feminists" answered this question in "a moral vacuum," she argued, Christian feminists should challenge two assumptions: first, that "the individual's self-interest is, in fact, the highest value," and second, that "a woman's rights" necessarily conflict with "a child's right to life." Soley claimed that abortion actually increased women's suffering through psychological, spiritual, and even physical damage. Ultimately, she rejected most feminists' conclusions that abortion offered a crucial solution to women's inequitable responsibility for children. Instead, Soley proposed, Christians should witness to the more just solution that men, women, and the community at large accept equal responsibility for children's welfare. In 1989 Joyce Hollyday prefaced *Sojourners'* forum on abortion legislation with a statement of the magazine's "feminist pro-life" interpretation of abortion as "violence—not only to unborn children but to women, who are also its victims." Thus *Sojourners* sustained its attempt "to protect a woman's right to equality as well as a child's right to life."[26]

As *Sojourners* expanded its coverage of abortion in the 1990s, these three established themes continued to shape the magazine's particular pro-life perspective. Editors and authors championed their "consistent ethic of life," remained ambivalent regarding anti-abortion legislation, and defended the compatibility of feminism and opposition to abortion. In 1992, for example, contributing editor Shelley Douglass described abortion as "almost always a moral wrong" for reasons she considered "feminist in nature as well as profoundly spiritual." Yet "mixed feelings about making any laws about abortion" made Douglass uncomfortable with polarized arguments "either enshrining it as an inalienable right or forbidding it under any circumstances." Likewise, in his 1994 book *The Soul of Politics*, Jim Wallis denied that "absolute support for unrestricted abortion on demand" represented "a litmus test for authentic feminism." He wanted to find solutions that did not criminalize women who made "painful and lonely decisions about abortion" based upon a lack of resources or support. While Wallis most often criticized the pro-life conservatives for their inconsistency in failing to combat other injustices, he charged political liberals with the opposite offense. They rightly supported "the battles for racial, economic, and gender justice" yet failed to recognize the defense of fetal life as a comparable, just cause. "The Left made a fundamental mistake in seeing a woman's right to choose as the only moral issue at stake in the abortion dilemma," Wallis stated. Building upon these three commitments, by the mid-1990s *Sojourners* developed a more focused strategy for opposing abortion.[27]

Uncomfortable with outlawing abortion, *Sojourners* began to champion the alternative goal of making abortions less desired and thus less common. This strategy combined a pragmatic regard for abortion's legality, a respect for the complex choices facing women with unwanted pregnancies, and an idealistic belief that better alternatives would decrease abortion's appeal. President Bill Clinton had pledged during his 1992 campaign to make abortion "safe, legal, and rare"—a combination that *Sojourners* seemed to accept even as it prioritized rareness. A 1995 cover article, "Women and Children First: Developing a Common Agenda to Make Abortion Rare," exemplified the magazine's attempt to articulate practical steps to bring together "the rights and dignity of women with the sanctity of all life." Associate editor Julie Polter proposed a combination of strategies and policies to address factors that led women to have abortions. Programs ranging from mentoring to abstinence and contraceptive education would reduce unintended pregnancies among teenagers and low-income families. If facing an unplanned pregnancy, women needed access to both emotional and financial resources—not only from the government but also from individuals, churches, and community groups. Social attitudes and public policies should make adoption a respected and feasible choice. Finally, poor women who refused abortion and wished to raise their children needed additional assistance to meet child-rearing costs. Polter denounced Republican proposals for welfare reforms that included "child exclusion" provisions that would deny benefits to needy children under certain circumstances. This plan "will serve to punish families and encourage, even coerce, abortions among women in poverty," she argued. For *Sojourners*, making abortion rare represented a principled and pragmatic pro-life strategy.[28]

Even when endorsing focused anti-abortion legislation, *Sojourners* regarded legal restrictions as only a piece of the puzzle in reducing abortions. Polter expressed outrage over President Clinton's 1996 veto of legislation to outlaw "partial birth abortions." Yet, she noted, this ban would have failed to make abortion rare since the procedure accounted for less than 0.4 percent of abortions performed. Polter accepted the need for "careful framing" of some "legislative restrictions on abortion," but she maintained that "pregnancy prevention and abortion alternatives" represented the most critical means for "creating a society where no one thinks that abortion is the only choice." Jim Wallis repeated this argument a year later when the Partial-Birth Abortion Ban Act again passed Congress. Agreeing that the "controversial" and "particularly abhorrent abortion procedure" should be illegal, he accepted some "restrictions to discourage but not totally outlaw abortion." Nevertheless, Wallis again emphasized preventive efforts—"combating teenage pregnancy, reforming adoption laws, providing needed alternatives to women"—as the decisive means "to reduce the tragic 1.5 million abortions per year." By portraying abortion reduction as a primary pro-life objective, *Sojourners* sought to transform controversies over legislation into conversations about diminishing abortion rates.[29]

Furthering such conversations to find "common ground" between pro-life and pro-choice advocates became one of *Sojourners'* principal goals in the 1990s and beyond. Leaders condemned the rhetorical hostility of extremists on each side that prevented respectful dialogue and possible consensus. As a result, the magazine committed itself "to encouraging open dialogue between the pro-life and the pro-choice sides of the issue who are concerned about the welfare of unborn children, as well as women and families." For example, *Sojourners* endorsed the Common Ground Network for Life and Choice. In the midst of conversations sponsored by this network, reported Frederica Mathewes-Green, abortion opponents and supporters offered each other "insights that help us move toward a society where abortion no longer looks like a grim necessity." In 1999 *Sojourners* offered a model of such dialogue by publishing excerpts from a conversation between the pro-life Mathewes-Green and pro-choice author Naomi Wolf. Ultimately, *Sojourners* hoped that these conversations would unite those who differed on abortion legislation around the shared goal of reducing the number of abortions. "If pro-life people know that one abortion is too many and many pro-choice people at least agree that there surely shouldn't be as many abortions as there are," asked

Julie Polter, "shouldn't we do what we can in the scope of that common territory?"[30]

Promoting consensus around abortion reduction as the most practical way to defend "the sanctity of life" continued as the core of *Sojourners'* abortion coverage in the early twenty-first century. Prior to the 2004 election, Jim Wallis suggested that Democrats could appeal not only to pro-choice advocates but also to millions of pro-life evangelicals and Catholics if they affirmed abortion reduction as "the basis for some new common ground." *Sojourners* contributors repeatedly proclaimed that "pro-life" and "pro-choice" had become tired slogans in electoral politics. But "voters are looking for solutions, not slogans," Amy Sullivan wrote in a 2006 cover article, and "there are ways to dramatically reduce abortion rates" through promoting policies that all parties could support. Indeed, that year Sojourners applauded two proposed bills—the Abortion Reduction Act and the Pregnant Women Support Act—that "advance the dialogue and moral framework for developing a reasonable, comprehensive strategy for making abortion rare in America." In both his 2005 bestselling book *God's Politics* and 2008 follow-up *The Great Awakening*, Wallis centered his analyses of abortion on ways to reduce the practice. "My religious and moral view is that abortion is wrong, even when the circumstances are wrapped up in great difficulties and inequities," he wrote. But abortion represents a "tragic and often desperate" choice, Wallis argued, and outlawing it would push "desperate women again into the back alleys of terribly dangerous illegal abortions." Thus he urged all parties to support policies that "dramatically reduce the shamefully high abortion rate in America."[31]

To many evangelicals, *Sojourners'* focus on reducing rather than ending abortion seemed a disappointing compromise. In a 2008 interview, *Christianity Today's* Ted Olsen asked Wallis why his ostensible "prophetic voice on social issues" did not lead him to treat abortion like slavery and to insist on its abolition. "I think the prophetic stance right now in the pitched legal stalemate on abortion is abortion reduction," he responded. Several months later, Wallis made this same case to audiences beyond evangelical circles. "Pro-life and pro-choice groups can support abortion reduction," he reiterated in an interview with *Newsweek*. "There's common ground in supporting aid to low-income women, preventing pregnancies, [and] reforming adoption." In lieu of making abortion illegal, *Sojourners* sought to develop pragmatic means to approximate pro-life ends.[32]

"Completely Pro-Life" Politics

Beginning in the mid-1980s the leaders of ESA became the most assertive pro-life proponents within progressive evangelical circles. They joined *Sojourners* in claiming that opposition to abortion represented only one front on which Christians must defend "the sacredness of human life." In the newsletter following its analysis of abortion in 1984, ESA published a "reaffirmation" of its commitments that described a broad range of political activities required by a "consistent pro-life agenda": oppose abortion practices that "destroy millions of lives each year," resist governments that violate human rights, protest nuclear weapons that threaten "to annihilate millions of human beings made in God's image," encourage "all strategies and agencies that strengthen the family," challenge economic injustice, and end institutionalized racism and discrimination based upon sex, age, or physical ability. Like *Sojourners*, ESA's interpretation of "consistency" in pro-life positions distinguished its anti-abortion ideology from politically conservative abortion opponents. As a result, ESA advocated means beyond legislative restrictions in its anti-abortion efforts. For example, a 1985 cover article encouraged members to join the pro-life Christian Action Council in boycotting a company that produced a drug to induce abortions. Months later, ESA lauded the group Pro-lifers for Survival for creating "nonviolent alternatives to abortion and nuclear arms." The article described their "goals and programs" as "parallel," for Pro-lifers for Survival supported abortion alternatives like pregnancy aid centers and appealed to "hearts and minds" rather than to legal constraints. By 1986, ESA's leaders were ready to spearhead an ambitious attempt to translate the organization's broad pro-life agenda into practical political activity.[33]

The political action committee JustLife brought together like-minded Protestants and Catholics to support candidates who upheld a "consistent pro-life ethic." The organization defined consistency by three criteria: opposing abortion, working for justice for the poor, and seeking nuclear arms reduction. JustLife drew from ecumenical circles and had a separate board of directors from ESA. Yet the "sister" organizations shared staff and office space, and in 1987 Ron Sider became executive director of both ESA and JustLife. By working through a registered political action committee, ESA's leadership could campaign on behalf of endorsed candidates without jeopardizing ESA's own tax-exempt status. "JustLife's unique contribution is to introduce [the consistent pro-life] agenda into electoral politics," Jack Smalligan, the initial executive director of JustLife, wrote in ESA's newsletter. From 1986 through 1992, JustLife supported targeted campaigns and published election study guides that contained articles examining "a consistent life ethic" and relevant voting records for congressional candidates.[34]

In its opposition to abortion, JustLife adopted a comprehensive strategy. While encouraging the expansion of abortion alternatives and support for underprivileged mothers and children, JustLife also embraced legislative efforts—including a constitutional amendment—that would prohibit abortion except in cases of danger to the mother, rape, and incest. To be sure, ESA clarified that it had not endorsed this "more specific stance" on abortion. "JustLife supports government efforts to limit the availability of abortion," wrote the editor of ESA's newsletter in 1988, "while ESA has no official position on abortion legislation." Nevertheless, the close ties between the organizations indicated that ESA had greater sympathy for such restrictions than did *Sojourners*. Ron Sider's support for anti-abortion legislation confirmed this implicit approval.[35]

In conjunction with JustLife's efforts, Sider published a book offering the most extended description of ESA's "consistent pro-life agenda." Published in 1987, *Completely Pro-Life: Building a Consistent Stance* began with an analysis of abortion. Sider built a biblical and scientific case that Christians "must act on the assumption" that the "developing fetus is truly a human being" created in God's image. Abortion is murder, he argued, and should be illegal except in exceptional cases "when the physical life of the mother is threatened." Sider recommended that abortion opponents attempt to reshape public policy in two ways. First, pro-life advocates should work to end most, if not all, abortions "through constitutional amendments and legislation which focus on the personhood or humanity of the unborn child." Thus Sider supported the reversal of *Roe v. Wade*, a human life amendment to the Constitution, and other legislative restrictions such as curtailed funding for abortions through federal programs. But Sider insisted that "the integrity of the pro-life movement" depended upon a second approach: "vigorously supporting changes in public policy that give women and families additional meaningful alternatives." Such policies would enhance family planning education, provide resources for women carrying children to term, offer services for disabled children, mandate paternal responsibilities, fund crisis pregnancy centers and adoption agencies, and develop programs to help poor people so that "they no longer feel like they have to choose between desperate poverty and abortion." Despite the cost of such initiatives, Sider pressed anti-abortion activists "to work as hard for pro-life programs designed to guarantee quality of life to the already living as we work for policies that will ensure life itself to the not yet born." As its title suggested, however, *Completely Pro-Life* did not focus exclusively on abortion. Subsequent chapters characterized economic injustice, family disintegration, and nuclear weapons as additional pressing threats to the "fullness of life in every area." By insisting that "a biblically informed pro-life agenda" comprised this array of issues, Sider challenged conservative abortion opponents to broaden their priorities.[36]

In the late 1980s and early 1990s, ESA's recurring attention to abortion in its newsletter reflected Sider's emphasis on both legislative restrictions and the development of viable alternatives. For example, in 1988 ESA urged readers to lobby Congress in support of the Hyde Amendment, an annual rider on appropriation bills that prevented federal funding of abortions. A year later the newsletter reported that more than two-thirds of women who had abortions indicated that their "inability to afford the baby" had influenced their decision. "Parents should not have to choose between aborting a child and raising him or her in poverty," ESA insisted. Leaders celebrated the extension of the Women, Infants, and Children benefits program as "a real pro-life victory" but continued to champion other policies that would diminish the effect of financial needs upon abortion decisions. ESA's response to the Supreme Court's 1989 *Webster* decision epitomized its broad anti-abortion strategy. The group endorsed states' legislative ability to restrict abortions, and it objected to bills introduced in the early 1990s—particularly the Freedom of Choice Act—intended to nullify such limitations. At the same time, ESA advocated additional legislation to support "genuine alternatives" such as a model set of bills developed by JustLife Education Fund. "We support the overturning of *Roe v. Wade*," ESA wrote in 1992, "but with a strong commitment to the simultaneous funding of support services for women and their children during and after pregnancy as well as private and public development of alternatives to abortion." While hoping to outlaw most abortions, ESA remained committed to addressing the factors that led women to terminate pregnancies.[37]

Although ESA's leaders addressed cultural assumptions regarding the tension between the feminist commitment to women's equality and opposition to abortion much less frequently than *Sojourners*, they remained dedicated to both causes. Sojourners' sensitivity to its feminist constituency contributed to its refusal to join ESA in the work of JustLife.

"Sojourners has decided not to have someone on the board of JustLife," Ron Sider told an interviewer in 1989, "not because they are really opposed to it, but because they are afraid it would give the wrong impression to some feminists." ESA had not published as extensively on feminist issues and thus felt less hesitancy about potentially offending feminists. Nevertheless, the leadership of ESA continued to affirm feminism and opposition to abortion as compatible. In *Completely Pro-Life*, Sider described the movement for women's equality as furthering a pro-life agenda and endorsed the Equal Rights Amendment as a beneficial legal reform. At the same time, Sider proposed a rider to the amendment that would prevent pro-choice advocates from using the ERA to defend abortion rights. ESA's newsletter also showed concurrent support for pro-life and feminist positions. In inaugurating its public policy analysis in 1988, ESA included separate categories for its congruent goals of both opposing abortion and promoting feminist concerns.[38]

In the early 1990s ESA addressed the issue more directly. Benjamin Davis, former director of ESA's Washington office, wrote an article titled "Protecting Everyone's Rights: One Man's Struggle with Feminism and Abortion." Davis confessed that guilt over his own and society's patriarchal past initially made him an uncritical advocate of the feminist movement. Yet Davis eventually concluded that in the process of exalting women's rights, feminists "had forgotten the third actor in this life-and-death drama, the unborn child." Therefore, he claimed, Christians must champion "the human rights of *all*"—"women as well as men" and "the unborn as well as the born." Several years later, Frederica Mathewes-Green shared her own "confessions of a pro-life feminist" with ESA members. Despite unequivocal support of women's equal rights, she too opposed abortion. "No matter how difficult a pregnancy made a woman's life," she wrote in ESA's *Prism* magazine, "dismembering her child was a violent and unjust solution." While lacking the frequency and force of *Sojourners'* articles, these analyses defended ESA's interpretation of pro-life feminism.[39]

Predictably, ESA criticized President Bill Clinton's pro-choice policies throughout his tenure in the White House. ESA reaffirmed opposition to the Freedom of Choice Act, which Clinton supported, and promised to challenge any inclusion of "unrestricted funding for abortion" in the health care reforms advocated by First Lady Hillary Clinton. Leaders saved their harshest words in response to President Clinton's perceived hypocrisy. Despite Clinton's open support for abortion rights, ESA's Keith Pavlischek noted, some pro-life evangelicals had voted for him based upon his pledge to make abortions "safe, legal, and rare." Yet the president immediately restored federal funding for abortion counseling, refused to support reauthorization of the Hyde Amendment, and insisted that abortion be covered in his proposed health care plans. As pro-lifers expressed outrage that none of these policies would make abortion "rare," Pavlischek argued that the Clinton administration had proven itself not merely pro-choice but rather "pro-abortion." Thus, he concluded, "consistently pro-life Christians" must view Clinton's claims about reducing abortion "as empty political rhetoric at best and a cynical attempt to win support and favor from evangelicals at worst."[40]

At the same time, ESA regarded pro-life conservatives as far from ideal. After Republicans regained a majority in Congress in the 1994 midterm elections, Ron Sider expressed gratitude that they favored "greater restrictions on abortion." But he claimed that Republicans' support for less stringent gun control, relaxed regulations on tobacco, elimination of the social "safety net," and vast reduction in nonmilitary foreign aid reflected "a strange idea of what it means to be 'pro-life.'" He encouraged evangelical voters to write congressional representatives and "remind them that being pro-life means not only protecting the unborn from abortion, but also guarding children from assault rifles, handguns, and seductive tobacco ads." As the new Congress began to tackle welfare reform, Sider criticized proposed reductions in benefits that he feared "will lead many women facing pregnancy, especially the young and poor, to the desperate choice of denying life to their children." To be sure, Sider occasionally collaborated with conservative abortion opponents. In 1996 both he and Jim Wallis (in a departure from Wallis's usual qualms regarding legislative restrictions) joined Religious Right leaders such as James Dobson and Ralph Reed and neoconservative Catholics such as Richard John Neuhaus and Robert George in signing an anti-abortion manifesto titled "The America We Seek: A Statement of Pro-Life Principle and Concern." The document identified abortion as "the civil rights issue of our time" and, in lieu of the ultimate goal of abolishing abortion through reversing *Roe v. Wade* or a constitutional amendment, called for both increased legal restrictions and enhanced "alternatives to abortion for women in crisis." Yet in a *Christianity Today* article that year, Sider also reminded mainstream evangelicals that "a pro-life ethic means more than being anti-abortion," for "it is unbiblical for pro-life Christians to overlook the sanctity of life of those who die unnecessarily because of tobacco, war, pollution, or starvation."[41]

While continuing to promote their broad pro-life agenda in the early twenty-first century, Sider and ESA increasingly joined *Sojourners* in endorsing pragmatic strategies for reducing abortions. With respect to electoral politics, for example, Ron Sider linked the defeat of Democratic presidential candidate John Kerry in 2004 to disillusionment among evangelicals and Catholics with his party's "extreme positions" on issues such as "the sanctity of human life." "Why can't the Democrats at least get serious about President Clinton's position that abortion should be rare?" he asked in a *Philadelphia Inquirer* op-ed. Sider soon joined Jim Wallis and other progressive evangelical leaders such as Tony Campolo and David Gushee in endorsing the efforts of Third Way, a centrist public policy think tank, to bring political progressives and evangelicals into agreement around "shared cultural values" such as "common ground" on abortion reduction. Indeed, Sider admitted in his 2008 book *The Scandal of Evangelical Politics*, "legislation that would totally abolish abortion is politically impossible." Therefore "people who believe in the sanctity of life should work to dramatically reduce the number of abortions." He reiterated his desire to make abortion not only less available through legislation but also less attractive through improved policies regarding adoption laws, services for disabled children, and educational and economic support for women "so they no longer feel they have to choose between desperate poverty and abortion." Sider concluded his chapter on "the sanctity of human life" by calling modern evangelicals to follow the example of the early church, as it "pleaded for the poor, the weak, children and the unborn" and "discarded hate in favor of love, war in favor of peace, oppression in favor of justice, bloodshed in favor of life." Thus Sider exemplified how most progressive evangelical leaders called upon Christians to base political engagement on what they regarded as a "consistent pro-life ethic."[42]

POLITICALLY HOMELESS

More than any other factor, progressive evangelicals' "consistent pro-life agenda" placed them on the margins of partisan politics from the 1980s into the twenty-first century. In 1980 the Republican Party opposed abortion unambiguously for the first time and called for a constitutional ban as part of its platform, while Democrats affirmed support of "reproductive freedom as a fundamental human right" and committed their party to opposing the reversal or restriction of abortion rights. As opposition to abortion increasingly became the political priority of the Religious Right, conservative evangelicals flocked to the support of Republicans. In turn, commitment to abortion rights by the political left inspired the loyalty of feminists and pro-choice advocates to Democrats. "Every two and four years abortion has been *the* determining issue for millions of American voters, on *both* sides of the issue, when they enter the voting booth," *Sojourners'* Vicki Kemper observed in 1988. The most militant members of the pro-life movement turned support for pro-life Republicans into a holy cause. "To vote for Bill Clinton is to sin against God," proclaimed Randall Terry, the founder of the anti-abortion group Operation Rescue, in 1992. Four years later, Religious Right leaders such as James Dobson of Focus on the Family and Ralph Reed of the Christian Coalition threatened Republicans that attempts to weaken the party's forceful anti-abortion plank would cost them the votes of evangelicals. Unlike conservative pro-life advocates, however, progressive evangelicals defined "pro-life" broadly and refused to let a candidate's position on abortion dictate their electoral decisions. Jim Wallis voiced the frustration of the progressive evangelical movement by criticizing Republicans' neglect of "other places where human life is now most threatened" and Democrats' insensitivity to the "moral tragedy of abortion." Believing that neither political party offered a thorough pro-life platform, evangelical progressives consistently felt politically homeless.[43]

As early as 1980, progressive leaders challenged other evangelicals to avoid "one issue politics" and balance opposition to abortion with other priorities. In its guide titled "Can My Vote Be Biblical?," ESA argued that Christians should support candidates "concerned about the whole range" of injustices rather than "focus exclusively on a few select issues to the neglect of other matters emphasized by the scriptures." In 1984 Sider reiterated this argument for mainstream evangelicals in a *Christianity Today* article. Rather than "judge political candidates almost exclusively by their stand on abortion," he argued, Christians should reflect a biblically balanced pro-life agenda that includes both opposition to abortion and attention to economic justice, world hunger, and nuclear proliferation. Writing in *Sojourners* that same year, Bill Weld-Wallis expressed the dilemma that pro-life progressive evangelicals faced. "Pro-lifers don't like us because we push them to embrace a consistent pro-life ethic," he observed. "Our friends in the peace and justice movement don't like us because we make them uncomfortable with our anti-abortion talk." In what would become a quadrennial ritual for progressive evangelical leaders, Weld-Wallis described the resultant political marginalization. In the presidential race, he wrote, "neither candidate comes close" to being "genuinely pro-life." The pro-choice Walter Mondale offered an end to military action in Central America and nuclear arms reduction but also "a continuation of the slaughter of innocents." Ronald Reagan symbolically opposed abortion but supported a "reprehensible" social agenda and a "war on the poor and the Third World." Though he still intended to vote and to "seek God's Spirit for counsel," Weld-Wallis concluded that support for either party would "seriously compromise some aspect of our pro-life stance." While a pro-choice perspective disturbed pro-life progressive evangelicals, mere opposition to abortion did not guarantee their support.[44]

In the late 1980s many progressive evangelical leaders further distinguished themselves from the conservative pro-life movement by gravitating toward Democrats. Most evangelical anti-abortion forces wove themselves into the fabric of Republican politics. They warned that votes for Democrats—even ones who opposed abortion—would damage the pro-life cause, for those Democrats might obstruct the judicial appointments of President Reagan. But pro-life progressive evangelicals found more Democrats than Republicans who agreed with their interrelated stands on life, peace, and justice. In fact, all but one of the sixty-eight candidates endorsed by JustLife in 1986 and 1988 were Democrats. In the 1986 Senate race in Nevada, for example, the Republican incumbent James Santini received the support of the anti-abortion Pro-Family Coalition. Yet Santini opposed both a nuclear freeze and increased funding for antipoverty programs, and thus JustLife backed the successful challenge of Harry Reid, a pro-life Democrat. Even a pro-choice Democrat could seem the most preferable candidate. In 1988 Jim Wallis called the presidential campaign of Jesse Jackson "the closest by far to the biblical priorities." He lauded Jackson for prioritizing the poor, supporting peaceful negotiations over military action, reversing the arms race, and denouncing apartheid in South Africa. Yet Jackson had abandoned a pro-life stance—one that *Sojourners* had printed in 1980—and adopted support for abortion rights. While the shift appeased the Democratic mainstream, Wallis characterized it as "a painful inconsistency on this sanctity of life question." Nevertheless, he regarded Republicans equally if not more inconsistent, for they proclaimed opposition to abortion but showed insensitivity to poverty, economic injustice, and military violence.[45]

As the partisan divide over abortion intensified in the early 1990s, pro-life evangelical progressives had good reasons for feeling ostracized. In 1992 both political parties rebuffed the attempts of evangelicals who promoted a "consistent ethic of life." Leaders of JustLife were denied the opportunity to testify before the Republican National Convention in favor of military cuts and increased social programs for the poor and marginalized. Likewise, the Democratic National Convention refused their request to testify against the party's pro-choice position. In fact, the Democratic Party prevented Bob Casey, the pro-life Democratic governor of Pennsylvania, from even speaking at its national convention. Because "the Democrats put so much pressure on their pro-life candidates," JustLife director Dave Medema stated, his organization found fewer candidates to endorse. A year later JustLife folded as a national organization. "In the polarized world of abortion politics," one analyst noted, "there was not a sufficiently sizable constituency for a PAC that endorsed a consistent ethic of life." Just before the 1992 presidential election, both Sider and Wallis again expressed disappointment with the inadequate options that each party offered. "Human life does not stop being precious at birth," Sider wrote. "It is a tragedy that we do not have presidential candidates linking opposition to abortion to other issues" within "a consistent life ethic." Also disillusioned, Wallis claimed that "Christians committed to peace and justice feel very marginalized" by both political liberals and conservatives.[46]

As two of the most prominent progressive evangelical leaders, Sider and Wallis reiterated these lamentations during subsequent presidential campaigns. Despite the ongoing efforts of many progressive evangelicals to promote their broad pro-life position, little changed during the two-term presidency of Bill Clinton. Democratic support for Clinton's pro-choice initiatives displeased them, but the persistently narrow pro-life definition of Republicans proved similarly disappointing. Thus Sider and Wallis acknowledged their familiar predicament prior to the 2000 presidential election. "The perennial problem is that neither the Democratic nor the Republican presidential candidate perfectly fits" with "a pro-life and pro-poor, pro-family and pro-racial justice agenda," Sider claimed. He preferred Republican George W. Bush's statements on abortion but favored Democrat Al Gore's promises on gun control, restrictions on capital punishment, military spending, and economic programs. Sider claimed that he remained "undecided" and "determined to vote for the person I sense will do less damage." Wallis encouraged *Sojourners* readers to ask, "How does the religious principle of the sacredness of human life challenge both candidates on, for example, abortion, capital punishment, military spending, missile defense, or gun control?" Believing that both Bush and Gore were only selectively pro-life, he too wrestled with the implications. "Is voting for candidates who are far from perfect a 'lesser of evils' compromise," Wallis questioned, "or an ethical decision to seek incremental change?" While his own answer remained unstated, progressive evangelicals' broad interpretation of "pro-life" created complex choices and compromised electoral decisions.[47]

The 2004 election offered little change. Both *Sojourners* and ESA repeated protests against the narrow connotation of "pro-life," the political polarization created by abortion, and the consequential complicated electoral decisions that evangelical progressives faced. A cover article of *Sojourners* explained yet again "why people who believe in the sanctity of life—all life—struggle to find a home in either political party." Wallis called it a "tragedy" that "in America today one can't vote for a consistent ethic of life." Arguing again that the goal of abortion reduction could bring consensus, he challenged Democrats to abandon their "rigid, ideological" pro-choice stance that cost them the votes of evangelicals and Catholics who otherwise appreciated their policies on "issues of justice and peace." Sider repeated his refusal to base his vote on a candidate's position on abortion. He considered the incumbent George W. Bush "much better on the sanctity of human life" but the Democratic challenger John Kerry "better on economic and racial justice, the environment, and American's international role." Without a clear determinative issue, Sider wrote, "I find this year's decision especially wrenching." After Kerry's defeat, he echoed Wallis's advice to Democrats. "If they would like to win again, they should ponder the fact that there are millions of evangelical and Catholic voters who prefer Democratic stands on many issues, including the tax structure, economic justice, overcoming poverty and the environment, but who also demand a centrist position on family, marriage and the sanctity of life," Sider claimed.[48]

Progressive evangelical leaders took a more proactive approach in 2008. Tony Campolo, a self-described "pro-life Democrat," reported on *Sojourners'* blog that he had joined his party's platform committee and, with the help of Wallis, successfully pressed for the inclusion of an abortion reduction plank. Wallis lamented Democrats' continued explicit opposition to "any and all efforts to weaken or undermine" a woman's "right to choose a safe and legal abortion." Nevertheless, he cheered the additional commitment to abortion reduction, for it reached out to "people, especially in the religious community, who have strong moral convictions about abortion." In an effort to avoid charges of partisanship, Wallis also attended the Republican National Convention. He, Ron Sider, and several Catholic leaders issued a statement urging Republicans "to demonstrate a willingness to bring Americans of diverse political backgrounds together behind common-ground solutions to the abortion crisis."[49]

Just before the 2008 election, Sider contrasted Republican candidate John McCain's "clearly anti-abortion" position with Democratic nominee Barack Obama's "strongly pro-choice" record. Yet neither candidate offered "a completely-pro-life agenda," he again concluded, and evangelicals should "not allow one issue to trump all others." While Wallis's friendship with Obama suggested his preference, he also declined to explicitly endorse a candidate. There is "no easy jump from God's politics to either the Republicans or Democrats," he argued, and thus Christians must make "the *imperfect choices* that always confront us in any election year." Wallis pledged to "choose candidates who have the most consistent ethic of life, addressing all the threats to human life that we face—not just one." Such threats included poverty, war, lack of heath care, the death penalty, and abortion. "On abortion," Wallis concluded, "I will choose candidates who have the best chance to pursue the practical and proven policies which could dramatically reduce the number of abortions in American and therefore save precious unborn lives." The perceived incongruities concerning "a consistent ethic of life" among both Republicans and Democrats left progressive evangelicals without a clear home in partisan politics.[50]

NASCENT COMMUNITY MEMBERS

To pro-life evangelical progressives, opposition to abortion fit naturally within their public theology once they concluded that unborn children represented nascent community members. As they mulled their responses to abortion in the late 1970s and early 1980s, the decisive issue for the leading progressive evangelical voices—as for many involved in abortion debates—was the status of fetuses. Because editors of *The Other Side* believed that the biblical and scientific "arguments for fetuses being human" proved "weak," they abstained from either approving or condemning legalized abortion. Both *Sojourners* and ESA reached a different conclusion that led them to their pro-life positions. By consistently describing the decision to oppose abortion as a principled commitment to the sacredness of human life, each group indicated that fetuses had rights and deserved protection as developing members of the human community. Several authors made the point explicit. "The most important strand in my conversion from pro-abortion to pro-life was the acknowledgement that the being growing in the womb was life, that life in all its fullness was apparent from conception," testified staff member Cathy Stentzel in *Sojourners'* inaugural analysis of abortion. "I know that it is a life and has a right to live." Likewise, ESA's executive director Bill Kallio insisted that "all human life is sacred and created in the image of God" and thus "must be protected from the moment of conception." To be sure, many evangelical progressives hesitated as they pondered abortion in light of their dedication to women's rights and substantive equality. But most determined that unborn persons' fundamental right to life overrode feminist concerns. "As Christians and feminists, we care deeply about the quality of life for women, especially poor women," wrote Bill Weld-Wallis in *Sojourners*. "But with the question of abortion, in the end, we feel that we must advocate for the person whose very existence, not just their quality of life, is at stake." Thus most progressive evangelical leaders grounded their pro-life commitments in the conviction that these nascent community members possessed the same sanctity and value as other people. In accord with their public theology of community, they believed that social conditions and political policies should affirm and protect vulnerable fetal life.[51]

At the same time, pro-life progressive evangelicals repeatedly argued that unborn children represent only one of many endangered and dehumanized groups. Their public theology inspired leaders' equal defense of the life and rights of *all* people, especially powerless and oppressed victims of injustice. "We attempt to take a consistent pro-life stance that regards all lives as precious and seeks to defend life everywhere and anywhere it is threatened, whether by weapons of war, abortion clinics, electric chairs, or the specter of poverty," proclaimed *Sojourners*. Thus progressive evangelical leaders rejected the narrow definition of "pro-life" held by conservative abortion opponents and promoted their opposition to abortion as a part of a comprehensive blueprint for social justice. "The human rights of *all* must be protected: women as well as men, non-whites as well as whites, the unborn as well as the born," Benjamin Davis wrote for ESA. "Before God, all of humankind stands equal and deserving full justice." In the public theology of pro-life progressive evangelical leaders, opposition to abortion represented a necessary but not sufficient part of a "consistently pro-life agenda" in defense of "persons created in the image of God."[52]

Just before the 2004 presidential election, a well-publicized campaign initiated by Sojourners epitomized how the progressive evangelical movement framed its objections to abortion. Titled "God is Not a Republican. Or a Democrat," the campaign attempted to discourage Christians from becoming "single-issue voters." Instead, Sojourners enjoined Christians to measure the policies of candidates "against a complete range of Christian ethics and values" that included not only "a consistent ethic of human life" but also care for human dignity, strong families, racial reconciliation, peace, and gender equality. By describing both the defense of human life and support for gender equity as Christian ideals, progressive evangelicals remained committed to harmonizing their anti-abortion and feminist convictions. In addition, the very name of the campaign indicated how progressive evangelicals remained unwilling to identify readily with either political party. Finally, Sojourners offered a broad range of criteria by which to measure the "consistent ethic of human life": "Do the candidates' positions on abortion, capital punishment, euthanasia, weapons of mass destruction, HIV/AIDS—and other pandemics—and genocide around the world obey the biblical injunction to choose life?" Balancing and prioritizing these issues regularly placed progressive evangelicals on the margins of both the broader evangelical movement and partisan political debates. But abortion did not represent the only issue that marginalized progressive evangelicals. The next chapter describes how their responses to homosexuality also distinguished them from both the Religious Right and political left.[53]

6. A Civil Right but Religious Wrong?

Although progressive evangelicals' harshest opposition usually came from the Religious Right, in early 2011 Jim Wallis and Sojourners found themselves under fire from religious and political liberals. Sojourners had refused to carry a video advertisement on the group's website from Believe Out Loud, an advocacy group dedicated to the full inclusion of lesbian, gay, bisexual, and transgender (LGBT) Christians within churches. In the video, a lesbian couple and their son enter a church but encounter silent hostility from the congregation. Yet the minister at the front of the sanctuary greets them warmly. "Welcome—everyone," he says before helping seat the family. While the video seemed only to urge the welcome of gays and lesbians within churches, Believe Out Loud as an organization promoted Christians' full affirmation of same-sex relationships as moral—a position with which most progressive evangelicals disagreed. Liberal Christians were disillusioned by Sojourners' rejection of the advertisement. Complaining that Wallis "wasn't necessarily progressive on issues like abortion and LGBT rights," they regretted partnering with Sojourners on other social justice issues and allowing Wallis to become the face of "Progressive Christianity in the eyes of the Obama administration and the Washington media." Indeed, one critic wrote ruefully, "It is entirely possible to do good work in the world and at the same time contribute to the ongoing bigotry and oppression of queer folk." To many on the political and religious left, Wallis and Sojourners appeared hypocritical for claiming dedication to social justice but refusing this sign of support for gays and lesbians.[1]

Wallis's response to this criticism reflected the fine line that most progressive evangelicals had drawn with respect to homosexuality over the previous three decades. On the one hand, Sojourners insisted that LGBT individuals deserve equal protection under the law, full civil rights, and a warm religious welcome from Christians. "Our message has always been that no matter what your theological perspective or biblical interpretation on the issue of homosexuality, every Christian has the obligation to defend the lives, dignity, and civil rights of gay and lesbian people" and "to be welcoming of all people," Wallis wrote. On the other hand, Sojourners refused to affirm same-sex sexuality as moral. Wallis acknowledged disagreement within "Sojourners' constituency, board, and staff" but at that time was still personally on record as supporting only heterosexual marriage. He feared that hosting the video from Believe Out Loud would suggest Sojourners' endorsement of same-sex relationships. In addition, he asserted that Sojourners' "core mission concerns" were focused on public "matters of poverty, racial justice, stewardship of the creation, and the defense of life and peace"—not on addressing particular theological disputes regarding sexuality. For Wallis and most other progressive evangelical leaders, the question of the morality of same-sex sexuality was a matter of *personal* ethics, not an issue of *social* justice. Even as their public theology inspired all progressive evangelicals' "commitment to civil rights for gay and lesbian people," most leaders believed that the Bible sanctions sexual activity only within heterosexual marriages.[2]

Determining whether or not to affirm covenantal same-sex unions proved a difficult and divisive issue within the progressive evangelical movement. In the late 1970s and early 1980s, sensitivity to the marginalized status of gay and lesbian Christians led some in the evangelical left to reconsider traditional biblical interpretations of homosexuality. Several scholars argued that scriptural condemnations of same-sex behavior either represented obsolete cultural taboos or denounced only exploitative practices. Without clear biblical guidance, they claimed, modern knowledge of homosexual orientations and the positive experiences of Christians in committed same-sex unions compel the church to affirm gays and lesbians' fully equal status. While conservative evangelicals quickly dismissed these arguments, a minority of progressive evangelicals found them persuasive. *The Other Side* expressed sympathy for these affirming arguments in 1978 before endorsing them in 1984. As the full acceptance of gays and lesbians within both the church and society became a central part of *The Other Side*'s mission, the journal grew increasingly estranged from the progressive evangelical movement. *Sojourners* and Evangelicals for Social Action (ESA) agreed that churches must welcome LGBT individuals, but their leaders joined conservatives in reaffirming biblical bans on same-sex behavior as relevant, clear, and authoritative. After prolonged silence, *Sojourners* stated in 1982 and then reiterated in 1985 its conviction that the Bible did not condone same-sex relationships. Because this stance generated backlash from many ecumenical partners and supporters, in subsequent coverage *Sojourners* muted this interpretation and instead promoted dialogue among Christians who took different positions. Nonetheless, the magazine continued to exasperate religious liberals by refusing to affirm gay and lesbian Christians. Without similar ecumenical contributors or constituents, ESA never equivocated in its own description of same-sex behavior as sinful. From the 1970s into the twenty-first century, ESA leaders consistently upheld heterosexual marriage as the only appropriate context for human sexuality.

While their theological standards for personal sexual practices led most progressive evangelicals to oppose all same-sex behavior, their theological standards for social justice inspired leaders to defend gays and lesbians' equal civil rights. *Sojourners* and ESA believed that *private* religious communities are free to restrict rights of ministry and membership to those who uphold their particular standards of sexual morality. Therefore they rejected the arguments of *The Other Side* and many religious liberals that social justice requires full religious affirmation of gays and lesbians. At the same time, progressive evangelicals unanimously insisted that all people— regardless of sexual orientation—must receive equal treatment in the *public* sphere. In turn, leaders denounced the Religious Right for promoting political initiatives to limit LGBT individuals' civil rights. As the AIDS crisis developed in the 1980s, evangelical progressives also criticized Christian conservatives who interpreted the disease as God's judgment on homosexuality. They decried such views as homophobic and promoted personal and political actions to care for victims. During debates about gay marriage in the 1990s and the first decade of the twenty-first century, however, almost all progressive evangelical leaders refused to endorse a legal right to marry a same-sex partner. Drawing upon their public theology, they believed that individual interests should not subvert the common good. Most evangelical progressives argued that the social purposes of marriage—producing and rearing children in stable environments—outweigh its individual benefits. Because covenantal heterosexual unions best serve these social purposes, they argued, the state rightfully restricted marriage and some benefits to heterosexual couples. Yet in an effort to ensure the access of same-sex couples to such entitlements as property and medical visitation rights, many progressive evangelicals came to accept the legal recognition of civil unions for gays and lesbians. This compromise illustrated how most leaders balanced their moral objections to same-sex behavior with support for gays and lesbians' civil rights.

GAY LIBERATION AND CHRISTIAN RESPONSES

Beginning in the late 1960s, gays and lesbians pushed with new vigor to end legal and social discrimination against them. The gay liberation movement gained both momentum and notoriety after a police raid on the Stonewall Inn, a gay bar in New York's Greenwich Village, sparked well-publicized riots in 1969. Within four years the number of organizations dedicated to securing gay rights grew from roughly fifty to over eight hundred. Such activism produced tangible results. In 1973, for example, the American Psychiatric Association overturned its classification of homosexuality as a mental disorder and repudiated therapies intended to "cure" gays and lesbians. Two years later the Civil Service Commission withdrew its ban on gay employees. By 1980 almost half of states with laws against sodomy repealed them. Gays and lesbians also gained further mainstream acceptance. In places beyond the historic hubs of New York and San Francisco, gay subcultures more and more operated openly and proudly. Media outlets portrayed homosexuality less derisively, and gay characters and themes began to appear throughout popular culture. The gay liberation movement instilled pride in participants and facilitated more favorable public attitudes toward homosexuals. As in the contemporary feminist movement, LGBT individuals employed the language of rights and equality to justify their cause.[3]

Most mainline Protestant and Catholic leaders came to support the civil rights of gays and lesbians while continuing to regard same-sex relationships as immoral. By the end of the 1970s, all of the mainline Protestant denominations except for the American Baptist Church issued formal statements in support of gay civil rights. Yet only the United Church of Christ fully affirmed gay and lesbian Christians and accepted openly gay ministers. Mainline Lutherans, Presbyterians, Methodists, Baptists, and Episcopalians maintained the traditional view of same-sex behavior as sinful. Within Roman Catholicism, the Vatican and the United States National Conference of Catholic Bishops reaffirmed that homosexual acts are "intrinsically disordered" even if same-sex attraction was involuntary. At the same time, the American bishops and a national council for priests vowed to oppose discrimination based on sexual orientation and to support gay civil rights. In response to official condemnations of homosexual behavior, grassroots organizations—such as the Episcopalian group Integrity, Presbyterians for Lesbian and Gay Concerns, and the Catholic organization Dignity—emerged to support gays and lesbians and to challenge their churches' positions. In addition, a few Protestant theologians began defending covenantal same-sex relationships, and a minority of Catholic theologians believed that the modernizing trends that emerged from the Second Vatican Council in the mid-1960s could cause the church to accept same-sex love as valid.[4]

To virtually all evangelicals, however, gay liberation loomed as both a religious and political threat. They had long regarded sexual sins as scandalous, but homosexuality seemed especially egregious. Unlike immoral heterosexual activity outside of marriage, evangelicals believed, same-sex intimacy perverted the "natural" attraction between men and women and represented a unique "abomination" (Leviticus 18:22). In response to the gay rights movement, therefore, evangelical leaders reiterated traditional biblical condemnations of homosexuality. In the public sphere, the emerging Religious Right increasingly reacted against perceived "gay militancy" by taking up public campaigns to deny that "the homosexual lifestyle" represented a morally acceptable and legally equal alternative. In 1977, for example, evangelical celebrity Anita Bryant led a conspicuous and successful crusade to repeal an ordinance in Dade County, Florida, that prohibited discrimination based on sexual preference. A year later, Tim LaHaye, a prominent Religious Right leader, published *The Unhappy Gays: What Everyone Should Know about Homosexuality*. "The homosexual community, by militance and secret political maneuvering, is designing a program to increase the tidal wave of homosexuality that will drown our children in a polluted sea of sexual perversion—and will eventually destroy America as it did Rome, Greece, Pompeii, and Sodom," he warned. Other leaders such as Phyllis Schlafly and Jerry Falwell portrayed the gay liberation and feminist movements as twin evils, for both sought to overturn traditional gender roles and family definitions. Thus attempts to combat growing public toleration of homosexuality became a prominent part of the Religious Right's "pro-family" political agenda.[5]

In contrast, progressive evangelical leaders hesitated in their response to gay rights activism. Their commitment to social justice and concern for marginalized groups inspired sympathy for the movement. In addition, they had already endorsed feminism in both society and the church—built upon similar calls for justice and equality—largely because they no longer accepted traditional interpretations of the Bible as promoting gender hierarchy. Now progressive evangelicals faced a similar issue that entailed theological and political questions. How convincing were reinterpretations of biblical condemnations of homosexuality as merely the culturally conditioned taboos of ancient authors that are no longer relevant in light of other biblical evidence and modern knowledge? If such prohibitions against same-sex behavior *are* still applicable, should Christians seek to enforce or to privilege heterosexuality in the public sphere? Can Christians support gay civil rights without affirming same-sex relationships as moral?

As with abortion, the leadership of Sojourners and *The Other Side* wrestled silently with these questions in the mid-1970s. Pioneering evangelical feminists, however, joined other feminists in grappling with the place of lesbianism in their struggle against patriarchal traditions. In 1974 Letha Scanzoni and Nancy Hardesty broached the subject in their groundbreaking *All We're Meant to Be: A Biblical Approach to Women's Liberation*. In a section devoted to the "sexual needs" of "the single woman," the authors commended celibacy but also considered the possibility of lesbianism. They claimed that biblical writers never addressed "homosexual orientation" but rather only same-sex activity, implying that scriptural admonitions against such acts applied only to heterosexuals but not those with homosexual orientations. At the first national meeting of the Evangelical Women's Caucus in 1975, Hardesty and Virginia Mollenkott led a session on "Woman to Woman Relationships" at which participants discussed without resolution the issue of lesbianism. Prominent biblical feminists such as Hardesty, Scanzoni, and Mollenkott expressed doubt that the Bible clearly denounced homosexuality. Their views laid the groundwork for conflict not only within evangelical feminism but also within the larger progressive evangelical movement in which they participated.[6]

THE OTHER SIDE: ACCEPTANCE AND AFFIRMATION

Before they were fully prepared to address controversies concerning homosexuality, *The Other Side*'s editors used letters from readers and contributors to acknowledge the issues. In April 1977 they published without comment an anonymous letter in which a gay Christian questioned why the magazine ignored the "psychological and sometimes physical suffering experienced by thousands of evangelical homosexuals." Four months later the editors printed four responses that reflected diversity of opinion among *The Other Side*'s constituency. Two letters reaffirmed the traditional evangelical view, expressing compassion while insisting that God "*can* heal homosexuality." In contrast, Ralph Blair, the director of a newly formed affirming organization called Evangelicals Concerned, assured the author that others shared his experiences and believed "a gay Christian life *is* viable." Finally, Scanzoni and Mollenkott, who served as associate editors for *The Other Side*, proclaimed that Christians must accept gays and lesbians and reported that they were completing a book on the subject. "A debate is brewing over the proper Christian response to homosexuality," the editors wrote in an accompanying statement. "Two groups claiming to be evangelicals are taking radically different stands." Unready to define their own view, they published contact information for both Evangelicals Concerned and Liberation in Jesus Christ, an ex-gay ministry.[7]

This ambivalence upset many readers. All three letters that *The Other Side* printed in response to the magazine's noncommittal statement rejected homosexuality as legitimate for Christians and criticized the editors' equivocation. "The Staff of *The Other Side* is in something of a turmoil over the question of whether or not homosexual activities can ever be an option for biblical people," editor Mark Olson replied. "Christians whom we respect are taking positions on different sides of the question." These respected Christians would have included Scanzoni, Mollenkott, and Hardesty—all associate editors of *The Other Side*. Their affirmation of gay and lesbian Christians balanced the traditional disapproval of homosexuality among evangelicals as the magazine's staff debated the issue. In 1978, in fact, Scanzoni and Mollenkott published the pioneering evangelical defense of homosexuality. In *Is the Homosexual My Neighbor?*, they offered alternative interpretations of biblical passages traditionally understood to condemn homosexuality. Mollenkott and Scanzoni argued that the ancient writers did not address monogamous homosexual relationships and were unaware of homosexual orientation. In addition, modern scientific and sociological evidence demonstrated that a minority of people have an involuntary, irreversible homosexual orientation that Mollenkott and Scanzoni considered analogous to left-handedness. Thus they asserted that Christians should affirm same-sex relationships. When *The*

Other Side finally published its awaited issue on homosexuality in June 1978, the influence of these arguments became clear.[8]

The Other Side adopted an unequivocal welcoming attitude toward gay and lesbian Christians, but staff members disagreed on whether or not to affirm same-sex relationships. "We all firmly adhere to the authority of Scripture" and "believe that most homosexual behavior is contrary to God's standards," Olson wrote in his introduction to the issue. "Our differences concern the legitimacy—or illegitimacy—of permanent, faithful homosexual relationships for people who feel they have no other viable sexual alternative." Therefore, Olson indicated, each article or column reflected the opinion of its author rather than "an official position of *The Other Side*." However, only a few authors voiced reservations, and even their articles adopted moderate tones. Coeditor John Alexander cautiously disapproved of same-sex behavior but admitted the issue's ambiguity. "In the end, I think the [biblical] evidence is against all genital homosexual practice," he wrote, "but I find the arguments just cloudy enough that I think sensible Christians can come down at somewhat different places." The majority of the issue served to affirm Christian homosexuality. Olson wrote a column recounting evangelicals' spiteful treatment of gay and lesbian Christians and urging instead their acceptance. Most prominent, the journal carried six testimonies of gay and lesbian Christians and an extended interview with Ralph Blair, director of the affirming group Evangelicals Concerned. The thrust of these supportive pieces largely overshadowed the few expressions of tolerant opposition. Although not espousing "official" affirmation of gays and lesbians, *The Other Side* had clearly identified itself as a sympathetic and welcoming forum for gay Christians.[9]

The Other Side's stance drew mixed reactions and undermined its credibility among many evangelicals. At first many readers expressed encouragement. "We've received an amazing number of letters in response to our June issue," Olson wrote in September. "The responses have been overwhelmingly supportive." Yet the editors also printed letters that expressed disappointment and even outrage with what some readers regarded as blatant biblical unfaithfulness. These criticisms increased in the coming months. Associate editor and evangelical statesman Frank Gaebelein communicated his disappointment, and *The Other Side*'s founders, John Alexander's parents, cut all ties with the magazine. A welcoming attitude and partial affirmation of gay and lesbian Christians proved literally costly as angry readers canceled their subscriptions. Not least, *The Other*

Side's reputation suffered. "Never again would the magazine be considered as 'evangelical' by many in the evangelical establishment," editors later wrote.[10]

Despite this criticism, over the next five years *The Other Side*'s leadership became fully convinced of the legitimacy of same-sex Christian relationships. During this period, the magazine carried cursory sympathetic coverage of gay and lesbian issues. At the beginning of 1984, however, the editors initiated a full-scale campaign to persuade Christians both to welcome and to affirm gays and lesbians. Over the course of several issues, *The Other Side* constructed a two-part case for its position.

First, editors argued that the Bible itself offers insufficient evidence for Christians to judge the morality of all expressions of same-sex love. Mark Olson endorsed works of biblical criticism such as Robin Scroggs's *The New Testament and Homosexuality*. Scroggs argued that the original meaning of scriptural injunctions against homosexuality referred only to pederasty or other ancient sexual practices—cases wholly dissimilar from and therefore irrelevant to contemporary loving, committed same-sex relationships. Olson also published his own lengthy exegetical article that reviewed all "the passages of Scripture that refer in one way or another to homosexual behavior." In each case, he concluded, either the biblical authors denounced only exploitative same-sex acts or the Old Testament passage in question no longer applied to Christians. John Alexander reached similar conclusions. "The Bible gives no indication that Jesus condemned homosexuality," "no Old Testament passage seems to apply," and only "three Pauline passages *may* condemn homosexuality," he wrote. Recognizing that "sensible" Christians could disagree, Alexander stated that the lack of clear biblical teaching against homosexuals in "permanent, covenant relationships" led him to cautious affirmation. Since they concluded that the Bible does not categorically condemn *all* expressions of homosexuality, the editors dismissed solitary appeals to scripture as inadequate—"not because the Bible is not authoritative, but simply because it does not address the issues involved," Olson clarified. Alexander proclaimed that they were not rejecting the evangelical commitment to biblical authority; they were rejecting only blanket condemnations of same-sex love that were based upon hermeneutical errors. "We're not talking about the authority of the Bible," Alexander maintained, "as much as we are about the authority of an *interpretation* of the Bible."[11]

Second, since they believed that Christians could not resolve contemporary debates about homosexuality by using only biblical evidence, *The*

Other Side promoted two other factors as determinative: social scientific research and the testimonies of gay and lesbian Christians. Letha Scanzoni wrote a two-part series on homosexuality based upon "careful scriptural, theological, historical, and scientific study." She cited research that demonstrated some people possess an involuntary homosexual orientation, a fact unknown to the ancient biblical authors. While sexual *behaviors* "may in some instances be changed," Scanzoni noted, studies revealed that sexual *orientations*, whether heterosexual or homosexual, are "deeply ingrained and resistant to change." In addition, she repeatedly referenced the experiences of gay and lesbian Christians—especially those who had tried unsuccessfully to change their orientation in ex-gay ministries—as compelling evidence for the need to affirm their sexuality. Thus Scanzoni concluded that the church must abandon misguided prejudice against gays and lesbians. *The Other Side*'s editors agreed. They believed that both the growing scientific and sociological consensus regarding innate homosexual orientations and the experiences of gay and lesbian Christians provided clarity in light of the Bible's ambiguity. "I hate to ignore even one passage of Scripture," Alexander stated. "But I also hate to condemn something that I don't see any harm in and that the Bible isn't terribly clear on." Olson argued that he had "seen God blessing and using homosexual Christians who have united with each other in loving sexual relationships. We must not be too attached to a few verses of Scripture— or our own interpretations of them—that we miss this witness of God's Spirit," he wrote. "God is still speaking." Without a clear sense of biblical guidance, therefore, *The Other Side* urged readers to adopt an affirming position on behalf of "those Christian brothers and sisters who differ from themselves only in the direction of their sexual feelings."[12]

Although public debates about same-sex marriage would not begin in earnest for another decade, *The Other Side* argued that Christians should honor covenantal same-sex relationships. Olson respected gays and lesbians who "have felt called to celibacy." But as a particular rather than universal calling, he claimed, celibacy was not the only moral option for those with a homosexual orientation. Likewise, Alexander wrote, "I can't finally see asking someone to be celibate for life on such flimsy [biblical] evidence." At the same time, *The Other Side* made clear that traditional Christian sexual morality must govern same-sex couples. "Both heterosexual and homosexual Christians are responsible before God to uphold the same ethical standards," Scanzoni assured readers. Alexander explicitly denied that a homosexual orientation allows one "a right to full sexual expression," for such logic could justify all forms of sinful sexual activity. But if, as *The Other Side* concluded, the Bible did not conclusively prohibit all homosexual behavior, then committed same-sex unions could parallel heterosexual ones. Olson cited both biblical and experiential evidence for affirming such same-sex relationships. While "the Bible assumes heterosexual relationships are the norm," he declared, no biblical principle "denies the validity of committed, caring homosexual relationships." In addition, Olson stated, "gay and lesbian Christians find God at work" in their "faithful, committed relationships." Alexander refused to believe that "homosexuals have any less right to sexual expression than heterosexuals." In fact, he argued, "forbidding permanent homosexual relationships seems more like a straight jacket than the loving provision of a wise God." *The Other Side* therefore regarded covenantal same-sex unions as appropriate analogues to heterosexual marriages.[13]

The editors acknowledged their controversial position by printing a balance of supportive and critical responses. At first, Olson noted, *The Other Side* received many "appreciative letters for our articles on homosexuality" from both heterosexual and homosexual Christians—a gratifying sign "in light of the storm of protest we've gotten on the subject in the past." But editors also allowed criticism by printing numerous letters in which readers rebutted their claims concerning both the nature of homosexual orientation and the Bible's ambiguity. "Former homosexuals" testified to their own transformations, while other readers compared homosexual orientations to other sinful inclinations. Most prominent, several respondents disputed *The Other Side*'s arguments that the biblical texts do not condemn all same-sex activity. "Scripture is clear on prohibiting homosexuality, adultery, and other sexual immoralities—no ifs, ands, or buts," a frustrated reader insisted.[14]

The Other Side's full acceptance of gay and lesbian Christians put the magazine in a distinct minority. In the mid-1980s, three-fourths of all Americans regarded homosexuality as "always wrong." Among mainline Protestants, the United Church of Christ remained the only denomination to affirm the full equality of gays and lesbians within the church. The Roman Catholic Church began to clamp down on dissent from its official position. Joseph Cardinal Ratzinger, the head of the Congregation for the Doctrine of the Faith who later became Pope Benedict XVI, issued a letter reminding Catholics that same-sex behavior is always immoral and that civil legislation should not condone homosexuality. Theologically conservative Protestants represented the religious group least likely to support gay civil rights and to affirm homosexuality as acceptable: 98 percent of Southern Baptists rejected homosexuality as a viable Christian lifestyle, and 90 percent of evangelicals regarded homosexual acts as "immoral behavior." As several critical letters to *The Other Side* suggested, the magazine's stance also began to alienate it from most other progressive evangelicals who concluded that the Bible offered sufficient evidence for reaffirming same-sex behavior as immoral. As one reader foresaw, "Homosexuality may become an issue of division among radical evangelicals." Indeed, *The Other Side* became an isolated voice for gay and lesbian evangelicals—a fact highlighted by the refusal of *Sojourners* and ESA to join it in adopting an affirming stance.[15]

SOJOURNERS: A DIVISIVE DEBATE

As *The Other Side*'s affirming position evolved in the late 1970s and early 1980s, *Sojourners* struggled to determine its own response. In 1977 contributing editor Donald Dayton first broached the subject of homosexuality in a review of three books that addressed Christian perspectives. One of these, *The Church and the Homosexual* by John J. McNeill, argued that God designs some people as homosexual and thus Christians should accept "the existence of an ethically responsible homosexual relationship." Although not endorsing this conclusion, Dayton believed that "those who would maintain a traditional position" faced a challenge in rebutting McNeill's argument. Yet *Sojourners* pursued the topic no further, leaving its position undefined. As with *The Other Side*, however, a reader criticized the magazine's apparent insensitivity to gays and lesbians. In a 1978 letter, an anonymous "evangelical Christian who is also a homosexual" expressed disappointment with *Sojourners'* silence on homosexuality and "the plight of many of your Christian brothers and sisters." While the editors' choice to print the letter represented a modest acknowledgment of the issue, *Sojourners* left the reader's hopes unfulfilled. For the next four years, leaders took no discernible steps to address either gay civil rights or the morality of same-sex relationships.[16]

Sojourners' reticence regarding homosexuality paralleled its initial indecisiveness regarding abortion. Despite the journal's reputation for tackling controversial and pressing social issues, its prophetic pretensions failed to produce a published analysis of homosexuality as a matter of either public policy or Christian ethics. In contrast, the other leading progressive evangelical journal, *The Other Side*, responded to its own readers by publishing its controversial 1978 issue welcoming gay and lesbian Christians. The most visible magazine of mainstream evangelicalism, *Christianity Today*, repeatedly addressed the topic. It named homosexuality its "Issue of the Year" in 1978, promoted the biblical case against same-sex relationships, and highlighted ex-gay ministries. Thus the absence of coverage within *Sojourners* represented a glaring omission and reflected how the issue of homosexuality perplexed its leadership. Leaders struggled to reconcile traditional notions of Christian sexual morality with their instinctual support for marginalized groups.[17]

The commitment to social justice at the heart of progressive evangelicals' public theology finally compelled *Sojourners* to address homosexuality in 1982. In an editorial titled "A Matter of Justice," publisher Joe Roos outlined *Sojourners'* interpretation of same-sex behavior as a civil right but religious wrong. He acknowledged the polarized responses to homosexuality among Christians: conservative Christians wanted to "exclude" gays and lesbians "from the life of the church" and to curtail their civil rights, while "the gay church movement" affirmed same-sex relationships as "entirely compatible with Christian faith." Yet *Sojourners* rejected both views. "While we do not believe that Scripture condones a homosexual lifestyle," Roos explained, "we do believe that homosexuals, like anyone else, deserve full human rights" that are not "conditional upon agreement over sexual morality." Within their own *private* communities, Roos argued, Christians must wrestle with "the biblical teachings and assumption on sexual morality," the "mysterious nature" of sexual orientation, and the pastoral needs of those "who feel they've never had a choice about their homosexuality." Within "the *public* arena," however, he insisted that "the first Christian duty is to love"—an act that need not entail approval but "must always include justice." And justice, Roos concluded, requires Christians to defend the full civil rights of gays and lesbians. As a result, he criticized recent attempts by the Religious Right "to legally deny the civil and political rights of homosexuals in this country" through legislation such as the Family Protection Act—a bill that would prevent gays and lesbians from receiving any federal funds (such as Social Security or student aid) or legal aid if they experienced discrimination based on their sexual orientation.[18]

Sojourners framed its position as a mediating path between "condemning the existence of Christians who are homosexual" and "simply accepting the verdict of a liberal culture that homosexuality is a lifestyle that should be affirmed and celebrated." As a matter of social justice, *Sojourners* argued, gays and lesbians must receive equal treatment and opportunities in public. But as a matter of sexual morality, Christians should welcome but not affirm gays and lesbians. Roos attempted to justify *Sojourners'* previous silence and even to forestall expectations that the journal would explore the legitimacy of same-sex relationships for Christians. "Certainly," he claimed, the subject of the proper Christian interpretation of homosexuality "is much more appropriately worked through in pastoral and confidential contexts than debated on the pages of a magazine." Yet the significance of the editorial remained clear as it set the course for *Sojourners'* subsequent coverage of homosexuality. The magazine attempted to champion gay civil rights while sensitively refusing to affirm the morality of same-sex behavior.[19]

In order to cultivate a reputation for open discussion, *Sojourners* published responses that ranged from indignation to appreciation. Two letters suggested that the editorial had been too lenient toward gays and lesbians. "If murderers and thieves, once convicted, must surrender their rights because of their lifestyle," one writer asked, "should not homosexuals also be denied certain privileges?" Other readers had the opposite reaction. "If your faith assumptions pronounce my sexuality 'sin,' you oppress me," a gay reader wrote bluntly. One writer expressed incredulity that the editors had "so shallowly dismissed serious research which challenges the old view that homosexual acts are automatically anti-biblical." Finally, several readers appreciated the editors' mediating position that reiterated "the Bible's clear teaching on this particular sin" but rejected "the destructiveness of hate." "You have pointed out that we can both love homosexuals by not denying them basic rights," one claimed, "and yet help them overcome their sin without condoning it."[20]

After this editorial, *Sojourners* did not address homosexuality for another three years. On the one hand, leaders appeared to take seriously the conviction stated by Roos that magazines do not offer fruitful contexts for discerning ethical guidelines regarding such a sensitive issue. On the other hand, not only conviction but also confusion contributed to this neglect. As the editors confessed when they finally returned to the subject in 1985, "We have found the issue of homosexuality a difficult and complex one." In particular, their empathetic relationships with "friends and family who are homosexuals" made them hesitant to issue definitive statements. The editors again lamented the dichotomous positions that "plagued" Christian discussions. Opponents "condemn homosexuals and attempt to deny them their God-given humanity and their civil rights," they complained, while advocates "celebrate a homosexual life-style as entirely consistent with God's intentions for sexual expression." *Sojourners'* leaders were certainly aware that their progressive evangelical allies at *The Other Side* had joined the vanguard of mainline Protestants who affirmed gay and lesbian Christians. They also acknowledged linger-ing internal disagreement among their staff. Nevertheless, by mid-1985, they decided that they needed to join ongoing theological debates among Christians concerning homosexuality.[21]

Despite professed love for gays and lesbians, *Sojourners* remained con-vinced that "a clear biblical word does not condone homosexual practice." The magazine used an article by popular evangelical author Richard Fos-ter as the medium for offering a theological response to homosexuality. In an excerpt from his forthcoming book *Money, Sex and Power*, Foster explored both "the joy and the responsibility of sexual expression" for Christians. He celebrated sexuality as part of "God's good creation" but also criticized "the sexual exploitation of a society that encourages sexual freedom without responsibility" and ignores biblical mandates of "mutuality, fidelity, and discipline." Not until the final section did the ar-ticle discuss homosexuality. Thus *Sojourners* endorsed Foster's belief that one must evaluate same-sex desire and relationships within the larger framework of Christian sexual ethics. While the editors introduced Fos-ter's treatment as "a clear word offered with sensitivity and compassion," they expected to receive criticism from both "those who take a more con-demnatory approach to homosexuals" and "those who have a more liberal perspective." Nevertheless, they published the article with hopes that it would prove "helpful to the dialogue around this difficult and sensitive issue." Their optimism would be short-lived.[22]

Foster attempted to construct a sympathetic but firm argument against Christian affirmation of same-sex practice. Although urging compassion for "homosexual persons who have been discriminated against and perse-cuted," he maintained that "the Bible is quite clear and straightforward" in its expectations. "From beginning to end," Foster wrote, "it views het-erosexual union as God's intention for sexuality and sees homosexual-ity as a distortion of this God-given pattern." Foster admitted that one could argue that biblical authors understood neither homosexual orien-tation nor covenantal same-sex relationships. "But it is not really pos-sible to say that the Bible is ambiguous about this matter," he claimed, for "homosexuality is rejected as 'unnatural' and a departure from God's intention." At the same time, Foster did not believe that homosexual orientation was "self-chosen." He accepted social scientific evidence that a small percentage of the population had "a confirmed sexual drive toward persons of their own sex." Yet Foster compared homosexual orientation to "clubfootedness"—a distinctly different analogy from the metaphor of left-handedness suggested by Letha Scanzoni and Virginia Mollenkott in *Is the Homosexual My Neighbor?* Left-handedness denotes difference. But a clubfoot, like homosexuality, represents a "distortion of God's intention," Foster concluded, albeit a distortion deserving empathy rather than condemnation from Christians.[23]

Even if gays and lesbians do not choose their orientation, Foster argued, they remain responsible for their actions. Despite questionable evidence, he remained hopeful that "genuine permanent change" in sexual orientation was possible. When such transformation did not occur, Foster suggested that gays and lesbians should choose "celibacy as the route of moral integrity" since "the practice of homosexuality is sin." Ultimately, gays and lesbians need both truth and grace from the church. "The Christian community cannot give permission to practice homosexuality to those who feel unable to change their orientation or to embrace celibacy," Foster wrote. But Christians must be "always ready to help" and "always ready to bring God's acceptance and forgiveness" to those who make a "tragic moral choice" to enter a same-sex relationship. By publishing Foster's analysis, *Sojourners* reaffirmed its commitment to welcome gays and lesbians while opposing same-sex practice.[24]

Many readers and prominent ecumenical supporters condemned Foster's article as hurtful rather than helpful. *Sojourners* published responses from several gays and lesbians who criticized the magazine's "blindness and arrogance" and appealed to their own experiences of divinely blessed same-sex relationships. Another reader accused *Sojourners* of entering "an unlikely alliance" with homophobic Christian conservatives by apparently agreeing that "homosexuality is both sick and sinful, if not downright disgusting." The most notable protest came from a prominent group of non-evangelical leaders who supported *Sojourners'* principled commitment to social justice. Among those jointly signing a critical response were Catholic peace activist and contributing editor Daniel Berrigan; celebrated social justice advocate William Sloane Coffin; theologian Walter Wink, a frequent contributor to *Sojourners*; and Virginia Mollenkott, coauthor of *Is the Homosexual My Neighbor?* The group denounced Foster's "uninformed and patronizing treatment of homosexuality" and appealed to "the reality of deep and abiding love between two gay persons" as evidence that God intended gays and lesbians to express their particular "gift of sexuality." These leaders also equated biblical condemnations of homosexuality with passages that supported slavery and patriarchy—neither of which now seemed "biblically justifiable." Prohibitions of same-sex activity should similarly yield to a progressive understanding of God's will, they argued, for "the Spirit has been and is leading us into new truth (John 16:12-13) and teaching us that what we once thought unacceptable is now clearly acceptable to God (Acts 10)." Like *The Other Side*, these ecumenical leaders viewed biblical statements on homosexuality as either ambiguous or irrelevant, and thus they championed the unqualified inclusion of gays and lesbians within both society and the church. For them, affirmation of same-sex relationships represented a basic "question of justice."[25]

At the same time, sympathetic readers offered support for what one praised as Foster's "compassionate and illuminating discussion of homosexuality." In issues after the initial negative letters appeared, editors published rejoinders from readers who defended Foster and *Sojourners* on the same grounds: fidelity to the Bible. One writer complained that the "criticism for the most part does not deal with the question, 'What is biblical?'" Like Foster, he could find "no compelling evidence that the Bible portrays God as condoning homosexual practice." Another reader accused critics of rebuking Foster "unjustly for his opinions, when he is being faithful to scripture." A third respondent objected to both the tone and the content of the reproachful letter from Berrigan, Coffin, Wink, Mollenkott, and others. "Why is it that such 'open-minded' Christians" resorted to characterizing Foster as "uninformed and ignorant" because he did not "share their acceptance of homosexual behavior?" he asked. The reader refused to give testimonies of "true love" in same-sex relationships equal evidential weight with what he regarded as clear biblical teachings. "The Bible only provides for sexual intimacy between a man and a woman who have committed to each other as wife and husband," he argued.[26]

For their own part, *Sojourners*' editors answered criticism by reiterating their dedication both to social justice for gays and lesbians and to upholding what seemed clear biblical expectations for heterosexuality. Alongside letters from readers, *Sojourners* published a response from Foster in which he again explained his opposition to same-sex activity. "I cannot endorse a homosexual lifestyle because I do not believe it squares with the witness we are given in the Bible and supremely in Jesus Christ," Foster reiterated. He encouraged readers to consult works that affirmed homosexuality such as *Is the Homosexual My Neighbor?* even if he had "not found these compelling." While Foster offered this public response, Jim Wallis wrote privately to Berrigan and his cosigners. "In hindsight," Wallis confessed, "the strong controversy generated by the publicity of the Foster article" confirmed that "the questions involved deserved more attention and discernment." He also conceded that "some of Foster's language and analogies proved unnecessarily hurtful, contrary both to his intentions and ours." But Wallis refused to retract the magazine's endorsement of Foster's intent: "to take a traditional biblical view" of same-sex activity as immoral but remain "deeply empathetic and pastorally sensitive." According to Ron Sider, head of ESA, "Wallis was appalled by the letter *Sojourners* received" from these non-evangelical supporters "that simply calls for setting scripture aside" regarding homosexuality. "He would never go for that," Sider told an interviewer. Under Wallis's evangelical leadership, *Sojourners* remained committed to giving its biblical interpretations the final word in its religious and political positions.[27]

Although *Sojourners'* stance aligned its leaders with most mainline Protestants in the mid-1980s, this criticism from their more theologically liberal allies foreshadowed the pressure they would increasingly face in the coming decades. Their refusal to affirm gay and lesbian Christians would clash with increasing numbers of religious and political liberals who fully accepted the morality of same-sex practice. At the same time, *Sojourners'* commitment to gay civil rights would frustrate leaders of the Religious Right who continued to fight public acceptance of homosexuality. While *The Other Side* had affirmed same-sex relationships as moral, *Sojourners* led the progressive evangelical movement to adopt a welcoming but not affirming stance. ESA joined *Sojourners* in this task.

ESA: PROMOTING TRADITIONAL FAMILIES

While Ron Sider and ESA supported the civil rights of gays and lesbians, they came closest to the Religious Right by framing criticism of same-sex practice as part of their defense of God's will for family life. In one of its earliest references, for example, the group declared in its 1980 voting guide that "the family is a divinely-willed institution" represents a "basic biblical principle" that should guide Christians' political participation. As part of its definition, ESA stressed the heterosexual and covenantal norms of family life: "It is God's will for one man and one woman to live together in a life-long commitment." The organization joined the Religious Right in supporting favorable policies such as tax deductions that would foster "the biblical understanding of marriage, family and sexuality." ESA also agreed with Christian conservatives that same-sex practice was sinful. In contrast to *The Other Side* and *Sojourners*, which each attracted more ecumenical audiences, ESA did not devote any space to deliberating this issue or to justifying its view. At the same time, ESA's leaders joined other evangelical progressives in opposing any public discrimination against gays and lesbians. "Homosexual sinners, like adulterous sinners, have inalienable civil rights (e.g. jobs and housing)," the group argued. Thus ESA walked a fine line. While objecting to policies that denied gays and lesbians equal treatment, it also opposed policies under which same-sex couples (and unmarried heterosexual partners) received the same *positive* benefits as heterosexual spouses. "Legislation and public funds should not promote sinful lifestyles," it insisted. This conviction—that it was not contradictory to defend gay civil rights while simultaneously advocating policies that benefited only heterosexual married couples—would define ESA's political responses to homosexuality into the twenty-first century.[28]

A 1983 survey indicated that ESA's members overwhelmingly approved of this strategy. Eighty-eight percent of respondents agreed that "basic civil rights, i.e. housing and medical care, etc., should be available to all persons regardless of sexual orientation" even as 93 percent affirmed that "a strong family is the basis of a strong society." Thus ESA's constituency remained unconvinced by the Religious Right's arguments that public toleration of homosexuality threatened the welfare of families. In other words, defending the importance of traditional families did not require restricting the civil rights of gays and lesbians. To be sure, ESA clearly believed that permanent heterosexual marriages best benefited children and society as a whole, and therefore the government should create policies that encourage such relationships. "We support all strategies and agencies that strengthen the family and support the view that marriage is a life-long covenant between one man and one woman," ESA's board of directors reiterated in 1984. Nevertheless, ESA's pronouncements on the family in the early 1980s never suggested that regulations against gays and lesbians should serve as positive means for "strengthening the family."[29]

As a leading voice within progressive evangelicalism, ESA president Ron Sider did not sit idly in the mid-1980s as debates over homosexuality occurred within the movement's primary journals. Sider served as a contributing editor for both *The Other Side* and *Sojourners*, and each magazine published his response to their respective stands on same-sex behavior. "I thank God for the tremendous contributions *The Other Side* has made, and I trust, will continue to make," Sider wrote after its affirmation of gays and lesbians in 1984. "But precisely my appreciation compels me to say that I disagree strongly with your stand on homosexuality, and I am frightened by its implications for biblical authority." He concurred that Christians should denounce homophobia and champion gay civil rights. But, Sider insisted, "I cannot agree that Scripture is ambiguous" concerning the morality of same-sex behavior. In addition to "infrequent prohibition," he wrote, "the primary biblical case against practicing homosexuality" resulted from "the constant positive assertion throughout the entire Bible that God's will for human sexuality is a man and a woman in life-long covenant." A year later Sider commended *Sojourners* for publishing Richard Foster's article that employed the same argument. "Thank you," he wrote, "for having the courage to take a gentle and sensitive but also forthright biblical stand on practicing homosexuality." Once again, Sider acknowledged that "we must repent of homophobia and insist on civil rights for all." But, once again, he claimed, "If we are to be biblical, we must gently yet firmly say no as Foster does to homosexual practice." Sider and ESA shared with *Sojourners* a sense of both biblical clarity and authority that shaped their mutual unwillingness to affirm same-sex relationships as moral.[30]

Working with ESA's staff in the mid-1980s to produce his book *Completely Pro-Life*, Sider offered his most sustained analysis of homosexuality within the church and the public sphere. He believed that a consistent pro-life agenda included not only opposition to abortion but also support for economic justice, peacemaking, and healthy and stable families. Regarding family life, Sider maintained that only traditional heterosexual marriages are "in the best interests of society." Distinguishing a morally neutral homosexual orientation from sinful homosexual practice, he briefly reviewed several "clear" and "explicit prohibitions" against same-sex behavior. In particular, Sider wrote, "it requires considerable exegetical gymnastics to argue plausibly" that Romans 1:26-27 "does not exclude all homosexual practice"—and he noted Scanzoni and Mollenkott's *Is the Homosexual My Neighbor?* as an example of "the special pleading of some recent pro-gay exegesis." To be sure, Sider argued, Christians should welcome gays and lesbians in the church, encourage their sexual abstinence, and support "those who fail and repent." But ultimately, same-sex behavior contravened "the constant, pervasive biblical teaching that sex is a gift intended only for the committed relationship of a man and a woman in lifelong covenant." Nevertheless, Sider claimed, as a matter of public policy Christians should not try to legislate such standards by punishing deviations such as homosexuality. "A pluralistic society" should not have "criminal laws against adultery, fornication, or homosexual practices between consenting adults conducted in private," he wrote. Likewise, "homosexual sinners" should have secure civil rights "coextensive with the rights of all other sinners," that is, *all* people. Still, Sider and ESA believed that only heterosexual families should receive positive benefits and legal recognition. Thus Sider sought to guard against public policies that promoted rather than merely permitted same-sex relationships.[31]

By the mid-1980s, then, progressive evangelical leaders concurred on the civil rights of gays and lesbians but disagreed on the Christian ethics of same-sex behavior. *The Other Side, Sojourners,* and ESA repudiated the antigay political agenda of the Religious Right. They also agreed that Christians must welcome and minister to gays and lesbians. Yet *The Other Side* went further and accepted the morality of gay unions, while neither *Sojourners* nor ESA affirmed same-sex behavior. Even as debates about homosexuality within churches and the broader culture were far from over, a new crisis arose that affected public perceptions and devastated the gay community: AIDS.

THE RESPONSE TO AIDS

In the early 1980s, acquired immunodeficiency syndrome, or AIDS, began to spread worldwide. Caused by the human immunodeficiency virus (HIV) and transmitted through bodily fluids such as blood and semen, AIDS destroys the immune system and has no cure. Because the disease in the United States initially spread most among gay men and drug users who shared needles, AIDS became stigmatized. Many Americans were uncomfortable discussing the disease. President Ronald Reagan largely ignored the issue and cut funding for AIDS research and prevention, and his administration even debated quarantining those with AIDS. When Surgeon General C. Everett Koop, an evangelical Christian, called for increased sex education and condom distribution to combat the spread of AIDS, previously supportive members of the Religious Right turned on him. They opposed these measures for ostensibly encouraging immoral behavior. In addition, several leaders openly identified AIDS as God's judgment on homosexuality. Jerry Falwell used fears about AIDS to justify opposition to gay rights. Homosexuals "have expressed the attitude that they know they are going to die and they are going to take as many people with them as they can," he wrote in a fund-raising letter. Therefore, Christians must combat legislation that would "force morally upstanding citizens to work alongside homosexual AIDS carriers." Besieged gay activists and allies responded by mobilizing to defend their rights and to push for federal funding for AIDS research, with groups such as ACT-UP (AIDS Coalition to Unleash Power) sponsoring public protests, parades, and political pressure. Yet the threat of AIDS grew. By 1989 the Centers for Disease Control reported 46,344 AIDS-related deaths, 82,764 confirmed cases, and possibly a million more unreported HIV infections.[32]

Progressive evangelicals refused to interpret AIDS as God's punishment on homosexuality. Drawing upon fundamental principles of their public theology—namely, the equal rights of all community members and the substantive equality of the disadvantaged—they responded empathetically to all victims of AIDS, including gay men. *Sojourners'* initial coverage set the tone. In 1986 associate editor Danny Collum lamented that the intensifying "public spotlight on AIDS" had created "a wave of panic and bigotry." He blamed the "AIDS hysteria" in part on the disease's association with gay men. In the best of times, Collum wrote, gays and lesbians "are victims of social discrimination, legal persecution, and violence." He now feared that "a witch hunt" would further erode their civil liberties, for Religious Right leaders inflamed an "incipient holy war by claiming that AIDS is God's punishment for sexual immorality." But Collum insisted that theological differences concerning homosexuality must not undermine commitments to care for the sick and to defend fundamental human rights. "Increasingly," he concluded, "issues of compassion and justice are the ones being raised by the AIDS crisis." A year later Jim Wallis echoed this appeal. "Ignorance and fear" were becoming "as dangerous as the disease itself," he wrote. Wallis notably avoided associating AIDS and homosexuality. He mentioned only that the confusion of "moral questions and health issues" contributed to a lack of political and educational resources committed to the crisis. Without easy answers or a foreseeable cure, Wallis argued that Christians must respond to those suffering with AIDS with the same compassion as Jesus would. *Sojourners* continued such coverage in 1990, calling for Christians to reject "homophobia" and demonstrate "compassion, not judgment, for those who suffer with AIDS." Condemning insinuations that gay men deserved AIDS, *Sojourners* urged greater efforts to search for a cure and to care for its victims.[33]

The Other Side's affirming position on homosexuality had attracted gay and lesbian readers and their allies, and therefore AIDS proved a poignant subject for the journal. Contributors focused more on the personal than on the political aspects of AIDS. In 1987 the journal highlighted both the tragic consequences and theological concerns created by the disease. For example, one author related the story of her friendship with a gay AIDS victim, whose suffering taught her lessons about the frailty of life and God's promise of love in the midst of tragedy. Another contributor, a gay man, offered a theological reflection on AIDS. Because God often used the oppressed to "lead the church and society toward whatever revelation they must embrace next," he suggested, perhaps God intended to use gays and lesbians to remind the world of "the holy truth of mortality" and refocus people on "the resurrection hope." *The Other Side* published several articles that sought to counteract the hostility that AIDS victims experienced from Christians. In response to suggestions "that AIDS was a scourge sent by God so that evil people would die in well-deserved ways," John Alexander reminded readers that God offered not only justice but also grace. He did warn against "cheap grace" that condoned sexual promiscuity. Nevertheless, he acknowledged that "society's harshness toward homosexuality" drove gays and lesbians "underground and made widespread promiscuity—and consequently the spread of the disease—among gays predictable." *The Other Side* culminated its initial sympathetic coverage with a 1990 article by an AIDS victim who told readers that their love and simple presence could help assuage the pain of living with the disease.[34]

Although addressing the issue less frequently, ESA likewise defended the dignity and rights of AIDS victims. A 1987 article by Ron Sider—published in both the *Christian Century* and ESA's newsletter—outlined what he identified as "an evangelical perspective on AIDS." Sider began with the premise that AIDS victims—regardless of their frailty, marginalized status, or even immoral choices—possess "inestimable worth" as persons "indelibly stamped with the divine image." Sider criticized pro-life Christian conservatives who hypocritically disdained efforts to help people with AIDS. "Precisely the people who speak most often about the sanctity of life should have been the first to champion" the right "to adequate health care rather than lobbying against government expenditure for AIDS research." Sider rejected both the "prejudicial untruth" that AIDS is "a homosexual disease" and arguments that "God created AIDS as a special divine punishment for the sin of homosexual practice." To be sure, Sider reasserted his view of same-sex behavior as immoral. *All sins have consequences*, he insisted, including the promiscuous practices and drug use by which AIDS often spread. Yet "sexual sin is no worse than other varieties," and Sider repeated a quip that "if AIDS is divine punishment, then surely the people who bring us economic oppression, environmental pollution and devastating wars should at least get herpes." Ultimately, Sider urged Christians to build compassionate ministries, to reject homophobia, and to support research and preventive measures. In promoting their "completely pro-life" agenda that linked opposition to abortion with other issues of social justice, Sider and ESA began to frame compassion and care for AIDS victims as a pro-life issue.[35]

Even as the AIDS crisis changed dramatically in the 1990s, progressive evangelicals remained committed to personal and political action on behalf of victims. In the United States, the number of new HIV infections declined, and the public focus on the disease's victims shifted away from gay men. Educational efforts and prominent cases of heterosexuals contracting HIV (such as basketball star Earvin "Magic" Johnson in 1991) helped to diminish popular perceptions of AIDS as a "gay disease." Activists successfully lobbied the government for prevention and research funding, and viable (albeit expensive) treatments for HIV slowed the death rates for carriers. At the same time, however, the worldwide spread of AIDS quickened, especially in Africa. By 1997 two-thirds of the 30 million HIV-positive people lived in sub-Saharan Africa; by 2001, 16 million of the 20 million people who had died from AIDS were African. As a matter of both compassion and justice, progressive evangelicals argued, American Christians must push their government to increase its AIDS-related aid to African nations. Regardless of where Africa fits into America's strategic interests, Jim Wallis wrote in 2000, "millions of God's children are dying, and the world is largely just passing by on the other side of the road." Leaders appreciated President George W. Bush's pledge in 2003 of $15 billion to combat AIDS in Africa and Caribbean nations but argued that more attention was needed to other injustices that exacerbated the epidemic. "The war against HIV/AIDS must be wrapped around underlying issues of poverty, inequality, and marginalization," *Sojourners'* Adam Taylor wrote. "HIV disproportionately impacts 'the least of these' in relation to both color and class." By 2005 more conservative evangelicals—with influential California pastor Rick Warren and his wife, Kay, taking the lead—also began promoting global HIV/AIDS activism as part of their public engagement. Yet progressive leaders had first championed this cause, even when the disease was most associated with gay men.[36]

SPHERES OF JUSTICE

In the 1990s and early twenty-first century, gays and lesbians witnessed substantial gains in their civic and cultural status. In 1996 the Supreme Court ruled in *Romer v. Evans* that the Equal Protection Clause of the Fourteenth Amendment extended to gays and lesbians. Seven years later, the Court issued another landmark ruling in *Lawrence v. Texas* by reversing a previous decision and declaring that laws against same-sex activity were unconstitutional. Public opinion polls showed increasingly tolerant attitudes toward homosexuality. By 2008 a majority of Americans viewed homosexuality as an "acceptable alternative lifestyle," supported legal recognition for same-sex couples, backed hate-crime protections for sexual minorities, and overwhelmingly endorsed gays and lesbians' equal civil rights.[37]

Over this period, religious groups remained divided in their responses to homosexuality. As more and more mainline Protestants fully affirmed gays and lesbians, intense controversies occurred within their denominations regarding the ordination of openly gay clergy and the blessing of same-sex unions. In 2003 the Episcopal Church installed Gene Robinson, a partnered gay priest, as bishop of New Hampshire. By 2011 the Evangelical Lutheran Church of America and Presbyterian Church, USA, also approved ordination for clergy in committed same-sex relationships. Even if not officially sanctioned by their respective churches, individual congregations across mainline denominations performed ceremonies for same-sex couples. Yet both the Roman Catholic Church and nearly all evangelicals remained staunchly opposed to same-sex practice as moral. In addition, leaders of the Religious Right continued to push for public restrictions on gay rights. They regularly supported ballot initiatives to prevent recognition of gays and lesbians as a protected class and to proscribe same-sex marriage. As Focus on the Family's Tom Minnery stated in 2003, Christian conservatives viewed the political victories and cultural acceptance of gays and lesbians as assaults on "the moral norms of our country" that imperiled both "the institution of marriage" and "the welfare of the coming generations of children." In the midst of these broader debates, different stances on homosexuality remained strong within the progressive evangelical movement. *The Other Side* continued to push for gays and lesbians' unqualified equality, while *Sojourners* and ESA supported only their equal civil rights.[38]

In the two decades prior to ceasing publication in 2004, *The Other Side* made its commitment to affirm gays and lesbians a conspicuous priority. By regularly printing supportive theological arguments, personal narratives, and other articles, the magazine became one of the most prominent Christian publications appealing to LGBT individuals. The addition of associate editor John Linscheid, a gay former Mennonite pastor, represented a symbolic and substantive expansion of the magazine's affirming efforts. Linscheid contributed multiple articles from the mid-1980s through the mid-1990s describing how gays and lesbians could interpret the Bible from a gay perspective. "The dynamics of sexual-minority life find profound expression in the Bible," he argued in one early example. By asking "what aspects of gay life helped me understand the gospel and what dynamics in the gospel threw light on my gay life," Linscheid wrote, he discovered new "interpretations of Scripture that fit gay experience with the risen Christ." *The Other Side* consistently published similar features that addressed specific biblical passages, broader hermeneutical principles, or gay theology. Other articles served as testimonials of self-acceptance. "I have come to understand myself as a gay man created by and for God," wrote a United Methodist minister in a paradigmatic piece. "To continually question this understanding is spiritually self-destructive and, I believe, an act of disobedience to God." Many of these affirming articles emphasized the experiences of gays and lesbians that inspired their biblical reinterpretations—a trend reflecting *The Other Side*'s more liberal theological evolution over this period that increasingly distanced the magazine from its evangelical heritage. Linscheid exhibited this methodology in an exegetical article on the "diverse paths of faithfulness" within the Gospel of John. While "popular evangelicalism cannot tolerate people who have new visions, interpret Scripture differently, or encounter Christ in non-traditional ways," he wrote, gay and lesbian Christians "examine our spiritual experiences in our own context" and "tell each other our own good news."[39]

The Other Side also defended its affirming position in didactic articles and testimonies designed to persuade skeptical readers. For example, Peggy Campolo—wife of prominent progressive evangelical leader Tony Campolo—described how she came to believe that "homosexuals are entitled to the same rights and privileges I claim for myself, including being able to marry legally and in the sight of the church." Although her husband agreed with *Sojourners* and ESA that churches should be welcoming but not affirming, Campolo urged heterosexual Christians to fully accept "our gay brothers and lesbian sisters." Likewise, Howard University School of Divinity professor Alice Ogden Bellis recounted how intensive study of biblical references to homosexuality led her to conclude "that a positive attitude toward homosexual marriage and ordination of gay men and lesbians is not only consistent with Scripture but *mandated* by it." Such articles framed *The Other Side*'s affirming position as a brave act of Christian faithfulness—a view shared by many gays and lesbians themselves. "Like the lonely prophets who refused to be silent even when the crowd condemned, jeered, or ignored them, *The Other Side* stands almost alone in its own clear, courageous commitment to Christ's call to justice, mercy, and truth," declared gay activist Mel White, a former ghostwriter for Billy Graham, Jerry Falwell, and Pat Robertson.[40]

These articles offered strategic responses not only to *The Other Side*'s external critics but also to those within its own constituency. Throughout the late 1980s and 1990s, the editors periodically printed letters from readers who insisted that the Bible prohibited same-sex relationships. "*The Other Side* has been a valued companion and teacher for me during the last thirteen or fourteen years," a typical disappointed reader stated. But "I am uneasy about what I see as a celebration of a gay/lesbian lifestyle" and "have concluded that we must part company." Yet almost always, the editors implicitly defended their stance by printing accompanying letters of praise. "Having seen letters from those who would have you change your stand on gay/lesbian issues, I felt that I must speak out," one supporter wrote. As a gay man contemplating suicide, he had received a collection of affirming articles from *The Other Side* that convinced him of God's love and acceptance. "When someone gives you grief over your stand on gay/lesbian issues, remember that *because of your stand, I am alive*," he declared.[41]

While *The Other Side*'s unapologetic affirming position won praise from gay and lesbian Christians and their allies, however, it contributed to the magazine's growing detachment from the progressive evangelical movement. From the late 1980s until the journal's end in 2004, collaboration between *The Other Side*'s leadership and *Sojourners*, ESA, and others in the evangelical left occurred less and less often. Over this period, *The Other Side* continued to promote other issues of social justice and peace central to evangelical progressivism. But its affirmation of gay and lesbian Christians clashed with former partners and pushed the implicit boundaries of evangelical identity. As progressive evangelical scholar and activist David Gushee noted in 2008, "If they are attempting to remain within the evangelical camp, left evangelicals do not normally break openly" with interpretations of same-sex activity as sinful. Both the editors and readers of *The Other Side* recognized the estrangement caused by the journal's affirmation of gay and lesbian Christians. Although he respected the sincerity of ESA president Ron Sider's opposition to same-sex practice, John Linscheid wrote openly of the painful need to confront him and other evangelical progressives who expressed "vocal opposition to the gay and lesbian movement in the church." One reader complained in a critical letter that *The Other Side*'s "unbiblical" stance on this one issue alienated potential progressive evangelical supporters. "I know *many* Christians who feel just as I do regarding nuclear weapons, war, racism, sexism, and justice," he lamented. "But I could *never* show them *The Other Side* as long as it has pro-homosexuality articles in it."[42]

What most marginalized *The Other Side* was its insistence that social justice for gays and lesbians could not be divorced from full religious affirmation of same-sex relationships. While the leadership of *Sojourners* and ESA endorsed gay civil rights but not the personal morality of same-sex behavior, *The Other Side* argued that this position fanned the public flames of homophobia. Linscheid explicitly faulted Ron Sider's forceful rejection of covenantal same-sex relationships. "Traditional evangelical positions such as his bolster oppression" and "indirectly create a climate that encourages antigay and antilesbian attitudes, legislation—and violence," Linscheid claimed. Mel White similarly alleged that "anti-gay rhetoric sanctioned and led (directly or indirectly) to the suffering and death of God's lesbian and gay children." While the Religious Right stood most guilty, he wrote, anyone who denies that God creates and fully accepts gays and lesbians was spreading "untruths used to justify their suffering." Just as leaders of the civil rights movement needed to combat biblical support for segregation, activist Rodney N. Powell wrote, sexual minorities also "must address the religious justifications for the persecution of the LBGT community." If gays and lesbians are "to achieve significant social and political equality," he declared, then they must challenge Christians who "quote the Bible in asserting that homosexuality is wrong." Over its final twenty years, *The Other Side* made this task central to its mission.[43]

Sojourners never renounced its unwillingness to affirm gay and lesbian Christians, but the criticism of its analysis of homosexuality in the mid-1980s chastened the editors and altered their subsequent coverage. They remained staunchly committed to gay civil rights. But, rather than officially endorsing a welcoming but not affirming position, *Sojourners* backtracked and declared itself committed to "dialogue" on the Christian ethics of same-sex unions. After six years of silence on the topic, in 1991 *Sojourners* published a forum dedicated to how churches should respond to "the complicated questions raised by gay and lesbian sexuality." Because of uncertainty and disagreement among both their staff and their ecumenical constituency, the editors now stated that *Sojourners* would not take an official position. Rather, they wanted to promote "a better dialogue" among Christians who disagreed on this sensitive subject. For the forum, editors invited only contributors who "share a common commitment to justice and human rights for all people, regardless of their sexual orientation, and to an inclusive church open to all who know their need for the grace of God." Articles ranged from calls for full affirmation of gays and lesbians within churches to theological arguments for gay Christians to remain celibate. For example, United Church of Christ minister Melanie Morrison—who had resigned as a contributing editor in protest after *Sojourners* published Richard Foster's article in 1985—defended "a lesbian feminist hermeneutic." In contrast, Duke Divinity School professor Richard B. Hayes outlined biblical justification for a welcoming but not affirming position. By adopting this approach, *Sojourners* balanced its reluctance to affirm homosexuality with its commitment to respect and to remain partners with Christians who championed the unqualified equality of gays and lesbians.[44]

Sojourners maintained this balancing act into the early twenty-first century, especially as it responded to increasingly divisive denominational debates. Occasional articles on the ethics of gay and lesbian sexuality modeled or promoted respectful discussions between opposing groups. In 1999, for example, the magazine published a "dialogue on the church and homosexuality" between Tony and Peggy Campolo in order to show how Christians can "differ intensely over this crucial issue and not separate." They agreed that churches must welcome gays and lesbians. But while Tony argued that "the Bible does not allow for same-gender sexual intercourse or marriage," Peggy explained her belief "that within the framework of evangelical Christianity, monogamous gay marriages are permissible." In the same issue, former associate editor Wesley Granberg-Michaelson, now general secretary of the Reformed Church in America, characterized "differences over the church's response to homosexual persons" as an important but secondary dispute that did not entail "the core definition of the Christian faith." Therefore, he claimed, such differences called for "theological dialogue and pastoral discernment" rather than "charges of heresy" and threats of denominational schism. In 2004 *Sojourners* published companion articles by two seminary presidents—Richard Mouw of the evangelical Fuller Theological Seminary and Barbara Wheeler of the mainline Auburn Theological Seminary. Mouw argued against affirming same-sex relationships, but Wheeler supported the full inclusion of LGBT members. They exemplified *Sojourners'* position, however, by agreeing that conflict "over the role of gays and lesbians in the church" should not fracture their denomination, the Presbyterian Church (USA).[45]

Yet even as *Sojourners* advocated dialogue and Christian unity, its sporadic coverage and editorial neutrality indicated that it viewed moral questions surrounding same-sex relationships as marginal to its social justice concerns—a perspective that frustrated more theologically liberal supporters. In the spirit of dialogue, *Sojourners* published a range of reader responses to its infrequent articles on homosexuality. Many letters thanked the editors for modeling respectful disagreement and "opening up a space for deep listening." In contrast, some conservatives rebuked *Sojourners* for no longer editorially describing same-sex relationships as immoral. "You have abandoned the evangelical, biblical vision that once was there and have embraced the lies of liberal theology," one complained. Yet most protests against *Sojourners* came from readers who criticized its ongoing refusal to affirm gay and lesbian Christians. Several explicitly accused the journal of tolerating unjust discrimination. "How can you miss that this homosexual/church thing is a justice issue, with the same dynamics as racism, sexism, or apartheid," one demanded. "Do not let the scriptural sanctions that exist for homosexual oppression somehow make our oppression legitimate." As affirming Christians recognized, *Sojourners'* regard for biblical interpretations of same-sex practice as sinful led them to support the right of churches to preclude non-celibate gays and lesbians from having equal status in their private religious contexts. Christians who refuse to affirm homosexuality "shouldn't be pressured to do so by their liberal denominational leaders," Jim Wallis assured the more conservative readers of *Christianity Today*. In practice, therefore, *Sojourners* still endorsed the welcoming but not affirming position. Although critics viewed this position as perpetuating injustice, *Sojourners* accepted that conservative Christians had legitimate theological justification for not granting equal religious rights to those sexually active outside heterosexual marriages.[46]

At the same time, *Sojourners* continued to view the public status of gays and lesbians as a distinct issue—one governed not by particular religious interpretations of sexual morality but by shared standards for social justice. "Regardless of what moral or theological positions churches hold regarding gay and lesbian sexual behavior," associate editor Jim Rice wrote, "all Christians can and should unite around a commitment to defend people's basic rights." *Sojourners* repeatedly condemned the antigay political agenda of the Religious Right, especially claims that gays and lesbians were seeking "special rights." Editors labeled ballot initiatives designed to repeal legal protections against discrimination based upon sexual orientation—such as Amendment 2 passed by Colorado voters in 1992—as "intolerance" and "bigotry." *Sojourners* also published several articles that described Christians' public responsibility to combat antigay attitudes that inspired violent attacks on gays and lesbians. "For Christians to advocate in defense of others' right to life, safety, and security doesn't necessarily mean agreement with their lifestyle," contributing editor Aaron McCarroll Gallegos insisted after the 1998 homophobic murder of college student Matthew Shepard gained national attention. For *Sojourners*, theological objections to same-sex behavior could not justify discrimination against gays and lesbians in the public sphere. "The issues of gay civil rights are fundamental matters of justice in a democratic society," explained Jim Wallis. As a result, *Sojourners* called for other like-minded Christians—those "who have raised biblically based arguments against gay and lesbian involvement in sexual relationships" but who also "stand for social action on behalf of human rights"—to join it in combating the Religious Right's "coordinated campaign against human dignity." While religious liberals criticized its theological reservations about same-sex relationships, *Sojourners'* vision for social justice clashed with the antigay political efforts of Christian conservatives.[47]

ESA continued to join *Sojourners* in this middle ground in the 1990s and early twenty-first century, but the organization remained vocally opposed to all same-sex practice. In contrast to *Sojourners*, ESA did not have an ecumenical constituency whose objections softened its refusal to affirm gay and lesbian Christians. Instead, ESA leaders consistently described same-sex behavior as immoral. "Homosexual practice is contrary to God's will," Ron Sider stated plainly. ESA's Keith Pavlischek offered more detailed criticism in reviewing Pim Pronk's *Against Nature: Types of Moral Argumentation Regarding Homosexuality*. Pavlischek commended Pronk as "intellectually honest" for conceding that "wherever homosexual intercourse is mentioned in the Bible it is condemned." Yet Pronk argued that "the Biblical teaching shouldn't matter" in light of the more authoritative experiences of those with same-sex attractions—an assertion that Pavlischek rejected as incompatible with the evangelical tenet that humans should interpret their experience based upon biblical data, not vice versa. Above all, ESA continued to frame its rejection of homosexuality within larger analyses of all sexual activity outside of heterosexual marriage as sinful. "Both biblical teaching and the long history of the church tell us that the only valid place for sexual intercourse is in a life-long marriage covenant between a man and a woman," Sider wrote.[48]

As with *Sojourners*, the refusal of ESA's leaders to adopt an affirming position (along with their pro-life stance) created tension when they partnered with more theologically liberal Christians. In the mid-1990s Sider and ESA board member Tony Campolo joined Jim Wallis in bringing together politically progressive evangelicals, African American Christians, mainline Protestants, and Catholics to form Call to Renewal as an alternative to the Religious Right. The coalition agreed on prioritizing economic justice, racial equality, and environmental issues. But many ecumenical participants grumbled about the progressive evangelical leadership's opposition not only to abortion but also to affirming the morality of same-sex unions. At Call to Renewal's 1996 national conference, for example, some members walked out in protest after Sider argued that the alliance should uphold biblical expectations for heterosexuality. To these dissenters, Call to Renewal's commitment to justice required participants to do more than "refuse the false choice" between "sexual morality or civil rights for homosexuals"—they needed to affirm same-sex relationships as equally moral and publicly acceptable. Like *Sojourners*, however, ESA's leaders demurred. They denied liberals' accusations that opposing the unqualified equality of gays and lesbians in all contexts discredited progressive evangelicals' commitment to social justice.[49]

But ESA also differed strongly with conservatives who attempted to curtail gay civil rights. While social justice does not entail theological approval and equal religious rights, the organization reiterated, it does prohibit public discrimination against gays and lesbians. "Those who engage in homosexual practice, like those who engage in adultery, still have basic civil rights," ESA's leaders repeated. They employed this analogy to persuade Christian conservatives that same-sex behavior represented a private sin rather than public peril, and they criticized the Religious Right for encouraging "crusades designed to deny gays any kind of protection from persecution and discrimination." To be sure, Tony Campolo wrote in ESA's *Prism*, progressive evangelicals should continue "to clearly state that the Bible speaks against same gender sexual eroticism" in order to avoid "the charge that we have drifted into the liberal stance which is characteristic of many mainline denominations." At the same time, he insisted, ending the "social oppression" of gays and lesbians represented one of the "dominant civil rights issue of the nineties." Sider even suggested that failure to differentiate between denying the affirmation of gays and lesbians in private Christian communities and restricting their rights in the public sphere tarnished progressive evangelicals' objections to same-sex relationships. "Our stand against homosexual practice," he argued, "would be far more credible if we were known for defending the civil rights of gay persons." Thus Sider and other ESA leaders challenged Christian conservatives to renounce public discrimination based upon sexual orientation.[50]

SOCIAL JUSTICE AND SAME-SEX MARRIAGE

Progressive evangelicals' principled defense of gays and lesbians' civil rights reflected the core commitments of their public theology of community. Gays and lesbians have the same "God-given human rights and dignity" as other community members, leaders insisted, and differences in sexual orientation or consensual same-sex behavior are not legitimate grounds for a society to withhold rights from some members. "To deny fundamental human rights to a group of people is to violate the core of professed theological integrity," Jim Wallis wrote regarding gays and lesbians. In particular, leaders argued that gays and lesbians were as deserving of love—expressed politically through protecting others' rights and dignity—as all other community members. "Christian love of neighbor demands respect for the civil rights of homosexuals," Ron Sider claimed. *Sojourners* contributing editor Aaron McCarroll Gallegos urged Christians to "work to change the atmosphere where gays are seen as less than complete human beings with the full civil privileges of other citizens." Therefore, progressive evangelicals interpreted the active prevention of public discrimination against LGBT individuals as integral to social justice. As a matter of "both justice and compassion," Wallis declared, "gay civil and human rights must be honored, respected, and defended for a society to be good and healthy." While *Sojourners* and ESA believed that Christians could legitimately restrict full participation in their private religious communities to those who met their theological standards for sexual morality, they could not use those particular standards as the basis for limiting gays and lesbians' rights in public. "In a pluralistic democracy," Wallis wrote, "we should support civil and human rights for all our citizens, regardless of our different interpretations of the complicated and thorny issues surrounding homosexuality."[51]

Yet, progressive evangelicals had to determine, do these civil and human rights include the right to marry a same-sex partner? Beginning in the 1990s, public debates regarding the legality and the morality of same-sex marriage became increasingly prominent. In 1993 Hawaii's supreme court ruled that the denial of marriage licenses to same-sex couples constituted discrimination under the state's constitution. In response, conservative activists and politicians began pushing for ballot initiatives and constitutional amendments that would preclude same-sex marriage. In 1996 Congress overwhelmingly passed the Defense of Marriage Act, a bill defining marriage in federal law as a "legal union between one man and one woman" and allowing states to refuse to recognize same-sex marriages licensed in other states. Over the next seven years, thirty-eight states adopted their own antigay marriage statutes. Yet when Massachusetts became the first state to legalize same-sex marriage in 2003, Religious Right leaders such as Focus on the Family's James Dobson and the Southern Baptist Convention's Richard Land urged evangelicals to prioritize opposition to gay marriage in their political agendas. "The homosexual activist movement is poised to administer a devastating and potentially fatal blow to the traditional family," warned Dobson in a direct-mail appeal to 2.5 million supporters. Galvanized by the issue, Christian conservatives helped pass antigay marriage amendments in twenty-six states between 2004 and 2008. Indeed, polls prior to these elections revealed that 81 percent of white evangelicals opposed allowing gay and lesbian couples to marry—the strongest opposition among all religious groups. To religious and political conservatives, heterosexual families served as the foundation for a healthy society, and any redefinition of marriage opened the door to legalized polygamy, incest, or even bestiality. In contrast, supporters of gay marriage argued that discrimination based upon sexual preference represent illiberal and unjust discrimination. Civil unions did not qualify for equal benefits offered to heterosexual couples, they protested, and therefore banning same-sex marriages denied equal civil rights and privileges to gays and lesbians.[52]

Because most progressive evangelicals interpreted marriage as primarily an institution for the common good rather than as an issue of individual rights, they refused to endorse same-sex marriage. Although a few individuals such as Peggy Campolo dissented, the most prominent progressive leaders and organizations joined conservatives in touting heterosexual marriage as the ideal structure not only for producing and rearing children but also for stabilizing society. "Marriage is the most basic unit of every social order because it is the best context for producing many things essential to a decent society," Sider claimed. Leaders argued that the communal benefits of restricting marriage to heterosexual couples outweighed individual interests. "Sometimes we confuse the social purposes of marriage with our culture's characteristic individualism and even narcissism," wrote Wallis. "Marriage has been institutionally established by the state to provide a structure and environment in which to raise, protect, and nurture children, much more than to ensure our personal happiness and fulfillment." Therefore, progressive evangelical leaders believed that the government rightfully licensed only heterosexual marriages. Since "a critical mass of families with male and female role models is crucial for the well-being of children and the stability of any society," Wallis stated, "traditional two-parent families must be strengthened and supported, even by public policy." Leaders rejected charges that their position represented an illegitimate political imposition of traditional Christian doctrine. "A commitment to the common good and to the wellbeing of all children, not a specific religious belief, compels us to insist that public law should retain the traditional legal definition of marriage," insisted Sider, who supported a federal marriage amendment as states began legalizing same-sex marriages. Inspired by their public theology of community to ensure that individual interests did not undermine the common good, nearly all progressive evangelical leaders opposed legal recognition of same-sex marriage into the early 2010s.[53]

At the same time, their opposition to discrimination against gays and lesbians led progressive evangelicals to break with conservatives and endorse other measures to secure rights for same-sex couples. The government should defend heterosexual marriage "in a way that doesn't scapegoat or discriminate against gay and lesbian citizens," Wallis declared during early debates over gay marriage. He subsequently concluded that civil unions offered the best compromise. "We can make sure that long-term gay and lesbian partnerships are afforded legitimate legal protections in a pluralistic society no matter what our views on the nature of marriage are," Wallis wrote in 2005. "The long-standing and deeply rooted concept of marriage as being between a man and a woman should not be changed, but same-sex couples should be granted the rights of 'civil unions.'" Other leaders proposed that the legal status of all couples should be distinct from the issue of marriage. "The government should get out of the business of marrying people and, instead, only give legal status to *civil unions*," Tony Campolo stated. "The government should do this for both gay couples and straight couples, and leave *marriage* in the hands of the Church." Dwight Ozard, editor of ESA's *Prism* magazine, suggested that such an approach "would allow the church to make a moral statement against same-sex marriages without denying what are perceived as civil rights." But Sider disagreed with such proposals. He argued that the state has a responsibility to recognize and to nurture stable heterosexual marriages through benefits such as exclusive tax incentives, and therefore legislation should not suggest that same-sex unions differed from heterosexual marriage only in name. "Society should not grant gay partners all the rights of marriage," Sider claimed. Nevertheless, he came to believe that legal recognition of civil unions could safeguard same-sex couples' rights to "own property together, make medical decisions for each other, have full hospital visitation rights, and inherit each other's property." Most progressive evangelical leaders believed that their proposals for civil unions justly ensured same-sex couples' rights while reserving marriage for heterosexuals.[54]

The responses of progressive evangelicals to same-sex marriage exemplified how their positions on homosexuality conflicted with both the political left and the Religious Right. To be sure, *The Other Side* illustrated how some progressive evangelicals joined many religious and political liberals in affirming the unqualified equality of gays and lesbians in both church and society. Yet the majority of the evangelical left refused to sanction same-sex behavior as a matter of personal morality and same-sex marriage as a matter of public welfare. As a result, liberals charged progressive evangelicals with perpetuating gays and lesbians' oppression. At the same time, evangelical progressives regarded the Religious Right's political agendas as dehumanizing and discriminatory toward gays and lesbians, and they criticized conservatives for sensationalizing the threat of homosexuality and attempting to curtail civil rights. Leaders especially rebuked Christian conservatives in the late 1990s and early twenty-first century for their preoccupation with same-sex marriage as one of the only religious and "moral values" at stake during political elections. "Many people of faith have grown weary of the Religious Right's attempts to narrow the moral litmus test to abortion and gay marriage," Wallis wrote after the 2004 presidential election. But progressive evangelical leaders not only promoted a broader set of moral issues; they also proclaimed a different set of priorities in their political agendas. "There were two [different] issues in the 2004 election year that most tugged at my heart, worry my Christian conscience, and compel me to faithful citizenship and discipleship," Wallis wrote. "The first is poverty, the second is war." The next two chapters analyze how progressive evangelicals addressed and emphasized these respective concerns.[55]

7. The Crusade against Poverty

George W. Bush may have seemed an unlikely ally in progressive evangelicals' campaigns for economic justice, but Sojourners' Jim Wallis and Evangelicals for Social Action president Ron Sider welcomed the possibility. Within a week of the December 2000 Supreme Court decision that secured his presidential victory, Bush invited Wallis and Sider to join a small group of religious leaders to discuss the role of faith-based organizations (FBOs) in providing federally funded social services. At the meeting, the Republican president-elect impressed both progressive evangelical leaders with his commitment to combating poverty through these "faith-based initiatives." Sider, who had voted for Bush based largely upon the candidate's support for faith-based initiatives, believed the president-elect's decision to devote this early meeting "to the issue of FBOs' overcoming poverty demonstrates that Bush intends to make this a high priority in his new administration." Wallis agreed that Bush "clearly believes in faith-based organizations and the important role they can play in solving social problems." When Bush confessed that he did not understand poor people and had no experience with impoverished communities, Wallis offered to give him a tour of his inner-city neighborhood in Washington, D.C., once the president settled twenty blocks away in the White House. To be sure, both Wallis and Sider promised to reserve judgment. "It was only a first meeting, and just an opening to further discussion," Wallis cautioned. Sider also challenged Bush "to use his Presidential 'pulpit' to tell everyone that expanding the role of FBOs does not eliminate the crucial need for effective government anti-poverty programs." Yet Bush's invitation and attitude afforded some measure of hope that his administration would advance economic justice. "Let's all pray that the next President learns to listen to the voices of the poor as much as God wants him to," Sider concluded.[1]

Bush's inaugural address the next month surprised Wallis even more. Drawing upon biblical allusions—from God's image as the basis for equality to the generosity of the Good Samaritan—the new president stated that "deep, persistent poverty is unworthy of our nation's promise." Bush urged compassion not only from private citizens but also from the government, pledging "to build a single nation of justice and opportunity." Wallis responded optimistically. "I didn't vote for George W. Bush," he admitted. But the new president impressed Wallis by referring to overcoming poverty as both a moral and political duty that included governmental responsibilities. "I can't remember a conservative Republican or, for that matter, a Democrat talking as much about poverty in an inaugural address," he wrote. Obviously encouraged, Wallis called for *Sojourners'* readers to give Bush a chance to fulfill his promises and even to "help him turn his words into reality." But Wallis also guaranteed accountability. "Words must be tested, and we will test Mr. Bush's," he vowed. "We will evaluate all of the Bush administration's policies by how they impact poverty."[2]

As Wallis suggested, progressive evangelicals viewed their mission to combat poverty as central in their broad social justice agenda. Leaders addressed no other issue as consistently and with such theological certainty, for they believed that God clearly called Christians to make economic justice a political priority. "It's difficult to understand how we can be biblical in our politics" and "not talk about poverty all the time," Wallis claimed. "This is the primary social issue in the Bible"—and "if our gospel isn't good news to the poor, it isn't an evangelical gospel." Their dedication to redress poverty through political actions stemmed from a set of biblical interpretations—what both Wallis and Sider labeled an evangelical "theology of liberation"—that leaders developed over the course of the 1970s. God sides with the poor, evangelical progressives argued, and God's people must join the work of liberating them from systemic oppression that produces and perpetuates poverty. Based upon their biblical interpretations, leaders claimed that God's design for economic justice calls for the redistribution of resources in order to meet basic needs of the poor, to ensure substantively equal economic opportunities, and to reduce inequalities in wealth and power. These biblical principles for economic justice should guide not only private practices but also public policies and social legislation, progressive evangelicals concluded. Therefore, leaders insisted that

Christians must work politically to promote governmental actions that provide for and empower the poor.[3]

This theology of liberation became the foundation for progressive evangelicals' economic analyses and public efforts to combat poverty. Throughout the 1970s and 1980s leaders argued that capitalism causes and compounds poverty, for capitalist economies allow the rich to monopolize economic power and prioritize profits over human needs. To counteract the resulting deprivation and inequalities, progressive evangelicals supported redistributive public policies that offered a social safety net and assisted the poor in moving toward economic independence. Support for social welfare programs, progressive tax rates, and nonmilitary foreign aid became their practical standard for judging politicians' concern for the poor. Leaders especially rebuked presidents when they increased military spending while cutting social programs. To the Religious Right, evangelical progressives' criticism of capitalism and enthusiasm for expanded welfare programs marked them as Marxist socialists. Yet progressive leaders denied these accusations and insisted that dedication to the poor should cause Christians to oppose the injustices within *all* economic systems.

After the collapse of state socialism in the former Soviet Union and Eastern Europe, however, progressive evangelicals did begin revising several parts of their economic analyses in the 1990s. Leaders acknowledged the ways in which capitalism could alleviate poverty, emphasized that irresponsible personal choices often contributed to poverty as much as systemic injustices, and supported increased antipoverty initiatives from the private sector and partnerships between the government and FBOs. Yet evangelical progressives still affirmed the core principles of their theology of liberation. Throughout the 1990s and into the twenty-first century, leaders remained critical of fiscal decisions that reduced social spending and seemingly increased economic inequalities. They protested policies such as the 1996 welfare reform law signed by President Bill Clinton and President George W. Bush's combination of tax cuts for the wealthy, funding for the "war on terror," and cuts to social programs.

Progressive evangelicals conducted their campaign for economic justice as a crusade. They defended their preferred policies with moralistic zeal, often denouncing opposite strategies and competing policies as immoral and unbiblical. Leaders viewed budgetary decisions regarding the funds for social programs through the lens of their theology of liberation, and they developed the slogan "Budgets are moral documents" as a way to challenge politicians to prioritize the poor in their fiscal decisions. Thus progressive evangelicals navigated complex economic debates by drawing upon the principles of their theology of liberation. Indeed, one cannot begin to understand the economic agenda and political activism of the contemporary progressive evangelical movement apart from this set of biblical interpretations that inspired its leaders.

"AN EVANGELICAL THEOLOGY OF LIBERATION"

Jim Wallis held aloft the holey Bible. "My friends, this *is* the American Bible—full of holes from all that we have cut out," he declared. As Wallis traveled and preached throughout the 1970s, he carried with him this shredded, fragile Bible. At the beginning of the decade, Wallis and other Post-Americans at Trinity Evangelical Divinity School had attempted to identify every biblical reference to the poor and oppressed. Having heard few if any sermons on poverty, they were astonished to find thousands of relevant Bible verses. In a symbolic act, one seminarian used scissors to cut out every biblical text about the poor and oppressed. The pile on the floor grew as he excised passage after passage: the Exodus narrative of God's deliverance of an enslaved people; Mosaic laws regarding the poor; the Hebrew prophets' denunciations of injustice; Mary's Magnificat; Jesus's inaugural sermon at Nazareth; the Sermon on the Mount; Jesus's identification with the poor and warnings against wealth; the economic sharing in the early church; Paul's collection for the poor in Jerusalem; and instructions in other epistles on ministering to those in need. Taking this Bible on the road, Wallis waved the decimated book before audiences and argued that American Christians had "cut poor people out of the Bible" by ignoring these biblical models and mandates to care for the poor. To Wallis and other progressive evangelicals, such passages on economic inequalities and injustices held the key to Christians' financial and political responsibilities. Beginning in the early 1970s, they developed a set of biblical interpretations and theological convictions—what Ron Sider described in 1980 as "an evangelical theology of liberation"—that shaped their expectations for economic justice and consequent political engagement.[4]

While early leaders independently identified poverty as a central issue of social justice, progressive evangelicals' theology of liberation had connections to Latin American liberation theology. Emerging in the 1960s and popularized in North America by the works of Gustavo Gutiérrez in the early 1970s, liberation theology reinterpreted the Christian faith from the perspective of the poor and oppressed. To exponents, the suffering of the poor in Latin America revealed an urgent need for liberation not only from individual sin but also from social sin manifested in political and economic oppression. Appropriating neo-Marxist analyses while rejecting Marxist materialism and atheism, liberation theologians accepted the reality of class struggle. They regarded poverty in their societies as the sinful results of exploitative capitalist systems that benefited only the powerful, rich elite. But, advocates proclaimed, the "good news" of the Christian gospel is that God works in history to overcome and to eradicate *all* forms of sin and injustice. In particular, God has a "preferential option for the poor" and favors them against their oppressors. Since sin is both individual and structural, they asserted, salvation entails both spiritual redemption and physical, political liberation. Thus liberation theologians insisted that the church must join God's work by identifying with the poor and working for their holistic salvation.[5]

Progressive evangelicals adopted an appreciative yet critical approach toward Latin American liberation theology. In articles and book reviews throughout the 1970s and 1980s, they defended the insights of liberation theologians regarding God's particular concern for the poor and Christians' responsibilities to fight economic exploitation. In addition, they argued, liberation theologians rightly challenged North Americans to assess how capitalist presumptions and economic self-interests distorted their theology to the point that many evangelicals perversely justified "the privilege of the powerful and poverty of the poor." Yet progressive evangelicals criticized the tendencies of Latin American liberation theologians to regard the experience of oppression and Marxist analyses rather than biblical revelation as the primary authority in theological interpretations. They also rejected any reduction of the meaning of liberation (or salvation) to political and economic emancipation. Finally, leaders faulted some liberation theologians for justifying violent revolutions. Nevertheless, progressive evangelicals endorsed the core conviction of Latin American liberation theology: the gospel's promise of "good news for the poor" requires Christians to combat oppression by the rich and unjust economic systems that produced poverty.[6]

As leaders developed their own evangelical theology of liberation, they too affirmed as a foundational principle that God sides with the poor and acts concretely to free them from oppression. Beginning in earnest in 1974, both *The Other Side* and the *Post-American* (subsequently renamed

Sojourners) consistently proclaimed this doctrine. Author after author asserted the maxim that "God is on the side of the poor and oppressed," defending this position with numerous biblical references to God's protection and provision for the needy. "The Scriptures are not neutral on questions of economics," Jim Wallis declared. "The God of the Bible is clearly and emphatically on the side of the poor, the exploited, and the victimized." In 1977 the most influential progressive evangelical proclamation of God's special concern for the poor and oppressed appeared in Ron Sider's best-selling *Rich Christians in an Age of Hunger*. Although insisting that biblical history reveals God uniquely identifying with and liberating poor and oppressed people, Sider qualified his argument with several caveats: material poverty is not the biblical ideal; God does not automatically offer or privilege the eternal salvation of the poor; and Christians must not reduce discipleship only to seeking justice for the poor and oppressed. Wallis also warned against glamorization of the poor. "Poverty is ugly and bitter, and the poor suffer from the same sinful human condition as the rest of us," he wrote. Still, Wallis maintained, "that God is on the side of the poor" is "much more clear biblically than most issues that have divided churches." To progressive evangelical leaders, this doctrine reflects a fundamental expression of God's compassion and justice.[7]

But God does more than merely side with the poor, evangelical progressives taught—God also opposes the rich and powerful. Leaders cited a litany of biblical support that ranged from the jeremiads of the Hebrew prophets to New Testament passages such as Luke 1:52-53 and 6:20-26 and James 5:1-6. Scripture teaches that "the God of the Bible wreaks horrendous havoc on the rich," Sider argued. "The rich may prosper for a time, but eventually God will destroy them." Authors explained God's opposition to wealthy elites by contending that the Bible overwhelmingly attributed poverty to their exploitation of the poor. "Both the Old Testament prophets and the New Testament apostles seem to take it for granted that the rich get that way by oppressing the poor," J. R. Burkholder claimed in the *Post-American*. In respective articles in *The Other Side* and *Sojourners*, Tom Hanks urged evangelicals to recover "the depth and intensity of the biblical witness against oppression," for "it must be recognized as the basic cause of poverty in biblical theology." Even when "Scripture does not charge the rich with direct oppression of the poor," Sider declared, it "accuses them of failure to share with the needy" with the same unjust result. Although Americans "insist that God could not be opposed to the rich and powerful" because "we want everyone to be treated equally, including the rich," *The Other Side*'s John Alexander wrote, such a belief "is repeatedly and flatly contradicted by Scripture."[8]

With confidence in the unquestionably *biblical* evidence for these doctrines, progressive evangelicals expected other Christians—especially evangelicals—to affirm them as well. "God's special concern for the poor and oppressed seems to me to be so clear that no serious person could dispute it," Alexander proclaimed. Leaders attributed their perception of God's participation in an apparent class struggle to a faithful reading of the Bible rather than to Marxist hermeneutics. "When we begin to examine the question of social justice from a biblical perspective, we are inevitably led to the division of the world into rich and poor," Wallis wrote. Yet, leaders complained, biblical teachings on "antagonistic classes and the struggle of the poor against their oppressors" had been "largely ignored and evaded in conservative evangelical theology." As a result, Sider charged, evangelicalism "has been unbiblical and therefore heretical." He explicitly denied that evangelical progressives "start with some ideologically interpreted context of oppression (for instance, a Marxist definition of the poor and their oppressed situation) and then reinterpret Scripture from that ideological perspective." But Sider knew how objectionable these doctrines sounded to evangelical audiences, and therefore he tried to offer a nuanced analysis in *Rich Christians in an Age of Hunger*. "Is God a Marxist?" Sider asked. "Is God engaged in class warfare?" Although answering neither question directly, he assured readers that God does not have class enemies and shows love impartially. At the same time, Sider explained, God's concern for the poor does *seem* biased—but only because of humans' sinful preference for the rich. Because the poor have greater needs for justice, God is not neutral. "The Bible clearly and repeatedly teaches that God is at work in history casting down the rich and exalting the poor," Sider summarized.[9]

Above all, progressive evangelical leaders believed that the Bible blames poverty on unjust economic systems that enable the oppressive acts of rich individuals and exacerbate inequality. "The biblical narratives speak clearly about the structural realities of oppression," Wallis claimed. "The poverty and misery people experience" is not "due to the failures of the poor" but rooted "in the political and economic power structures and the lifestyle of the affluent that makes such structures possible and even necessary." Sider lamented most evangelicals' "neglect of the biblical teaching on structural injustice" such as "sinful social institutions and bad economic structures." Indeed, progressive evangelicals argued that ostensibly amoral economic systems often became immoral "social structures that tolerate and foster great poverty." Any economic system that allows privileged classes to exploit or to neglect the poor—all while "the rich work within the law and follow accepted business practices"— amounts to "legalized oppression." Ultimately, leaders warned that systemic economic injustice incurs God's wrath. "God works in history to destroy evil social structures and sinful societies, where wealthy classes grow richer from the sweat, toil, and grief of the poor," Sider declared.[10]

Like Latin American liberation theologians, progressive evangelicals believed that God expects Christians also to side with and seek justice for the poor and oppressed. "The biblical mandate is clear in instructing the people of God to identify with and support the cause of the poor and oppressed," Wallis contended. "The scriptures claim that to know God is to do justice and to plead [their] cause." In fact, evangelical progressives elevated this solidarity and activism to a defining mark of Christian discipleship. "The people of God, if they really are the people of God, are *also* on the side of the poor and oppressed," argued Sider. "Those who neglect the needy are not really God's people at all—no matter how frequent their religious rituals or how orthodox their creeds and confessions." Yet as progressive evangelical leaders identified the pursuit of justice for the poor as a religious obligation, the question remained: how should Christians translate this theoretical commitment into practice? As evangelicals, they again mined their Bibles for guiding principles and practices.[11]

Four biblical paradigms determined how progressive leaders interpreted God's blueprint for economic justice. First, they emphasized Mosaic legislation on tithing, gleaning, and loaning that provided for the poor and mitigated economic inequalities. In particular, evangelical progressives highlighted the Year of Jubilee (every fiftieth year) that required Israelites to cancel debts and to return land to the family of its original owners (Leviticus 25). Such legislation regularly provided equal access to economic resources and opportunities. While industriousness, laziness, or calamity led in the interim to different incomes, "the Year of Jubilee guaranteed that such a system would not continue indefinitely, nor would it develop into a permanent structure of inequality," explained Frank Breisch in *The Other Side*. Second, leaders argued that Jesus transformed economic attitudes and relationships among his followers. As signs of disciples' dependence upon God and love for others, Jesus instructed them to renounce money and possessions (for example, Matthew 6:24, Luke 14:33) in order to share resources freely within the community and with the poor (for example,

Luke 6:30 and 12:33-34). Peter Davids summarized Jesus's teaching: "One must give up wealth and invest in heaven—by giving to the poor—if one is to serve God single-mindedly." Third, authors idealized the communitarian practices of the early church as described in Acts 2:42-47 and 4:32-37. After Pentecost, the initial Christian community established a "common life" that included financial sharing and the voluntary sale of private resources to meet other members' needs. In this context, Sider claimed, discipleship entailed "unlimited economic liability for, and total economic availability to, the other members of Christ's body." Passages such as James 2:15-16 and 1 John 3:14-18 suggested similar expectations for all local churches. Finally, progressive evangelicals argued that Paul's collection for the impoverished Jerusalem church extended economic sharing from *intra*-community assistance to *inter*-community aid across ethnic and geographic lines (for example, Romans 15:26, 2 Corinthians 7-9). "The collection 'as a matter of equality' [2 Corinthians 8:14] was to symbolize the organic unity of the universal Christian church," Bill Faw wrote in *Sojourners*.[12]

To progressive evangelicals, the collective force of these passages revealed a fundamental principle: God's design for economic justice entails the redistribution of socioeconomic resources in order to meet everyone's needs, to empower equal opportunities, and to prevent gross inequalities. "The people of God are committed by the teaching of scripture and the command of their master to a redistribution of wealth," summarized Davids. Evangelical progressives affirmed that the Bible sanctions private property. But, they argued, individuals must use economic resources for the common good. "From the perspective of biblical revelation," Sider wrote, "property owners are not free to seek their own profit without regard for the needs of their neighbor." Likewise, God approves the acquisition of wealth—but only for legitimate ends. "We must distinguish between the accumulation of capital for one's personal benefit—that's the 'riches' which the Bible condemns—and the accumulation of capital as an economic resource, as a productive capacity that may indeed be a tool in the work of God's kingdom—or at least in the enhancement of human welfare," J. R. Burkholder asserted. Wallis urged readers to imitate the "new system of distribution" developed in the apostolic church and to reject individualistic assumptions about property rights. "The early believers realized that the way of Christ militated against the private use and disposition of resources and led to the sharing of all money, property, possessions, and assets as needs arose in the community," he claimed.

Leaders expected the redistribution of wealth and the ideal of economic equality to liberate the poor from oppressive poverty and to create just economic relationships within Christian communities.[13]

But in addition to guiding Christians' interpersonal practices, progressive evangelicals concluded, biblical principles of distributive economic justice should also shape public policies. To be sure, leaders believed that God desires private charitable sharing of economic resources with the poor so that "all needs are met, outside as well as inside the church." Yet they also argued that Mosaic laws designed to benefit the poor demonstrate that God's will for economic justice includes social legislation and not only "charitable courtesy that the wealthy may extend if they please." These laws represented "institutionalized mechanisms and structures that promote justice," Sider argued, and therefore "Scripture prescribes justice rather than mere charity." Progressive evangelicals admitted the difficulty in applying economic principles based upon ancient Israel's legislation and the apostolic church's example to contemporary societies. Nevertheless, they contended that the purposes of these biblical practices were not arbitrary norms but rather models for economic justice that all societies should apply. Sider reasoned that God would only institute ideals in Israel that should characterize and benefit *all* people, and he pointed to examples of God's judgment of other ancient societies as proof that "Yahweh applies the same standards of social justice to all nations." Thus to liberate the poor from economic injustice, evangelical progressives determined, Christians should promote economic structures and public policies modeled after the biblical principles of redistribution and economic equality. At the heart of a just economic system "is a divine demand for regular, fundamental redistribution of the means for producing wealth," Sider wrote. "We must discover new, concrete models for applying this biblical principle in our global village."[14]

As a result of these theological principles concerning economic justice, progressive evangelicals taught that Christians must "exercise political influence" in order to promote redistributive public policies that alleviate poverty and moderate inequalities. Over and over, leaders identified the fair distribution of socioeconomic resources as crucial in their political vision for a just society. "In areas where struggles for social justice are occurring," Wallis wrote, "the central questions concern the need for the fundamental redistribution of wealth and power." Clark Pinnock's address to the 1975 Evangelicals for Social Action Workshop exemplified how early progressive leaders placed economic justice at the foundation of their public engagement. He outlined a "systematic theology for public discipleship" predicated upon "an evangelical theology of human liberation." Christians should imitate God's "passionate hatred of injustice" by seeking to free others from "suffering, injustice, and inequality." In particular, because of God's especial compassion for the poor, Christians must promote economic justice as a communal, political ideal. "God's concern for the needy suggests that our nations will be judged according to the way in which they have treated the poor and needy," Pinnock declared.[15]

By the end of the 1970s, then, progressive evangelical leaders had developed an evangelical theology of liberation that shaped their interpretation of economic justice, guided their economic analyses, and motivated their political engagement. "For the last decade, *Sojourners* has been working out a theology of liberation for North American Christians," Wallis wrote in 1981. "We have learned that siding with the poor brings us into conflict with the institutions and arrangements that oppress them." Both *The Other Side* and Evangelicals for Social Action (ESA) joined *Sojourners* in promoting this theological vision for economic justice. Through changing circumstances from the 1970s into the twenty-first century, this evangelical theology of liberation inspired progressive evangelicals to prioritize the poor and to support public policies for economic redistribution.[16]

COUNTERACTING CAPITALISM

In the summer of 1972 *The Other Side* published a foil to the economic analyses developing among early progressive evangelical leaders. The article by H. Edward Rowe, editor of the right-wing journal *Christian Economics*, presented a full-throated defense of the economic conservatism that had become predominant among twentieth-century evangelicals. "Capitalism is more consistent with the Word of God than any other system of economics," Rowe declared. "God is the God of freedom, and free enterprise capitalism is simply freedom in the economic realm." He defended not only the "productive efficiency" but also the beneficence of capitalism: "It has conquered more human misery and poverty than any other economic system." Rowe condemned the "War on Poverty" initiated by President Lyndon Johnson as a "socialist scheme" and "legislated theft" that entailed "redistribution of wealth from the more productive to the less productive elements of society." Despite altruistic intentions, he argued, federal antipoverty programs hurt the poor by discouraging work. In fact, Rowe insisted that the government should play *no* role in addressing poverty since he believed that the Bible mandates only charitable aid from individuals and the church. By printing this article, *The Other Side* reminded readers that most contemporary evangelicals revered capitalism, abhorred the expansion of the welfare state, and advocated charity as the proper response to poverty.[17]

Yet the emerging progressive evangelical movement was reaching radically different conclusions. Following Rowe's piece, *The Other Side* published an "antidote to the preceding article." Board member Bill Pannell noted how easily "the wealthy spout the rhetoric of free enterprise" as they "enjoy the benefits of power through the control of the nation's economic assets." He argued that the rich and powerful systematically excluded the poor from access to socioeconomic resources, thereby ensuring their subjugation. In reality, Pannell wrote, "economic corruption" and inequality flourished under the guise of capitalism's purported freedoms. Other progressive evangelicals offered even more strident criticism. That same year, the *Post-American* decried the "pathological process of capitalism" that put the pursuit of profits before human needs. Editor Jim Wallis described America's capitalist economy as a "domestic colonialism which locks 30 million of its own people into poverty and misery"; meanwhile, the government ignored "the needs of the poor, the old, the sick, the unemployed, [and] the homeless" in order to build "the most destructive war machine in human history." Evangelical progressives also began criticizing the "unjust economic structures" of global capitalism that "produced suffering and starvation." Ron Sider argued that affluent North Americans were "exploiting the poor of the world" through unfair trade patterns and grossly disproportionate consumption of resources. Wallis identified this oppression as America's economic imperialism. "People of the non-industrialized world are poor because we are rich," and "the poverty and brutalization people experience is maintained and perpetuated by our political and economic systems and by the way we live our lives," he wrote in 1973. As these judgments hardened, condemnations of capitalism and proposals to counteract its consequences became hallmarks of evangelical progressivism through the 1980s.[18]

These criticisms of capitalism reflected the interpretations of poverty and expectations for economic justice that emerged from progressive evangelicals' theology of liberation. "The primary standard the Bible gives us for judging any economic system is the priority of the poor," *Sojourners'* Danny Collum claimed. To leaders, therefore, evidence of widespread poverty and inequality revealed the failures of capitalism. Throughout the 1970s and 1980s, progressive evangelicals consistently highlighted statistics and stories of suffering. The official poverty rate in America rose from a historic low of 11.1 percent in 1973 to 15.2 percent (35.3 million people) in 1983. The numbers for children and blacks proved even more distressing: 22 percent of Americans under age eighteen, almost half of all black children, and 36 percent of all African Americans lived in poverty. The stagnant economy, inflation, and escalating unemployment threatened to impoverish millions more. Unequal distributions of wealth also increased. By 1984, the top 20 percent of Americans possessed nearly half the nation's resources; the bottom half owned only 1 percent. "U.S. Christians need to begin a 'radical' analysis of capitalism and its effects," urged contributors to *The Other Side*, for "in a trillion-dollar economy, we still have over thirty million Americans living in poverty and millions more with no real financial security." Progressive evangelicals also repeatedly emphasized desperate circumstances abroad. A global recession, debt crises, crop failures, less profitable exports, and decreased foreign aid exacerbated poverty in underdeveloped countries. In Third World nations, almost a billion people suffered from malnutrition. "Hunger and starvation stalk the land. Famine is alive and well on planet earth. Millions of people die of starvation each year," Ron Sider wrote in his somber opening to *Rich Christians in an Age of Hunger*. The gap in standards of living between affluent and impoverished nations continued to widen, as 20 percent of people held 80 percent of the world's wealth. Because they believed that the Bible attributed most poverty to oppressive economic systems, progressive evangelicals concluded that this evidence exposed the fatal flaws of global capitalism.[19]

As a result, throughout the 1970s and 1980s leaders consistently decried how capitalism allowed powerful elites to exploit the poor. Oppression of the poor by the rich represented a central theme in their theology of liberation, and progressive evangelicals—especially the staff of *Sojourners*—embraced analyses of capitalism by leftist critics such as C. Wright Mills and G. William Domhoff that coincided with these biblical interpretations. They argued that wealthy elites manipulated the American economy and politics to enrich themselves at the expense of the poor. "Certain people, classes, and institutions possess an enormous and illegitimate amount of power which is exercised for their own benefit and against social justice and especially against the poor," Jim Wallis declared. Rich businessmen monopolized resources, depressed workers' wages, and used political connections to prevent redistributive policies. In turn, economic inequality worsened and trapped millions in poverty. Evangelical progressives also blamed Western countries and multinational corporations for poverty in the Third World. "In our increasingly interlocking global economy," *Sojourners*' Phil Shenk wrote, "the poor of far-off lands essentially are the serfs of lords living in richer nations." Perpetuating colonialism, wealthy countries established lopsided trade patterns, imposed high tariffs, and consumed vastly disproportionate amounts of the earth's food and resources. In addition, powerful multinational corporations exploited cheap materials and labor in developing countries, hindered indigenous economic development, and produced exports rather than necessities for the local poor. Most egregious, these multinational corporations and Western governments often supported oppressive regimes in poor nations in order to ensure access to resources and business stability. Thus progressive evangelical leaders largely attributed economic injustice to the consequences of global capitalism. "In good measure, mass poverty is the effect of our world-wide economic system and of the political structures that support it," Nicholas Wolterstorff asserted in *The Other Side*.[20]

Evangelical progressives criticized capitalism not only as oppressive in practice but also as immoral in purpose. Leaders believed that economic systems should prioritize people's welfare, but the pursuit of profits that drives capitalism seemed to foster greed, materialism, and indifference toward human needs. "There is a glaring dissonance between the life Christ calls his disciples to in his Kingdom and the values enshrined daily by capitalism," stated Wes Michaelson in *Sojourners*. "While Christ warns us against the worship of money, capitalism encourages first the accumulation of money and then its rampant expenditure through breeding a national psychology of endless material desire." *The Other Side*'s John Alexander criticized capitalism for serving "mammon" rather than people. "That cannot be tolerated," he insisted. "We must have a system with different priorities" that promotes "the needs of the people of the world, those made in God's image." Danny Collum explicitly blamed capitalism's profit motive for economic injustice. "The gross inequalities of wealth and poverty in the U.S. are the natural result of a social, political, and economic system that places the maximization of private profit above all other social goals," he wrote. "The human, social, cultural, and spiritual benefits that would result from a more just distribution of wealth and power will never show up on the all-important quarterly profit and loss statement." Progressive evangelicals challenged other Christians to recognize the immorality of capitalism. "Judged on the basis of God's revelation through the Bible, American capitalism is an abomination," declared George Mc-Clain in *The Other Side*. "It enables some to gain and retain great wealth at the expense of others," "leaves most people pretty much on their own to scrape for a living," and "almost forces us to act in a selfish, un-Christian way."[21]

This vilification of capitalism infuriated leaders of the burgeoning Religious Right. As an array of evangelical conservatives, libertarians, and Christian Reconstructionists rushed to defend free enterprise in the 1970s and 1980s, competing economic analyses became one of the most divisive political issues among evangelicals. Christian conservatives drew upon the free market economic theories of Ludwig von Mises, Friedrich Hayek, Milton Friedman, and P. T. Bauer to argue that capitalism had proven itself the most just and efficient system for expanding economic opportunities, creating wealth, and maximizing freedom. They insisted that voluntary economic exchanges, not coercion, drove capitalist activity. Legitimate self-interest, not greed, inspired the pursuit of profits. Private ownership of property checked exploitative power. In fact, conservatives declared, capitalism *decreases* poverty by offering the poor opportunities for economic advancement and producing ample wealth for charity. The Religious Right also defended capitalism on biblical grounds. "The Bible promotes free enterprise," Jerry Falwell declared. "The Book of Proverbs and the parables of our Lord clearly promote private property ownership and the principles of capitalism." In turn, conservative authors rebutted the biblical interpretations of evangelical progressives. For example, they argued, the Jubilee redistribution of land was limited in scope, likely never instituted, and no longer applicable; Jesus targeted only spiritual poverty and spiritual liberation; and economic sharing within the early church reflected temporary emergencies rather than models for subsequent Christians. "Capitalism is quite simply the most moral system, the most effective system, and the most equitable system of economic exchange," summarized Ronald Nash.[22]

Though progressive evangelicals longed for a more just system, they also accepted the pragmatic need to promote practices and policies that counteracted capitalism's unjust consequences. To begin, leaders advocated personal efforts to help the poor. Without such actions, they believed, their political advocacy would lack integrity. Christians should not "lobby for government programs for the poor while failing to make room for them in our own lives," argued Danny Collum. First and foremost, evangelical progressives urged Christians to live more simply in order to side with the poor. Americans must "break away from the patterns of overconsumption and waste which characterize our lifestyles and play such a significant role in perpetuating poverty around the world and at home," *Sojourners* proclaimed. Simple living defied consumer capitalism and freed personal resources to redistribute, and therefore leaders published numerous articles and books highlighting "the biblical meaning of material simplicity and sharing with the poor." Second, they promoted and participated in intentional living communities. Individuals and families shared housing or lived near each other in order to facilitate simple living and economic sharing. For several years the families of Ron Sider, John Alexander, and other progressive evangelical leaders were members of Jubilee Fellowship in the Germantown area of Philadelphia. The Sojourners community lived together first in Chicago and then Washington, D.C., and the group's journal regularly featured stories about members' own practices and those of similar communities. Finally, progressive evangelicals urged sacrificial personal giving to the poor. In response to Americans' relative affluence, Sider promoted the idea of a graduated tithe in which Christians increased the percentage of their charitable aid as their incomes grew. *The Other Side*'s staff founded Jubilee Fund, an aid organization designed to "play a small part in transferring wealth to poor parts of the church" by channeling funds to "poor and oppressed Christians." Progressive evangelicals also endorsed gifts to relief and development organizations such as World Vision and Bread for the World.[23]

At the same time, leaders insisted that economic justice required changes in public policies and not just personal solutions. They denounced the Religious Right and Republican politicians for promoting charity as the best if not only way to help the poor. Unlike progressive evangelicals, conservatives believed that poverty primarily stemmed from either unfortunate circumstances or personal moral failures. In their view, short-term charity would enable individuals who were willing to work to have another opportunity to become self-supporting; the lazy or profligate "undeserving poor" would rightly remain impoverished. Thus conservatives expressed confidence that America's economic, political, and social systems offered sufficient opportunities to avoid poverty—an optimism that progressive evangelicals rejected. Their own biblical and sociological analyses led evangelical progressives to attribute most poverty to oppressive conditions created by systemic injustices and social inequalities. Charity addresses only the consequences and not causes of poverty, leaders argued; it meets "immediate needs" but leaves unaltered the "root causes" of poverty such as exploitation and lack of socioeconomic resources. "Feeding the hungry is crucial, and I mean that," John Alexander wrote. "But handing them food does nothing to change a system in which those with money get richer and those without it get poorer." By contrasting charity with justice, progressive evangelicals sought to discredit conservatives' response to poverty as both inadequate and immoral. "To say that the needs of the poor should be met by private charity is to say that the basic necessities of life are not a God-given right of each person," Collum claimed in *Sojourners*. Wallis also maintained that "charity requires no fundamental or systemic change, while justice challenges root assumptions, popular attitudes, and basic structures. The prophets and Jesus cry for justice, not for charity." For evangelical progressives, repeated calls for "structural change" reflected their conviction that political actions were vital to redressing systemic patterns and social causes of poverty.[24]

Drawing upon their broader public theology and specific biblical interpretations of economic justice, leaders declared that the government should act as "an agent for justice" by redistributing resources in order to empower the poor, to mitigate inequalities, and to care for the helpless. They regarded the state's authority, economic interventions, and public programs as necessary to counter unjust concentrations of economic power that flourished under unbridled capitalism. While progressive evangelicals usually remained vague regarding comprehensive policy prescriptions, they consistently championed certain types of statist interventions and actions. In addition to regulating corporate power, leaders believed that the government should fund social welfare programs and adopt tax laws that reduce economic inequality. Social programs should "meet the basic needs of those unable to care for themselves" and "redistribute resources so that the poor have genuine equality of economic opportunity to earn a decent living," Ron Sider explained. Such programs included financial supplements through Aid to Families with Dependent Children; Medicaid; food stamps; nutritional aid programs such as Women, Infants, and Children; and housing assistance. To help fund these programs for the poor, evangelical progressives advocated higher taxes on wealthy individuals and corporations. "Taxes are necessary if government is to continue to fulfill its role as an instrument of justice," Sider wrote. "The biblical teaching that God is opposed to extremes of wealth and poverty would seem to favor progressive taxes on income and wealth." In response to global poverty and economic inequality, leaders advocated both fair trade policies and forms of foreign aid that encouraged indigenous economic development—especially among the poor—in developing countries. In fact, they argued, affluent nations such as the United States should privilege the welfare of the global poor over their own economic and military self-interests. Christians should "demand a foreign policy that unequivocally sides with the poor" by pushing their government to "be more concerned about hungry people abroad than with economic convenience at home," Sider claimed.[25]

Based upon these expectations, progressive evangelicals measured politicians' concern for the poor by how extensively they supported redistributive and equalizing policies. Leaders denounced politicians who cut social programs, for such acts denied the poor vital resources, services, and opportunities. To be sure, evangelical progressives did not uncritically champion extensive welfare programs. Wallis admitted that in practice some antipoverty programs served "more to control poor people than to help them" and "are often wasteful." Leaders wanted to avoid "government paternalism," "cycles of dependency," and eligibility requirements that discouraged work and two-parent households. But until better alternatives became feasible, they argued, well-designed social programs provided an "essential safety net" and helped to "empower the poor to move toward self-sufficiency." In fact, progressive evangelicals attributed much of these programs' lack of success to insufficient funding. "The Great Society commitments to a more just society can hardly be said to have failed" when "its programs have never been adequately funded," Collum claimed. Leaders invariably blamed spending on the military rather than on social programs as the paramount problem. "While it has become politically chic to criticize the failure of government spending to solve social problems," Wallis wrote, "the deadly escalation of the military budget" represented "the principal reasons that so few public resources have been left for the poor." Thus progressive evangelicals rebuked politicians who seemingly robbed the poor to pay for war. Ultimately, leaders believed, Christians have the public duty to hold all politicians accountable for how their policies affect the poor. God calls Christians not to "partisanship for a particular political party" but "to partisanship for the poor," George Chauncey wrote in *The Other Side*. "In light of that sort of partisanship, we are to examine and evaluate the proposals and policies of any administration and of any Congress, regardless of which political party is in control."[26]

This nonpartisan prioritization of the poor led progressive evangelicals to criticize presidents from both political parties in the 1970s. Leaders of the emerging evangelical left attacked Republican president Richard Nixon for prioritizing financial commitments to warfare over welfare, as the costs of the Vietnam War prevented adequate funding of social programs. "Is it right to spend billions for a wasteful military establishment in the face of so much domestic need?" asked Robert Clouse in *The Other Side*. "We should demand that national resources be reallocated to meet the desperate needs" of the poor. Richard Pierard derided Nixon's tax breaks for wealthy individuals and corporations as "welfare for the affluent." In the 1972 election Jim Wallis portrayed support for Nixon as a vote "for the rich against the poor" and insisted that people who "really care about the poor" should vote for Democratic candidate George McGovern. Although Democratic president Jimmy Carter's policies in the late 1970s seemed more favorable than those of Nixon and his successor Gerald Ford, progressive evangelicals judged him a failure as well. "Carter gets himself elected on promises to help the poor," wrote *The Other Side*'s John Alexander, but "you can't tell him from other corrupt, status quo politicians." Leaders censured Carter for breaking his pledge to decrease defense spending, balancing the budget through cutting social programs, and enhancing tax breaks for the wealthy. Carter was perpetuating "a system which allocates most of its resources to make war and subsidize the rich," Wallis complained. He labeled Carter's budget proposals that cut social programs while increasing military spending "more proof to the poor that they don't count in this society."[27]

Yet no politician seemed as callous toward poverty as Ronald Reagan. Soon after the Republican president took office, progressive evangelical leaders began accusing him of superintending "an assault on the poor." Reagan championed free-market capitalism, believing that reductions in government spending, regulation, and tax rates would stimulate the economy after a decade of weak growth and mild recessions. The immediate benefits to the wealthy would ostensibly "trickle down" to the poor and compensate for cuts in social programs. Yet progressive evangelicals condemned "Reaganomics" for inverting the biblical principle that a society should redistribute resources to the poor. The Reagan administration planned "to redistribute income from lower income working people to rich people and big business through tax cuts and to redirect federal spending from the poorest people in the U.S. to an already bloated military establishment," Danny Collum declared. As a result, leaders claimed, Reagan flouted the biblical prioritization of the poor. "Instead of a strong commitment to the defense of the poor and powerless," ESA executive director

Bill Kallio protested, "we find only tax incentives for the rich and a strong bias against the needs of the poor and unemployed."[28]

Throughout the 1980s, author after author in *Sojourners, The Other Side*, and ESA's publications denounced Reagan's policies. "The Reagan budget cuts will drastically increase the number of people who are poor, hungry, sick, ill-housed or homeless, uneducated, and without hope," Collum declared. As the president increased defense spending as part of the Cold War arms race, Wallis urged Christians to raise "the basic questions of justice for the world's poor who are daily robbed by nuclear weapons." Although supporters of "Reaganomics" claimed vindication after the economy began recovering in 1983, progressive evangelicals responded by pointing to persistently high poverty rates. "It is no recovery when 35 million U.S. citizens are living below the official poverty line," insisted *The Other Side*'s Mark Olson. Based in large part upon the perceived "insensitivity of the Reagan administration toward the poor," Wallis and other leaders preferred Democratic nominee Walter Mondale during the 1984 election. Reagan's reelection and even slight declines in poverty rates during his second term did nothing to temper progressive evangelicals' criticism. ESA president Vernon Grounds complained in 1985 when Reagan "proposed cuts in our national budget which will snatch from millions of marginalized Americans the life-buoys they need to keep from drowning in a sea of poverty." Other leaders continued to decry that Reagan's policies compounded poverty and economic inequalities. "Trickle-down Reaganomics has only worsened the lot of the poor" by leading to "low welfare benefits, low wages, and drastic reductions in other social programs," *Sojourners*' Vicki Kemper wrote in 1988. More than any other modern politician, leaders concluded, Reagan had aggravated rather than alleviated economic injustice.[29]

To leaders of the Religious Right, progressive evangelicals' economic proposals and political preferences throughout the 1970s and 1980s betrayed their Marxist sympathies and socialist schemes. Confident that laissez-faire policies worked for the benefit of all, Christian conservatives insisted that the statist interventions in the free market and redistributionist policies favored by progressive evangelicals invariably led to socialism—a system of collective control of the means of production and distribution of wealth that conservative critics condemned as economically inefficient, politically repressive, and immorally reliant upon governmental theft. Especially in the 1980s, conservative critics sought to stigmatize progressive leaders as thinly veiled socialists who were "parroting the 'received wisdom' of secular liberalism." Former *Christianity Today* editor Harold Lindsell alleged that "*Sojourners* favors socialism" and was dedicated to "undermining America's belief in the free enterprise system," while Ronald Nash identified Jim Wallis as an "evangelical who can hardly restrain his enthusiasm for Marxism." In a scathing parody of Ron Sider's popular *Rich Christians in an Age of Hunger*, Christian Reconstructionist David Chilton attacked what he labeled "the ESA philosophy of Christian socialism." Chilton's *Productive Christians in an Age of Guilt Manipulators*—a book that mimicked the style and appearance of Sider's book—ridiculed Sider for constructing "superficially biblical" arguments in support of the "socialistic redistribution of wealth" and governmental "theft in the name of social justice." Though "perhaps sincere in their Christian concern for the poor," Franky Schaeffer charged, "Ronald Sider, Tony Campolo, Jim Wallis, and John Alexander have allowed their zeal for a socially conscientious gospel to lead them towards leftist dogma in one guise or another." These polemics by the Religious Right stemmed from concerns that progressive leaders not only peddled socialism but also led gullible evangelicals to view Democratic politicians' proposals for redistributive economic policies as "more closely aligned with Christian ideals of 'justice and compassion.'" As a result, Schaeffer complained in the mid-1980s, some evangelicals voted for Democrats even though their platforms "clashed with basic views of Bible-believing Christians concerning such issues as abortion [and] homosexuality."[30]

Progressive evangelical leaders rejected accusations that they endorsed socialism. Evangelicals had fallen into an uncritical "capitalist captivity," they argued, and must avoid a similar situation with socialism. "Our final allegiance is to God, not systems," John Alexander argued. "Christians must remain free to call all systems and programs to account for how they treat the poor; so we can't get attached to any of them, whether capitalist, socialist, or whatever." Wallis admitted that "the impossibility of making capitalism work for justice and peace" made the promises of a "new socialist society" appealing. However, he implored Christians to resist conformity to *all* human economic or political systems in order to sustain the church's independence and prophetic calling. While they spent much more time criticizing capitalism, evangelical progressives argued that economic injustices also flourished under socialism—especially as implemented in totalitarian communist states. Christians must not sanction "an economic order that tries to autocratically impose material equality by vesting the state with religious authority and assuming that the unbridled power of its high-priestly rulers will be righteous," *Sojourn-ers'* Wes Michaelson warned. Wallis claimed that "the biblical suspicion of concentrated wealth and power" applies to both "collectivist bureau-cracies" and "large corporations," while Sider criticized "both Marxist totalitarianism and multinational corporations" that "centralize power in the hands of a tiny group of individuals." Indeed, in the late 1980s and early 1990s, evangelical progressives cautiously welcomed the demise of state socialism and communism in Eastern Europe. Even as leaders main-tained many reservations concerning capitalism, these historic changes and their own evolving analyses of poverty led progressive evangelicals to begin modifying their antipoverty proposals.[31]

REFINED PROPOSALS, REITERATED PRINCIPLES

"The world has changed, and so have I," Ron Sider declared in prefac-ing a substantially revised edition of *Rich Christians in an Age of Hunger* in 1997. "Communism has collapsed. Expanding market economies and new technologies have reduced poverty. 'Democratic capitalism' has won the major economic/political debate of the twentieth century." Sider con-fessed in a companion article that he was "not now as critical of capital-ism," for market economies had proven most successful in producing the wealth necessary to alleviate poverty. Therefore, he wrote in the updated edition, "those who care for the poor should endorse market-oriented economies—rather than state-owned, centrally planned ones—as the best basic framework currently known for economic life." To be sure, Sider remained convinced that Christians must not ignore "the problems and injustices of today's market-oriented economies"—especially the fact that many "economically and socially marginalized" people lacked the capital necessary "to earn decent livings and live as dignified members of a community." Therefore he continued to defend strategic "governmen-tal intervention in the economy" and to endorse "substantial government programs designed to lift the poorest." But Sider had grown "more cau-tious and suspicious" concerning the state's role in combating poverty. "With disturbing frequency," he claimed, "government bureaucracies and regulations mess things up more than they make things better." As a re-sult, Sider championed expanded, complementary roles for voluntary and community organizations. "Both private and public programs to provide capital so that the poor have genuine opportunity to earn their own way are absolutely indispensable if today's market economies are to work with even minimal justice," he declared. Finally, Sider added a chapter devoted to "poverty's complex causes." Although he had never attributed poverty solely to unjust economic structures and oppression, in the updated *Rich Christians in an Age of Hunger* Sider analyzed the impoverishing effects of "wrong personal choices, misguided cultural values, disasters, and inadequate technology" before his chapter on "structural injustice."[32]

These conspicuous revisions to the most iconic book of the contemporary progressive evangelical movement reflected three primary ways in which Sider and other progressive evangelical leaders began refining their economic evaluations and political proposals in the early 1990s. They moderated their criticism of capitalism, accepted broader interpretations of the causes of poverty, and championed antipoverty partnerships between the government and private organizations and ministries. Even so, leaders remained resolute in defending the core principles of their evangelical theology of liberation: in their personal lives and public engagement, faithful Christians must emulate God's special concern for the poor; and a just society empowers the poor through redistributive policies that reduce gross inequalities and provide substantively equal economic opportunities. Well into the twenty-first century, evangelical progressives continued to apply these principles in the midst of changing economic conditions and political debates.

In the wake of the collapse of state-directed socialism in Eastern European communist states, progressive evangelical leaders refused to join conservatives in celebrating the triumph of capitalism. "The fact that there is no longer any clear alternative does not take away capitalism's own evident failures to resolve the problems of injustice and inequality," Wallis maintained. Despite the fall of communism, *Sojourners'* Wesley Granberg-Michaelson warned, Christians must not believe "that capitalism—and an unfettered market—can solve human aspirations for economic and social liberation." Although their criticisms of capitalism during the 1990s and early twenty-first century were less frequent and less fiery than in previous decades, progressive evangelicals reiterated three primary objections to free market economies. First, capitalism fails to redress the poor's debilitating lack of socioeconomic resources and thus perpetuates economic inequalities. Without adequate access to "the resources necessary to participate" in market economies, Granberg-Michaelson argued, many people would remain unable to escape "dependency, debt, and the exploitation that now characterizes the relationship between the affluent and the poor." Second, capitalism allows and even encourages people to put the desire to make money and other self-interests ahead of moral obligations to help the poor. "Just as communism violated ethics out of ideological necessity," Wallis claimed, "so free-market capitalism violates ethics when its devotion to profits overrides every other human consideration." Finally, leaders charged capitalism with fueling "materialism and consumerism," in which possessions "become more important than God, neighbor, and the creation." Even as they acknowledged "communism's state ownership and central planning" as "inefficient and totalitarian," progressive evangelical leaders remained wary of free-market capitalism.[33]

Yet they also began expressing greater respect for both the productivity and the economic freedom associated with capitalism. For example, in a reflective piece on what progressive Christians could learn from the sweeping changes that delegitimized state socialism, *Sojourners* contributing editor Richard Taylor argued that those "who rely too heavily on a leftist analysis of capitalism" fail to notice how "modern capitalism might offer something worthwhile to humanity." He urged readers to remain committed to "the equitable *distribution* of wealth" while also exploring "how an economy must be organized to *create* wealth"—an ability for which capitalism showed "special genius." Sider agreed that market economies had proven the most productive. Therefore, "since poor nations need economic growth in order to provide a modestly decent standard of living for the world's poorest people," he concluded, a "mixed economy" that combines market-driven economic activity with strategic government intervention offered the best-known framework "for empowering the poor." Progressive evangelicals also endorsed one of the primary reasons that conservatives had long extolled capitalism: free enterprise allows people to exercise their God-given liberties. "God wills us to have the freedom to make those decisions that determine our own destinies, including our economic lives," Tony Campolo wrote in ESA's magazine. Finally, the impressive results of nongovernmental organizations and aid programs that provided the poor with capital persuaded many leaders that such opportunities could lift them out poverty. "One of the greatest success stories of the last twenty years is the explosion of micro-loans" that "empower millions of desperately poor people" and "produce stunning transformations in poor communities," Sider exclaimed in the new edition of *Rich Christians in an Age of Hunger*. Wallis heralded such programs as "especially effective in creating new jobs and economic activity in abandoned sectors of the global economy." Thus progressive evangelicals acknowledged the transformative potential of capitalism.[34]

In addition to softening their stance toward capitalism, leaders began offering more balanced analyses of the causes of poverty. Evangelical progressives had previously joined political liberals in primarily blaming systemic factors such as unjust distributions of wealth, the oppressive power of corporations and wealthy individuals, unfair trade patterns, and the narrow profit motive of capitalism. Yet their decades of antipoverty activism and relationships with the poor persuaded many leaders to concede that conservatives were partly right in blaming irresponsible personal decisions and broken families. "There is no single cause of poverty," Sider stated explicitly. "Personal sinful choices and complex social structures cause poverty," along with "misguided cultural ideas, natural and human disasters, and lack of appropriate technology." In his 1999 book *Just Generosity: A New Vision for Overcoming Poverty in America*, Sider explained his centrist position. "I have lived and worshiped with the poor far too long to side either with the liberal who quickly dismisses the way personal choices contribute to poverty or with the conservative who ignores the way complicated structural barriers make it difficult for many hardworking people to escape poverty." Wallis admitted that as a younger activist he had viewed the causes of poverty as "primarily structural, the consequences of unjust social and economic forces that powerfully define people's chances for success." But "having tried to combat poverty and violence for three decades now," he wrote in 2000, "I'm coming back to a more balanced view." He now affirmed that "poverty as a larger economic issue is related to many personal and relational factors" such as "dysfunctional or abusive domestic relationships, chemical addiction, irresponsible and destructive sexual behavior, deficiencies in work habits or job experiences, emotional instability or depression, [and] bad financial habits and choices." As they increasingly acknowledged the multifarious causes of poverty, progressive evangelicals sought strategies to "confront both personal and political realities" and to promote both "personal responsibility and social justice."[35]

Successful approaches should include partnerships between the government and private sector, leaders concluded. They remained committed to public policies that addressed larger structural injustices and provided necessary finances and coordination for antipoverty programs. But by the mid-1990s evangelical progressives also accepted that private organizations generally delivered more effective services and better helped the poor develop responsible lifestyles. "It is undeniably true that government alone cannot do what must be done," Wallis wrote. "Many of the problems caused by a breakdown of family, community and values cannot be solved only or even best by government action." He regarded many private programs as "more personal, compassionate, and effective—and far less costly—than comparable government programs." Yet "'churches and charities' alone cannot possibly solve the enormous social problems we now confront," Wallis insisted. Because private antipoverty organizations almost always struggle financially, he argued, "local, state, and federal governments must play a critical role both in helping to convene new partnerships and in mobilizing resources." Sider also viewed the co-operative work of private and public initiatives as crucial. "Smaller non-governmental agencies (many of which are faith-based) often do a better job than large state bureaucracies in providing the actual delivery systems for government-funded services" and in "demanding individual responsibility," he claimed. But because "it is totally unrealistic to suggest that churches and other voluntary agencies provide all the funds and staff to care for the poor in America," Sider stated, "it is both morally right and in each person's long-term self-interest for the government to tax us all so that it can provide funding for effective programs that empower and care for the needy." Leaders hoped that partnerships between the government and private organizations could gain the support of both liberals "who see policy and funding issues at the heart of reducing poverty" and conservatives "who point to the deep cultural roots in family breakdown, sexual behavior, or personal responsibility."[36]

Even as they refined their economic analyses and antipoverty strategies, progressive leaders reaffirmed the foundational tenets of their evangelical theology of liberation. Christians must work to liberate the poor from oppressive, impoverishing forces by promoting redistributive practices and policies that provide equal opportunities and mitigate extremes of wealth. Sider defended these doctrines in both the revised edition of *Rich Christians in an Age of Hunger* and subsequent publications. "To endorse market economies without redistributing resources so the poorest have the capital to earn a decent living is damnable defiance of the biblical God of justice," he declared. While *Sojourners* and *The Other Side* offered fewer biblical exegeses of economic justice than in the 1970s and early 1980s, their leaders also continued to promote this theology of liberation. "Compassion and justice for the poor is the *first principle of biblical politics*," Wallis proclaimed again in 1997. At the same time, progressive evangelical leaders did make several adjustments in their interpretations and presentations of these doctrines. Most notably, even though they had always denied that Marxist ideology had distorted their theology, after the fall of communism leaders sought to avoid any perceived sympathy for Marxism. In the new edition of *Rich Christians in an Age of Hunger*, for example, Sider excised the rhetorical question "Is God a Marxist?," which had appeared in previous editions, and he offered an explicit negative reply to another question—"Is God engaged in class warfare?"—that he had previously left unanswered. In addition, Sider added qualifications to re-emphasize the merits of private property and wealth and to clarify further God's desire for equality of economic opportunities rather than outcomes. Despite such modifications, leaders still warned that "God judges nations by what they do to the poorest." Therefore, progressive evangelicals' theology of liberation and interpretation of economic justice continued to shape their political judgments and proposals.[37]

In the early 1990s progressive evangelicals regularly criticized politicians from both parties for neglecting the poor in order to reduce budget deficits and to appeal to the middle class. After the Cold War, leaders expected less defense spending to free more government funds for social programs. As a result, they decried President George H. W. Bush's pledge to apply savings from decreased military budgets to the rising national debt rather than to spending on "affordable housing, education, job and anti-poverty programs, and health care." During the 1992 presidential election, Sider and Wallis lamented that both Bush and Democratic candidate Bill Clinton were focused on attracting middle-class voters rather than on addressing growing socioeconomic inequalities and "the poverty that now imprisons 35 million Americans." Nevertheless, Clinton's victory initially seemed a welcome change from his Republican predecessors' conservative policies. For example, Wallis wrote appreciatively that he no longer routinely feared that the White House would "proudly announce another cut in a domestic social program." But Clinton began disappointing the evangelical left by making political compromises that scaled back antipoverty initiatives and prioritized federal debt reduction over substantial social spending. Progressive evangelicals' dismay grew after the 1994 midterm elections. Republicans regained control of the House of Representatives for the first time in forty years, offering a "Contract with America" that promised tax cuts, balanced budgets, and welfare reform. To progressive evangelical leaders, the new Republican majority's priority on downsizing "big government" rather than on helping the poor appeared hypocritical and unbiblical. Because "the poor, with little or no political clout, are an easy target," Wallis complained, conservatives cut "government entitlements that affect the poor" but left untouched "middle-class and corporate subsidies." Sider denounced Congress's 1995 proposals to "slash $380 billion dollars from programs for the poor and grant about $245 billion in tax cuts to the rich and middle class," for he insisted that "cutting funding for the poor in order to buy middle-class votes with a deficit-fueled tax cut blatantly defies biblical priorities."[38]

The battle over welfare reform in the mid-1990s produced progressive evangelicals' harshest rebukes of both Clinton and congressional Republicans. The Republican majority sought to dismantle social programs, which they believed were wasteful, encouraged dependency, and rewarded out-of-wedlock births. To be sure, progressive evangelical leaders agreed that reforms were needed, and they criticized most Democrats for simply defending a broken system. "The institutions of the welfare state have not resolved the crushing issues of poverty," Wallis acknowledged. "For too many, welfare has become not another chance but a way of life that results in dependency and despair." Sider concurred that "caring for the poor is not the same as simply endorsing the centralized, bureaucratic welfare programs of the last forty years" that were often "foolish" and "anti-family to boot." Yet politicians should seek *better* programs, they insisted, not merely abandon or gut existing ones. Leaders argued that Republican efforts to radically reduce social spending would punish the poor for the welfare system's failures and remove important (albeit imperfect) forms of assistance. *"It is absolutely immoral, from a Christian perspective, to slash and burn systems and safety nets without offering anything to replace them,"* Wallis exclaimed. Despite such criticism, Clinton signed the Republican-sponsored Personal Responsibility and Work Opportunity Reconciliation Act in 1996. The new law replaced the federal cash-assistance program with smaller grants to states, allowed states discretion in designing and operating programs, required recipients to find work within two years, limited lifetime benefits to five years, restricted eligibility for food stamps and nutrition programs, and ended many benefits for legal, noncitizen immigrants. Progressive evangelical leaders expressed outrage. "A great national sin has just been committed," Wallis declared. He berated Clinton for failing "the most serious moral test of his presidency" by signing a pernicious but popular bill in order to win reelection. The law may reduce welfare expenditures, evangelical progressives protested, but it would increase poverty by restricting benefits without expanding other programs that aided the poor in moving from welfare to work.[39]

Yet progressive evangelicals found a silver lining in the new legislation. As part of their own prescriptions for welfare reform, leaders had endorsed strategies in which the government partnered with private agencies—both religious and secular—that not only offered social services such as job training but also taught "the values and behaviors that translate into economic well-being." Indeed, Sider and others claimed, studies demonstrated that "rechanneling federal support through such mediating agencies could be less costly and far more effective" in relieving and preventing poverty. Therefore, despite other flaws in the 1996 welfare legislation, leaders embraced the inclusion of a "Charitable Choice" provision that allowed faith-based organizations to provide federally funded social services. Progressive evangelicals denied accusations that the provision violated the separation of church and state, for regulations precluded the use of funds for religious activities such as worship and proselytism and prohibited religious discrimination against beneficiaries. Working through Call to Renewal, a new ecumenical antipoverty group headed by Wallis, leaders began promoting the benefits of Charitable Choice to both state officials and religious social agencies. They also set aside ideological differences with conservatives regarding the government's responsibilities to combat poverty in order to find common ground in supporting Charitable Choice. For example, Sider and Republican senator Rick Santorum of Pennsylvania coauthored an article in which they agreed that "an effective response to poverty will be more than mere cash assistance—it will encourage choices and behavior that enable people to escape poverty." Because FBOs "nurture transformed people making choices that help them overcome poverty," they concluded, Charitable Choice has "the potential to be a powerful instrument to help empower the poor." While progressive evangelical leaders pushed for more government resources and better programs, they also championed Charitable Choice as a pragmatic, promising antipoverty initiative.[40]

At the turn of the century, both international and domestic poverty remained a primary concern in progressive evangelicals' political agenda. ESA and *Sojourners* enthusiastically promoted the global grassroots movement Jubilee 2000. Based upon the cancellation of debts during the Year of Jubilee prescribed in Leviticus 25—a passage central in progressive evangelicals' interpretation of economic justice—the campaign called for wealthy nations and international creditors to forgive the crippling debts of poor countries that hindered spending on education, health care, and other human needs. On the domestic front, the number of people in poverty dropped from 36.5 million in 1996 to 32.3 in 1999 during a period of economic growth. Yet millions remained impoverished, progressive evangelicals emphasized, and leaders highlighted troubling statistics: the poverty rate for blacks remained three times higher than for non-Hispanic whites; one in six children lived below the poverty line; and economic inequality had worsened. In the midst of the 2000 presidential election, therefore, Wallis, Sider, and others affiliated with Call to Renewal developed a new campaign to "put poverty on the national agenda." They encouraged Christians across the political spectrum to sign a "Covenant to Overcome Poverty" and to "evaluate public policies and political candidates by how they affect people who are poor." On behalf of Call to Renewal, Wallis published an open letter to Democratic candidate Al Gore and Republican candidate George W. Bush and thanked both for promising to enhance the work of FBOs. But he also challenged the election winner to lead the nation in mobilizing resources—both public and private—in order to reduce child poverty by half. "As you fulfill your commitments to increase partnerships between government and the faith community," he concluded, "we look forward to working with you."[41]

Despite this pledge, the working relationship between progressive evangelicals and President Bush soured quickly after his inauguration. Leaders initially praised Bush for establishing the Office of Faith-Based and Community Initiatives in order to expand social services provided by FBOs. Yet they professed increasing indignation at the perceived neglect of the poor caused by tax cuts for the wealthy and the costs of the "war on terror" after the 9/11 attacks. Sider condemned Bush's tax cuts as "outrageous and immoral." "Biblical principles of justice support a graduated, progressive tax system," he reiterated in 2001, but the president's proposals gave "40 percent of the total benefit to the richest 1 percent while the bottom 40 percent got a piddling 4 percent." Sider insisted that the poor "need a living wage, health insurance, educational opportunity, and social security, and all of that costs tax dollars that are rapidly disappearing as Bush gives one huge tax cut after another to a rich and tiny minority." Progressive evangelicals also renewed their protests that increased military spending diverts funds from social programs for the poor. In early 2003 Wallis anticipated the financial consequences of the impending invasion of Iraq. "The urgent need to overcome poverty, at home and around the world, will literally be pushed off the agenda in favor of the resources, attention, and priority that war demands," he declared. In light of America's costly military commitments in Afghanistan and Iraq, Wallis subsequently claimed, "the poor are also becoming war casualties."

Ultimately, progressive evangelicals charged that Bush's policies reversed God's special concern for the poor. "The administration's priorities are a disaster for the poor and a windfall for the wealthiest," Wallis argued, "and thus directly conflict with biblical priorities."[42]

As poverty rates rose during the remainder of Bush's two-term presidency, progressive evangelicals campaigned to make economic justice a political priority. During the 2004 election, leaders challenged Christian conservatives to view poverty as a nonpartisan "moral issue" as important as abortion and same-sex marriage. "We must show that people of faith are united in believing that 35 million people living in poverty is a moral and religious issue that our political debate must address," Wallis urged. Several prominent progressive evangelicals—including Wallis, Sider, community development leader John Perkins, and activist Shane Claiborne—were arrested as they protested in front of the U.S. Capitol against a proposed 2006 budget that expanded tax cuts and military funding but dramatically decreased social spending. "Do evangelical Christians really want to support tax cuts for millionaires paid for by cuts in food stamps, healthcare, housing vouchers, and nutritional programs for poor Americans?" Sider exclaimed. In articles and monographs—including Wallis's bestselling books *God's Politics* and *The Great Awakening* and updated editions of Sider's *Rich Christians in an Age of Hunger* and *Just Generosity*—leaders continued to report statistics and stories that illustrated the "scandal" of both domestic and global poverty. America's worsening recession in 2008 only reinforced their commitment to prioritize economic justice. During that year's election, Sojourners sponsored a "Vote Out Poverty" campaign to guide Christians' participation. Both Wallis and Sider criticized Republican John McCain for supporting many of Bush's economic policies but commended Democratic nominee Barack Obama for his pledges to repeal tax cuts for the wealthy, to achieve universal health care, and to double foreign aid. "It is time to lift up practical policies and practices that help the poor escape their poverty and clearly challenge the increasing wealth gap between rich and poor," Wallis declared again in 2008. To progressive evangelicals, the crusade to promote economic justice represented a perennial part of Christians' public discipleship.[43]

"BUDGETS ARE MORAL DOCUMENTS"

Progressive evangelical leaders viewed economic debates as theological disputes. Their theology of liberation led them to insist that particular types of public policies and redistributive programs—ones that provide for the destitute, enable substantively equal opportunities, and reduce gross inequalities in wealth and power—best embody biblical principles for economic justice. As a result, evangelical progressives defended their policy prescriptions with moral conviction. To be sure, some leaders, especially Ron Sider, periodically acknowledged the difference between affirming biblical principles and agreeing upon how to implement them. "We must constantly remember the large gulf between revealed principles and contemporary application," claimed Sider in each edition of *Rich Christians in an Age of Hunger*. "Objecting to my application of biblical ethics to contemporary society is not at all the same as rejecting biblical principles." Although not "all applications are equally valid," he wrote, Christians should show "humility and tolerance" as they develop and debate specific proposals. Yet most progressive evangelical leaders displayed little tolerance for economic programs that flouted what they regarded as clear biblical principles. They insisted that God expects the government, not only individuals and churches, to play a vital role in caring for and empowering the poor. Therefore, leaders refused to treat conservatives' commitment to help the poor almost exclusively through private charity as a prudential disagreement regarding how best to reduce poverty. Instead, they denounced opposition to redistributive public policies and substantial social spending as unbiblical and sinful. In the midst of heated economic debates, progressive evangelical leaders regularly accused Republicans and the Religious Right of ignorantly disobeying or immorally defying God's command to seek justice for the poor.[44]

Over and over, progressive evangelicals used theological terms to condemn combinations of social spending cuts, lower taxes on the rich and corporations, and increased military budgets. For example, in the early 1980s Jim Wallis castigated the Religious Right for ignoring a "radical social vision rooted in the Bible's concern for the poor" in their support of "tax breaks for the middle class and big corporations, as well as increased military spending and budget balancing by cutting the amount of public resources allocated for the poor." In 1984 *The Other Side*'s John Alexander urged Christians to vote against political candidates who disregarded clear biblical guidelines. "If they give tax cuts to the rich and benefit cuts to the poor, they are violating a basic Christian principle and must be put out of office," he wrote in an implicit rebuke of Ronald Reagan. Because the Hebrew prophets' condemnations of economic injustice shaped progressive evangelicals' theology of liberation, leaders invoked them as allies. *Sojourners'* Danny Collum criticized Reagan's policies by imagining "the rage of the prophet Amos at the prospect of $60 billion in corporate tax cuts paid for by cutting infant nutrition programs" and "the weeping of Micah and Isaiah at our country's $300 billion military budget" while millions starved worldwide. A decade later, Sider similarly argued that the efforts of congressional Republicans to slash successful social programs while cutting taxes on the rich "would make Amos and Isaiah weep and rage" because they represented "blatant, sinful defiance of the God of the Bible." Likewise, Wallis claimed that Amos and Isaiah would have protested President George W. Bush's tax policies by "screaming on the White House lawn about the justice of God." Christian conservatives likely chafed at such moralistic certainty regarding how the Hebrew prophets would evaluate modern levels of social spending, tax rates, and military expenses by a democratic, industrialized nation. Yet progressive evangelical leaders remained confident that their preferred policies represented the best applications of biblical principles.[45]

No slogan better revealed the theological enterprise at the heart of progressive evangelicals' economic analyses than their frequent claim that "budgets are moral documents." Leaders interpreted fiscal decisions as ethical choices that reflect the priorities and values of those who design budgets. Because God expects political leaders and governments to foster economic justice, they concluded, budgets must prioritize robust funding for the poor in order to be moral. While progressive evangelicals had implicitly used this standard from the beginning of their movement, Wallis introduced it explicitly in the mid-1990s. He labeled as immoral the budget proposals by congressional Republicans that lowered income and corporate taxes, increased military spending, and severely reduced funds for social programs. "A budget is also a moral document," Wallis declared. "The morality of further benefiting the rich while balancing the budget on the backs of the poor, the young, and the old is simply unacceptable from a Christian point of view." Progressive evangelical leaders began proclaiming that "budgets are moral documents" as part of their advocacy for greater public funding of antipoverty initiatives, and they especially made the slogan central to their criticism of President George W. Bush's policies. "Paying for war by cutting needed spending for the poor while giving unneeded tax cuts to the rich is morally unconscionable," Wallis insisted in response to Bush's 2004 proposed budget. "Let me say this again in my clearest evangelical language: this federal budget is unbiblical." Sider echoed this judgment two years later. God "demands that rulers seek justice for the poor," he proclaimed, and "every budget is a moral document." Yet Bush's 2006 budget again reduced taxes on the wealthy, expanded military spending, and cut social programs. "Does God really want poor Americans to bear the burden of paying for the war in Iraq and balancing the federal budget?" Sider demanded. In measuring morality by allocation of dollars, progressive evangelicals reduced complex analyses of government spending—that is, the rationale behind, impact of, and relationship between diverse allocations—to a simple but rhetorically powerful theological formula.[46]

By insisting that Christians must seek justice for both the domestic and global poor, progressive evangelicals made their theology of liberation a central plank in their public theology of community. Leaders believed that the suffering caused by poverty represented an affront to the dignity and equality that each person possesses as a bearer of the *imago Dei*. Since "the radical assertion of the image of God in every human being lies at the heart of our best religious traditions," Wallis wrote, we should "fashion a global economy and conduct our politics as if every human being had equal and sacred value." They repeatedly argued that Christians must enter into relationships with the poor, properly recognize them as fellow community members, and fulfill their communal responsibilities to meet their needs and to enable their equal economic opportunities. "Most of the biblical insights about overcoming poverty seem to have to do with inclusion, bringing people into the community and incorporating their needs into the common life," stated Wallis. *Sojourners'* Danny Collum argued that the biblical theme of community—which emphasizes the common good, or "the collective well-being of the entire people"—could help counteract many consequences of capitalism that produced economic injustice. "The need for community and interdependence can be a powerful force for countering an economic direction that places corporate profit before people, families, and neighborhoods and fosters growing inequality," he claimed. In order to ensure the common good, progressive evangelicals defended the role of public policies and programs in ensuring the just distribution of socioeconomic resources. "Governmental action to empower the poor is one way we promote the common good," Sider claimed. "A theology of distributive justice grounded in scripture" emphasizes "structural arrangements that guarantee the basic needs for life in community." Writing in *Sojourners*, Richard Taylor summarized the biblical themes that inspired both the broader public theology and the specific vision for economic justice of progressive evangelicals: "the sacred dignity of the human person, the prophets' passionate protest against exploitation and injustice, concern for the poor, working for the common good, and building institutions to serve human needs and liberate human capacities."[47]

Of course, the building of such institutions to advance economic justice requires money—and evangelical progressives believed that they knew the best place to find it. Throughout the course of their crusade against poverty, they again and again argued that reductions in the military budget would enable robust social spending. To leaders, the grossly higher levels of spending on the military rather than helping the poor revealed America's immoral priorities. *Sojourners* quoted from Martin Luther King Jr.'s 1967 speech "Beyond Vietnam" as a prophetic warning: "A nation that continues year after year to spend more money on military defense than on programs of social uplift is approaching spiritual death." But, as the next chapter demonstrates, progressive evangelicals did not denounce the military budget only for its effects on the poor. As advocates for peacemaking, they also condemned America's nationalistic militarism for perpetuating violence and oppression in other countries throughout the world.[48]

8. Make Peace, Not War

"Vietnam. The word still sparks deep emotion within me," Sojourners' Jim Wallis wrote in 1980. Five years after the Vietnam War ended, Wallis recounted how it became the prism through which progressive evangelicals viewed American foreign policy. "The war was a tutor to me and many others," he explained, for the United States' policies and practices seemingly laid bare the country's hypocrisy and imperialism. "Many were convinced we were fighting against communism," but "this was not a war for democracy or freedom or self-determination," Wallis claimed. Instead, the war unmasked "a large and powerful nation trying to impose its control over the destiny of a small and weak nation" as demonstrated by America's ruthless intervention. "We installed and maintained a succession of corrupt and brutal dictators as our client regimes," "killed two million" Vietnamese, and "turned 12 million more into refugees, devastated their land, and corrupted their culture," Wallis stated. By 1980 most Americans wanted to leave behind the Vietnam War as a tragic mistake in the otherwise honorable ongoing Cold War against communism. Yet Wallis believed that Americans must never forget their country's depravity. "It was illegal and immoral to seek to control the destiny of Vietnam," he declared. "In biblical perspective it was a sin, a national act of selfish cruelty." Wallis criticized human rights abuses by the victorious Vietnamese communists, but he also insisted that American Christians "apply a single standard of judgment to all governments"—including their own. And by the standard of respect for the lives, rights, and self-determination of *all* people, he concluded, the United States deserved denunciation. "The sin of Vietnam is still with us," Wallis concluded. "Our foreign policy continues to be based on the desire to control the political economies of other nations."[1]

Wallis's editorial exemplified how progressive evangelicals consistently challenged American nationalism and militarism from the early 1970s through the United States' "war on terror" in the early twenty-first century. Disillusioned by the Vietnam War, leaders opposed America's apparent arrogance and aggression during the final phases of the Cold War. They criticized the United States for hypocritically supporting anticommunist yet repressive regimes in developing countries. The evangelical left also denounced America's nuclear arms buildup as a jingoistic, immoral strategy. As Ronald Reagan declared that the threat of communism justified military incursions in Central America in the 1980s, leaders organized protests and direct action campaigns against what seemed further examples of the United States' imperial interventions. While the Religious Right enthusiastically supported Cold War militarism as a necessary part of America's divinely ordained mission to defend freedom and democracy, progressive evangelical leaders charged *both* the United States and the Soviet Union with using coercive measures and violent means to secure their interests at the cost of human rights.

Although they welcomed the fall of communism, evangelical progressives wanted the United States to use its unrivaled power and influence in the post-Cold War era to promote justice worldwide rather than to fulfill selfish ambitions. Leaders especially repeated their long-standing conviction that America should press for peace in the Middle East by helping resolve the Israeli-Palestinian conflict. Sympathetic to Palestinian grievances, they reiterated calls for the United States to persuade its ally Israel to withdraw from occupied territories and to recognize a Palestinian state. But the Gulf War of 1991 convinced progressive evangelicals that America remained more concerned for its own geopolitical interests—especially access to affordable Middle Eastern oil—than to justice and international partnerships. After unsuccessfully trying to prevent the invasion of Iraq, leaders feared that America's swift and decisive victory would inspire the use of military might and unilateral actions to enforce a "Pax Americana"—a self-interested and coercive peace. These concerns arose with new urgency after the terrorist attacks of September 11, 2001. Progressive evangelicals unequivocally condemned the acts as evil. But they also objected to the militaristic and indiscriminate "war on terror" pursued by the administration of President George W. Bush. Instead, they argued for both multilateral efforts to bring terrorists to justice under international law and alternative strategies to undermine terrorist networks. Heralding such policies as the best solution to the ongoing threat posed by Iraqi president Saddam Hussein, Jim Wallis and other leaders criticized the Iraq War as unjust and subsequent American occupation as impracticable and immoral.

Progressive evangelicals' opposition to American nationalism and militarism stemmed from key principles in their public theology and straightforward interpretations of biblical commands to love one's neighbor, to love one's enemies, and to make peace. Nationalism exalted the welfare of one's own country and people, they argued, thus preventing Christians from fulfilling their responsibilities to promote the common good of *all* their neighbors in the global community. The leadership of *Sojourners*, Evangelicals for Social Action (ESA), and *The Other Side* also concluded that biblical teachings on nonviolence and love for enemies should guide Christians' public engagement and not only their personal actions. As a result, these pacifist progressive evangelicals protested the lethal nature of militaristic policies and warfare. While others within the evangelical left accepted the legitimacy of just wars, politically progressive evangelicals united in their commitment to the public task of active peacemaking. Pacifist leaders promoted various forms of "nonviolent resistance" as faithful and effective strategies for confronting evil and making peace. The conviction that peace and justice represented intertwined goals stood at the heart of the contemporary progressive evangelical movement.

PROTESTING THE COLD WAR

Opposition to the Vietnam War and disillusionment with the United States played a galvanizing role in the rise of the contemporary progressive evangelicalism. Originally naming their publication the *Post-American*, Wallis and others who founded the magazine that became *Sojourners* drew upon the analyses and rhetoric of the New Left in composing damning critiques of America's apparent imperialism. "The government's policy of genocide in Southeast Asia is symptomatic of its economic, military, and political exploitation throughout the world," Wallis wrote in early 1972. "American intervention in the Third World on the side of repressive regimes serves to block change and make the world safe, not for democracy but for American business." Frustrated by President Richard Nixon's prosecution of the war and proclamations of America's superiority, a cadre of early leaders formed Evangelicals for McGovern during the 1972 election and championed the Democratic candidate's commitment to ending the Vietnam War. In the early manifesto of the progressive evangelical movement—the 1973 Chicago Declaration of Evangelical Social Concern—signers rejected "a national pathology of war and violence which victimizes our neighbors at home and abroad." They also urged fellow evangelicals to "resist the temptation to make the nation and its institutions objects of near-religious loyalty." Ultimately, resistance to the Vietnam War forged progressive evangelicals' resolve to challenge perceived abuses of American power. "When our own nation is a principal actor and causal agent in creating destruction, killing, and suffering," Wallis wrote in 1975, "then we have to act against the policies of the government."[2]

The war convinced many in the evangelical left that a fundamental tension existed between being faithful Christians and being loyal, patriotic members of any nation—including the United States. "What Vietnam has taught the Christian is that allegiance to country often involves disobedience to God" and "that the basic governing principles of citizenship in the secular society and citizenship in the Kingdom of God are mutually exclusive," Post-American Bill Lane claimed. Influenced by Anabaptist contributors such as theologian John Howard Yoder and activist Art Gish, *Post-American* authors especially urged evangelicals to embrace a distinct, countercultural identity. They wanted audiences to recognize America's unjust policies rather than accept "the comfortable notion that their nation acts out of righteous or, at worse, mistaken motivations." Wallis argued that "being separate from the world—a break with the prevailing idolatries and mythologies of American life and society—is a necessary part of responsible political action." For the Post-Americans, leftist analyses of American imperialism reinforced their sense of religious alienation from the United States. They cited books such as William Appleman Williams's *The Tragedy of American Diplomacy*, Gabriel Kolko's *The Roots of American Foreign Policy*, and *Roots of War* by future contributing editor Richard Barnet in describing America's responsibility for many global conflicts and injustices. The denouement of the Vietnam War seemed to validate these judgments. "Not to face up to the violence and injustice of the role of American power in the world is not to have learned anything from Vietnam," Wallis declared. Thus early progressive evangelical leaders came to expect that their foundational Christian commitments to peace and justice would consistently run counter to the United States' bellicose foreign policies.[3]

In contrast, the Vietnam War did little to dampen most evangelicals' patriotic support for Cold War militarism. Standing within a long tradition of viewing the United States as a "redeemer nation," they commonly portrayed America as providentially chosen to spread and to defend the blessings of liberty and democracy. Such confidence in America's righteous role in world politics stemmed in part from conservative evangelicals' belief that the United States had been founded as a "Christian nation." In the 1970s, books such as Peter Marshall and David Manuel's *The Light and the Glory* and conservative Christian leaders popularized accounts of Christianity's influence upon America's foundational events and the Founding Fathers' personal lives. "Any diligent student of American history finds that our great nation was founded by godly men upon godly principles to be a Christian nation" with "a special destiny in the world," Moral Majority leader Jerry Falwell proclaimed. Since the mid-twentieth century, this destiny seemed most manifest in America's resistance to "godless communism." Evangelicals had championed aggressive Cold War policies from the conflict's beginning, for they interpreted it as an ideological clash between Christianity and Marxist atheism. "Either communism must die, or Christianity must die," evangelist Billy Graham declared in the 1950s. Therefore, most evangelicals believed, in order to defend the Christian ideals of political and religious freedom against the totalitarian threat of communism, the United States was justified in fighting proxy wars in Korea and Vietnam, intervening in developing nations to buttress anticommunist regimes, and maintaining superiority in the Cold War arms race. After Vietnam, conservative evangelicals acknowledged their country's imperfections but still praised American power as the world's greatest force for freedom. As the Religious Right gained prominence in the late 1970s, its leaders elevated patriotic nationalism to an article of faith. "I love America because she, above all nations of the world, has honored the principles of the Bible," Falwell declared in 1980. "America has been great because she has been good."[4]

Progressive evangelicals repudiated the tendency among evangelicals to merge Christian faith and American allegiance. The Post-Americans chose their magazine's name as a protest against what they regarded as "the disastrous equation of the American way of life and the Christian way of life." Writing in *The Other Side*, Ron Sider rebuked the National Association of Evangelicals for blurring "the distinction between the people of God and the citizens of the United States" when its convention combined "patriotic, nationalistic songs" with Christian hymns and wove together scripture and history in support of American exceptionalism. As many evangelicals celebrated the nation's bicentennial in 1976 and Jerry Falwell conducted "I Love America" rallies nationwide, *Sojourners'* Wes Michaelson warned against the idolatrous "worship of American nationalism." Christians must recognize how "America has systematically attempted to crush the 'life and liberty' of people both at home and abroad who have resisted its dominant interests and threatened its structures of power," he claimed, and pray for "a spiritual detachment from the destiny of their nation." After Religious Right leaders gained national attention for helping boost Ronald Reagan's election in 1980, Jim Wallis disowned them as "evangelical nationalists." Their "religious vision of zealous nationalism" has "all but destroyed the integrity of the term evangelical," he complained. "The evangelical nationalists are perpetuating a theology of empire" that baptizes America's "global system of economic and political domination." Thus progressive evangelicals' withering analyses of the United States and its global influence estranged them from Christian conservatives.[5]

In the wake of the Vietnam War, progressive evangelical leaders turned much of their criticism upon America's support for repressive foreign regimes. They decried how the United States overlooked gross abuses of human rights in other countries in order to preserve both its economic dominance and Cold War containment of communism. In a unique collaborative effort in 1976, for example, *The Other Side* and newly renamed *Sojourners* jointly published accounts of torture in allied nations such as Brazil, Uruguay, Chile, the Philippines, Iran, and South Korea. "When put to the test," claimed *Sojourners'* Wes Michaelson, "the United States regularly allows its political and economic interests to override any concern for how governments are treating their citizens." Although they appreciated President Jimmy Carter's commitment—based upon his own Christian faith—to aligning America's foreign policy with its democratic ideals, progressive evangelicals initially criticized his administration for increasing economic and military aid to "key American fiefdoms" such as the Philippines and South Korea "where human rights are crushed with impunity." On occasion *Sojourners* and *The Other Side* acknowledged the oppressive practices and conditions of the Soviet Union and other communist states. Yet, as Michaelson wrote, leaders sought "to draw the attention of concerned Christians in America particularly to repression in those nations in which the United States weaves its web through protective economic, military, and diplomatic relationships" in order to disabuse audiences of uncritical patriotism and to inspire protests against American complicity in such practices.[6]

At times, progressive evangelical leaders even held the United States partly responsible for provoking revolutions, humanitarian crises, and repressive policies in places such as Cambodia, Vietnam, and Iran. To be sure, they denounced the Khmer Rouge in Cambodia for its mass killings, Vietnamese communists for committing human rights violations, and the new Islamic leaders of Iran for their executions and taking of American hostages. Yet in each of these countries, they argued, America's unjust intervention and backing of the previous tyrannical government precipitated these violent backlashes. During the Iranian hostage crisis in 1980, for example, Wallis criticized the inexcusable captivity of the hostages and demanded that "their safety and release must remain a central priority." At the same time, he and John Alexander each insisted that American leaders should confess that Iranians had just grievances against the United States. "What if we asked the Iranian people to forgive us," Wallis asked, "for installing and maintaining the shah, for interfering in their country," and "for equipping and training the police that tortured and killed them?" The United States, progressive evangelicals continued to declare, must repent of its oppressive, self-interested foreign policies.[7]

The evangelical left considered America's nuclear arms buildup one of its most egregious offenses. Despite a détente between the United States and the Soviet Union during most of the 1970s, both superpowers expanded their nuclear arsenals. Hawkish advisers persuaded Presidents Gerald Ford and Carter that America's security and global interests even required the willingness to use nuclear weapons first. In response, progressive evangelicals began conspicuous campaigns to convince Christians to oppose the nuclear arms race. While "resistance to the military aggression of nation-states is always a Christian responsibility," Wallis declared in 1977, "the fact that world rulers are now marching us all into nuclear oblivion makes Christian resistance to that insanity an imperative." Leaders rejected pragmatic arguments that Soviet capabilities warranted America's nuclear readiness. "A biblical view does not justify one nation's possession of nuclear weapons because of another's," wrote Wes Michaelson. "To plan and prepare for the destruction of millions of lives is an abomination in the eyes of the Lord for any group, at any time, for any reason." In 1978 *Sojourners* issued a declaration—endorsed by leaders across the evangelical left, mainline Protestants, and Catholic peace activists such as Dorothy Day and the Berrigan brothers—that described America's nuclear weapons not as tools "for a righteous purpose, for peace and self-defense," but as a means "for protecting our wealth and power in a global order that is fundamentally unjust." Ultimately, the signers insisted, Christians' "primary allegiance to Jesus Christ and his kingdom commits us to total abolition of nuclear weapons." A year later, *Sojourners* persuaded Billy Graham, whom editors had previously criticized for endorsing American militarism, to describe in an interview his recent repudiation of nuclear arms. For progressive evangelicals, the absolutist slogan "It's a sin to build a nuclear weapon" encapsulated their objections. "No matter what," Wallis stated in 1980, "preparing to annihilate millions of people is wrong."[8]

Leaders encouraged Christians to oppose the nuclear arms race through prayers, protests, and practical financial resistance. *Sojourners* regularly condemned support for nuclear weapons as idolatrous trust in America's military strength. But through prayer, Wallis argued, Christians remember and proclaim that true security comes only through the victory of Christ over evil. "Given the enormity of the nuclear danger," he wrote, "let us give ourselves to a renewal of prayer" in order to "deepen our identity as peacemakers." Strengthened by such religious resolve, progressive evangelicals organized vigils and protests, and they joined groups such as the Fellowship of Reconciliation in broader antinuclear rallies. In May 1978, for example, members of Sojourners demonstrated outside both the United Nations in New York and a nuclear weapons plant in Colorado. A year later, Sojourners hosted a Memorial Day service of "prayer and worship to confront the idolatry of nuclear weapons," and in September the group protested outside a nuclear weapons exposition in Washington, D.C. As a financial form of protest, both *Sojourners* and *The Other Side* also promoted war tax resistance. The government uses tax revenue "to underwrite military destruction" and preparations for war, Wallis charged, and thus Christians face "a dilemma in which peace claims our commitment but war claims our money." *Sojourners* devoted two issues—March 1977 and February 1979—and numerous other articles to exploring theological justifications for tax resistance and practical strategies such as keeping income below the taxable threshold, withholding the percentage of taxes used for military purposes, or even refusing to pay all federal taxes. Despite "pressure and intimidation" from the IRS, publisher Joe Roos wrote in 1979, Sojourners members defended their own tax resistance as "a vigorous 'no' to global preparation for nuclear holocaust."[9]

Progressive evangelicals' antinuclear activism intensified in the early 1980s as President Ronald Reagan escalated the Cold War arms race. Promising "peace through strength," Reagan increased defense spending by 34 percent in his first term; launched the costly Strategic Defense Initiative, a space-based antimissile system that critics derided as "Star Wars"; and sought to intimidate the "evil empire" of the Soviet Union. Religious Right leaders and even the moderate National Association for Evangelicals enthusiastically supported Reagan's nuclear policies. In turn, progressive evangelicals joined other peace activists in voicing their opposition to nuclear weapons with even more vigor. *The Other Side* and especially *Sojourners* published article after article that decried the nuclear arms race. Wallis edited two books devoted to building a grassroots movement of Christian peacemakers against nuclear bombs. ESA president Ron Sider and board member Richard Taylor coauthored *Nuclear Holocaust and Christian Hope* in which they argued that nuclear weapons' massive, indiscriminate destructiveness should cause even just war advocates to become nuclear pacifists. Leaders also promoted and participated in protests such as ongoing tax resistance, symbolic acts of civil disobedience, and demonstrations at nuclear testing sites. In 1983 prominent members of the evangelical left helped organize a conference, "The Church and Peacemaking in a Nuclear Age," at which they condemned nuclear weapons as immoral. While supportive of the broader nuclear freeze movement, progressive evangelicals advocated the more ambitious goal of disarmament. Sojourners and ESA inaugurated similar campaigns that encouraged Christians to "covenant together to abolish nuclear weapons as an urgent matter of faith." By the mid-1980s leaders of both groups also began promoting opposition to nuclear arms—with their potential to kill more people more quickly than ever—as necessarily part of a "completely pro-life" agenda.[10]

Based upon America's interventionist foreign policies and militarism throughout the 1970s and early 1980s, progressive evangelical leaders often portrayed the United States and the Soviet Union as equally unjust. The Cold War was not a clear contest between democratic defenders of freedom and evil communists, they declared, but rather a power struggle between similarly oppressive empires. The "two superpowers" attempt "to shape the world in their own image, each accusing the other of doing what they themselves are doing," Wallis claimed. "Both use the other's [nuclear arms] escalations as the justification for their own"; "neither cares much for freedom, for truth or for peace"; and "each pursues its own self-interest through manipulations, violence, and power politics, then arrogantly pro-claims its cause as righteous." Leaders chided those who denounced the Soviet Union's totalitarianism but ignored injustices committed by the United States. John Alexander agreed that "the history of the Soviet Union is appalling," but he also highlighted America's own sordid record by cit-ing atrocities in Vietnam, support for dictators, and other "repression in-flicted on the third world." When the Soviet Union invaded Afghanistan in 1979, progressive evangelicals decried the attack but dismissed the United States' condemnation as hypocritical. "How can the U.S. take the lead" in opposing Soviet aggression when "we have invaded more third world countries than it is easy to count?" Alexander asked. *Sojourners'* Danny Collum acknowledged that "the USSR is an imperialist power that subjugates the basic rights and needs of other peoples to its own real or imagined security needs, economic self-interest, and lust for power." But, he declared, "moral outrage at Soviet imperialism has been used to blind us to the United States' very similar actions in Iran, Vietnam, Chile and El Salvador." Indeed, progressive evangelicals began arguing in the early 1980s, the United States' increasing interventions in Central America were demonstrating America's imperial instincts once again.[11]

IMPERIAL INTERVENTION IN AMERICA'S "BACKYARD"

As civil conflicts and guerrilla wars beset several Central American na-tions in the 1980s, President Reagan and his advisers viewed the region as a Cold War battleground. In 1979 the left-wing Sandinista National Lib-eration Front in Nicaragua overthrew the brutal dictatorship of Anastasio Somoza, a West Point graduate whose family had ruled for over forty years with American backing. Establishing ties with both the Soviet Union and Cuba, the Sandinistas also encouraged the leftist Farabundo Martí Front for National Liberation (FMLN) fighting against the violently repressive, pro-American government in neighboring El Salvador. Anxious to reas-sert the United States' power in the aftermath of Vietnam—and blaming the USSR for fomenting these revolutions in America's "backyard"—the Reagan administration became obsessed with stopping the spread of com-munism in the Western Hemisphere. "Central America is the most im-portant place in the world for the United States today," declared United Nations ambassador Jeane Kirkpatrick in 1981. Reagan, CIA director Wil-liam Casey, and other leaders viewed the Sandinistas and FMLN rebels as treacherous, totalitarian Marxist-Leninists. Therefore, they not only

supported overt military force rather than negotiations but also justified covert and even unauthorized operations to eradicate the threat of
communism in Central America. In order to avoid public outcry and congressional opposition, the Reagan administration limited America's involvement to strengthening anticommunist governments and guerrillas
through economic aid, training troops, deploying small numbers of special
forces, and providing clandestine military assistance. In El Salvador, the
United States increased financial support for the right-wing government
while training and equipping its military groups. In Nicaragua, Reagan authorized the CIA and National Security Council to organize and to assist
counterrevolutionaries—or "Contras"—to overthrow the Sandinista government. Despite increasing evidence that Salvadoran government forces
and the Contras were routinely assassinating opponents and torturing
civilians, Reagan referred to them as "freedom fighters" and even (in the
Contras' case) "the moral equal of our Founding Fathers."[12]

Already cynical regarding the United States' motives and militarism,
progressive evangelicals dismissed Reagan's portrayal of the problems in
Central America as a Cold War morality play. Leaders insisted that, along
with long-standing socioeconomic inequality in the region, America's
past and present interventions—not communist expansionism—were
primarily fueling the political unrest and violence. As Central America
moved to the forefront of progressive evangelicals' concerns in the early
1980s, *Sojourners* and *The Other Side* repeatedly highlighted the United
States' long record of military invasions and political impositions in the
region. These interventions included the "lusty colonial power play" of
seizing control of the Panama Canal; the establishment of the Somoza
dictatorship in Nicaragua; the 1954 CIA-planned coup in Guatemala; the
1965 invasion of the Dominican Republic in the name of anticommunism;
and the decades-long backing of El Salvador's repressive regime. "Since
[the Spanish-American War of] 1898, the countries of Central America
and the Caribbean have had their existence defined in terms of U.S. interests rather than their own," *Sojourners'* Danny Collum declared. By sup-
plying "hundreds of millions of dollars in military aid" to "dictatorial regimes," progressive evangelicals argued, America created or compounded
what Jim Wallis identified as the true roots of the region's problems: "the
grinding poverty of the majority of people, the control of the country by
an elite of wealthy landowners, and the reign of terror being carried out
by the military to enforce the rule of the few over the many." Thus leaders countered arguments that communists bore primarily responsibility

for the recent violence. "The United States is the largest offender in the import of weapons and military aid into the region and the primary ally of terrorism, carried out by right-wing governments," Joyce Hollyday wrote in *Sojourners*. While the Reagan administration invoked the "specters of communism," she argued, "a search for the source of Central America's brutality eventually takes us home, to the doorsteps of the White House, the Capitol, the Department of State, and the Pentagon."[13]

Progressive evangelical leaders initially focused on the United States' complicity in El Salvador's violence. In a wave of articles beginning in 1980, *Sojourners* and *The Other Side* recounted stories and statistics of atrocities committed by American-supported Salvadoran troops. After the newly inaugurated President Reagan increased aid to the right-wing government—despite the murders of Archbishop Oscar Romero, numerous political opponents, four female American Catholic missionaries, and over 10,000 civilians in 1980 alone—over fifty prominent leaders of the evangelical left issued "An Evangelical Response to El Salvador." Printed in *Sojourners*, the statement decried that "U.S. weapons are being used by the Salvadoran military to persecute the poor" through "terror, torture, rape, and mutilation." Signers rebutted the Reagan administration's efforts to blame communists for the violence and "to depict the Salvadoran regime as a moderate government force committed to reform," and they called "upon our government to suspend all military aid and refrain from any further intervention in El Salvador." Despite these protests, American aid to the country grew. Meeting a congressional condition, the Reagan administration began to certify twice a year that the Salvadoran government was improving its human rights record—claims that progressive evangelical leaders repeatedly disputed. Wallis cited Amnesty International reports of "sadistic, demonic violence" carried out "by the forces receiving military aid and political support from the United States." A doctor who spent a year in El Salvador testified in *The Other Side* to "war crimes" committed by government troops. "I am amazed that Congress continues to silently listen to those certifications every six months while thousands are being killed by U.S. arms," he wrote. In 1983 Reagan pushed Congress for more funding by contending that "we cannot turn our backs" on the purported democracy emerging in El Salvador. Yet the president seemed quite willing, Hollyday retorted, "to turn his back on the 30,000 Salvadorans killed by government security forces in the last three years."[14]

As details of Reagan's funding of the Contras emerged in 1982, progressive evangelicals quickly made opposition to the United States' "low-intensity" war against Nicaragua one of their foremost causes. The president justified his actions by maligning the Sandinistas as "Marxist-Leninist bands" who were denying democratic rights, exacerbating poverty, and arming the leftist guerrillas in El Salvador. Progressive evangelical leaders rejected these charges as part of an "extensive propaganda campaign." On the invitation of Nicaragua's Evangelical Committee for Aid and Development (CEPAD), Wallis, Hollyday, Ron Sider, and several other evangelical leaders traveled to the country in 1982 and met with both religious and political leaders, including Sandinista head Daniel Ortega. The Sandinistas did embrace socialism, they reported, but the majority were not totalitarian Marxist-Leninists. The new government appeared in the process of vastly improving Nicaraguans' welfare and held widespread popular support. Not least, progressive evangelicals declared, the Reagan administration had failed to produce credible evidence that the Sandinistas were providing substantial weaponry to Salvadoran rebels. "Ronald Reagan is lying about Nicaragua," *Sojourners* bluntly proclaimed on its cover. To be sure, leaders criticized the Sandinistas' treatment of the Miskito Indian minority, press censorship, initial tolerance of church seizures, and delayed elections. Nevertheless, they insisted that American efforts to sabotage the Sandinista government by supporting the Contras represented an imperialistic attack on Nicaragua's sovereignty. "What gives you the right to intervene in the affairs of another country and seek to overthrow its government?" Wallis asked in an open letter to Reagan. Hollyday called the president hypocritical. "While accusing the Soviet Union and Cuba of intervention in Central America," she wrote, "the Reagan administration is perpetuating massive interference in a legitimate government and plotting its demise."[15]

Reagan ignored such concerns. Throughout 1983, his administration escalated support for the Contras, attacked Nicaragua's economy through more sanctions, conducted military exercises in neighboring Honduras to intimidate the Sandinistas, and authorized the invasion and overthrow of the procommunist government of Grenada to indicate the United States' willingness to use direct military force. In turn, progressive evangelical leaders intensified their criticism and helped develop two national campaigns—Witness for Peace and the Pledge of Resistance—to protest Reagan's Central American policies.[16]

Witness for Peace mobilized delegations of activists who traveled to Nicaragua to thwart attacks by the U.S-backed Contras. This direct action campaign grew out of the experiences of American Christians who recognized during previous visits that Contra forces did not attack towns in which they were present. Progressive evangelical leaders were crucial in establishing and promoting Witness for Peace. Sojourners' Wallis and Hollyday helped organize and promote the group, while ESA's Sider and Vernon Grounds served as initial advisers. Wallis drafted Witness for Peace's statement of purpose that committed participants to "stand with the Nicaraguan people by acting in continuous nonviolent resistance to U.S. policy" and "to mobilize public opinion and help change U.S. foreign policy." Leaders drew upon their relationships with Nicaraguan religious groups, especially CEPAD, to coordinate activities in the country. In December 1983 Wallis and Hollyday traveled with the first delegation, while Sider visited a year later. *Sojourners* and *The Other Side* published reports from these trips in addition to other firsthand accounts of the Contras' terrorist acts and brave resolve of the Nicaraguan people. Beyond offering their bodies as human "shields of love," Witness for Peace also captured the attention of national news media. Major newspapers, magazines, and even television networks reported on their peacemaking efforts and relied upon their accounts of CIA-directed Contra attacks. Progressive evangelicals helped Witness for Peace grow into an influential grassroots organization that sent over 4,000 delegates to Nicaragua, mailed newsletters to 40,000 readers, and contacted over a million people in its fund-raising efforts.[17]

Sojourners also played a primary role in the Pledge of Resistance, a campaign that inspired tens of thousands of Americans to join protests against Reagan's policies in Central America. At a retreat with other Christian activists just after the 1983 American invasion of Grenada, Sojourners' Wallis and Jim Rice drafted a statement in which many attendees promised "to initiate and support demonstrations of public opposition to any invasion attempt" in Nicaragua—an event they feared as imminent. Momentum for this contingency plan spread among religious and peace organizations, and leaders established regional contacts and a communications network coordinated by Sojourners and Witness for Peace offices. In mid-1984 *Sojourners* published more detailed plans for "a credible and coordinated plan of massive public resistance" in order to "prevent a direct U.S. invasion of Nicaragua or to make such military action so politically costly it will have to be halted." By 1985 more than 50,000 people had signed the Pledge of Resistance through the efforts of a growing national campaign, and leaders broadened their plans to oppose any military escalation in Central America. After the Reagan administration implemented a full trade embargo of Nicaragua and Congress passed a $27 million aid package for the Contras in June, pledge protests occurred in hundreds of American cities and resulted in over 2,000 arrests for civil disobedience. Over the next two years, the number of pledge signers grew to 80,000. Activists participated in thousands of demonstrations and vigils that included occupying congressional offices, blocking military bases and arms shipments, conducting dramatized funerals for Central American victims, running "Stop the Lies" advertising campaigns, and organizing 100,000 protesters in April 1987 to march for peace in Washington, D.C. Combined with their antinuclear activism, progressive evangelicals' leadership and participation in the Pledge of Resistance and Witness for Peace made them significant contributors to the American peace movement in the final decade of the Cold War.[18]

At the same time, these campaigns demonstrated how progressive evangelicals' activism routinely clashed with both the Religious Right and the political left. On the one hand, opposition to American intervention in Central America put them at odds with Christian conservatives who enthusiastically backed Reagan's aggressive anticommunism. For example, Christian Broadcasting Network founder Pat Robertson visited El Salvador and defended its government, praised Contra soldiers as "God's army," and helped to send over $20 million in private aid to Central American allies when Congress refused Reagan's requests for increased funding. In response, progressive evangelical leaders denounced the Religious Right for exhibiting a "triumphal, gospel-thumping Christian nationalism" and supporting the United States' "terroristic militarism" in Central America. On the other hand, progressive evangelicals' religious inspirations and idioms produced conflict with other factions in Witness for Peace and the Pledge of Resistance. Sojourners' leaders, who had helped found each campaign, fought to maintain the campaigns' religious natures. "If the identity were more liberal and secular, or, even more problematic, left[ist] or Marxist in character, it would be easily written off by the U.S. government and press and would not attract the numbers and kind of people whom we need," Wallis claimed regarding Witness for Peace. In addition to concern for mainstream credibility, progressive evangelicals wanted their protests to include prayers, religious symbols, and nonviolent actions. Yet non-Christian and secular activists challenged the campaigns' religious exclusivity and rejected religious styles of protest. Despite consistent debates, Witness for Peace retained its self-designation as "a prayerful, biblically based community" that "welcomes others in this endeavor who vary in spiritual approach but are one with us in purpose." But progressive evangelical leaders lost organizational control of the Pledge of Resistance as the campaign embraced a secular constituency and style in order to attract broad participation in its mass protests. Ultimately, tension between progressive evangelical and other activists hindered the potential strength of their collaborative resistance to Reagan's policies.[19]

Through the end of the 1980s, progressive evangelical leaders continued to publish reports of heinous acts committed by the Contras and Salvadoran government in order to sustain pressure on politicians to end American intervention in Central America. The Iran-Contra scandal—in which Reagan officials secretly sold arms to Iran and transferred the profits to the Contras after Congress passed the Boland Amendments that prohibited such funding—reconfirmed progressive evangelicals' view of American policies as imperialistic and immoral. *Sojourners'* Danny Collum labeled the affair yet another example of the "unresolved contradiction between the United States' profession of democratic ideals at home and the undemocratic conduct that comes with empire building." During congressional hearings in 1987, Reagan officials reasserted that support for the Contras was necessary to combat communist brutality—claims that Wallis called "morally corrupt and politically indefensible" since the region's violence primarily stemmed from "the endemic poverty and repression" perpetuated by "economic oligarchies and military elites supported by the U.S. government." At the same time, progressive evangelicals offered ongoing objections to injustices committed by the region's leftist groups. Leaders condemned the violent tactics of FMLN rebels battling the pro-American Salvadoran government, and both *Sojourners* and ESA periodically distanced themselves from repressive actions taken by the Sandinista government. Wallis admitted his hesitancy to voice criticism since the Reagan administration would use it to justify its policies. Yet "true friends are not uncritical," he wrote, and thus he protested the Sandinistas' human rights abuses, increased militarization, and closer ties to the Soviets. In an open letter in 1987, ESA also rebuked Nicaragua's president Daniel Ortega for suppressing democratic and religious freedoms. Thus progressive evangelicals sought to demonstrate that they opposed *all* forms of injustice, whether produced by American support for right-wing militarism or by leftist governments and groups.[20]

These attempts to offer balanced coverage of Central America coincided with leaders' conscious efforts in the final years of the Cold War to denounce communist totalitarianism more candidly. By the mid-1980s, progressive evangelicals' strong criticism of both capitalism and American foreign policy had led many conservatives to brand them as Marxist sympathizers and Soviet supporters. For example, a *National Review* article derided *The Other Side* and *Sojourners* for giving "every benefit of the doubt" to communist regimes while ignoring their oppression and poverty. The conservative watchdog group Accuracy in Media distributed a report claiming that *Sojourners* followed the "Soviet party line" in economic and political issues. Religious Right leaders made similar allegations, with Franky Schaeffer identifying Jim Wallis, Ron Sider, John Alexander, and Tony Campolo as members of "the evangelical Hate America Club." Theologian Clark Pinnock, an early mentor to the Post-Americans and contributing editor to *Sojourners*, repudiated his former views and accused the evangelical left of naively serving the Soviet Union's "foreign policy interests." While progressive evangelicals rejected these charges as distortions—*Sojourners'* editors insisted that they had published "at least 20 articles about repression in communist countries"—leaders did begin to censure Soviet oppression more frequently and forcefully. "The Marxist-Leninist system is evil," Alexander declared in *The Other Side*, and "the Christian left must be clear on that." Sider challenged fellow progressives to denounce "the evils of Marxist regimes" as clearly as the "injustices committed by Western powers." In 1988 *Sojourners'* Danny Collum acknowledged that peace activists had the tendency to "gloss over and play down militaristic behavior of the Soviet Union and the repressive nature of the Soviet system." But, he argued, Cold War militarism would not end without peace movements that were "grassroots, democratic, non-aligned, and critical of *both* superpowers."[21]

As the Cold War drew to a close at the end of the 1980s, progressive evangelicals expressed cautious enthusiasm. They heralded "the winds of democracy" that were bringing reforms in the Soviet Union and communism's collapse in Eastern Europe. Wallis praised the changes as a "salvation event" in which God was bringing freedom, justice, and liberation to oppressed people. At the same time, leaders worried that a sense of victory in the Cold War would inspire the United States to maintain its aggressive foreign policies—a fear that seemed justified by the American invasion of Panama and overthrow of Manuel Noriega's regime in December 1989. Like other anticommunist dictators, Noriega had received economic and military aid while American officials ignored his government's corruption and drug trafficking. However, after Noriega annulled the results of a presidential election, U.S. policy makers perceived his government as a threat to America's strategic access to the Panama Canal. President George H. W. Bush authorized over 24,000 troops to invade the country and to capture Noriega. While most Americans approved, progressive evangelicals condemned the attack as self-serving and the rationale as insincere. "Only when the dictator no longer serves U.S. purposes or becomes an albatross do American officials speak about democracy," Wallis declared. Instead of American intervention, Collum argued, Noriega "deserved to be overthrown by the Panamanian people and brought to Panamanian justice" as had occurred in the domestic democratic revolutions in Eastern Europe. At the end of the Cold War, therefore, progressive evangelicals believed that the United States faced a choice: "Standing alone as the sole surviving superpower, will we now try to play global Rambo, dominating the post-Cold War world for our own self interest?" asked Ron Sider. "Or will we help lead the way to a new world order of international cooperation and partnership, with greater justice and power for all?" The Gulf War in 1991 soon offered progressive evangelical leaders a disappointing answer.[22]

PEACE IN THE MIDDLE EAST

One year after the invasion of Panama and ouster of Noriega, the United States was preparing for war against another formerly allied dictator: President Saddam Hussein of Iraq. Coming to power in 1979, the megalomaniacal Hussein established a corrupt, ruthless regime that murdered hundreds of thousands of its own citizens. When he provoked an inconclusive war with neighboring Iran that lasted from 1980 to 1988, however, Reagan officials viewed Iraq as the lesser threat to American interests in the Middle East. They periodically provided Hussein with economic and military aid while largely overlooking his tyrannical rule and use of chemical weapons against enemies. In August 1990 Iraq invaded its smaller, oil-rich neighbor Kuwait. Hussein apparently believed that American diplomats had pledged that the United States would not oppose this attack. Instead, President Bush quickly denounced the invasion, imposed economic sanctions, and eventually secured authorization from the United Nations for an international coalition to use force if Iraq did not withdraw from Kuwait. In the wake of the Cold War, Bush hoped to promote "a new world order" in which "nations recognize the shared responsibility for freedom and justice" and "the strong respect the rights of the weak." But the president also admitted another priority: to assure "the security and stability of the Persian Gulf," a region essential to the United States' access to affordable oil.[23]

As Hussein refused to withdraw and an American-led invasion seemed imminent at the end of 1990, progressive evangelical leaders sought to build an antiwar movement. To be sure, they abhorred Hussein's brutality and agreed that Iraq must leave Kuwait. But leaders argued that solutions should come through multilateral, nonmilitary responses. In addition, progressive evangelicals accused the United States of hypocrisy for not only accepting but also enabling another, more long-standing injustice in the region: Israel's oppressive treatment of Palestinians. "The U.S.'s one-side support of Israel contributes significantly to the total Middle East dilemma," Ron Sider argued. "If the United States is so concerned about international aggression, why did we not send in troops when Israel seized the West Bank and Gaza strip from Jordan? Why have we allowed a repressive military occupation of these territories for over twenty years?" he asked. Jim Wallis called Bush's outrage at Iraq's actions "full of contradictions," for the United States "gave the green light for Israel's invasion of Lebanon, subsidizes Israel's 23-year occupation of the West Bank and Gaza, and acquiesces in the face of increasing oppression of the Palestinians." Thus progressive evangelical leaders used the Gulf War crisis to reiterate one of their long-standing convictions: the United States must promote peace in the Middle East by pressing Israel to end its unjust treatment of Palestinians.[24]

The contentious founding of the modern state of Israel in 1948 and subsequent American support for the embattled nation had produced deep resentment in the region. At the end of World War II, Great Britain relinquished colonial control over Palestine. Both religious and humanitarian concerns after the Holocaust inspired the United States to cosponsor a United Nations resolution for the creation of an autonomous Jewish state alongside an Arab Palestinian one. Yet Palestinians and the predominantly Muslim nations in the Middle East rejected this plan. When Israel nevertheless declared its independence, several surrounding Arab countries attacked the new nation. Israel not only successfully defended itself in the ensuing war but also enlarged its territory. As a result, the Palestinian state never materialized, and hundreds of thousands of Palestinians fled from areas they considered their rightful homeland. In the following decades, Israel warred several more times with neighboring states. During the Six-Day War of 1967, for example, Israel preemptively attacked Egypt, Jordan, and Syria and seized the Gaza Strip, the West Bank, and the Golan Heights from these respective nations as protective buffer zones. Six years later during the Yom Kippur War, Israel rebuffed its enemies' attacks and defended these occupied territories. Throughout the 1970s and 1980s, Israeli troops also periodically battled across the country's borders with Palestine Liberation Organization (PLO) forces and eventually Islamic groups such as Hezbollah and Hamas. In addition to hostilities directed at Israel, both Palestinians and their Arab allies seethed at the United States' steadfast support for Israeli policies. America developed an unusually close alliance with Israel in the midst of the Cold War, backed its military efforts, and provided over $36 billion in vital economic and military aid by 1983. In addition, while the United States rhetorically opposed Israel's control of the occupied territories, it did nothing to require its withdrawal, accepting that Arab nations must first recognize Israel's right to peaceful existence. Such policies had strong support from the American public, as polls consistently revealed overwhelming sympathy for Israel in the Arab-Israeli conflict.[25]

No group outside of Jewish circles supported Israel with as much zeal as American evangelicals. With a love for biblical stories of ancient Israel and the place of Jesus's ministry, evangelicals revered the "Holy Land" as the site of God's former mighty deeds. Yet many evangelicals also viewed modern Israel as integral to God's *future* plans. Beginning in the late nineteenth century, a complex system of biblical interpretations known as premillennial dispensationalism had become popular among evangelicals. In short, advocates of this theology taught that God dealt differently with humans in different historical dispensations, or eras. After Jews rejected Jesus as the messiah, they argued, God postponed the promised restoration of Israel's kingdom and worked through the Gentile church. But according to dispensationalists' interpretations of biblical prophecies, the reestablishment of the nation of Israel set the stage for history's final era in which Jesus would return to "rapture" Christians from the earth prior to the apocalyptic battle of Armageddon and inauguration of God's millennial kingdom. Based upon this theology, most evangelicals celebrated both the founding of modern Israel in 1948 and its seizure of territories — especially Old Jerusalem in the West Bank—during the Six-Day War. "This return constitutes a preparation for the end of the age, the setting for the coming of the Lord for His Church and the fulfillment of Israel's prophetic destiny," exclaimed Dallas Theological Seminary president John F. Walvoord in 1967. As part of their growing political participation in the 1970s, Religious Right leaders staunchly defended the Jewish state, arguing that God judges nations by their treatment of Israel. "To stand against Israel is to stand against God," announced Moral Majority's Jerry

Falwell. In turn, the Israeli government nurtured a strategic relationship with these Christian conservatives, as prime ministers and other officials often met with prominent evangelical leaders to sustain their endorsements. By the 1980s American evangelicals as a whole had become Israel's "best friend."[26]

Members of the evangelical left abstained, however, from intimacy with Israel. They insisted that most evangelicals' love for Israel blinded them to injustices committed against Palestinians. In the late 1970s progressive leaders began regularly criticizing the theological bases and political consequences of Christian conservatives' biased dedication to Israel. *Sojourners'* Wes Michaelson declared that the "biblical injunctions to seek justice for all peoples"—not dispensationalists' "spurious interpretations of Old Testament 'prophecy'"—should be "the guiding principle for a Middle East settlement, including justice for the Palestinians whose discarded lives have been so lightly regarded by past U.S. policy and so grossly ignored by evangelicalism." Although Israel has the clear "right to exist," he declared in 1977, there are "equally moral imperatives for the displaced and persecuted people of Palestine to also have their own homeland." *Sojourners* printed a corresponding biblical exegesis that rebutted claims that "the modern state of Israel is the fulfillment of Old Testament prophecy." Progressive evangelicals repeatedly claimed that "real peace" requires justice for all parties and that the United States should use its influence to promote a balanced solution that combined "a totally trustworthy arrangement for Israel's security" and "the creation of some form of Palestinian state." Therefore, Michaelson criticized the 1978 Camp David Accords—negotiated by President Carter and leading to a historic peace treaty between Egypt and Israel—for leaving unresolved "the primary issue" fueling "unrest and violence" in the Middle East: the present suffering and "political destiny of the Palestinians." At the end of the 1970s, leaders from across the evangelical left, mainline Protestants, and Catholics reiterated these convictions in the "La Grange Declaration." Published in *Sojourners*, this document again lamented dispensationalist biblical interpretations used to support Israel's occupation of Palestinian territories. For both Israelis and Palestinians to "find peace and true security," signers declared, Israel must accept Palestinians' right to "political self-determination" and "a sovereign state."[27]

Throughout the 1980s progressive evangelicals remained determined to counterbalance the prejudiced attitudes of other evangelicals and to challenge the pro-Israeli policies of the United States. *Sojourners* and *The*

Other Side published a number of interviews with and articles by Israeli and Palestinian peace activists—especially Palestinian Christians—in order to encourage support for a two-state solution. Leaders also continued to offer biblical analyses intended to debunk dispensationalism, which ESA labeled a "sensationalized brand of pop eschatology" that replaced "a biblical concern for peace and justice with a misguided attempt to fulfill speculative end-times scenarios." Most often, progressive evangelicals criticized Israeli and American policies for exacerbating rather than alleviating violence in the Middle East. For example, when Israel invaded Lebanon in 1982 in order to combat PLO troops based there, *Sojourners'* Danny Collum blamed Israel's "basic injustice" and "brutality" in the occupied territories for inciting the PLO's admittedly "terrible actions." At the same time, he charged that "the United States bears a heavy responsibility" for Middle Eastern tensions since it supplied Israel's weapons and "failed to take any concrete actions" against Israel's oppressive occupation of the West Bank and Gaza. In the late 1980s *Sojourners, The Other Side*, and ESA published multiple sympathetic accounts of the prolonged Palestinian intifada, or uprising. After respective visits to the Palestinian territories, Jim Wallis, Ron Sider, and other leaders condemned "acts of terrorism" by a minority of Palestinians but heralded the intifada's primarily nonviolent tactics and the PLO's stated willingness to recognize Israel. They once again censured the United States for failing to use its influence to push for a settlement that guaranteed both Israel's security and justice for Palestinians. "As we support the right of Israel to exist," ESA wrote in 1989, "we must also demand that the legitimate rights of the Palestinians be respected, including the right to self-rule."[28]

These objections to American policies in the Middle East—combined with fears of unchecked American ambitions after the Cold War—shaped progressive evangelicals' protests against President Bush's preparations for war after Iraq's invasion of Kuwait in 1990. Leaders opposed a counterinvasion for three primary reasons. First, they joined other critics in charging that the desire for affordable oil—not an altruistic commitment to combat tyranny—primarily motivated the United States. Though Bush likened Saddam Hussein to Adolf Hitler and portrayed the intervention as necessary to thwart tyrants, evangelical progressives highlighted America's past and present readiness to protect autocratic Arab monarchies as long as they favorably provided access to oil. "The U.S. commitment to restore a Kuwaiti royal family that has suppressed every democratic impulse in that country—and to defend a Saudi monarchy with one of the more dismal human rights records in the world—suggests that we are making the world safe more for feudalism and gas guzzling than for democracy," Wallis argued. Second, leaders accused the United States of having "a double standard" by overlooking Israel's ongoing subjugation of Palestinian territories. President Bush must "confront injustice not only in the occupation of Kuwait but also in the Israel/Palestine conflict," ESA proclaimed. Third, progressive evangelicals warned against resolving the crisis through American aggression. The United States must reject "the jingoistic nationalism and military-industrial complex that would prefer the role of unilateral global policeman to cooperative partner," Sider insisted. Following a weeklong peace pilgrimage to the Middle East, Wallis and other antiwar church leaders "condemned the brutal aggression of Saddam Hussein and called for the withdrawal of Iraq from Kuwait," but they also "urged a reliance on the international economic embargo, diplomatic pressure, political initiatives, and multilateral action as alternatives to the U.S. military escalation." Despite such proposals, progressive evangelicals and other critics failed to persuade the Bush administration that "there must be an alternative to war."[29]

The United States' quick, decisive victory in the Gulf War earned overwhelming popular support but unsettled progressive evangelicals. After a devastating thirty-nine-day bombing campaign that began on January 17, 1991, American and coalition ground forces routed Iraqi troops and liberated Kuwait in only 100 hours. (President Bush suspended the fighting, however, without taking Baghdad or capturing Hussein.) Most Americans, including evangelicals, responded enthusiastically, as Bush's approval rate reached above 90 percent. Billy Graham offered his implicit blessing by spending the night at the White House as the bombing began. Prominent Christian conservatives such as the Southern Baptist Convention's Richard Land and *First Things* editor Richard John Neuhaus argued that the conflict met just war criteria and dismissed objectors as irrelevant. But progressive evangelicals' opposition remained firm. Both Wallis and Sider rebutted just war arguments, accusing Bush of failing to treat war as the last resort. Sojourners organized marches for peace and prayer vigils at the White House in protest. Despite the minimal number of American casualties, progressive evangelicals lamented reports of 100,000 Iraqi troops killed and the "collateral damage" of civilian deaths. Ultimately, leaders feared that this militaristic success paved the way for the United States to establish a self-interested vision of peace—a "Pax Americana"—in the "new world order" after the Cold War. "The imposition of Pax Americana is the ultimate purpose of the war in the Persian Gulf," Wallis wrote, and "will be enforced and controlled by the military supremacy and political direction of the United States." To counter this impulse, Sider encouraged Christians to demand "that President Bush's 'new world order' means working as genuine global partners rather than strutting as self-serving global policeman." He and other evangelical progressives wanted political leaders to use "this moment of unusual U.S. influence" in the post-Cold War era "to work for the economic well-being and national dignity of all people."[30]

For the rest of the 1990s, this vision for the benevolent use of American power led progressive evangelicals to call for the United States to support international peacemaking efforts, especially in the Middle East. The country faced virtually no large-scale threats to its security or primary interests during this period, and after his election in 1992 President Bill Clinton adopted a more restrained foreign policy. Loath to risk American lives in global conflicts, Clinton either largely stayed out of ethnic and civil wars in places like Rwanda or worked through NATO and UN campaigns in areas such as the Balkan states. For progressive evangelicals, such situations created what *Sojourners* characterized as "a moral dilemma for those committed to peacemaking." While leaders advocated UN interventions to stop genocides and ethnic cleansings, they objected to militaristic campaigns and other means that seemed to increase rather than alleviate suffering. Progressive evangelicals' responses to Saddam Hussein after the Gulf War illustrated this tension. They supported both UN efforts to monitor Hussein's weapons and proposals to try him in an international court. But leaders opposed economic sanctions that most affected Iraqi civilians, and they denounced U.S. bombing campaigns when Hussein rebuffed UN inspectors. "Saddam Hussein is a real threat, and his potential for using chemical and biological weapons is a great danger to countless numbers of people," Wallis claimed. "But continuing to bomb and starve the children of Iraq will neither remove him nor his weapons of mass destruction." Well into the twenty-first century, progressive evangelicals also repeatedly addressed the unresolved Israeli-Palestinian conflict, urging "the United States to be much tougher on the present Israeli government." In fact, after the 1998 bombings of American embassies in Kenya and Tanzania by Muslim extremists, Wallis argued that outrage over the Palestinians' plight had contributed to the new global threat of Islamic terrorism. If the United States failed to support a Palestinian state, democratic reforms, and military withdrawal in the Middle

East, he warned, "terrorism could become the new enemy that we have 'lacked' since the fall of communism." The events of September 11, 2001, proved Wallis prescient.[31]

OPPOSING TERRORISM, OPPOSING WAR

American foreign policy inalterably changed on the day known thereafter as simply 9/11. Nineteen terrorists hijacked four airplanes, crashed into the World Trade Center and the Pentagon, and killed nearly 3,000 people. Intelligence officials quickly identified the group responsible for the attacks: the global militant Muslim network of al Qaeda, led by disillusioned Saudi scion Osama bin Laden, that promoted violent jihad (holy war) against enemies. Members targeted the United States in retaliation for its perceived aggression against Muslims, including support for Israel's unjust policies and America's desecrating military presence near Islam's holiest sites in Saudi Arabia. Al Qaeda had already successfully executed attacks such as the bombings of the American embassies in 1998 and the USS *Cole* in Yemen in 2000. In the days after 9/11, President George W. Bush committed the United States to a "war on terror." He vowed not only to bring al Qaeda to justice but also to "pursue nations that provide aid or safe haven to terrorism." This threat most immediately applied to Afghanistan's Taliban regime, the fundamentalist Islamic group that theocratically controlled the country and sheltered al Qaeda leaders. When the Taliban refused to hand over bin Laden, the first phase of America's war on terror began on October 7 with a bombing campaign aided by Britain and other NATO allies. On the ground, the United States primarily relied upon the indigenous Northern Alliance—a volatile coalition of dissident Afghan warlords and their tribes—that quickly captured major cities with the aid of American Special Forces and CIA operatives. On December 6 the final Taliban militia surrendered, and the United States helped to install Afghanistan's new interim government and to begin rebuilding and securing the country. Although bin Laden had fled into Pakistan and the Bush administration was already eyeing Iraq as the next theater of war, the American public celebrated this initial success.[32]

Progressive evangelical leaders joined in condemnations of the terrorist attacks as evil, but they insisted that the United States remain focused and restrained in its response. The day after 9/11, Jim Wallis, Ron Sider, and several ecumenical coauthors issued "Deny Them Their Victory: A Religious Response to Terrorism." The statement acknowledged the country's suffering and affirmed "that those responsible for these utterly evil acts be found and brought to justice." At the same time, the authors urged President Bush to "seek the wisdom of God" in determining the nation's response and to avoid vengeful, violent, and indiscriminate retaliation. Therefore, after Bush subsequently pledged to prosecute a "war on terror," progressive evangelicals expressed unease. Leaders believed that America's commitment to such an open-ended war would promote revenge rather than justice, endanger innocent lives, take precedence over economic and diplomatic strategies to combat terrorism, and infuriate millions of other Muslims who shared the terrorists' resentment of American global dominance. Instead, they proposed, the United States should immediately concentrate on cooperative efforts to bring terrorists to justice under international law and ultimately redress the global injustices and grinding poverty that produced "the breeding and recruiting ground for terrorism." To evangelical progressives, the amorphous nature and indefinite scope of Bush's planned "war on terror" would exceed the justifiable and precise goal of holding terrorists accountable to the rule of law.[33]

In turn, leaders criticized the war in Afghanistan for its misdirected priorities and troubling consequences. Less than a week after the start of the war, Sojourners began calling for an end to America's bombing campaigns. The first waves of air strikes had successfully diminished the Taliban's military, Wallis argued, and sustained bombing would only kill more civilians and distract from "what should be our only goal: bringing terrorists to justice." Rather than escalating the war, he wrote in the *Washington Post*, the United States should refocus on "intensifying worldwide police and intelligence activity and using international law to convict, isolate and discredit the terrorists—and then carefully targeting search and capture operations to find and stop them." In November Sojourners launched a campaign—"Feed the People, Halt the Bombing, Honor Ramadan"—that urged officials to suspend bombing during Muslims' holiest month in order to address looming humanitarian crises, to demonstrate respect for Islam, and to reconsider the best means for bringing al Qaeda leaders to justice. As the Taliban prepared to surrender, President Bush called Afghanistan "just the beginning on the war against terror," for "there are other nations willing to sponsor" terrorists. But progressive evangelicals insisted that the war in Afghanistan not set a precedent. "New and costly wars against countries that may contain terrorist bases or training camps, but where the government is not synonymous with those networks, would inevitably raise serious international legal, political, and, of course, moral questions," Wallis responded. "Wars against whole nations, even ones with repressive governments, are a blunt instrument in defeating terrorism." Wallis and other leaders would employ these arguments to oppose the turn in America's "war on terror" to its next front: Iraq.[34]

While the Bush administration developed plans to invade Iraq throughout 2002, progressive evangelicals championed alternatives and protested the potential war's injustice. In his State of the Union address, Bush identified Iraq as part of an "axis of evil" and accused the country of continuing "to flaunt its hostility toward America and to support terror." Administration officials courted public and political support for a war against Iraq, claiming that evidence revealed Iraqi links to al Qaeda and Saddam Hussein's development of weapons of mass destruction. Polls indicated that the majority of Americans trusted the administration, and in October Congress passed the "Joint Resolution to Authorize the Use of United States Armed Forces Against Iraq" by over a 2-1 margin. Yet progressive evangelicals voiced objections. In their own journals, ecumenical statements, and op-eds in major newspapers, leaders challenged both the prudence and the justice of attacking Iraq. They agreed that Hussein posed a substantial threat. Like other critics, however, progressive evangelicals maintained that international diplomacy and continued UN weapons inspections represented better means for disarming Iraq. They warned that a preemptive war would undermine international cooperation against terrorist networks, inflame anti-Americanism among Muslims and fuel more terrorist attacks, destabilize the Middle East and sabotage the Israeli-Palestinian peace process, and require years of occupation and investment in order to rebuild Iraq. "The potential social and diplomatic consequences of a war against Iraq make it politically unwise," Sojourners stated in an antiwar declaration signed by Ron Sider, Tony Campolo, and other prominent American and British church leaders. But in addition to pragmatic concerns, progressive evangelicals and many other Christians opposed the war on religious grounds. They repeatedly insisted that a preemptive war to overthrow Hussein's regime failed to meet just war criteria: it lacked a just cause, was not a last resort, and would produce disproportionate civilian suffering. Thus the war would be more than imprudent, leaders proclaimed. It would be immoral.[35]

With war appearing imminent in early 2003, progressive evangelicals mounted final attempts to build enough religious resistance to forestall an attack on Iraq. Jim Wallis, who began his activist career protesting the Vietnam War, especially rode the wave of public debates about the potential invasion to become a leading voice against the war. "We call upon all churches and all individual Christians to refuse their consent to this war," for "it would dishonor our nation, disregard morality, and violate international law," proclaimed Wallis and prominent Christian figures such as theologian Stanley Hauerwas, activist William Sloane Coffin, and ethicist Glen Stassen in another declaration. In February Wallis led a delegation of American religious leaders to meet with British prime minister Tony Blair, who supported Bush's war plans. They discussed with Blair "the moral and even theological issues at stake" and argued that the proposed preemptive war represented "both bad theology and bad policy." Although the majority of evangelicals viewed the potential war as justified and even necessary—evangelicals as a whole supported an invasion of Iraq more strongly than any other religious group—leading media outlets such as the *New York Times* regularly quoted Wallis as a spokesman for the opposition of nearly all other Christian communities, including the evangelical left. As a final initiative in early March, Wallis and several mainline Protestant leaders developed a six-point plan "to defeat Saddam Hussein without war." Published in the *Washington Post*, it called for an international coalition to indict Hussein for war crimes, disarm Iraq through further weapons inspections, establish a temporary UN-led government, provide immediate humanitarian aid, commit to establishing a Palestinian state, and reinvigorate a coordinated campaign against terrorist networks. Yet the president and his advisers ignored both domestic opposition and overwhelming worldwide disapproval. On March 20 Bush ordered "Operation Iraqi Freedom" to begin.[36]

After the Bush administration's initial thrill of victory over Iraq gave way to the agony of occupation, progressive evangelicals claimed vindication. The American-led invasion started with a "shock and awe" bombing campaign, and ground forces swiftly defeated the Iraqi military. Hussein fled into hiding as American troops captured Baghdad on April 9 and secured more of the country in the following weeks. On May 1 Bush buoyantly declared victory over Iraq while standing aboard an aircraft carrier under a banner that proclaimed "MISSION ACCOMPLISHED." Although those in the Bush administration expected to easily reconstruct Iraq into a democratic, economically self-sufficient state, they soon realized that the United States' mission was far from over. The country's infrastructure collapsed; internecine sectarian violence grew; and by the summer an insurgency exploded against Americans, whom many Iraqis resented as invaders rather than welcomed as liberators. To progressive evangelicals, this instability and violence confirmed their conviction that the international community, not American military leaders, could best address Iraq's problems. Rather than pour more money and troops into Iraq, the United States should "give up its occupation and allow the U.N. to take a leadership role in the reconstruction and transition [of power] in Iraq," wrote *Sojourners'* Duane Shank. In addition, progressive evangelical leaders repeatedly argued that the lack of weapons of mass destruction found in Iraq validated their objections to the war. "The president of the United States misled the American people" and waged "a pre-emptive and largely unilateral war that has proven to be both unnecessary and unjust," Wallis declared in early 2004, summarizing the frustrations of the antiwar movement. "Iraq is now a big mess, with no clear or responsible exit strategy in sight, and is likely to remain so for a very long time."[37]

Through the end of Bush's presidency in 2008, progressive evangelicals continued to portray the Iraq war as a fiasco. Over and over, leaders called for the United States to end its incendiary occupation and allow international authorities such as the United Nations to repair Iraq. "The American occupation has become more the catalyst than the solution to a violent and bloody insurgency," Wallis wrote in 2006. The United States should "give up control over Iraq"—for only "international involvement will ultimately achieve security and stability"—and then fulfill its "political and moral responsibility to assist the Iraqi people to secure and rebuild their country." In contrast to claims by the Bush administration, evangelical progressives charged that the war in Iraq had increased rather than diminished the threat of terrorism by inflaming anti-Americanism and diverting resources from targeted campaigns against al Qaeda. Leaders also regularly cited the mounting tragic costs—in terms of both human lives and financial debts—as more evidence that the war must end. "We mourn 4,000 Americans and hundreds of thousands of Iraqis who have died," all while "the war is squandering billions of dollars that are urgently needed for other domestic and international needs," stated Wallis, Sider, Tony Campolo, and other progressive evangelical leaders in a 2008 statement. Not least, they condemned the Bush administration's approval of "enhanced interrogation techniques"—what they and other critics regarded as torture—in the broader war on terror. In response, leaders from across the evangelical left and center issued "An Evangelical Declaration Against Torture: Protecting Human Rights in an Age of

Terror." Not even a successful troop surge that reduced violence in 2007 altered progressive evangelicals' opinion of the war. "I think it was the worst policy mistake in American foreign-policy history, with the exception of Vietnam," Wallis claimed in 2008. "The war in Iraq cannot be won, should never have been fought in the first place, makes everything it promised to solve even worse, and continues to be pursued at the cost of America's soul."[38]

Beyond condemning the spurious rationale for the Iraq war and its calamitous consequences, evangelical progressives abhorred President Bush's use of theology to justify his foreign policy. As an evangelical himself, Bush routinely drew upon Christian idioms in declaring that America had a "divine appointment" to defend freedom by "rid[ding] the world of evil." "Freedom is God's gift to everybody," the president claimed, and "I believe the United States is *the* beacon for freedom in the world." Thus Bush characterized the war on terror as "a confrontation between good and evil" and confidently aligned American military actions with God's will. While Christian conservatives who formed the president's political base cheered these reassertions of the United States' role as a "redeemer nation," progressive evangelicals were appalled. They regularly chastised Bush for distorting theological language to construct a "nationalist religion" that baptized American ambition and aggression. *Sojourners* pictured a bust of Bush arrayed as a Roman emperor on its cover and published articles that criticized his "theology of empire." The president "confuses the identity of the nation with the church, and God's purposes with the mission of American empire," Wallis wrote. Prominent progressive evangelicals helped initiate a statement endorsed by a range of ecumenical leaders—"Confessing Christ in a World of Violence"—that described the commands of Jesus to serve as peacemakers and to love one's enemies as incompatible with the "militarism and nationalism" inherent in Bush's "theology of war." They also rejected Bush's simplistic theological dualism. "To name the face of evil in the brutality of terrorist attacks is good theology," Wallis wrote, "but to say 'they are evil and we are good' is bad theology" and "rules out self-reflection and correction." Finally, progressive evangelicals rebuked Bush for defending the United States' global responsibilities in messianic terms. "America is not the hope of the earth and the light of the world. Jesus Christ is!" Wallis exclaimed. "And it is his way that we follow, not the flawed path of our nation's leaders who prosecute this war." Bush's bad theology, leaders contended, had inevitably produced bad policy.[39]

As in all areas of political engagement, progressive evangelicals believed that constructing a just foreign policy requires the proper theological foundation. Leaders viewed the eager endorsement of the Iraq war by many Christians—especially the majority of evangelicals—as a result of a fundamental theological error that had long plagued American Christianity: placing allegiance to one's country before faithfulness to the commands of Jesus and the kingdom of God. "Support for U.S. wars and foreign policy is still the area where American Christians are most 'conformed to the world' (Romans 12:2)," Wallis proclaimed in 2008. "This is our Achilles' heel, our biggest blind spot, our least questioned obedience, the worst compromise of our Christian identity, and the greatest failing of our Christian conscience." From the beginning of their movement, progressive evangelical leaders repudiated American chauvinism and militarism—promoting instead commitments to anti-nationalism and nonviolence—based upon their own underlying public theology of community and the responsibilities of Christians to love their neighbors, to love their enemies, and to make peace.[40]

Progressive evangelicals rejected nationalism as antithetical to God's expectations for Christians to love all people across all nations, who are bound together as neighbors in a global community. Whereas nationalism encourages people to prioritize the welfare of their compatriots and own country, leaders argued, Christians must imitate God's impartial love of people worldwide and take responsibility for the common good of neighbors who live beyond humanly constructed national borders. "The Christian community's concern for the rights of others is grounded in God's compassion for all humanity," which "knows no limits" and "is constrained by no national boundaries," Wes Michaelson stated in *Sojourners*. Ron Sider described his commitment "to a global perspective rather than a narrow nationalism" as foundational in his political philosophy. "As Christians, we are global citizens before we are patriotic Americans," he wrote. "Therefore, we must insist on the well-being of all our neighbors, not only those living in the United States," and "resist nationalistic public policies that so easily forget about the needs and rights of people elsewhere." Leaders differentiated morally neutral love for the United States and its best ideals from chauvinistic support for American superiority. "The self-centered jingoism of much modern patriotism is simply sin," Sider claimed. Ultimately, progressive evangelicals wanted all

Christians to prioritize the common good of every global neighbor in their own public theologies and consequent political engagement. "Nationalism doesn't go well with the kingdom of God," and "'God Bless America' is not found in the Bible," Jim Wallis declared. "To take a global perspective, to value other countries' interests as much as our own, and, perhaps most critically, to count all the world's children as important as ours—all will significantly alter our political views."[41]

Because leaders of *Sojourners*, ESA, and *The Other Side* incorporated biblical teachings on nonviolence into their *public* theology and not only personal ethics, they also denounced American militarism and warfare. They portrayed pacifism as the corollary to respect for the sanctity of each individual person. Sider explained that "war kills persons created in the image of God," while Wallis described principled nonviolence as a consequence of *Sojourners'* commitment to uphold "the sacred value of human life." Influenced by the pacifist Anabaptist tradition, these progressive evangelical leaders highlighted New Testament commands to imitate Jesus's example of a suffering servant who nonviolently reconciled enemies. They also appealed to eschatological visions for nations beating "their swords into plowshares" and training for war no more (Isaiah 2:1-4, Micah 4:1-5). Most important, leaders repeatedly emphasized Jesus's directive to love one's enemies and his "radical extension of neighbor love to include even enemies" (Matthew 5:38-48, Luke 6:27-36). They insisted that global neighbors included enemies of the United States; these enemies' malevolence did not negate Jesus's instructions to love them; and love precludes killing, whether done by private individuals or military agents. "All people everywhere are neighbors to Jesus' followers and therefore are to be actively loved," Sider proclaimed. "And that even extends to enemies—even violent oppressive foreign conquerors!" Therefore, these progressive evangelicals believed that Christians must refuse to support—and, of course, participate in—violent military actions. During the Cold War, for example, Sider proclaimed, "Jesus' command to love even our enemies means that even totalitarian Marxist leaders are neighbors whom Christ commands us to understand and love." Similarly, he objected to attacks on American enemies in the 1991 Gulf War since "every person in the Middle East—including Saddam Hussein and the Iraqi soldiers—are neighbors to be loved."[42]

To be sure, pacifist progressive evangelical leaders recognized their minority status, for most Christians since the fourth century had embraced the just war tradition. Indeed, others active in the evangelical left—especially those affiliated with the Reformed theological tradition—did not support unconditional nonviolence. While acknowledging Jesus's command to love enemies as a personal requirement, they interpreted the Bible to allow governments to conduct just wars as a last resort in order to restrain evil, to defend the innocent, and ultimately to reestablish peace and justice. Even as leaders of *Sojourners*, ESA, and *The Other Side* offered biblical rebuttals of just war theory, they respected Christians who "reluctantly" condoned or participated in violence as a last resort "for what they believe is the sake of justice." Pacifist progressive evangelicals showed less patience, however, with those who appeared to embrace the "Christian realism" of Reinhold Niebuhr, the most influential public theologian of the mid-twentieth century. Niebuhr had renounced his early pacifism and taught that Jesus's nonviolent ethic was impractical for securing justice in a sinful world. In doing so, *Sojourners'* Bill Kellerman argued, he tragically justified the "lesser" evil of military violence in order to combat "greater" evils such as communist totalitarianism. Progressive evangelicals decried Niebuhr's influence among contemporary Christians. They especially criticized the Religious Right for viewing Jesus's commands as "unrealistic" or "ineffective," thus accepting that the goal of American security justified militaristic means to thwart enemies' hostilities. While rejecting "Christian realism" outright, on occasion pacifist progressive evangelicals such as Sider and Wallis did pragmatically apply just war criteria to American foreign policy in order to engage other Christians on their own terms. In each case, however, they argued that American militarism—including Cold War interventions, nuclear arms buildup, and wars against Iraq—failed to meet just war criteria (a fact that led critics to complain that they employed impossibly high standards). Despite this strategic willingness to entertain just war theory, many prominent progressive evangelical leaders remained committed to principled pacifism as part of their public theology.[43]

But pacifism does not entail passivity, they insisted. Leaders across the evangelical left united in promoting Christians' public responsibilities to make peace. For example, both just war defender Richard Mouw and Sider agreed that "all Christians, whether pacifist or non-pacifist," should acknowledge "that our Lord Jesus summons us all to be active peacemakers." To this end, progressive evangelicals stressed the imperatives of *action* in resolving conflicts and confronting evil. Peacemaking "has more to do with action than with theory," Wallis stated. "Jesus didn't say, 'Blessed are the peace lovers.' He said, 'Blessed are the peacemakers.' Peace must be *made*." In attempts to counter accusations that opposition to defensive violence against belligerent enemies rendered them irrelevant, pacifist leaders adopted the language of "nonviolent resistance." "We prefer to use the word *nonviolence*, rather than *pacifism*," explained Sider and Richard Taylor, "because pacifism suggests acquiescence in the face of evil whereas nonviolence connotes an active but loving confrontation of injustice and evil." Sider defended "activist nonviolence rather than nonresistance" as "the more faithful application of New Testament teaching," for "Jesus' own actions show that a quietist interpretation of his commands is mistaken." Pacifist progressive evangelicals repeatedly cited models for nonviolent peacemaking. Although "the 20th century was the bloodiest in human history," Sider claimed, it included "numerous and stunningly successful examples of nonviolent victories over injustice and oppression": the Indian independence movement led by Mahatma Gandhi, the American civil rights movement, several countries' resistance to the Nazis during World War II, Solidarity's undermining of Soviet communism in Poland, and more. Progressive evangelicals' own nonviolent activism entailed prayer vigils, protest demonstrations, civil disobedience, and direct action campaigns such as Witness for Peace in Central America and Christian Peacemaker Teams in other global areas of conflict. "The path of active peacemaking is where we are likely to find the alternatives to war and violence that are so desperately needed," Wallis proclaimed. Thus these progressive evangelical leaders championed nonviolent resistance as a theologically faithful and politically realistic means to create peace in a world full of war and terrorists.[44]

Peacemaking represented an integral part of progressive evangelicals' comprehensive dedication to social justice, for they characterized peace and justice as inseparably linked. Multiple leaders described the Hebrew word "shalom," often translated simply as "peace," as conveying a far more expansive biblical "call to justice." "Shalom means not only the absence of war" but also "just economic relationships with the neighbor," "fair division" of economic resources, and limitations on "great extremes of wealth and poverty," Sider stated. "The result of such justice, Isaiah says, is peace (32:16-17)," and "if we try to separate justice and peace, we tear asunder what God has joined together." This view of the intimate connection between peace and justice led progressive evangelicals in the late twentieth century to begin championing the work of Fuller Theological Seminary professor and *Sojourners* contributor Glen Stassen to develop a theory and practices for "just peacemaking." In addition to recommended steps such as arms control and enhancing international cooperation, the "just peacemaking" paradigm promoted several principles to increase social justice and thus advance the abolition of war: "support nonviolent action"; "acknowledge responsibility for conflict and injustice and seek repentance and forgiveness"; "advance democracy, human rights, and religious liberty"; and "foster just and sustainable economic development." *The Other Side*'s Mark Olson summarized well the distinctive "peace and justice" mission of his magazine, *Sojourners*, and ESA: "Christian pacifists are those people committed to joining hands with God in the movement toward a world where justice and righteousness prevail, where lion and lamb cavort together, where enemies embrace and tools of war become tools of hope, where God, earth, and humanity sing together in perfect harmony." It was this radical vision of peace and justice that originally inspired the contemporary progressive evangelical movement—and it was this same vision that sustained it well into the twenty-first century.[45]

Epilogue

Through the first five years of President Barack Obama's presidency, progressive evangelical leaders enjoyed more attention from politicians and the public than they ever had before. While the Religious Right remained a strong political force, evangelical progressives had raised the profile of their own movement as a visible alternative. Their distinctive public theology remained the inspiration for leaders' vigorous participation in political debates as they addressed a wide range of issues in order to advance their comprehensive vision of social justice and the common good. In the process, progressive evangelicals continued to take positions that alternately clashed with the Religious Right and political left.

Articles addressing injustices and inequalities faced by both racial minorities and women remained regular features within *Sojourners* and Evangelicals for Social Action's *Prism* magazine. Progressive evangelicals criticized insensitivity to racial issues and the lack of minority leadership within the predominantly white circles of evangelicalism and the emerging church movement. In the public sphere, *Sojourners* challenged the illusion of a "colorblind" society after Obama's election by calling attention to ongoing racialized inequalities in incomes and incarceration rates. In 2013 Jim Wallis, Lisa Sharon Harper, and other contributors decried both the Supreme Court decision that struck down part of the 1965 Voting Rights Act and the controversial acquittal of George Zimmerman for the 2012 killing in Florida of black teenager Trayvon Martin as evidence of persistent systemic racism. Progressive evangelicals also maintained their commitment to promoting feminist causes within both religious and broader social contexts. *Sojourners* and Evangelicals for Social Action (ESA) published numerous articles by Christian feminists that criticized ongoing patriarchal resistance among conservative evangelicals and Catholics to women's ministries within the church. In addition, both groups called for political actions to address violence against women, sex trafficking, and the repression of women's rights in other countries.[1]

Debates surrounding the Patient Protection and Affordable Care Act—the health care expansion and reforms colloquially labeled Obamacare—illustrated the ways in which many progressive evangelicals continued to balance their opposition to abortion with other commitments in their comprehensive pro-life agenda. Leaders heralded Obama's commitment to universal coverage. "Morally it is unacceptable for the richest nation in history to have 47 million uninsured people with no guarantee of adequate health care," Ron Sider wrote just after Obama's election. Many also described health care expansion as a pro-life strategy. They argued that providing low-income women with adequate, accessible coverage would reduce abortions by offering substantive support for their decisions to bring children to term. After the president introduced his proposals in mid-2009, however, they were soon mired in fierce debates. One of these regarded whether patients who receive federal subsidies could use the money to purchase plans that covered abortion. Jim Wallis complained that the issue was a distraction that could doom the legislation. Because he insisted that current law—the Hyde Amendment—already prohibited the use of federal funds for abortion, Wallis portrayed the health care bill as "abortion neutral" so neither pro-life nor pro-choice factions would object and undermine its passage. Yet abortion opponents remained unconvinced. When pro-life Democratic senator Bob Casey of Pennsylvania proposed compromise language that more clearly guarded against abortion coverage in the health care legislation, a group of leading progressive evangelicals that included Wallis, Sider, David Gushee, and Glen Stassen endorsed a statement encouraging other pro-life Christians to accept the language and thus support the bill. After several more rounds of negotiations, President Obama issued an executive order that explicitly reaffirmed the Hyde Amendment and thus secured enough support among pro-life Democrats for the passage of the bill. Progressive evangelicals praised the legislation not only for extending health care to millions of uninsured Americans but also for remaining consistent with restrictions on abortion funding while offering hope for pragmatic abortion reduction.[2]

While most progressive evangelical leaders remained unwilling to affirm the morality of same-sex relationships, they continued to promote dialogue among differing Christians and to defend social justice for lesbian, gay, bisexual, and transgender (LGBT) individuals. Ron Sider and ESA maintained their conviction that the state should recognize only traditional heterosexual unions as marriages, and they reiterated the belief that "the Bible teaches that sexual activity belongs exclusively in a lifelong marriage between a man and a woman." In 2009 Sider joined prominent Christian conservatives in signing the Manhattan Declaration, a manifesto that warned against assaults on traditional marriage (along with human life and religious freedom) and promised civil disobedience against potential laws compelling them to treat "immoral sexual partnerships" as marriages. At the same time, ESA began to imitate Sojourners' longstanding commitment to dialogue. Sider commended the dedication to "bridge building" and loving communication between Christians and the LGBT community promoted by evangelical activist Andrew Marin. In this spirit, ESA leaders pledged to establish empathetic relationships with gay Christians and "to discover what committed Christians, both gay and straight, have to offer and teach each other." At the end of 2012, ESA published an entire issue of *Prism* devoted to "listening to and learning from sexual minorities in the church."[3]

Even as Sojourners maintained a commitment to honest conversations on LGBT issues, a notable shift occurred in 2013 when Jim Wallis endorsed same-sex marriage. He regarded his previous support of civil unions as no longer sufficient to guarantee same-sex couples' equal protection under the law, and thus he expressed gratitude for the Supreme Court's invalidation of the federal Defense of Marriage Act. Wallis also claimed that his new position reflected his concern for the disintegration of covenantal marriages and the number of young Christians leaving the church in response to its apparent hostility toward LGBT people. While he insisted upon churches' religious freedom to define marriage in accord with their particular biblical and theological interpretations, Wallis hinted at an openness to if not acceptance of arguments in favor of affirming the morality of gay marriages. "Sincere Christians who take the Bible seriously can reach different interpretations of how the scriptures apply to committed same-sex couples," he wrote. "We should always be open to what God is speaking to a new generation of Christians as they seek to be faithful to the call of Christ in their lives." Yet Wallis stopped short of explicitly endorsing theological arguments that churches should bless covenantal same-sex marriages—either he remained undecided, or he wanted to avoid alienating those who regarded an affirming position as a rejection of biblical authority. To be sure, between 2008 and early 2014 a few of the most progressive figures associated with the evangelical left—such as emerging church theologian Tony Jones, former Sojourners board member Brian McLaren, and provocative author Rob Bell—followed in the pioneering footsteps of *The Other Side* and declared support for the full affirmation of LGBT Christians and religious recognition of same-sex marriages. Yet most progressive evangelical leaders appeared still dedicated to a welcoming but not affirming position within the church.[4]

As greater numbers of Americans accept not only same-sex marriage as a civil right but also the morality of such relationships, however, it seems likely that a divide will grow among progressive evangelicals—and perhaps even within evangelicalism as a whole—regarding both the legal and the moral status of same-sex marriage. Many will surely remain opposed to both public and religious recognition of gay marriages. But one can anticipate more and more progressive evangelicals endorsing the *legal* right to same-sex marriage while continuing to view same-sex acts as a *personal* sin. Greater numbers may also become convinced by biblical and theological arguments in support of affirming covenantal gay marriages and the full inclusion of LGBT people within churches. Indeed, survey results released by the Public Religion Research Institute in early 2014 indicated that "white evangelical Protestant Millennials are more than twice as likely to favor same-sex marriage as the oldest generation of white evangelical Protestants (43% vs. 19%)," and thus this divide may have already begun.[5]

Progressive evangelicals remained undivided and resolute in championing their theological interpretation of economic justice and the government's critical role in alleviating poverty, especially as the American economy struggled throughout President Obama's first term. During budget debates in 2010 and 2011 that focused upon reducing the growing national deficit, leaders developed overlapping campaigns that urged Obama and Congress to let the Bush tax cuts expire and to slash other spending rather than cut programs for the poor. In early 2011, for example, Sojourners published an ad campaign titled "What Would Jesus Cut?" "The moral test of a society is how it treats the poor," Wallis, Ron Sider, Tony Campolo, David Gushee, activist Shane Claiborne, and other supporters declared. While politicians must avoid bankruptcy and burdening future generations with debt, "our budget should not be balanced on the backs of poor and vulnerable people," they insisted. These leaders also joined centrist evangelicals and other representatives of the evangelical left in a similar initiative co-sponsored by ESA and the Center for Public Justice titled "A Call for Intergenerational Justice: A Christian Proposal for the American Debt Crisis." Endorsers called for a progressive tax code and cuts in areas such as defense spending and corporate subsidies, but they proclaimed that "to reduce federal debt at the expense of our poorest fellow citizens would be a violation of the biblical teaching that God has a special concern for the poor." Sider developed even more detailed proposals for balancing the budget while reducing poverty and economic inequality in his subsequent book *Fixing the Moral Deficit*. Finally, Sojourners developed another campaign, the "Circle of Protection," designed to safeguard government "programs that meet the essential needs of hungry and poor people." As part of this initiative, Wallis led an ecumenical coalition of religious leaders to meet with Obama, who endorsed the campaign's theme that vital debt reduction should not harm the poor. In each of these efforts, progressive evangelicals based their proposals upon the conviction that "budgets are moral documents."[6]

Leaders sustained their opposition to the ongoing wars in Afghanistan and Iraq, pressing President Obama to move more quickly to withdraw American troops. "Soldiers are dying for a failed, arrogant, theologically unjust, and immoral war policy," Wallis wrote in 2010. "To begin a war and then an occupation of Afghanistan was the wrong policy, killing more Afghan innocents than American innocents who died on 9/11. It was then further compromised by the morally unjustifiable war in Iraq." Contributors to *Sojourners* explored proposals for withdrawing from Afghanistan "in a responsible manner, with an enduring commitment to development and human rights" for its people. Wallis regularly cited the sobering statistics of the two wars: over 40,000 American casualties, hundreds of thousands of Iraqi and Afghan dead, millions of refugees, and an estimated cost of almost $4 billion. When most of the final troops left Iraq in December 2011, Wallis called upon the country to "learn from this horrible and costly mistake" that "terrorism is not defeated by wars of mass occupation." While rejecting unilateral militarism, progressive evangelicals repeated calls for the United States to use its influence to promote global peace and justice—especially in the Middle East. *Sojourners* and ESA's *Prism* continued to publish articles in support of nonviolent means to resolve the Palestinian-Israeli conflict. Tony Campolo, ESA's Paul Alexander, Ron Sider, and Shane Claiborne participated in "Christ at the

Checkpoint" conferences, hosted by Palestinian Christians at Bethlehem Bible College in 2010 and 2012, to promote peacemaking and reconciliation. On a political level, Sider, Campolo, and Wallis joined ecumenical religious leaders in endorsing open letters to Obama that encouraged "immediate and bold American leadership" in reviving negotiations in order to achieve "a just, lasting and comprehensive peace with a viable Palestinian state living side by side with Israel in peace and security."[7]

In addition to these long-standing concerns, two additional causes served as conspicuous parts of progressive evangelicals' political engagement. First, leaders championed environmental stewardship and sustainability, or what some supporters called "creation care." After scattered articles in *The Other Side* and *Sojourners* concerning environmental issues in the 1980s, progressive evangelicals began to declare more and more regularly in the following decades that Christians must make protection of the environment a political priority—especially because environmental problems particularly hurt the poor. They accepted not only the scientific consensus regarding humans' role in global warming and other environmental degradation but also the need for governmental regulations in response. During elections, leaders urged Christians to evaluate political candidates' positions on public policies to protect the environment. "We believe the environment—caring for God's earth—is a religious issue" that should be among Christians' political priorities, Sojourners proclaimed in its 2004 "God is Not a Republican. Or a Democrat" campaign. In 2008 both Wallis in *The Great Awakening* and Ron Sider in *The Scandal of Evangelical Politics* devoted a separate chapter to outlining the biblical imperatives for creation care and to defending appropriate public policies. Throughout Obama's first term, *Sojourners* and *Prism* published numerous articles on environmental concerns such as the dangerous realities of climate change, deforestation, mountaintop-removal mining, and animal suffering.[8]

Second, justice and rights for immigrants also became a political priority for progressive evangelicals in the early twenty-first century. Though they had occasionally addressed immigrant issues prior to 2006, broader public debates about illegal immigration began to capture the attention of evangelical progressives as well. Numerous leaders identified immigrants as analogous to "aliens" for whom God's people must care (for example, Leviticus 19:34) or "strangers" whom Jesus instructed his disciples to welcome (Matthew 25:31-46). Others characterized immigrants as among the "neighbors" whom Christians must love as themselves. In

Obama's early presidency, progressive evangelicals particularly took up calls for humane immigration reform that would secure national borders while keeping families intact and putting undocumented immigrants on a path to legal status or citizenship. *Sojourners* and *Prism* printed a flood of articles in support. Wallis took part in a protest against Arizona's 2010 strict anti-immigrant law, which he called "a social and racial sin" that "should be denounced as such by people of faith and conscience across the nation." In 2012 Wallis also helped establish a coalition of evangelical leaders from across the political spectrum as the Evangelical Immigration Table. Group members issued an "Evangelical Statement of Principles for Immigration Reform" and mobilized their respective constituencies to pray and to lobby for legislation based upon the principles of human dignity, family unity, and respect for the rule of law. President Obama met with Wallis and other representatives in March 2013, and Wallis believed that the political diversity of the group helped persuade the president to incorporate its proposals in his own bill.[9]

Four decades after the 1973 Chicago Declaration of Evangelical Social Concern that helped launch contemporary progressive evangelicalism, the movement stands as strong as ever. Leaders successfully created and sustained a notable form of biblically based public engagement. In the process, they developed a public theology that became the foundation for their movement's distinctive political positions, distinguishing themselves from both the Religious Right and the political left. During the 2012 presidential election season, Jim Wallis summarized well the perennial vision of the contemporary progressive evangelical movement. "For me and a growing number of others, it is precisely because we are Bible-believing and Jesus-following evangelical Christians that we have a fundamental commitment to social, economic, and racial justice and are called to be good stewards of God's creation, peacemakers in a world of conflict and war, and consistent advocates for human life and dignity," he wrote. "And because we are members of the global body of Christ, we don't believe God blesses and loves our country more than others."[10]

As different leaders become the most prominent advocates for progressive evangelicalism, the foundational work of Wallis, Ron Sider, Tony Campolo, and other representatives has prepared the movement to remain an important part of America's religious and political landscape in the coming years. In 2013 Sider retired as president of ESA. Although his successors, co-presidents Paul Alexander and Al Tizon, have less of a national profile than Sider, they pledged to sustain the group's dynamic activism in addressing racism, "human trafficking and sexual justice, immigration reform, the Israeli/Palestinian situation, economic justice, creation care, animal welfare, and other crucial issues." In early 2014, Campolo announced that he would also retire as president from his organization, the Evangelical Association for the Promotion of Education. Even at the age of seventy-nine, however, he planned to remain an active public speaker and leader within the "Red Letter Christian" network for the foreseeable future. As Wallis prepared to turn sixty-six in 2014, he kept an active schedule of writing, lobbying, media appearances, and conducting a book tour in support of his new work, *On God's Side: What Religion Forgets and Politics Hasn't Learned about Serving the Common Good*. After recovering from cancer surgery in mid-2013, Wallis resumed his prominent public activism and leadership of Sojourners—a role he will likely continue in as long as his health and age allow. To be sure, new leaders will emerge and inevitably take the progressive evangelical movement in new directions as they confront changing religious and political contexts. But as they do, and as younger generations of evangelicals construct their own pursuits of social justice and the common good, they can draw upon the practical models and the public theology developed by Sider, Wallis, Campolo, and many others associated with Sojourners, ESA, and *The Other Side* over the past forty years.[11]

Notes

ABBREVIATIONS

BGCA Billy Graham Center Archives
    CC *Christian Century*
    CT *Christianity Today*
  ESA Evangelicals for Social Action
    FN *Freedom Now*
  LAT *Los Angeles Times*
  NYT *New York Times*
   P-A *Post-American*
    PI *Philadelphia Inquirer*
  Sojo *Sojourners*
  TOS *The Other Side*
WCSC Wheaton College Special Collections
  WP *Washington Post*

INTRODUCTION

1. Vicki Kemper, "'It Won't Be Long Now,'" *Sojo*, Aug.-Sept. 1985, 32-35; "Police Arrest Christians in Capital Protest," *LAT*, May 28, 1985; Jim Wallis, "A Consistent Ethic of Life," *Sojo*, July 1985, 4-5.

2. George Curry, "248 Seized in Capital in Day of Protests," *Chicago Tribune*, May 30, 1985.

3. James Ridgeway, "Evangelical Group Is Rooted in Radical Movement," *LAT*, Jan. 19, 1985; "Evangelicals to Protest in Washington," *PI*, May 28, 1985; Curry, "248 Seized"; Ann Monroe, "Devout Dissidents," *Wall Street Journal*, May 24, 1985.

4. Monroe, "Devout Dissidents"; Curry, "248 Seized"; Wallis, "Consistent Ethic of Life"; David Holmberg, "Right or Left, They Follow the Bible," *PI*, June 14, 1985.

5. Wallis, "Consistent Ethic of Life"; Holmberg, "Right or Left"; George Curry, "Religion: Convert to Social Activism," *Chicago Tribune*, June 11, 1985; Monroe, "Devout Dissidents."

6. Ron Sider, "Why ESA Is Stubbornly Multi-Issue," *ESA Advocate*, Jan. 1989, 2; Wallis, *Soul of Politics*, 39.

7. Howard Kohn, "Ideal Politics," *LAT*, Nov. 6, 1994; Gary Scott Smith, "The Men and Religion Forward Movement of 1911-12: New Perspectives on Evangelical Social Concern and the Relationship Between Progressivism and Religion," *Westminster Theological Journal* 49 (Spring 1987): 91-118.

8. Dayton, *Discovering an Evangelical Heritage*, 21 (Finney quotation); T. Smith, *Revivalism and Social Reform*, 8, 151, 252; Young, *Bearing Witness against Sin*.

9. T. Smith, *Revivalism and Social Reform*, 163-77; Dayton, *Discovering an Evangelical Heritage*, 99-119; Magnuson, *Salvation in the Slums*; Hardesty, *Women Called to Witness*, 1-12; Kazin, *Godly Hero*, 124 (Bryan quotation). For a case study of progressive evangelicalism in Boston in the late nineteenth and early twentieth centuries, see Hartley, *Evangelicals at a Crossroads*.

10. Wallis, *Great Awakening*, 304-6.

11. Marsden, *Fundamentalism and American Culture*; Moberg, *Great Reversal*.

12. Marsden, *Fundamentalism and American Culture*; Schmidt, *Souls or the Social Order*; Carpenter, *Revive Us Again*.

13. "The Gospel's Continuing Relevance," *CT*, Nov. 5, 1965, 34; Marsden, *Understanding Fundamentalism and Evangelicalism*, 1-96; Hollinger, *Individualism and Social Ethics*; Fowler, *New Engagement*.

14. "The Chicago Declaration of Evangelical Social Concern," in Sider, *Chicago Declaration*, 1-2.

15. Martin, *With God on Our Side*; Williams, *God's Own Party*.

16. Wallis, "Recovering the Evangel," *Sojo*, Feb. 1981, 3-5.

17. Wallis, *Who Speaks for God?*, 14, 198-99; Tony Campolo, "Faith in Search of a Home," *Sojo*, Mar.-Apr. 1995, 19-20; Jim Wallis, "Who Speaks for God?," *Sojo*, Mar.-Apr. 1995, 16-18.

18. Wallis, *God's Politics*, xvi-xxviii, 3-4; "For the Health of the Nation," in Sider and Knippers, *Toward an Evangelical Public Policy*, 363-75; David Kirkpatrick, "Democrats Turn to Leader of Religious Left," *NYT*, Jan. 17, 2005; Wes Stephenson, "The Amazing True Story of the Liberal Evangelical," *Boston Globe*, Jan. 23, 2005; David Paul Kuhn, "The Gospel According to Jim Wallis," *WP*, Nov. 26, 2006; Stephanie Simon, "Evangelicals Branch Out Politically," *LAT*, Jan. 31, 2006.

19. Wallis, *Great Awakening*, 25; Claiborne, *Irresistible Revolution*; Sullivan, *Party Faithful*; Harper, *Evangelical Does Not Equal*; Campolo, *Red Letter Christians*, 21-23; Francis Fitzgerald, "The New Evangelicals," *New Yorker*, June 30, 2008; Chris Smyth, "Obama Evangelicals Are Closing the God Gap," *London Times*, Mar. 8, 2008; Dan Gilgoff, "Evangelical Minister Jim Wallis Is in Demand in Obama's Washington," *U.S. News & World Report*, Mar. 31 2009, http://www.usnews.com/news/religion/articles/2009/03/31/evangelical-minister-jim-wallis-is-in-demand-in-obamas-washington (Dec. 31, 2013).

20. David Van Biema, "The Birth of the New Evangelicalism," *Time*, Nov. 3, 2008, http://www.time.com/time/specials/packages/article/0,28804,1855948_1855958_1862091,00.html (Dec. 31, 2013)

21. Sojourners, "2013 Media Kit," http://sojo.net/sites/default/files/SojournersMediaKit%202013.pdf (Dec. 31, 2013); Swartz, *Moral Minority*.

22. [Self statement], *TOS*, Oct. 1988, 9; "History and Vision," *TOS*, July-Aug. 1989, 4.

23. Ted Olsen, "Where Jim Wallis Stands," *CT*, May 1, 2008, 55; Ron Sider, "I'm Not a Social Activist," *Prism*, Nov.-Dec. 2003, 36; Jim Wallis, "An Evangelical Manifesto," *Sojo*, July 2008, 5-6; "An Evangelical Manifesto," http://www.anevangelicalmanifesto.com/docs/Evangelical_Manifesto.pdf (Dec. 31 2013).

24. Quebedeaux, *Young Evangelicals*; Fowler, *New Engagement*; Campolo, "Faith in Search of a Home," 19; Wallis, *Great Awakening*, 25.

25. Nash, *Why the Left Is Not Right*; Gushee, *Future of Faith*; Swartz, *Moral Minority*; Janet I. Tu, "Is There a Great Awakening?," *Seattle Times*, Jan. 31, 2008; Olsen, "Where Jim Wallis Stands," 52; Tony Campolo, "What's a 'Red-Letter Christian'?," Beliefnet.com, http://www.beliefnet.com/Faiths/Christianity/2006/02/Whats-A-Red-Letter-Christian.aspx (Dec. 31, 2013).

26. [Editorial response], *Sojo*, Nov. 1977, 39; Jim Wallis, "Ten Years," *Sojo*, Sept. 1981, 5; Wallis and Hollyday, *Cloud of Witnesses*.

27. Larsen, "God's Gardeners"; Wilkinson, *Between God and Green*.

CHAPTER 1

1. "The Chicago Declaration of Evangelical Social Concern," in Sider, *Chicago Declaration*, 1-2.

2. Coffman, *Christian Century*; Hulsether, *Building a Protestant Left*; Quebedeaux, *Young Evangelicals*; Swartz, *Moral Minority*.

3. Fred Alexander, "Integration Now," *FN*, Dec. 1965, 3; Fred Alexander, "Our Name," *FN*, Aug. 1965, 4. On white evangelical attitudes toward segregation and civil rights, see Emerson and Smith, *Divided by Faith*, 45-49.

4. Fred Alexander, "Christ Is Not the Answer," *FN*, May-June 1967, 9.

5. F. Alexander, "Our Name," 4.

6. "Social Concern," *FN*, May-June 1967, 3; John Alexander, "A Christian World View," *FN*, May-June 1967, 11. See also Robert Krueger, "Evangelical Retreat from the Social Gospel," *FN*, Dec. 1965, 6-7.

7. For example, see *FN*, Aug.-Sept. 1966, devoted to the theme "The Bible and the Curse."

8. John Alexander, "The Problems of Integration in the Community," *FN*, Apr. 1966, 4; John Alexander, "These Things Ought Not Be So," *FN*, Oct.-Nov. 1966, 3; John Alexander, "What the Christians Must Do," *FN*, Dec. 1966, 6; Fred Alexander, "Understanding," *FN*, Dec. 1966, 8.

9. John Alexander, "A Time to Act," *FN*, May-June 1968, 3.

10. For example, see Fred Alexander, "Do Bible Believers Believe the Bible?," *FN*, Apr. 1966, 3; J. Alexander, "These Things Ought Not Be So," 2; F. Alexander, "Christ Is Not the Answer," 9.

11. Bill Pannell, "Memorial to Dr. Martin Luther King," *FN*, May-June 1968, 4; Fred Alexander, "Memorial," *FN*, May-June 1968, 7; John Alexander, "Day of the Evil Gun," *FN*, July-Aug. 1968, 19; John Alexander, "The Old Testament in Today's Society," *TOS*, May-June 1970, 4.

12. F. Alexander, "Memorial," 7; Fred Alexander, "The American Dream," *TOS*, Nov.-Dec. 1970, 29; John Alexander, "Not That Separate," *FN*, Sept.-Oct. 1968, 25; Arthur Glasser, "The Cultural Mandate," *FN*, Jan.-Feb. 1969, 19. See also *FN*, Nov.-Dec. 1968, devoted to the theme "Law and Order."

13. Coffman, *Christian Century*; Hulsether, *Building a Protestant Left*; Martin, *With God on Our Side*, 69-70 (Falwell quotation).

14. "The Other Side," *TOS*, Sept.-Oct. 1969, 31; John Alexander, "The Authority of Scripture," *TOS*, Jan.-Feb. 1973, 45; John Alexander, "Evangelism," *TOS*, Mar.-Apr. 1972, 3-4, 48.

15. William Lunch and Peter Sperlich, "American Public Opinion and the War in Vietnam," *Western Political Quarterly* 32 (Mar. 1979): 25; Settje, *Faith and War*; Hulsether, *Building a Protestant Left*, 125-34; Loveland, *American Evangelicals*, 118-64; Williams, *God's Own Party*, 79 (Graham quotation).

16. John Alexander, [response], *TOS*, Sept.-Oct. 1971, 7; John Alexander, "A Politics of Love," *TOS*, July-Aug. 1972, 42-44.

17. Peter Ediger, "Explo '72," *P-A*, Fall 1972, 13; Wallis, *Revive Us Again*, 83-85; "The Jesus Woodstock," *Time*, June 26, 1972, 66.

18. Jim Wallis, "Post-American Christianity," *P-A*, Fall 1971, 2-3; "What Is the People's Christian Coalition?," *P-A*, Winter 1972, 7.

19. Wallis, *God's Politics*, 34-35; Wallis, *Revive Us Again*, 19-51.

20. Wallis, *Revive Us Again*, 52-73.

21. Ibid., 72-76.

22. Ibid., 77-91.

23. Wallis, "Post-American Christianity," 2; Jim Wallis, "The Issue of 1972," *P-A*, Fall 1972, 2; Jim Wallis, "Babylon," *P-A*, Summer 1972, 8-9; William Stringfellow, "The Relevance of Babylon," *P-A*, Jan.-Feb. 1973, 8-9; People's Christian Coalition, "Bibliography," Nov. 1971, box 7, folder 7, Sojourners Collection, WCSC; Clark Pinnock, "The Christian Revolution," *P-A*, Fall 1971, 10: Jim Wallis, "The Movemental Church," *P-A*, Winter 1972, 3.

24. Wallis, "Post-American Christianity," 3; Joe Roos, "American Civil Religion," *P-A*, Spring 1972, 8-10; Mark Hatfield, "Piety and Patriotism," *P-A*, May-June 1973, 1-2; "What Is the People's Christian Coalition?," *P-A*, May-June 1973, 15.

25. Wallis, "Babylon," 9; Peggy Herbert, "Cost of Silence," *P-A*, Summer 1972, 5; Wallis, "Post-American Christianity," 3; Jim Wallis and Bob Sabath, "In Quest of Discipleship," *P-A*, May-June 1973, 3.

26. Donald Oden, "Psalm 23 of the Black Man," *P-A*, Fall 1972, 7; Glen Melnik, "Awake Thou That Sleepest," *P-A*, Fall 1971, 7; Dick and Joyce Boldrey,

"Technocracy and Women's Liberation," *P-A*, Summer 1972, 11; "Jesus Was No Chauvinist," *P-A*, Summer 1972, 11; Glen Melnik, "Lettuce Boycott," *P-A*, Fall 1972, 7; Wallis, "Babylon," 8; Jim Wallis, "Airwar," *P-A*, Spring 1972, 4-5; Wallis and Sabath, "In Quest of Discipleship," 3.

27. "Signs of a New Order," *P-A*, Summer 1972, 13; John R. Stott, "The Conservative Radical," *P-A*, Nov.-Dec. 1973, 5.

28. Wallis, "Post-American Christianity," 3 (emphasis added).

29. Bill Pannell, "How Blacks Must Change," *TOS*, Jan.-Feb. 1971, 20; Tom Skinner, "[Untitled]," *TOS*, July-Aug. 1970, 34. See also, for example, William Bentley, "The Other America," *TOS*, Jan.-Feb. 1970, 30-33; and John Perkins, "Black Religion," *TOS*, Jan.-Feb. 1972, 24-29.

30. Moberg, *Inasmuch*; Moberg, *Great Reversal*; Pierard, *Unequal Yoke*, 179; Clouse, Linder, and Pierard, *Protest and Politics*, 2.

31. Richard J. Mouw, "Reflections on My Encounter with the Anabaptist-Mennonite Tradition," in *Engaging Anabaptism: Conversations with a Radical Tradition*, ed. John D. Roth (Scottdale, Pa.: Herald Press, 2001), 118; Mouw, *Political Evangelism*, 7; Richard J. Mouw, "Weaving a Coherent Pattern of Discipleship," *CC*, Aug. 20-27, 1975, 729; Richard J. Mouw, "Evangelicals and Political Activism," *CC*, Dec. 27, 1972, 1316-19.

32. Grounds, *Evangelicalism*, 11, 28; Yoder, *Politics of Jesus*.

33. Hatfield, *Conflict and Conscience*, 27; Swartz, *Moral Minority*, 68-85.

34. Barrie Doyle, "Backing Their Man," *CT*, Oct. 27, 1972, 38-39; Walden Howard, EFM letter, n.d., ESA Collection, box 1, folder 4, BGCA; "The Evangelical Vote," *Newsweek*, Oct. 30, 1973, 93; Williams, *God's Own Party*, 102; Ron Sider to Stephen Charles Mott, Nov. 14, 1972, ESA Collection, box 1, folder 4, BGCA.

35. Mouw, "Weaving," 729; Sider to Mott.

36. "Signs of a New Order," *P-A*, May-June 1973, 12. The planning committee included Sider, John Alexander, Jim Wallis, Richard Pierard, David Moberg, Bill Pannell, Paul Henry, former *Christianity Today* coeditor Frank Gaebelein, Fuller Seminary theologian Lewis Smedes, Conservative Baptist Home Mission director Rufus Jones, and Eastern Mennonite College president Myron Augsburger.

37. Mouw, "Reflections," 118.

38. Richard Pierard, Lecture Notes, Feb. 15, 1974, ESA Collection, box 2, folder 1, BGCA; Henry, *Uneasy Conscience*, 13-14. On Henry's influence, see Swartz, *Moral Minority*, 13-25.

39. Ronald J. Sider, "An Historic Moment for Biblical Social Concern," in Sider, *Chicago Declaration*, 24-30.

40. "Chicago Declaration."

41. Ibid.

42. Ibid.

43. Sider, "Historic Moment," 15, 29; Paul B. Henry, "Reflections," in Sider, *Chicago Declaration*, 137; William H. Bentley, "Reflections," in Sider, *Chicago Declaration*, 135-36; Jim Wallis, "The Lesson of Watergate," *P-A*, Jan. 1974, 1; Joel A. Carpenter, "Compassionate Evangelicalism," *CT*, Dec. 2003, 41. For reaction to the Chicago Declaration, see Sider, "Historic Moment," 31-33.

44. Sider, "Historic Moment," 28-29; Swartz, *Moral Minority*, 187-212.

45. Sullivan, *Party Faithful*, 16 (Sider quotation); Williams, *God's Own Party*.

46. Seth Dowland, "'Family Values' and the Formation of a Christian Right Agenda," *Church History* 78.3 (Sept. 2009): 606-31.

CHAPTER 2

1. Wallis, *Soul of Politics*, 52-53.

2. Ibid., 40, xvii.

3. Sider, *Scandal of Evangelical Politics*, 25, 78, back cover; Wallis, *Agenda*; Jim Wallis, "What Does Washington Have to Say to Grand Rapids?," *Sojo*, July 1977, 3-4; Marlin VanElderen, "Setting Aside Common Stereotypes," *Sojo*, June 1978, 32; Wallis, *God's Politics*, back cover. On the evolution of Wallis's public theology, see Geoffrey C. Bowden, "The Evangelical-Anabaptist Spectrum: The Political Theologies of Francis Schaeffer, John Howard Yoder, and Jim Wallis," in *The Activist Impulse: Essays on the Intersection of Evangelicalism and Anabaptism*, ed. Jared S. Burkholder and David C. Cramer (Eugene, Ore.: Pickwick Publications, 2012), 292-320.

4. Victor Anderson, "The Search for Public Theology in the United States," in *Preaching as a Theological Task: World, Gospel, Scripture*, ed. Thomas G. Long and Edward Farley (Louisville: Westminster John Knox Press, 1996), 20; E. Harold Breitenberg Jr., "What Is Public Theology," in *Public Theology for a Global Society*, ed. Deirdre King Hainsworth and Scott R. Paeth (Grand Rapids, Mich.: Eerdmans, 2010), 5; Thiemann, *Constructing a Public Theology*, 21; Sider, *Scandal of Evangelical Politics*, 257n50, 39.

5. Ron Sider, "Why Public Policy Research in ESA?," *ESA Update*, Aug. 1982, 3; Wallis, *God's Politics*, 28; Wallis, *Great Awakening*, 8; Sider, *Scandal of Evangelical Politics*, 37, 41.

6. Ronald J. Sider, "Toward an Evangelical Political Philosophy," in *Christians and Politics Beyond the Culture Wars: An Agenda for Engagement*, ed. David P. Gushee (Grand Rapids, Mich.: Baker Books, 2000), 87; Ronald J. Sider, "Justice, Human Rights, and Government," in Sider and Knippers, *Toward an Evangelical Public Policy*, 167; Wallis, *God's Politics*, 5; Wallis, *Soul of Politics*, 72. See also Wallis, *Great Awakening*, 213-14; and Sider, *Scandal of Evangelical Politics*, 128.

7. Sider, *Scandal of Evangelical Politics*, 53-54; Stephen Mott and Ronald J. Sider, "Economic Justice: A Biblical Paradigm," in *Toward a Just and Caring Society: Christian Responses to Poverty in America*, ed. David P. Gushee (Grand Rapids, Mich.: Baker, 1999), 19; Sider, "Justice, Human Rights, and Government," 167; Wallis, *Who Speaks for God?*, 83; Wallis, *Soul of Politics*, 40.

8. Sider, *Scandal of Evangelical Politics*, 231; "The Chicago Declaration of Evangelical Social Concern," in Sider, *Chicago Declaration*, 1; Vernon Grounds, "Justice," *Prism*, May-June 1999, 18.

9. Mott and Sider, "Economic Justice," 19; Wallis, *Who Speaks for God?*, 86; Wallis, *Great Awakening*, 81, 85-86, 92; Sider, *Scandal of Evangelical Politics*, 59; Duane Shank, "Seeking Common Ground," *Sojo*, Jan. 2005, 9.

10. Mott and Sider, "Economic Justice," 19; Wallis, *Who Speaks for God?*, 139; Sider, *Scandal of Evangelical Politics*, 129.

11. Wallis, *God's Politics*, 6; Bill Kallio, "Frank Talk about ESA," *ESA Update*, Jan.-Feb. 1983, 5; Stephen Monsma, "Is Christian Engagement in Electoral Politics Any Different?," *ESA Update*, Nov.-Dec. 1987, 6; Wallis, *Great Awakening*, 59; Jim Wallis, "What Is 'Biblical Politics'?," *Sojo*, Nov. 2011, 7; Mott and Sider, "Economic Justice," 24; Sider, *Scandal of Evangelical Politics*, 106, 101.

12. Sider, *Scandal of Evangelical Politics*, 114-15, 134-37, 264n32; Wallis and Gutenson, *Living God's Politics*, 36.

13. Sider, *Scandal of Evangelical Politics*, 113-14, 122.

14. Ibid., 109, 114, 116, 125; Sider, *Just Generosity*, 55; Wallis, *God's Politics*, 240.

15. Sider, *Scandal of Evangelical Politics*, 90; Jim Wallis, "All Hands on Deck," *Sojo*, Apr. 2007, 5; "Here We Stand," *ESA Update*, Sept.-Oct. 1984, 2.

16. Wallis, *Soul of Politics*, 26-27; Sider, *Scandal of Evangelical Politics*, 90-91; Ronald J. Sider and Fred Clark, "Should We Give Up on Government?," *CT*, Mar. 2, 1998, 53-54; Wallis, *Great Awakening*, 70-71. See also Wallis, *Faith Works*, 166-67; and Wallis, *God's Politics*, 226-29.

17. Sider, *Scandal of Evangelical Politics*, 100; Wallis, *On God's Side*, 5.

18. Isaiah Berlin, "Two Concepts of Liberty," in *Four Essays on Liberty* (New York: Oxford University Press, 1969), 118-72; Ryan, *Making of Modern Liberalism* (especially 21-44). For a succinct account of varieties of the broad liberal tradition, see Gerald Gaus and Shane D. Courtland, "Liberalism," in *The Stanford Encyclopedia of Philosophy*, ed. Edward N. Zalta (Spring 2011 ed.), http://plato.stanford.edu/archives/spr2011/entries/liberalism/ (Dec. 31, 2013).

19. Bellah et al., *Habits of the Heart*, 142; Mark Olson, "A Perversity of Freedom," *TOS*, Feb. 1984, 13; Sider, *Scandal of Evangelical Politics*, 55, 130; Wallis, *Soul of Politics*, 72-73.

20. Audi and Wolterstorff, *Religion in the Public Square*, 25, 29; Rawls, "The Idea of Public Reason Revisited," *University of Chicago Law Review* 64.3 (Summer 1997): 765-807. For an overview of diverse liberal theorists who defend restraints and restrictions on religious rationales in public arguments, see Eberle, *Religious Conviction*.

21. Wallis, *God's Politics*, 31-32; Sider, *Scandal of Evangelical Politics*, 180-82; Wallis, *Great Awakening*, 57-69; Jim Wallis, "From a Shoebox to a Movement," *Sojo*, Nov. 2011, 15.

22. Sider, *Scandal of Evangelical Politics*, 38-40; Audi and Wolterstorff, *Religion in the Public Square*, 94. See also the exchange between Wolterstorff and philosopher Richard Rorty in *Journal of Religious Ethics*, 31.1 (Mar. 2003): 129-49.

23. Wallis, *God's Politics*, 56, 4, 69, 7; Wallis, *Soul of Politics*, xvi; Neuhaus, *Naked Public Square*; Carter, *Culture of Disbelief*. For additional critiques of proposals to restrain or to restrict the role of religion in liberal democracies, see Eberle, *Religious Conviction*.

24. Jim Wallis, "Signs of the Times," *Sojo*, Nov. 1988, 19; Wallis, *Great Awakening*, 302; Wallis, *God's Politics*, 3, 67-68; Jim Wallis, "Dangerous Religion," *Sojo*, Sept.-Oct. 2003, 25. On the Religious Right's democratic commitments, see

Shields, *Democratic Virtues.* On the shared Christian antiliberalism of progressive evangelicals, the Religious Right, and Catholic social activists, see Bivins, *Fracture of Good Order.*

25. Ellen Willis, "Freedom from Religion," *The Nation*, Feb. 19, 2001, 11-16; Americans United for the Separation of Church and State, "Political Leaders Should Resist Pressure to Take Up Preaching, Says Church-State Expert," Feb. 1, 2005, http://www.au.org/media/press-releases/political-leaders-should-resist-pressure-to-take-up-preaching-says-church-state (Dec. 31, 2013); Hunter, *To Change the World*, 147-48. For another theological critique of the Religious Right and evangelical left, see Collins, *Power.*

26. Wallis, *God's Politics*, 71; Sider, *Scandal of Evangelical Politics*, 39.

27. Wallis, *God's Politics*, 7; Sider, "Towards a Political Philosophy," *ESA Advocate*, Oct. 1988, 2; Wallis, *Great Awakening*, 308. In challenging liberal philosophers' individualistic assumptions and attempts to justify a theory of justice independent of any comprehensive moral or religious doctrines, progressive evangelical leaders expressed objections similar to those developed by philosophers such as Michael Sandel, Alasdair MacIntyre, Charles Taylor, and others who became known as communitarians. See Mulhall and Swift, *Liberals and Communitarians.*

CHAPTER 3

1. David Hilfiker, "Still Separate, Still Unequal," *Sojo*, May 2004, 7.

2. Findlay, *Church People in the Struggle*; Emerson and Smith, *Divided by Faith*, 45-48.

3. "John Alexander: Taking Jesus Seriously," *TOS*, Oct. 1985, 10; John Alexander, "Negro Intelligence," *FN*, Nov.-Dec. 1967, 9; William Bentley, "The Other America," *TOS*, Jan.-Feb. 1970, 30-33; John Alexander, "Racism," *TOS*, Mar.-Apr. 1970, 3-4; Bill Pannell, "Lawlessness Administration Style," *TOS*, Sept.-Oct. 1971, 32-35; Tom Skinner, "Black Power," *TOS*, Jan.-Feb. 1972, 6-11.

4. Jim Wallis, "Post-American Christianity," *P-A*, Fall 1971, 2; Glen Melnik, "Awake Thou That Sleepest," *P-A*, Fall 1971, 7; "What Is the People's Christian Coalition?," *P-A*, Winter 1972, 7.

5. Jones, "Ronald Sider," 406; "Ron Sider: Working for Kingdom Values," *TOS*, Oct. 1986, 11; "The Chicago Declaration of Evangelical Social Concern," in Sider, *Chicago Declaration*, 1.

6. Fred and John Alexander, "A Manifesto for White Christians," *TOS*, Jan.-Feb. 1974, 51; John Perkins, "Integration or Development," *TOS*, Jan.-Feb. 1974, 12, 48; Ron Potter, "Black Christian Separatism," *TOS*, Jan.-Feb. 1974, 42; Jim Wallis, "Putting Flesh on Words," *P-A*, May 1974, 23.

7. Patterson, *Restless Giant*, 15-19, 62-66; Wilson, *Declining Significance.*

8. Jim Wallis, "Mammon's Iron Thumb," *Sojo*, Feb. 1978, 3-4; John Perkins, "Stoning the Prophets," *Sojo*, Feb. 1978, 8-9; Mark Olson, "White Follies, Black Shackles," *TOS*, June 1979, 14, 28.

9. Schaller, *Right Turn*, 132; Mayer, *Running on Race*, 150-72.

10. Jim Wallis, "Lord Have Mercy," *Sojo*, Oct. 1980, 5; John Alexander, "Welcome to the Election Circus," *TOS*, Sept. 1980, 10-13; John Alexander, "Did We Blow It?," *TOS*, Feb. 1981, 10-14; Jim Wallis, "The Children Are Getting Hurt," *Sojo*, May 1981, 3. See also Lucius Outlaw, "Down to the Crossroads," *Sojo*, May 1981, 12-16.

11. Bill Kallio, "Editorial," *ESA Advocate*, Feb. 1982, 2; Danny Collum, "Clear Signals," *Sojo*, Mar. 1982, 4, 6; Danny Collum, "Prophet of Hope for the Sick and Tired," *Sojo*, Dec. 1982, 4.

12. Bill Pannell, "Catsup and Baloney," *TOS*, Oct. 1985, 33; Jim Wallis, "A Great Prophet of God," *Sojo*, Jan. 1986, 4; James H. Cone, "A Dream or a Nightmare?," *Sojo*, Jan. 1986, 28-29.

13. Jim Wallis, "America's Original Sin," *Sojo*, Nov. 1987, 15-16.

14. Perry Perkins, "The Loss of Steve Biko," *Sojo*, Nov. 1977, 7; Ron Sider, "What If Ten Thousand," *TOS*, Nov. 1979, 14-16; Muhammad Isaiah Kenyatta, "Time to Take Offense," *TOS*, Nov. 1981, 20.

15. Culverson, *Contesting Apartheid*, 87-88; Robert Pear, "Falwell Denounces Tutu as a 'Phony,'" *NYT*, Aug. 21, 1985; Elizabeth Schmidt, "Greasing the Wheels of Apartheid," *Sojo*, Oct. 1983, 10-12; Jim Wallis, "A Lesson for the Long Haul," *Sojo*, Oct. 1986, 5. See additional articles in *Sojo*, Feb. 1985, and *TOS*, Dec. 1985.

16. Wallis and Hollyday, *Crucible of Fire*; "Issues in Christian Perspective: South Africa," insert in *ESA Update*, May 1986; "Hundreds Sign Kabare," *ESA Update*, Apr. 1988, 5.

17. Sharon Temple, "Apartheid in America," *ESA Update*, July-Aug. 1988, 4; "Peace Pentecost 1988," *Sojo*, Nov. 1987, 6; Johnny Edward Tolliver, "American Education," *TOS*, Sept.-Oct. 1989, 20-24.

18. Jim Wallis, "From Integration to Transformation," *Sojo*, Aug.-Sept. 1990, 4-5; John Perkins, "Restless Vigilance," *TOS*, May-June 1991, 26. See additional articles in *Sojo*, Aug.-Sept. 1990.

19. Phil Shenk, "The Longest Walk," *Sojo*, July 1978, 10-12; Charlie Garriott, "Captives in Their Homeland," *Sojo*, July 1978, 12-13; Charlie Garriott, "Land, Sin, and Repentance," *TOS*, June 1985, 23; "A Call to Action," *TOS*, June 1987, 36-37.

20. Bob Hulteen, "Unsettled Scores of History," *Sojo*, Jan. 1991, 4, 6; "Special Focus on Native Americans," *ESA Advocate*, Jan.-Feb. 1992, 9. See also Carol Hampton, "A Heritage Denied," *Sojo*, Jan. 1991, 11-13; Kathleen Hayes, "Columbus and the Great Commission," *ESA Advocate*, Jan.-Feb. 1992, 1-7; and Little Rock Reed, "Broken Treaties, Broken Promises," *TOS*, May-June 1992, 48-54.

21. Jim Wallis, "Time to Listen and Act," *Sojo*, July 1992, 12; Jim Wallis, "A New Conversation on Race," *Sojo*, Nov.-Dec. 1995, 10; Rodney Clapp, "One Afternoon in the Sun," *Prism*, Nov.-Dec. 2000, 5; Wallis, *Who Speaks for God?*, 111, 113.

22. Yvonne V. Delk, "To Move Beyond Denial," *Sojo*, July 1992, 16; Eugene F. Rivers, "Blocking the Prayers of the Church," *Sojo*, Mar.-Apr. 1997, 26-31; Bob Hulteen, "As Long As You Think You're White, There's No Hope for You," *Sojo*, Mar.-Apr. 1997, 28-29; Jim Wallis, "Why?" *Sojo*, Mar.-Apr. 1998, 9; Yvonne Delk,

"A Time for Action," *Sojo*, Mar.-Apr. 1998, 25; Harold Dean Trulear, "I've Been to the Edge," *Prism*, Mar.-Apr. 1998, 8.

23. Patterson, *Restless Giant*, 305-8; Jim Wallis, "Evangelicals and Race," *Sojo*, Mar.-Apr. 1997, 11; Andres Tapia and Rodolpho Carrasco, "The High Stakes in Promise Keepers' Bid to Reconcile Races," *Prism*, Jan.-Feb. 1998, 28-29; Bill Wylie-Kellermann, "Exorcising an American Demon," *Sojo*, Mar.-Apr. 1998, 16-20.

24. "Race in America," *Prism*, July-Aug. 2001, 5-11; Franklin D. Raines, "40 Acres and a Mortgage," *Sojo*, Sept.-Oct. 2002, 24-29; Meg E. Cox, "Living beyond Hatred," *Sojo*, Dec. 2006, 24-28; Elizabeth Palmberg, "Seeing Green," *Sojo*, May-June 2003, 17-18; Alexis Vaughan, "A Nation of Jenas," *Sojo*, Jan. 2008, 7; Harold Dean Trulear, "Jena 6 Surprise," *Prism*, Mar.-Apr. 2008, 39; Danny Duncan Collum, "Color Lines and Party Lines," *Sojo*, Aug. 2004, 25.

25. Shailagh Murray and Peter Slevin, "As Minister Repeats Comments, Obama Tries to Quiet Fray," *WP*, Apr. 29, 2008; John W. Kennedy, "Preach and Reach," *CT*, Oct. 2008, 26-30; Jim Wallis, "Defending the Facts on Obama's Faith," *Huffington Post*, Feb. 29, 2008, http://www.huffingtonpost.com/jim-wallis/defending-the-facts-on-ob_b_89271.html (Dec. 31, 2013); Jim Wallis, "Healing the Wounds of Race," *Sojo*, May 2008, 5-6; Ron Sider, "Wright, Obama, and the Future: We Must Choose," *Prism*, July-Aug. 2008, 40.

26. Sider, "Wright, Obama, and the Future," 40; Jeff Zeleny, "Obama Urges U.S. to Grapple with Race Issue," *NYT*, Mar. 19, 2008; Wallis, "Healing the Wounds of Race," 5; Jim Wallis, "A Transformational Moment," *Huffington Post*, June 5, 2008, http://www.huffingtonpost.com/jim-wallis/a-transformational-moment_b_105495.html (Dec. 31, 2013); Kennedy, "Preach and Reach," 30; Jim Wallis, "A New Faith Coalition," *Sojo*, Jan. 2009, 5-6; Mary Nelson, "Post-Racial?," *God's Politics Blog*, http://sojo.net/blogs/2008/11/05/post-racial-no-not-yet-so-lets-get-work (Dec. 31, 2013).

27. "The Truth about All of You," *TOS*, Apr. 1978, 6-7; "Who You Are," *TOS*, Sept. 1982, 7; Joe Roos, "Into 1980 Together," *Sojo*, Jan. 1980, 4; "1984 ESA Member Survey Results," *ESA Update*, Jan.-Feb. 1984, 3; "Who We Are," *ESA Update*, Apr. 1988, 1.

28. "Growing Together," *TOS*, July-Aug. 1975, 31; Lincoln and Mamiya, *Black Church*; Marsden, *Understanding Fundamentalism and Evangelicalism*. For a recent analysis of African Americans and evangelicalism, see Gilbreath, *Reconciliation Blues*.

29. William H. Bentley, "Reflections," in Sider, *Chicago Declaration*, 136; "Growing Together," *TOS*, 45.

30. Ron Sider, "Called to Be Servant Advocates," *ESA Advocate*, Sept. 1988, 1; Ron Sider, "Why ESA Is Stubbornly Multi-Issue," *ESA Advocate*, Jan. 1989, 2; Swartz, *Moral Minority*, 187-95.

31. "The Chicago Declaration," 1; Wallis, "Time to Listen and Act," 12; Wallis, "The Children Are Getting Hurt," 3; Wallis, *Soul of Politics*, 91-92.

32. Bentley, *National Black Evangelical Association*, 104; Danny Collum, "Filling Out the Vision," *Sojo*, Oct. 1984, 3; Michael McKinley, "Telling the Truth," *Prism*, May-June 2000, 12-15.

33. Emerson and Smith, *Divided By Faith*, 76-79, 90, 112.

34. Wallis, "Why?," 9; Gilbreath, *Reconciliation Blues*, ix; John Alexander, "Racism," *TOS*, Mar.-Apr. 1970, 33; "Chicago Declaration," 1; Collum, "Clear Signals," 6; Wallis, "America's Original Sin," 17.

35. "Can My Vote Be Biblical?," *ESA Update*, Sept.-Oct. 1984, 4; "Here We Stand," *ESA Update*, Sept.-Oct. 1984, 2 (emphasis added); Ronald J. Sider, "Mischief by Statute," *CT*, July 16, 1976, 14; Sider, *Rich Christians* (1977), 133; Craig Wong, "MLK's Message Revisited," *Prism*, Nov.-Dec. 2007, 33.

36. John Alexander, "Reverse Racism," *TOS*, Mar. 1978, 12-13; Jim Wallis, "The 'Equality' of the Hard-Hearted," *Sojo*, Aug. 1978, 4-5.

37. Van Temple, "Affirmative Action Is Good Business," *ESA Advocate*, Dec. 1991, 12; Jim Wallis, "Is Affirmative Action Obsolete?," *Sojo*, July-Aug. 1998, 12; Barbara Reynolds, "Playing the Race Card," *Sojo*, May-June 1995, 10-11; Timothy Tseng, "Affirmative Action," *Prism*, Jan.-Feb. 1996, 12.

38. Vernon Grounds, "Sharing South Africa's Agony," *ESA Update*, May 1986, 3; "Peace Pentecost 1988," *Sojo*, Apr. 1988, 23; Wallis, *Who Speaks for God?*, 117, 118, 123.

CHAPTER 4

1. "Jesus Was No Chauvinist," *P-A*, Summer 1972, 11; "What Is the People's Christian Coalition?," *P-A*, Summer 1972, 6; Dick Boldrey and Joyce Boldrey, "Technocracy and Women's Liberation," *P-A*, Summer 1972, 5-6.

2. Hardesty, *Women Called to Witness*; Dayton, *Discovering an Evangelical Heritage*, 85-98; Gallagher, *Evangelical Identity*, 19-37.

3. Gallagher, *Evangelical Identity*, 37-44; DeBerg, *Ungodly Women*; Bendroth, *Fundamentalism and Gender*.

4. Andre S. Bustanoby, "Love, Honor, and Obey," *CT*, June 6, 1969, 3; Mary Bouma, "Liberated Mothers," *CT*, May 7, 1971, 4.

5. Letha Scanzoni, "Woman's Place," *Eternity*, Feb. 1966, 14-16; Letha Scanzoni, "Elevating Marriage to Partnership," *Eternity*, July 1968, 11-14; Ruth A. Schmidt, "Second-Class Citizenship in the Kingdom of God," *CT*, Jan. 1, 1971, 13; Nancy Hardesty, "Women: Second Class Citizens," *Eternity*, Jan. 1971, 14-16.

6. "Eve's Second Apple," *CT*, Aug. 24, 1973, 29; Billy Graham, "Jesus and the Liberated Woman," *Ladies' Home Journal*, Dec. 1970, 42; Gallagher, *Evangelical Identity*, 46-49.

7. John Alexander, "Thinking Male," *TOS*, July-Aug. 1973, 3-4, 43-47; Judy Alexander, "Servanthood and Submission," *TOS*, July-Aug. 1973, 2, 40-43; Letha Scanzoni, "Mystique and Machismo," *TOS*, July-Aug. 1973, 12-15; Nancy Hardesty, "Gifts," *TOS*, July-Aug. 1973, 22-26; "Jesus Was no Chauvinist"; Boldrey and Boldrey, "Technocracy and Women's Liberation."

8. Nancy Hardesty, "Blessed the Waters That Rise and Fall to Rise Again," *EEWC Update*, Summer 2004; "The Chicago Declaration of Evangelical Social Concern," in Sider, *Chicago Declaration*, 2; "Action Proposals Accepted at the

Second Thanksgiving Workshop," ESA Collection, box 2, folder 16, BGCA; Cochran, *Evangelical Feminism*, 14-16.

9. Jim Wallis, "Our Common Struggle," *P-A*, Aug.-Sept. 1974, 3-4; Wes Michaelson, "Neither Male nor Female," *Sojo*, Jan. 1976, 12; John Alexander, "A Conversation with Virginia Mollenkott," *TOS*, May-June 1976, 24; Virginia Mollenkott quoted in *TOS*, Apr. 1977, 43.

10. "The Chicago Statement on Biblical Inerrancy," in *Evangelicals and Inerrancy*, ed. Ronald Youngblood (Nashville, Tenn.: Thomas Nelson, 1984), 231.

11. Scanzoni and Hardesty, *All We're Meant to Be*, 18-19; Cochran, *Evangelical Feminism*, 11-31.

12. Phyllis E. Alsdurf, "Evangelical Feminists," *CT*, July 21, 1978, 47; Gundry, *Woman Be Free!*, 38.

13. Harold Lindsell, "Egalitarianism and Scriptural Infallibility," *CT*, Mar. 26, 1979, 46; Quebedeaux, *Worldly Evangelicals*, 125; Gundry, *Woman Be Free!*, 37; Cochran, *Evangelical Feminism*, 64-69.

14. Jim Wallis, "Our Common Struggle," *P-A*, Aug.-Sept. 1974, 4; Lucille Sider Dayton, "The Feminist Movement and Scripture," *P-A*, Aug.-Sept. 1974, 10-11; Boyd Reese, "Review," *P-A*, Aug.-Sept. 1974, 26; Thomas Howard and Donald W. Dayton, "Dialogue on Women, Hierarchy and Equality," *P-A*, May 1975, 8-15; Nancy Hardesty, "Toward a Total Human Theology," *Sojo*, May-June 1976, 35-36; J. Alexander, "A Conversation with Virginia Mollenkott," 30.

15. Patterson, *Restless Giant*, 45-58.

16. Falwell, *Listen, America!*, 150-52; Williams, *God's Own Party*, 105-11, 143-46.

17. "The New Housewife Blues," *Time*, Mar. 14, 1977, 62-69; Sharon Gallagher, "The Soul of the Total Woman," *Sojo*, May 1977, 31; Letha Scanzoni and John Scanzoni, "Liberated, but . . . ," *TOS*, Mar. 1978, 52-53.

18. Joyce Hollyday, "Toward One Freedom," *Sojo*, July 1980, 5; Joyce Hollyday, "Walking through Death Valley Days," *Sojo*, June 1981, 3; Joyce Hollyday, "Just Where Is the ERA?," *Sojo*, Feb. 1982, 6; Dana Mills Powell, "Count-down for ERA," *Sojo*, Feb. 1982, 10-11; Edith Holleman, "The ERA," *TOS*, Aug. 1982, 10-12.

19. Virginia Mollenkott, "Feminism and the Kingdom," *Sojo*, June 1977, 28-30; Hollyday, "Toward One Freedom," 5.

20. Patterson, *Restless Giant*, 271-72; Phyllis Korkki, "A Slow Narrowing of the Pay Gap," *NYT*, Oct. 21, 2007; Center for American Women and Politics, "Women in Elective Office 2008," http://www.cawp.rutgers.edu/fast_facts/levels_of_office/documents/elective08.pdf (Dec. 31, 2013); Evans, *Tidal Wave*, 4-5.

21. Claudia Wallis, "Onward, Women," *Time*, Dec. 4, 1989, 82; Joyce Hollyday, "Frontrunners and Backlashers," *Sojo*, Nov. 1992, 19-20; "Robertson Letter Attacks Feminists," *NYT*, Aug. 26, 1992; Davis, *Moving the Mountain*, 433-512; Evans, *Tidal Wave*, 176-238.

22. Joyce Hollyday, "Trials and Triumphs for Feminism," *Sojo*, June 1992, 4-5.

23. Vicki Kemper, "Poor and Getting Poorer," *Sojo*, Mar. 1986, 14-18; Joyce Hollyday, "Women at Work, " *Sojo*, Apr. 1987, 4; Joyce Hollyday, "Gender Gap at Work," *Sojo*, May 1987, 12; "Washington Update," *ESA Advocate*, Sept. 1988, 5;

"Washington Update," *ESA Advocate*, June 1989, 7; "Washington Update," *ESA Advocate*, May 1992, 12; Margaret Randall, "Gender, Money, and Power," *TOS*, Sept.-Oct. 1998, 46-48.

24. Donna Schaper, "Imbalance of Power," *Sojo*, Nov. 1981, 26-29; "Violence against Women," *Sojo*, Nov. 1984, 10-27; Joyce Hollyday, "Breaking the Silence," *Sojo*, Apr. 1990, 6-7; Joyce Hollyday, "Ending the War against Women," *Sojo*, Aug.-Sept. 1990, 7; Karen Lattea, "Ending the Stigma and the Silence," *Sojo*, July 1991, 5; Philip Brasfield, "Stranger to Our Town," *TOS*, Sept.-Oct. 1990, 21; James Moore, "Bread and Roses," *ESA Advocate*, Oct. 1992, 4; Katherine Clark Kroeger, "An Agenda for Biblical Feminism at the End of the Century," *Prism*, Sept.-Oct. 1995, 11.

25. Molly Marsh, "Out of Harm's Way," *Sojo*, June 2008, 9; Al Miles, "Domestic-Violence Intervention and Prevention," *Prism*, May-June 2004, 11. See also, for example, Dee Dee Risher, "Violence: Personal and Political," *TOS*, May-June 2002, 42-45; and Gail Martin, "Breaking the 'Holy Hush,'" *Sojo*, Jan. 2007, 24-29.

26. Mary P. Burke, "Hope for the Future," *TOS*, May 1983, 21; Moore, "Bread and Roses," 2; Ron Sider, "Injustice against Women," *Prism*, Jan.-Feb. 2007, 40. See also, for example, Vicki Kemper, "'The Unique Concerns of Women,'" *Sojo*, Oct. 1985, 5-6; Dee Dee Risher, "Bread and Tortillas: A Dialogue of Women," *TOS*, Nov.-Dec. 1988; Rosemary Radford Ruether, "The Art of Survival," *Sojo*, July 1993, 18-21; Rose Marie Berger, "Women Building Peace," *Sojo*, Nov. 2004, 38-41; Elizabeth Palmberg, "'Teach a Woman to Fish ... and Everyone Eats,'" *Sojo*, June 2005, 28-34; Asra Q. Nomani, "A Faith of Their Own," *Sojo*, Mar. 2007, 8; and Laurel Rae Mathewson, "Women's Work: The Better Half of Peacemaking, *Sojo*, June 2007, 9.

27. Gallagher, *Evangelical Identity*; Cochran, *Evangelical Feminism*.

28. Barbara Hargrove, "A Place in the Church," *Sojo*, July 1987, 14; Gretchen Gaebelein Hull, "New Creations," *ESA Advocate*, Dec. 1990, 15; Kari J. Verhulst, "Are Women Redeemed?," *Sojo*, Sept.-Oct. 1994, 11; Gretchen Gaebelein Hull, "Human Rights, Civil Rights, Discrimination and the Church," *Prism*, Sept.-Oct. 1995, 15.

29. Lareta Halteman Finger, "Women in Pulpits," *TOS*, July 1979, 14-27; Dana Powell, "Review: *Our Struggle to Serve*," *Sojo*, July 1979, 31-32; "To Know Herself Well," *ESA Update*, July-Aug. 1983, 3-5; Jim Wallis to Roberta Hestenes, Oct. 23, 1986, Sojourners Collection, WCSC; "Making a New Way," *Sojo*, July 1987, 14-37; Nan Arrington Peete, "A First for the Episcopal Church," *Sojo*, Dec. 1988, 10; Vicki Kemper, "Nancy Hastings Sehested," *Sojo*, Feb. 1988, 22-24.

30. "At the Well: Where the Daughters Gather," *TOS*, Jan.-Feb. 1998, 31; Kari Verhulst, "Lifting Up Women," *Sojo*, Nov.-Dec. 1996, 14; Julie Polter and Anne Wayne, "From the Inside Out," *Sojo*, July-Aug. 1997, 16-21; Rose Marie Berger, "The World as God Intends," *Sojo*, May-June 1999, 18-23; "Your Daughters Will Prophesy," *Prism*, July-Aug. 2000, 13-18; Elizabeth D. Rios, "Beyond Labels, toward Calling," *Prism*, Mar.-Apr. 2005, 12; "Leading Ladies," *Prism*, Mar.-Apr. 2006, 8-15.

31. "Gifted with Hope," *Sojo*, Apr. 1985, 12-22; Joan Chittister, "Yesterday's Dangerous Vision," *Sojo*, July 1987, 21; Joan Chittister, "The Balance of Time," *Sojo*, Aug.-Sept. 1987, 32-36; "Joan Chittister," *TOS*, Apr. 1986, 12-15; Joe Nangle, "'New Grace' in the Church," *Sojo*, May 1991, 7; Joe Nangle, "Pastoring Those Excluded by the Pope," *Sojo*, Aug. 1994, 35; Joan Chittister, "A Dangerous Discipleship," *Sojo*, Jan.-Feb. 2002, 42-45; Rose Marie Berger, "Rocking the Boat," *Sojo*, Mar. 2007, 30-35.

32. Nancy Hardesty, "And God Said, 'Let Us Make Woman in Our Image,'" *TOS,* Oct. 1977, 62; Virginia Mollenkott, "Unlimiting God," *TOS*, Nov. 1983, 11; Karen Torjesen and Leif Torjesen, "Inclusive Orthodoxy," *TOS*, Dec. 1986, 14-18; Reta Halteman Finger, "Your Daughters Shall Prophesy," *TOS*, Oct. 1988, 34; Patricia McBee, "Misfit No More," *TOS*, Mar.-Apr. 2004, 43.

33. Sharon Gallagher, "Why God Is Not (Just) Father," *Sojo*, Nov. 1993, 9; Julie Polter, "When Body Meets Soul," *Sojo*, Sept.-Oct. 1994, 22. See also, for example, Virginia Ramey Mollenkott, "In Memory of Her," *Sojo*, Oct. 1983, 35-36; Rosemary Radford Ruether, "Of One Humanity," *Sojo*, Jan. 1984, 17-19; Madonna Kolbenschlag, "The Feminine Face of Creation," *Sojo*, May 1991, 25-28; and Rosemary Radford Ruether, "The Image of God's Goodness," *Sojo*, Jan.-Feb. 1996, 30-31.

34. Jones, "Ronald Sider," 436; Ron Sider, "All I Want for Christmas," *ESA Advocate*, Dec. 1989, 1; Laura Coulter, "Using the 'F' Word," *Prism*, May-June 2004, 24-27.

35. Evans, *Tidal Wave*, 24-32; Tong, *Feminist Thought*, 1-95.

36. Ginny Earnest, "On a Firm Foundation," *Sojo*, Oct. 1988, 30; Sider, "Injustice against Women," 40; Miles, "Domestic-Violence Intervention and Prevention," 11.

37. Earnest, "On a Firm Foundation," 30; Wallis, *Soul of Politics*, 104-7; Moore, "Bread and Roses," 21; Kathy McGinnis, "Lifting the Yoke," *TOS*, Dec. 1980, 34; Jeannie Wylie-Kellermann and Bill Wylie-Kellermann, "More Than a Coin Toss," *Sojo*, Jan.-Feb. 1998, 21; Hollyday, "Toward One Freedom," 5; Polter, "When Body Meets Soul," 21.

38. Davis, *Moving the Mountain*, 454.

CHAPTER 5

1. Joyce Hollyday, "Walking Through Death Valley Days," *Sojo*, June 1981, 4.

2. Evans, *Tidal Wave*, 46-47, 139-42; Hull and Hoffer, Roe v. Wade, 97, 149; "What Next for U.S. Women," *Time*, Dec. 5, 1977, 18-24.

3. Martin, *With God on Our Side*, 193-94; Williams, *God's Own Party*, 111-20, 207-10; Hull and Hoffer, Roe v. Wade, 185-88.

4. Schlafly, *Power of the Positive Woman*, 88; Falwell, *Listen, America!*, 153; LaHaye, *I Am a Woman*, 27, 29; Luker, *Abortion*, 194.

5. Jones, "Ronald Sider," 407; Scanzoni and Hardesty, *All We're Meant to Be*, 143-44.

6. Charles Fager, "Abortion Impasse," *Sojo*, Dec. 1976, 8-10; Jim Stentzel, "A Way Out of the Abortion Impasses," *Sojo*, Apr. 1979, 8; "Postmark," *Sojo*, Jan.

1977, 34; "Postmark," *Sojo*, May 1979, 39; "Letters," *TOS*, Apr. 1980, 47; "Letters," *TOS*, May 1980, 46.

7. John Alexander, "No Easy Answers," *TOS*, June 1980, 10-19; Mark Olson, "Back to the Bible," *TOS*, June 1980, 34-44; Mark Olson, "Editorial," *TOS*, June 1980, 5-6.

8. J. Alexander, "No Easy Answers," 10-19.

9. Mark Olson, "Editor's Response," *TOS*, Oct. 1980, 5; Mark Olson, "Editor's Response," *TOS*, Dec. 1980, 46.

10. Kay Lindskoog, "Our Foundlings' Fathers," *TOS*, June 1982, 38-39; Charles Fager, "Building Bridges between Peace and Life," *TOS*, Sept. 1982, 34-35; "Letters," *TOS*, Dec. 1982, 2; "Letters," *TOS*, Sept. 1983, 2.

11. Jim Wallis, "Coming Together on the Sanctity of Life," *Sojo*, Nov. 1980, 3-4; "Abortion: A Convergence of Concerns," *Sojo*, Nov. 1980, 13-25.

12. Wallis, "Coming Together," 3; Cathy Stentzel, "A Quiet Conversion," *Sojo*, Nov. 1980, 4-6.

13. Wallis, "Coming Together," 3-4.

14. Ibid.; "Postmark," *Sojo*, Jan. 1981, 38-39.

15. Walter Isaacson, "The Battle over Abortion," *Time*, Apr. 6, 1981, 20-28; "Postmark," *Sojo*, Aug. 1984, 41; Martin, *With God on Our Side*, 226-27.

16. "Abortion: The Political Dilemma," *Sojo*, Oct. 1984, 4.

17. "Can My Vote Be Biblical?," *CT*, Sept. 19, 1980, 14-17; "For Your Perusal," *ESA Update*, Summer 1980, 10; Ron Sider, "A Letter from ESA's President," *ESA Update*, Aug. 1981, 5.

18. Bill Kallio, "From Ambivalence to Action," *ESA Update*, July-Aug. 1984, 5; "Interview with Dr. Thomas and Susan Hilgers," *ESA Update*, July-Aug. 1984, 4-6; Norman Bendroth and Peggy Bendroth, "Speak Out," *ESA Update*, July-Aug. 1984, 6-7; "Justice in Action," *ESA Update*, July-Aug. 1984, 7; "Resources on Abortion," *ESA Update*, July-Aug. 1984; "1984 ESA Member Survey Results," *ESA Update*, Jan.-Feb. 1984, 4; "Here We Stand," *ESA Update*, Sept.-Oct. 1984, 2.

19. Joyce Hollyday, "No Easy Answers," *Sojo*, Nov. 1989, 14-16.

20. Mark Olson, "A Cause for Sadness," *TOS*, Oct. 1986, 34, 36; Kathleen Hayes, "A Cause for Hope," *TOS*, Oct. 1986, 35, 37; "Letters," *TOS*, Dec. 1986, 4-6; "Letters," *TOS*, Jan.-Feb. 1987, 4-5.

21. Nancy Rockwell, "Scripture and Morality," *TOS*, Mar.-Apr. 1990, 24-27; Niki Amarantides, "Fighting for Survival," *TOS*, Mar.-Apr. 1990, 29-30.

22. Donna Schaper, "Those Abortion Battles," *TOS*, May-June 1990, 50; "Letters," *TOS*, Mar.-Apr. 1991, 4.

23. "Abortion: The Political Dilemma," 4.

24. Liane Rozzell, "An Affirmation of Life," *Sojo*, June 1985, 34-37; Ginny Earnest Soley, "To Preserve and Protect Life," *Sojo*, Oct. 1986, 34-37; Vicki Kemper, "Abortion and the Front Lines," *Sojo*, Nov. 1988, 5-6; Hollyday, "No Easy Answers," 14. On Operation Rescue, see Martin, *With God on Our Side*, 320-25.

25. Kemper, "Abortion and the Front Lines," 5-6; Rozzell, "Affirmation of Life," 36; "Abortion and the Law," *Sojo*, Nov. 1989, 14-22.

26. Soley, "To Preserve and Protect Life," 35-37; Hollyday, "No Easy Answers," 16.

27. Shelley Douglass, "The Abortion Battle," *Sojo*, July 1992, 5; Wallis, *Soul of Politics*, 109-10; Jim Wallis, "Common Ground Politics," *Sojo*, Jan.-Feb. 1997, 8.

28. Julie Polter, "Women and Children First," *Sojo*, May-June 1995, 16-18.

29. Julie Polter, "Outrage over the Abortion Veto," *Sojo*, July-Aug. 1996, 9-10; Jim Wallis, "Unexpected Allies," *Sojo*, July-Aug. 1997, 8.

30. "Sojourners Fact Sheet," 1993, Sojourners Collection, WCSC; Frederica Mathewes-Green, "Pro-Life, Pro-Choice," *Sojo*, Dec. 1994-Jan. 1995, 13; Naomi Wolf and Frederica Mathewes-Green, "Getting to Disagreement," *Sojo*, Jan.-Feb. 1999, 32-35; Polter, "Women and Children First," 9-10.

31. Jim Wallis, "Pro-life Democrats?," *Sojo*, June 2004, 5-6; Amy Sullivan, "Abortion: A Way Forward," *Sojo*, Apr. 2006, 12-13; "Jim Wallis Statement on 95/10 Abortion Rate Bills in U.S. House of Representatives," Sept. 20, 2006, http://sojo.net/press/jim-wallis-statement-9510-abortion-rate-bills-us-house-representatives (Dec. 31, 2013); Wallis, *Great Awakening*, 194-95.

32. Ted Olsen, "Where Jim Wallis Stands," *CT*, May 2008, 54; "Wallis, the Democrats and the Abortion Debate," *Newsweek*, June 26, 2008, http://www.newsweek.com/wallis-democrats-and-abortion-debate-90593 (Dec. 31, 2013).

33. "Here We Stand," 2; "Prolife Groups Organize Upjohn Boycott," *ESA Update*, Aug. 1985, 1; "'That All May Live in Peace,'" *ESA Update*, Feb. 1986, 1.

34. Jack Smalligan, "JustLife: A Christian PAC," *ESA Update*, Nov.-Dec. 1987, 3.

35. "Where Do Evangelicals Really Stand on Abortion and a Nuclear Freeze?," *ESA Update*, May 1988, 1; Beth Spring, "A New Political Group Will Oppose Abortion, Poverty, and Nuclear Arms," *CT*, June 13, 1986, 36-37.

36. Sider, *Completely Pro-Life*, 49, 56, 69, 70, 189.

37. See the "Washington Update" in the following *ESA Advocate* issues: Sept. 1988, 2; Nov. 1989, 4; May 1990, 4; June 1990, 5; May 1992, 5; and Sept. 1992, 6. See also "ESA Legislative Priorities for 1992," *ESA Advocate*, Mar. 1992, 5.

38. Jones, "Ronald Sider," 428; Sider, *Completely Pro-Life*, 151; "Washington Watch," *ESA Advocate*, Sept. 1988, 1.

39. Benjamin Davis, "Protecting Everyone's Rights," *ESA Advocate*, June 1991, 14-15; Frederica Mathewes-Green, "Not Quite a Perfect Fit," *Prism*, Sept.-Oct. 1994, 10.

40. "ESA Legislative Priorities for 1993," *ESA Advocate*, Mar. 1993, 5; "From the Capitol: Abortion and Health Care," *Prism*, Nov. 1993, 32; Keith Pavlischek, "Public Policy Rhetoric," *Prism*, Feb. 1994, 14-17.

41. Ron Sider, "Hopes (and Fears) for the 104th Congress," *Prism*, Jan. 1995, 38; Ron Sider, "An Open Letter to the U.S. House of Representatives," *Prism*, Feb. 1995, 28; "The America We Seek," *First Things*, May 1996, 40-44; Ron Sider, "Our Selective Rage," *CT*, Aug. 12, 1996, 14. In 2009 Wallis disclaimed his endorsement of the 1996 antiabortion statement "The America We Seek." See Sarah Posner, "Jim Wallis Rejects 1996 Pro-life Declaration," *Religion Dispatches*, Oct. 30, 2009, http://www.religiondispatches.org/blog/1979/jim_wallis_rejects_1996_pro-life_Declaration/ (Dec. 31, 2013).

42. Ronald J. Sider, "Dems: Change or Stay on Sidelines," *PI*, Nov. 19, 2004; Jim Wallis, "'Come Let Us Reason Together,'" *Sojo*, Dec. 2007, 5-6; Sider, *Scandal of Evangelical Politics*, 145-56.

43. Kemper, "Abortion and the Front Lines," 5; Martin, *With God on Our Side*, 325, 357-59; Wallis, "Coming Together on the Sanctity of Life," 3; Jim Wallis, "Lift Every Voice," *Sojo*, July-Aug. 1996, 7.

44. "Can My Vote Be Biblical?"; Ronald J. Sider, "Let's Get the Church Off the Soapbox," *CT*, Mar. 16, 1984, 54; Bill Weld-Wallis, "Abortion: The Political Dilemma," *Sojo*, Oct. 1984, 4.

45. Phil Gailey, "Abortion Knits Religious Right into G.O.P. Fabric," *NYT*, June 19, 1986; Smalligan, "JustLife"; Terry Mattingly, "Too Conservative? Too Liberal? No, It's JustLife," *St. Petersburg Times*, Oct. 31, 1992; Mary E. Bendyna, "Just-Life Action," in *Risky Business? PAC Decisionmaking in Congressional Elections*, ed. Robert Biersack, Paul S. Herrnson, and Clyde Wilcox (Armonk, N.Y.: M. E. Sharpe, 1994), 199; Jim Wallis, "Signs of the Times," *Sojo*, Nov. 1988, 15-21.

46. Mattingly, "Too Conservative?"; Bendyna, "JustLife Action," 200; Ron Sider, "The Key Issues," *ESA Advocate*, May 1992, 16; Jim Wallis, "Can Politics Be Moral?," *Sojo*, Nov. 1992, 11.

47. Ron Sider, "A Tough Call," *Prism*, Sept.-Oct. 2000, 24; Jim Wallis, "Should Joe Lieberman Keep His Faith to Himself?," *Sojo*, Nov.-Dec. 2000, 20-21.

48. Heidi Schlumpf, "No Place to Stand," *Sojo*, June 2004, 12-16; Wallis, "Pro-life Democrats?," 5; Ron Sider, "Bush vs. Kerry," *Prism*, Sept.-Oct. 2004, 36; Sider, "Dems: Change or Stay on Sidelines."

49. Tony Campolo, "Moving the Abortion Debate beyond Partisan Purists," *God's Politics Blog*, Sept. 10, 2008, http://sojo.net/blogs/2008/09/10/moving-abortion-debate-beyond-partisan-purists (Dec. 31, 2013); Jim Wallis, "A Step Forward on Abortion," *God's Politics Blog*, Aug. 14, 2008, http://sojo.net/blogs/2008/08/14/step-forward-abortion (Dec. 31, 2013); Jim Wallis, "Searching for Common Ground on Abortion at the Republican Convention," *God's Politics Blog*, Sept. 2, 2008, http://sojo.net/blogs/2008/09/02/searching-common-ground-abortion-republican-convention (Dec. 31, 2013).

50. Ron Sider, "McCain or Obama?," *Prism*, Sept.-Oct. 2008, 46-48; Jim Wallis, "My Personal Faith Priorities for this Election," *God's Politics Blog*, Oct. 23, 2008, http://sojo.net/blogs/2008/10/23/my-personal-faith-priorities-election (Dec. 31, 2013).

51. J. Alexander, "No Easy Answers," 16; Stentzel, "Quiet Conversion," 5-6; Kallio, "From Ambivalence to Action," 3; Weld-Wallis, "Abortion," 4.

52. Weld-Wallis, "Abortion," 4; Davis, "Protecting Everyone's Rights," 15; Sider, *Scandal of Evangelical Politics*, 155.

53. Wallis, *God's Politics*, xxvi-xxviii.

CHAPTER 6

1. Robert Chase, "LGBT 'Welcome' Ad Rejected by Sojourners," *Religion Dispatches*, May 7, 2011, http://www.religiondispatches.org/archive/politics/4583

(Dec. 31, 2013); Sarah Posner, "Progressive Christian: Wallis 'No Longer Speaks for Us,'" *Religion Dispatches*, May 9, 2011, http://www.religiondispatches.org/dispatches/sarahposner/4592 (Dec. 31, 2013).

2. Jim Wallis, "A Statement on Sojourners' Mission and LGBTQ Issues," *God's Politics Blog*, May 9, 2011, http://sojo.net/blogs/2011/05/09/statement-sojourners-mission-and-lgbtq-issues (Dec. 31, 2013).

3. Jenkins, *Decade of Nightmares*, 31-32; Hirshman, *Victory*.

4. Wendy Cadge, "Vital Conflicts: The Mainline Denominations Debate Homosexuality," in *The Quiet Hand of God: Faith-Based Activism and the Public Role of Mainline Protestantism*, ed. Robert Wuthnow and John H. Evans (Berkeley: University of California Press, 2002), 267-69; Howell Williams, "Homosexuality and the American Catholic Church: Reconfiguring the Silence, 1971-1999" (Ph.D. diss., Florida State University, 2007), 20-26.

5. Martin, *With God on Our Side*, 100-101; Herman, *Antigay Agenda*, 25-59; LaHaye, *The Unhappy Gays*, 179; Schlafly, *Power of the Positive Woman*, 12; Falwell, *Listen, America!*, 183-85.

6. Scanzoni and Hardesty, *All We're Meant to Be*, 152-57; Cochran, *Evangelical Feminism*, 200n31, 92.

7. "Letters," *TOS*, Apr. 1977, 6; "Letters," *TOS*, Aug. 1977, 4; "Sidelines," *TOS*, Aug. 1977, 37-38.

8. "Letters," *TOS*, Dec. 1977, 3; Scanzoni and Mollenkott, *Is the Homosexual My Neighbor?* See also Cochran, *Evangelical Feminism*, 77-91.

9. Mark Olson, "About This Issue," *TOS*, June 1978, 4; John Alexander, "Homosexuality: It's Not That Clear," *TOS*, June 1978, 8.

10. "Letters," *TOS*, Sept. 1978, 64; "Letters," *TOS*, Dec. 1978, 5-7; "Years of Expanding Vision: 1975-1979," *TOS*, May-June 1995, 47.

11. Mark Olson, "Review," *TOS*, Feb. 1984, 50; Mark Olson, "Untangling the Web," *TOS*, Apr. 1984, 24-29; John Alexander, "What Harm Does It Do?," *TOS*, Apr. 1984, 30-31.

12. Letha Scanzoni, "Can Homosexuals Change?," *TOS*, Jan. 1984, 12-15; Letha Scanzoni, "Putting a Face on Homosexuality," *TOS*, Feb. 1984, 8-10, 48; J. Alexander, "What Harm Does It Do?," 31; Olson, "Untangling the Web," 29.

13. Olson, "Untangling the Web," 29; John Alexander, "On Defending Homosexual Behavior," *TOS*, Aug. 1984, 6-7; Scanzoni, "Putting a Face on Homosexuality," 10; J. Alexander, "What Harm Does It Do?," 31.

14. Mark Olson, "A Commitment to Hope, a Commitment to Justice," *TOS*, June 1984, 26-27; "Letters," *TOS*, Apr. 1984, 2-3; "Letters," *TOS*, May 1984, 2-3; "Letters," *TOS*, July 1984, 3.

15. "Letters," *TOS*, Apr. 1984, 3; Jeni Loftus, "America's Liberalization in Attitudes toward Homosexuality, 1973-1998," *American Sociological Review* 66.5 (Oct. 2001): 762-82; Cadge, "Vital Conflicts," 269-70; Williams, "Homosexuality and the American Catholic Church," 111-12; Scott Thumma, "Negotiating a Religious Identity: The Case of the Gay Evangelical," *Sociological Analysis* 52.4 (Winter 1991): 338.

16. Donald Dayton, "Reviews," *Sojo*, June 1977, 39; "Postmark," *Sojo*, Feb. 1978, 39.

17. Tim Stafford, "Issue of the Year," *CT*, May 5, 1978, 36-40; Herman, *Antigay Agenda*, 44-54.

18. Joe Roos, "A Matter of Justice," *Sojo*, July-Aug. 1982, 6 (emphasis added).

19. Ibid.

20. "Postmark," *Sojo*, Sept. 1982, 40-41.

21. "In This Issue," *Sojo*, July 1985, 2.

22. Ibid.

23. Richard Foster, "God's Gift of Sexuality," *Sojo*, July 1985, 18-19.

24. Ibid.

25. "Postmark," *Sojo*, Oct. 1985, 48.

26. Ibid., 49; "Postmark," *Sojo*, Nov. 1985, 49; "Postmark," *Sojo*, Dec. 1985, 52-53.

27. "Postmark," *Sojo*, Oct. 1985, 48; Jim Wallis, Letter to Berrigan et al., Aug. 2, 1985, Sojourners Collection, WCSC; Jones, "Ronald Sider," 433.

28. "Can My Vote Be Biblical?" *CT*, Sept. 19, 1980, 14-17.

29. "ESA Member Survey Results," *ESA Update*, Jan.-Feb. 1984, 4; "Here We Stand," *ESA Update*, Sept.-Oct. 1984, 2.

30. "Letters," *TOS*, July 1984, 2; "Postmark," *Sojo*, Oct. 1985, 49.

31. Sider, *Completely Pro-Life*, 114-15, 132-33, 218n12.

32. Patterson, *Restless Giant*, 179-82; Martin, *With God on Our Side*, 238-57 (Falwell quotation, 254); Schaller, *Right Turn*, 164.

33. Danny Collum, "Addressing the AIDS Crisis," *Sojo*, Feb. 1986, 6; Jim Wallis, "AIDS: The Need for Compassion," *Sojo*, Nov. 1986, 6; Calvin Morris, "AIDS: Does the Church Care?," *Sojo*, May 1990, 20; Joyce Hollyday, "A Deeper Response to AIDS," *Sojo*, Feb. 1990, 7.

34. Mary Beth Danielson, "Transfiguration," *TOS*, Dec. 1987, 12-13; John Fortunato, "Mortal Journey," *TOS*, Dec. 1987, 14-15; Robert Hirschfield, "Out of the Palace," *TOS*, Apr. 1988, 10-11; John Alexander, "Cheap Grace and AIDS," *TOS*, Mar.-Apr. 1989, 48-49; Terry Boyd, "Sunflowers in Small Places," *TOS*, May-June 1990, 44-46.

35. Ronald J. Sider, "AIDS: An Evangelical Perspective," *CC*, Jan. 6, 1988, 11-14; Leslie K. Tarr, "Evangelist Offers 'Completely Pro-life' Agenda," *Toronto Star*, Oct. 24, 1987.

36. Patterson, *Restless Giant*, 182; Robert Pear, "New U.N. Estimate Doubles Rate of Spread of AIDS Virus," *NYT*, Nov. 26, 1997; Richard E. Stearns, "Mercy Impaired," *CT*, Sept. 3, 2001, 100; Jim Wallis, "Our Strategic Interest in Africa," *Sojo*, July-Aug. 2000, 9; Adam Taylor, "The Devil's in the Details," *Sojo*, May-June 2003, 18; Rebecca Barnes, "The Church Awakens," *CT*, Jan. 2005, 22-23. See also Sider, *Rich Christians* (2005), 13-14.

37. Hirshman, *Victory*; Lydia Saad, "Americans Evenly Divided on Morality of Homosexuality," June 18, 2008, Gallup.com, http://www.gallup.com/poll/108115/americans-evenly-divided-morality-homosexuality.aspx (Dec. 31, 2013).

38. Laura R. Olson, Paul A. Djupe, and Wendy Cadge, "American Mainline Protestantism and Deliberation about Homosexuality," in *Faith, Politics, and Sexual Diversity in Canada and the United States*, ed. David Rayside and Clyde

Wilcox (Vancouver: UBC Press, 2011), 189-203; Ted Olsen and Todd Hertz, "Does *Lawrence v. Texas* Signal the End of the American Family?," *CT*, June 1, 2003, http://www.christianitytoday.com/ct/2003/Juneweb-only/6-30-11.0.html (Dec. 31, 2013).

39. John Linscheid, "Our Story in God's Story," *TOS*, July-Aug. 1987, 33; Frank Wulf, "Getting to the Point," *TOS*, May-June 1996, 40; John Linscheid, "A Thousand Trains to Heaven," *TOS*, Sept.-Oct. 1993, 8-15. See also, for example, Jeffery P. Dennis, "Liberating Gay Theology," *TOS*, Sept.-Oct. 1993, 56-58; and John Linscheid, "Looking Down on Sodom," *TOS*, Nov.-Dec. 1996, 13-17, 51.

40. Peggy Campolo, "The Holy Presence of Acceptance," *TOS*, Mar.-Apr. 1994, 16-22; Alice Ogden Bellis, "When God Makes a Way," *TOS*, Mar.-Apr. 1995, 44; Mel White, "Bringing in the Beloved Community," *TOS*, Jan.-Feb. 1998, 18-21.

41. "Letters," *TOS*, Jan.-Feb. 1991, 3-4; "Letters," *TOS*, Mar.-Apr., 1995, 2-3; "Letters," *TOS*, May-June 1995, 1.

42. Gushee, *Future of Faith*, 59; John Linscheid, "Wounded in the Sider Boycott," *TOS*, Mar.-Apr. 1989, 10; "Letters," *TOS*, July-Aug. 1989, 10.

43. Linscheid, "Wounded in the Sider Boycott," 11; White, "Bringing in the Beloved Community"; Rodney N. Powell, "Nothing Less Than Freedom," *TOS*, Jan.-Feb. 2003, 41.

44. "The Need for a Better Dialogue," *Sojo*, July 1991, 10-28.

45. Tony Campolo and Peggy Campolo, "Holding It Together," *Sojo*, May-June 1999, 28-32; Wesley Granberg-Michaelson, "Many Members, One Body," *Sojo*, May-June 1999, 24-27; Richard Mouw, "Why the Evangelical Church Needs the Liberal Church," *Sojo*, Feb. 2004, 14, 16, 18; Barbara Wheeler, "Why the Liberal Church Needs the Evangelical Church," *Sojo*, Feb. 2004, 15, 17, 19.

46. See the following "Postmark" sections in *Sojo*: Oct. 1991, 8-10; Nov. 1991, 8-9; Dec. 1991, 8-9; July-Aug. 1999, 5-6; Sept. 1999, 5-6. See also Ted Olsen, "Where Jim Wallis Stands," *CT*, May 2008, 57.

47. Jim Rice, "When Dignity Is Assaulted," *Sojo*, Feb.-Mar. 1994, 6-7; Jim Rice, "Saying No to Bigotry," *Sojo*, Feb.-Mar. 1993, 4-5; Aaron McCarroll Gallegos, "Practicing What We Preach," *Sojo*, Jan.-Feb. 1999, 9-10; Wallis, *God's Politics*, 332.

48. Ron Sider, "Who Is Destroying the Family?," *Prism*, Mar. 1994, 10; Keith Pavlischek, "Authority and Experience," *Prism*, Jan. 1995, 29-30; Sider, *Scandal of Evangelical Politics*, 168.

49. Ted Olsen, "Call to Renewal Alliance Divided over Its Agenda," *CT*, Apr. 8, 1996, 87; Wallis, *Who Speaks for God?*, 205.

50. "Washington Update," *ESA Advocate*, Mar. 1993, 8; Tony Campolo, "What about Homophobia?," *Prism*, Feb. 1994, 20; Sider, *Scandal of Evangelical Politics*, 168.

51. Rice, "When Dignity Is Assaulted"; Wallis, *Soul of Politics*, 112; "Clash over Gay Marriage," *CC*, Dec. 18, 1996, 1246; Gallegos, "Practicing What We Preach"; Wallis, *God's Politics*, 331; Wallis, *Great Awakening*, 229.

52. Cahill, *Same-Sex Marriage*; David Kirkpatrick, "Conservatives Using Issue of Gay Unions as Rallying Tool," *NYT*, Feb. 8, 2004; David Masci, "An Overview

of the Same-Sex Marriage Debate," Pew Forum on Religion and Public Life, Nov. 21, 2008, http://www.pewforum.org/Gay-Marriage-and-Homosexuality/An-Overview-of-the-Same-Sex-Marriage-Debate.aspx (Dec. 31, 2013).

53. Sider, *Scandal of Evangelical Politics*, 159, 169; Wallis, *Great Awakening*, 229; Jim Wallis, "What Next for Call to Renewal?," *Sojo*, Mar.-Apr. 1996, 7-8; Ronald J. Sider, "The Anabaptist Perspective," in *Church, State, and Public Justice*, ed. P. C. Kemeny (Downers Grove, Ill.: InterVarsity Press, 2007), 190-91.

54. Wallis, "What Next for Call to Renewal?"; Wallis, *God's Politics*, 332-34; Campolo, *Red Letter Christians*, 94; Randy Frame, "Seeking a Right to the Rite," *CT*, Mar. 4, 1996, 64-66, 72-73; Sider, *Scandal of Evangelical Politics*, 166-69; Sider, "Bearing Better Witness," *First Things*, Dec. 2010, 50.

55. Wallis, *God's Politics*, 11, 17.

CHAPTER 7

1. Ronald J. Sider, "My Meeting with the President-Elect," *CT*, Dec. 2000, http://www.christianitytoday.com/ct/2000/Decemberweb-only/54.0b.html (Dec. 31, 2013); Jim Wallis, "An Unexpected Meeting with Mr. Bush," *Sojomail*, Dec. 22, 2000, http://sojo.net/sojomail/2000/12/22 (Dec. 31, 2013); Lindsay, *Faith in the Halls of Power*, 68.

2. "Bush Speech," *NYT*, Jan. 21, 2001; Jim Wallis, "Give Bush a Chance," *Sojomail*, Jan. 26, 2001, http://sojo.net/sojomail/2001/01/26 (Dec. 31, 2013); Jim Wallis, "We Will Test President Bush's Words," *Sojomail*, Feb. 2, 2001, http://sojo.net/sojomail/2001/02/02 (Dec. 31, 2013).

3. "Interview: Jim Wallis," *PBS Frontline*, Apr. 29, 2004, http://www.pbs.org/wgbh/pages/frontline/shows/jesus/interviews/wallis.html (Dec. 31, 2013).

4. Wallis, *Soul of Politics*, 149-51; Wallis, *God's Politics*, 212-14; Ronald J. Sider, "An Evangelical Theology of Liberation," *CC*, Mar. 19, 1980, 314-18.

5. C. Smith, *Emergence of Liberation Theology*, 26-50.

6. Jim Wallis, "Liberation and Conformity," *Sojo*, Sept. 1976, 3; Reese, "Resistance and Hope," 87-102. See also, for example, other articles in *Sojo*, Sept. 1976; Ronald J. Sider, "Evangelism, Salvation and Social Justice," *International Review of Mission*, July 1975, 251-67; "Socialism and the Christian Witness: An Interview with Orlando Costas," *TOS*, Jan.-Feb. 1976, 27-30, 39-43; Kathleen Hayes, "Gustavo Gutierrez: Opting for the Poor," *TOS*, Nov. 1987, 10-13.

7. Wallis, *Agenda*, 88; Sider, *Rich Christians* (1977), 59-85; Sider, "Evangelical Theology of Liberation," 314-15; Ronald J. Sider, "Is God Really on the Side of the Poor?," *Sojo*, Oct. 1977, 11-14; Jim Wallis, "Idols Closer to Home," *Sojo*, May 1979, 11; Jim Wallis, "A Meditation on Suffering," *Sojo*, Feb. 1976, 4. See also John Alexander, "The Bible and the Other Side," *TOS*, Sept.-Oct. 1975, 56-65.

8. Sider, *Rich Christians* (1977), 73, 77; J. R. Burkholder, "Money: Master or Servant," *P-A*, Dec. 1974, 19; Tom Hanks, "Oppressors on the Run," *TOS*, Feb. 1981, 23; Tom Hanks, "Why People Are Poor," *Sojo*, Jan. 1981, 22; Sider, "Evangelical Theology of Liberation," 316; J. Alexander, "The Bible and the Other Side," 61-62.

9. J. Alexander, "The Bible and the Other Side," 60; Jim Wallis, "Of Rich and Poor," *P-A*, Feb.-Mar. 1974, 1; Hanks, "Why People Are Poor," 21; Sider, "Evangelical Theology of Liberation," 315, 318; Sider, *Rich Christians* (1977), 72-84.

10. Wallis, "Meditation on Suffering"; Wallis, "Of Rich and Poor"; Ronald J. Sider, "Mischief by Statute," *CT*, July 16, 1976, 14-16; Sider, *Rich Christians* (1977), 133-38; Peter Davids, "God and Mammon, Part I," *Sojo*, Feb. 1978, 14. Drawing upon the work of Hendrikus Berkof, some leaders associated oppressive economic systems with the Pauline conception of fallen "principalities and powers" that were intended to serve but now seek to enslave people. See Gay, *With Liberty*, 48-50.

11. Wallis, "Of Rich and Poor," 11; Wallis, "Meditation on Suffering"; Sider, "Evangelical Theology of Liberation," 316.

12. Frank Breisch, "Proclaim Liberty Throughout the Land," *TOS*, Jan.-Feb. 1975, 13; Davids, "God and Mammon, Part I," 17; Sider, *Rich Christians* (1977), 101; Bill Faw, "Our Daily Bread," *Sojo*, Jan. 1980, 24. See also, for example, articles in *P-A*, June-July 1975; Ronald J. Sider, "Sharing the Wealth," *CC*, June 8-15, 1977, 560-65; and Merold Westphal, "Sing Jubilee," *TOS*, Mar. 1978, 29-35.

13. Peter Davids, "People of God and the Wealth of the People," *P-A*, June-July 1975, 16; Sider, *Rich Christians* (1977), 114; Burkholder, "Money," 20; Wallis, *Agenda*, 98-99.

14. Faw, "Our Daily Bread," 24; Sider, *Rich Christians* (1977), 89-95, 205-23. See also John Alexander, "The Distribution System," *TOS*, Jan.-Feb. 1976, 6-11; Sider, "Mischief by Statute"; Sider, "Is God Really on the Side of the Poor?"; John Alexander, "The Economics of Jesus," *TOS*, Oct. 1978, 14-18.

15. Sider, *Rich Christians* (1977), 206; Wallis, "Of Rich and Poor," 1; Clark Pinnock, "An Evangelical Theology of Human Liberation," *Sojo*, Feb. 1976, 31.

16. Jim Wallis, "Ten Years," *Sojo*, Sept. 1981, 5.

17. H. Edward Rowe, "Poverty," *TOS*, July-Aug. 1972, 23-29; Gay, *With Liberty*, 10-14; Fowler, *New Engagement*, 26-30, 184-88.

18. Bill Pannell, "Paint, or Get Off the Ladder," *TOS*, July-Aug. 1972, 30-32; Herb McMullan, "Man and Technocracy," *P-A*, Winter 1972, 4; Jim Wallis, "The Movemental Church," *P-A*, Winter 1972, 2; Ron Sider, "A Call for Evangelical Nonviolence," *CC*, Sept. 15, 1976, 753; Sider, *Rich Christians* (1977), 138-62; Jim Wallis, "The Invisible Empire," *P-A*, Nov.-Dec. 1973, 1.

19. Danny Collum, "The Way America Does Business," *Sojo*, Nov. 1985, 15; Eugene Toland, Thomas Fenton, and Lawrence McCulloch, "World Justice and Peace," *TOS*, Jan.-Feb. 1976, 56-57; Sider, *Rich Christians* (1984), 11-49; Stricker, *Why America Lost*, 117-206; Clark, *Victory Deferred*, 69-101; Sider, *Completely Pro-Life*, 83-85.

20. Wallis, *Agenda*, 85; Phil Shenk, "Give Me Your Poor?," *Sojo* Aug. 1980, 5; Nicholas Wolterstorff, "Until Justice and Peace Embrace," *TOS*, May 1984, 23. See also, for example, J. Alexander, "Distribution System"; George DeVries Jr., "Trade on the High Seize," *TOS*, Jan.-Feb. 1976, 59-62; Richard Barnet, "Interview on Multinational Corporations," *Sojo*, Feb. 1976, 14-19; Bill Tabb, "The Demise of Our Free Enterprise System," *TOS*, Dec. 1979, 44-49; and Sider, *Rich*

Christians (1984), 124-58. For the influence of leftist critiques of capitalism, see Wallis, *Call to Conversion*, 182-83; and "Justice: The Economics of Oppression," *Sojo*, Nov. 1985, 38-39.

21. Wes Michaelson, "Liberating the Church," *Sojo*, Sept. 1976, 4-5; J. Alexander, "Distribution System," 10-11; Danny Collum, "Assault on the Poor," *Sojo*, July 1981, 16; George McClain, "Money Trouble," *TOS*, Mar. 1978, 20.

22. Gay, *With Liberty*, 64-113 (Nash quotation, 82); Lienesch, *Redeeming America*, 95-138; Carl Schoettler, "Elder Statesman Falwell Says Evangelicals Political Force," *Houston Chronicle*, Apr. 5, 1987, 7.

23. Collum, "Assault on the Poor," 16; Joe Roos, "Economic Koinonia," *Sojo*, Aug. 1979, 24-25; Jim Stentzel, "That Others May Simply Live," *Sojo*, Feb. 1979, 5; Sider, *Living More Simply*; Bob Sabath, "A Community of Communities," *Sojo*, Jan. 1980, 17-19; Sider, *Rich Christians* (1984), 165; John Alexander, "Good News about Our New Jubilee Fund," *TOS*, Nov.-Dec. 1975, 2-4.

24. John Alexander, "Hard Heads and Soft Hearts," *TOS*, Jan.-Feb. 1975, 3, 54; Collum, "Assault on the Poor," 16; Jim Wallis, "Poverty Is a Scandal," *Sojo*, Nov. 1985, 4; Lienesch, *Redeeming America*, 124-38. See also J. Alexander, "Distribution System."

25. Sider, *Completely Pro-Life*, 86-95; Jim Stentzel, "'The Watts Riot of the White Middle Class,'" *Sojo*, July 1978, 6; Jim Wallis, "The Cry of the Poor," *Sojo*, July 1980, 6; Sider, *Rich Christians* (1984), 196, 203; Gay, *With Liberty*, 33-34. See also Collum, "Assault on the Poor."

26. Stentzel, "'Watts Riot'"; Wallis, "Cry of the Poor"; Sider, *Completely Pro-Life*, 89; Collum, "Assault on the Poor," 15; Jim Wallis, "Mammon's Iron Thumb," *Sojo*, Feb. 1978, 3; George Chauncey, "Responding in Faith," *TOS*, May 1984, 8.

27. Robert Clouse, "America's National Priorities," *TOS*, Sept.-Oct. 1972, 35-38; Richard Pierard, "Is Richard Nixon Still a Conservative?," *TOS*, Sept.-Oct. 1972, 42; Jim Wallis, "The Issue of 1972," *P-A*, Fall 1972, 2-3; John Alexander, "Kingdom Work," *TOS*, Aug. 1979, 12; Jim Wallis, "'The Outsider' in the White House," *Sojo*, Jan. 1978, 3; Wallis, "Mammon's Iron Thumb," 3-4; Wallis, "Cry of the Poor," 6.

28. Collum, "Assault on the Poor," 12-13; Bill Kallio, "Editorial," *ESA Update*, Feb. 1982, 2.

29. Collum, "Assault on the Poor"; 15; Jim Wallis, "Crossroads for the Freeze," *Sojo*, Jan. 1983, 5; Mark Olson, "On Hearing the Cries of Recovery," *TOS*, June 1983, 16; Jim Wallis, "The President's Pulpit," *Sojo*, Sept. 1984, 20; Vernon Grounds, "Pondering Poverty," *ESA Update*, May 1985, 3; Vicki Kemper, "Welfare Reform," *Sojo*, Dec. 1988, 6. See also, for example, Chauncey, "Responding in Faith"; Danny Collum, "The Big Picture," *Sojo*, May 1986, 14-19; and Danny Collum, "The Crash of '87," *Sojo*, Jan. 1988, 4-5.

30. Franky Schaeffer, "Introduction," in Schaeffer, *Is Capitalism Christian?*, xxii-xxiv; Lindsell, *Free Enterprise*, 31; Nash, *Social Justice*, 158; Chilton, *Productive Christians*, 5, 7, 9, 20.

31. Michaelson, "Liberating the Church," 5; J. Alexander, "Economics of Jesus," 18; Wallis, "Liberation and Conformity," 4; Wallis, "Poverty Is a Scandal,"

5; Sider, *Rich Christians* (1984), 195; Boyd Reese, "Christ and Capitalism," *Sojo*, May 1984, 36-37.

32. Sider, *Rich Christians* (1997), xiii-xiv, 125, 135-36, 232, 236; Ronald J. Sider, "Rich Christians in an Age of Hunger Revisited," *Prism*, May-June 1997, 11.

33. Jim Wallis, "History's New Opening," *Sojo*, Nov. 1991, 4; Wesley Granberg-Michaelson, "Economics: Searching for Alternatives," *Sojo*, July 1991, 4-5; Wallis, *Soul of Politics*, 27; Sider, *Rich Christians* (1997), 144, 140.

34. Richard Taylor, "Seeing the World through New Lenses," *Sojo*, Jan. 1993, 24; Sider, *Rich Christians* (1997), xiv-xv, 141; Ronald J. Sider, "A Response to Ronald Nash," *Prism*, Mar.-Apr. 1997, 26; Tony Campolo, "Is There Anything Wrong with Capitalism?," *Prism*, Mar.-Apr. 1997, 23; Wallis, *Who Speaks for God?*, 102.

35. Sider, *Rich Christians* (1997), 123; Sider, *Just Generosity*, 35; Wallis, *Faith Works*, 133-34. See also Jim Wallis, "Poverty Is Not a Left-Wing Issue," *Sojo*, Sept.-Oct. 2000, 7-8.

36. Wallis, *Who Speaks for God?*, 76-77; Sider, *Just Generosity*, 92-93; Wallis, *God's Politics*, 230.

37. Sider, "Rich Christians in an Age of Hunger Revisited," 10; Sider, *Rich Christians* (1997), 41-120, 233; Jim Wallis, "The Church Steps Forward," *Sojo*, Mar.-Apr. 1997, 7-8; Ron Sider, "The Congress That Stole Christmas," *Prism*, Nov.-Dec. 1995, 38. See also Sider, *Just Generosity*, 49-75.

38. Ron Sider, "Can Bush Help End the Cold War?," *ESA Advocate*, Mar. 1989, 1-3; Shelley Douglass, "What Peace Dividend?," *Sojo*, Apr. 1990, 35; "Washington Update," *ESA Advocate*, Nov. 1990, 5-6; Ron Sider, "The Key Issues," *ESA Advocate*, May 1992; 16; Jim Wallis, "A Cry for Change," *Sojo*, Jan. 1993, 4; Jim Wallis, "The First Quarter," *Sojo*, Jan. 1994, 4-5; Jim Wallis, "What to Do about the Poor," *Sojo*, Mar.-Apr. 1995, 10-11; Sider, "Congress That Stole Christmas," 38; Ronald J. Sider, "Hopes (and Fears) for the 104th Congress," *Prism*, Jan. 1995, 38.

39. Wallis, "What to Do about the Poor"; Sider, "Hopes (and Fears)," 38; Sider, "Congress That Stole Christmas," 38; Jim Wallis, "God Hears the Cry of the Poor," *Sojo*, Jan.-Feb. 1996, 7-8; Jim Wallis, "A Great National Sin," *Sojo*, Sept.-Oct. 1996, 7-8.

40. Ron Sider and Heidi Rolland, "Correcting the Welfare Tragedy," *Prism*, Nov.-Dec. 1994, 19; Ron Sider, "Public Dollars, Private Efforts," *CT*, Sept. 11, 1995, 18; Stanley Carlson-Thies, "Charitable Choice: Bringing Religion Back into American Welfare," *Journal of Policy History* 13.1 (2001): 109-32; Laurie Goodstein, "Religious Groups See Larger Role in Welfare," *NYT*, Dec. 14, 1997; Rick Santorum and Ron Sider, "'Charitable Choice' Addresses the Spiritual Roots of Social Problems," *PI*, Jan. 23, 1999. See also Jim Wallis, "What's an FBO?," *Sojo*, Sept.-Oct. 1999, 7-8.

41. Fred Clark, "Proclaiming Jubilee," *Prism*, May-June 1999, 22-23; Martin Wroe, "An Irresistible Force," *Sojo*, May-June 2000, 18-22; Jim Wallis, "Lifting All Boats," *Sojo*, Nov.-Dec. 2000, 7-8; Jim Wallis, "If Not Me, Who?," *Sojo*, May-June 2000, 7; Ron Sider, "Send Them a Message," *Prism*, May-June 2000, 28; Carter Echols, "Quiz the Candidates, Then Vote!," *Sojo*, Nov.-Dec. 2000, 48; Jim Wallis, "But What Does All the Faith Talk Mean?," Beliefnet.com, Nov. 1, 2000,

http://www.beliefnet.com/News/Politics/2000/11/But-What-Does-All-The-Faith-Talk-Mean.aspx (Dec. 31, 2013).

42. Ron Sider, "Grossly Unfair," *Prism*, May-June 2001, 30; Ron Sider, "Compassionate Conservatism or Blatant Injustice," *Prism*, Mar.-Apr. 2003, 36; Jim Wallis, "A Momentous Choice," *Sojo*, Mar.-Apr. 2003, 7-8; Jim Wallis, "This War Isn't Over," *Sojomail*, Apr. 24, 2003, http://sojo.net/sojomail/2003/04/24 (Dec. 31, 2013); Jim Wallis, "The Things That Make for Peace," *Sojo*, July-Aug. 2003, 7.

43. Jim Wallis, "Values and the 2004 Election," *Sojomail*, Mar. 4, 2004, http://sojo.net/sojomail/2004/03/04 (Dec. 31, 2013); Wallis, *Great Awakening*, 116, 125; Ron Sider, "Evaluating President Bush's 2006 Budget," *Prism*, July-Aug. 2005, 39; Frank James, "'Christmas Scandal' Outcry," *Chicago Tribune*, Dec. 15, 2005; Wallis, *God's Politics*, 47-48; Ron Sider, "Holy Week, American Poverty, and Faithful Discipleship," *Prism*, Mar.-Apr. 2006, 40; Elizabeth Denlinger, "Vote Out Poverty," *Sojo*, Sept.-Oct. 2008, 7; Ron Sider, "McCain or Obama?," *Prism*, Sept.-Oct. 2008, 46-48.

44. Sider, *Rich Christians* (1977), 210; Sider, *Just Generosity*, 14-15.

45. Jim Wallis, "Recovering the Evangel," *Sojo*, Feb. 1981, 3-5; John Alexander, "On Stopping Bullies," *TOS*, Oct. 1984, 5; Collum, "Way America Does Business," 16; Sider, "Congress That Stole Christmas," 38; Jim Wallis, "Mr. President, You Should Be Ashamed," *Sojomail*, June 4, 2003, http://sojo.net/sojomail/2003/06/04 (Dec. 31, 2013).

46. Wallis, "God Hears the Cry of the Poor"; Gutterman, *Prophetic Politics*, 131; Sider, "Evaluating President Bush's 2006 Budget," 40.

47. Wallis, *Soul of Politics*, 72; Wallis, *Great Awakening*, 105; Collum, "Way America Does Business," 16; Ron Sider, "Do We Care Enough?," *Sojo*, Sept.-Oct. 1999, 30-31; Taylor, "Seeing the World," 25.

48. "A Prophecy for the '80s," *Sojo*, Jan. 1983, 13.

CHAPTER 8

1. Jim Wallis, "Vietnam," *Sojo*, Apr. 1980, 3-5.

2. Jim Wallis, "The Movemental Church," *P-A*, Winter 1972, 2; Barrie Doyle, "Backing Their Man," *CT*, Oct. 27, 1972, 38-39; "The Chicago Declaration of Social Concern," in Sider, *Chicago Declaration*, 2; Jim Wallis, "No Peace, No Honor," *P-A*, Apr. 1975, 5.

3. Bill Lane, "Lessons from Vietnam," *P-A*, Mar.-Apr. 1973, 8; Jim Wallis, "Biblical Politics," *P-A*, Apr. 1974, 3; Jim Wallis, "The Invisible Empire," *P-A*, Nov.-Dec. 1973, 1; Boyd Reese, "America's Empire," *P-A*, Nov.-Dec., 1973, 10-11; Jim Wallis, "Vietnam and Repentance," *P-A*, May 1975, 19.

4. Settje, *Faith and War*; Lienesch, *Redeeming America*, 139-219; Falwell, *Listen, America!*, 29, 263; Martin, *With God on Our Side*, 33-34 (Graham quotation).

5. Jim Wallis, "Post-American Christianity," *P-A*, Fall 1971, 3; Ron Sider, "Where Have All the Liberals Gone?," *TOS*, May-June 1976, 42-43; Martin, *With God on Our Side*, 203; Wes Michaelson, "No King but Caesar," *Sojo*, Jan. 1976, 4-6; Jim Wallis, "Recovering the Evangel," *Sojo*, Feb. 1981, 3-4.

6. Wes Michaelson, "Suffering with the Victims," *Sojo*, July-Aug. 1976, 3; Wes Michaelson, "Human Rights," *Sojo*, Apr. 1977, 3; Wes Michaelson, "Persecution Visited upon the Body," *Sojo*, Jan. 1977, 7. See also John Alexander, "How Free Is Free," *TOS*, July-Aug. 1976, 56-62.

7. Wes Michaelson, "Reaping a Whirlwind," *Sojo*, Sept. 1978, 5-6; Jim Wallis, "Compassion, Not Politics," *Sojo*, Sept. 1979, 4-5; John Alexander, "The Ominous Eighties," *TOS*, Apr. 1980, 8-12; Jim Wallis, "We Could Just Ask Them to Forgive Us," *Sojo*, Jan. 1980, 3-4.

8. Patterson, *Restless Giant*, 102-3, 122-23; Jim Wallis, "Nuclear War by 1999?," *Sojo*, Feb. 1977, 4; Wes Michaelson, "Curiouser and Curiouser Bomb Logic," *Sojo*, Feb. 1977, 5; "A Call to Faithfulness," *Sojo*, June 1978, 19-21; "A Change of Heart," *Sojo*, Aug. 1979, 12-14; Jim Wallis, "Offensive Simplicity," *Sojo*, Feb. 1980, 6.

9. Jim Wallis, "The Work of Prayer," *Sojo*, Mar. 1979, 3-5; "Please Come to New York," *Sojo*, May 1978, 6; Jim Wallis, "Waging Peace," *Sojo*, Aug. 1978, 19-21; "Nuclear Arms Bazaar," *Sojo*, Aug. 1979, 4; Jim Wallis, "Accountability and April 15," *Sojo*, Mar. 1977, 3; Joe Roos, "'Let Your Nay be Nay,'" *Sojo*, Feb. 1979, 5. See also John Schuchardt, "Why I Say No to Terror," *TOS*, Jan. 1979, 15-16; Jim Wallis, "Refusing the Call to Arms," *Sojo*, Mar. 1980, 3-5.

10. Patterson, *Restless Giant*, 193-217; Williams, *God's Own Party*, 204-5; Wallis, *Waging Peace*; Wallis, *Peacemakers*; Sider and Taylor, *Nuclear Holocaust*; Joyce Hollyday, "Bathed in the Spirit," *Sojo*, Aug. 1983, 24-28; Jim Douglass, "Tracking the White Train," *Sojo*, Feb. 1984, 12-25; "A Confrontation in the Desert," *Sojo*, July 1985, 12; Jean Caffey Lyles, "Evangelicals Confront the Arms Race," *CC*, July 20-27, 1983, 668-70; Wallis, "Bound Together for Peace," *Sojo*, Aug. 1981, 17; "An Evangelical Commitment to Nuclear Disarmament," *ESA Update*, May-June 1983, 2; Patricia Narciso, "Consistency for the Sake of Life," *Sojo*, Aug.-Sept. 1985, 12; Sider, *Completely Pro-Life*, 152-86; Jim Wallis, "Crossroads for the Freeze," *Sojo*, Jan. 1983, 5-6.

11. Jim Wallis, "Against the Consensus," *Sojo*, Oct. 1981, 6; J. Alexander, "How Free Is Free"; J. Alexander, "Ominous Eighties," 10; Danny Collum, "The Height of Irresponsibility," *Sojo*, May 1981, 6. See also Wes Michaelson, "The Plank in Our Eye," *Sojo*, Aug. 1978, 3-4.

12. C. Smith, *Resisting Reagan*, 18-56 (Kirkpatrick quotation, 18); Schaller, *Right Turn*, 94-96 (Reagan quotation, 96).

13. Wes Michaelson, "U.S. Imperial Instincts in Panama," *Sojo*, Nov. 1977, 8; Blase Bonpane, "The Vietnamization of Central America," *TOS*, Jan. 1981, 26-31; Danny Collum, "Trespassing in the Basin," *Sojo*, Apr. 1982, 19-23; Jim Wallis, "An Open Letter to President Reagan," *Sojo*, Apr. 1982, 3-4; Joyce Hollyday, "The Grandest of Bellicose Errors," *Sojo*, Jan. 1982, 5-6; Joyce Hollyday, "El Salvador, 'The Savior,'" *Sojo*, Apr. 1981, 5-6.

14. Joyce Hollyday, "A Martyr's Abiding Hope," *Sojo*, May 1980, 3-5; Joyce Hollyday, "Murderous Stability," *Sojo*, Jan. 1981, 5-6; Bonpane, "Vietnamization of Central America"; Hollyday, "El Salvador"; "Speaking Out on El Salvador," *Sojo*, May 1981, 4-5; Wallis, "Open Letter"; Charles Clement, "Ministering for

Life, Calling for Peace," *TOS*, Sept. 1983, 39-41; Joyce Hollyday, "Misleading the Nation," *Sojo*, June-July 1983, 3.

15. Joyce Hollyday, "The Battle for Central America," *Sojo*, Apr. 1982, 12-16; Wallis, "Open Letter"; Joyce Hollyday, "Undoing Nicaragua," *Sojo*, Dec. 1982, 5; Ronald J. Sider, "Who Is My Neighbor?," *TSF Bulletin*, Mar.-Apr. 1983, 11-13; Jim Wallis and Joyce Hollyday, "A Plea from the Heart," *Sojo*, Mar. 1983, 3-5; Hollyday, "Misleading the Nation," 3; Joyce Hollyday, "Gunboats and Butter," *Sojo*, Sept. 1983, 3; Chris Moss, "Faulty Deductions," *TOS*, Nov. 1983, 25; Richard Shaull, "The Prophetic Challenge to Imperial America," *TOS*, Feb. 1984, 14-16; Jim Wallis, "Challenging the Lie," *Sojo*, Aug. 1984, 1.

16. C. Smith, *Resisting Reagan*, 30-32.

17. Griffin-Nolan, *Witness for Peace* ("Statement of Purpose," 235); C. Smith, *Resisting Reagan*, 70-78; Swartz, *Moral Minority*, 237; Jim Wallis, "Witness for Peace," *Sojo*, Nov. 1983, 3-4; Joyce Hollyday, "A Shield of Love," *Sojo*, Nov. 1983, 10-13; Joyce Hollyday, "The Long Road to Jalapa," *Sojo*, Feb. 1984, 26-30; Ron Sider, "Why Me, Lord?," *TOS*, Apr.-May 1985, 20-25.

18. "A Promise of Resistance," *Sojo*, Dec. 1983, 6; Jim Wallis, "A Pledge of Resistance," *Sojo*, Aug. 1984, 10-11; Steven Hall-Williams, "Pledge Says 'No' to *Contra* Aid," *Sojo*, June 1986, 10; C. Smith, *Resisting Reagan*, 78-85.

19. David Marley, "Ronald Reagan and the Splintering of the Christian Right," *Journal of Church and State* 48.4 (Autumn 2006): 851-68; Steven Hall-Williams, "Robertson's *Contra* Chaplains," *Sojo*, Apr. 1986, 10-11; Lienesch, *Redeeming America*, 205-17; William O'Brien, "Oh God!," *TOS*, Oct. 1985, 2; Griffin-Nolan, *Witness for Peace*, 60-61 (Wallis quotation, 60); C. Smith, *Resisting Reagan*, 219-23, 329-36; Vicki Kemper, "Pledge Network Renews Commitment," *Sojo*, Feb. 1986, 10.

20. Danny Collum, "A State of Secrecy," *Sojo*, Mar. 1987, 4; Jim Wallis, "The Policy Is Still Wrong," *Sojo*, Oct. 1987, 4-5; Beth Spring, "The Government's Heavy Hand Falls on Believers," *CT*, Dec. 13, 1985, 51-52; Jim Wallis, "A Friend of Nicaragua," *Sojo*, Jan. 1986, 4-5; "An Open Letter to Presidents Ronald Reagan and Daniel Ortega," *ESA Update*, Nov.-Dec. 1987, 4-5; Patterson, *Restless Giant*, 210-13. See also, for example, Jack Nelson-Pallmeyer, "Low-Intensity Conflict," *TOS*, Nov. 1987, 24-29; and Vicki Kemper, "A Resurgence of Repression," *Sojo*, Jan. 1988, 8-10.

21. Lloyd Billingsley, "First Church of Christ Socialist," *National Review*, Oct. 28, 1983, 1339; Dennis Marker, "Under Attack," *Sojo*, Mar. 1985, 5-6; Franky Schaeffer, "Introduction," in Schaeffer, *Is Capitalism Christian?*, xxii-xxv; Reese, "Resistance and Hope," 268-70; Danny Collum, "Critical Imbalance," *Sojo*, Oct. 1983, 6; John Alexander, "Resisting Evil," *TOS*, Sept. 1984, 8; Ronald J. Sider, "A Plea for Conservative Radicals and Radical Conservatives," *CC*, Oct. 1, 1986, 834-35; Danny Collum, "Neither East nor West," *Sojo*, Oct. 1987, 4; Danny Collum, "'New Thinking' for the Peace Movement," *Sojo*, Mar. 1988, 5 (emphasis added).

22. Jim Rice, "The Winds of Democracy," *Sojo*, June 1989, 4; Jim Wallis, "Salvation Events," *Sojo*, Apr. 1990, 50; Jim Wallis, "The Dictators Hall of Fame," *Sojo*, July 1989, 5; Danny Collum, "Under Bush's Thumb," *Sojo*, Apr. 1990, 4-5;

Ron Sider, "Global Rambo or Cooperative Partner," *ESA Advocate*, Nov. 1990, 1; Patterson, *Restless Giant*, 225-29.

23. Patterson, *Restless Giant*, 230-33; Anderson, *Bush's Wars*, 19-35; George H. W. Bush, "Transcript of President's Address to Joint Session of Congress," *NYT*, Sept. 12, 1990.

24. Sider, "Global Rambo," 2-3; Jim Wallis, "What Price Oil?," *Sojo*, Oct. 1990, 5.

25. Carenen, *Fervent Embrace*; Yaacov Bar-Siman-Tov, "The United States and Israel since 1948: A 'Special Relationship'?," *Diplomatic History* 22.2 (Spring 1998): 231-62.

26. Weber, *On the Road*; Carenen, *Fervent Embrace* (Walvoord quotation, 133; Falwell quotation, 189); Falwell, *Listen, America!*, 113.

27. Wes Michaelson, "Evangelical Zionism," *Sojo*, Mar. 1977, 3-5; Dewey Beegle, "The Promise and the Promised Land," *Sojo*, Mar. 1977, 24-27; Wes Michaelson, "A Shaky Shalom," *Sojo*, May 1979, 3-4; Wes Michaelson, "Biblically Buttressed Land Grab," *Sojo*, July 1979, 22-24; Wes Michaelson, "The Necessities of Peace," *Sojo*, Oct. 1979, 4-5; Wes Michaelson, "The Unresolved Issue at Camp David," *Sojo*, Nov. 1978, 4-5; "La Grange Declaration," *Sojo*, July 1979, 24-25.

28. William J. McConnell, "Prophecy and Politics in the Holy Land," *ESA Advocate*, July-Aug. 1990, 1A; Danny Collum, "Tangled Roots of Conflict," *Sojo*, Sept. 1982, 8-10; Vicki Kemper, "A Plea from Palestine," *Sojo*, Apr. 1989, 4; Jim Wallis and Charles Kimball, "The Clock Is Ticking," *Sojo*, Nov. 1989, 31-32; Ron Sider, "A Pilgrimage to the Holy Land," *ESA Advocate*, July-Aug. 1990, 1-4; "Washington Update," *ESA Advocate*, July-Aug. 1989, 6. See also, for example, "Elias Chacour: Persecution and Peace in the Middle East," *TOS*, Sept. 1986, 8-11; Mubarak Awad, "A Victory within Ourselves," *Sojo*, Jan. 1989, 26-30; and William O'Brien, "Beneath Their Vine and Fig Tree," *TOS*, Jan.-Feb. 1988, 19-27.

29. Wallis, "What Price Oil?," 4-5; John Alexander, "On Hating Arabs," *TOS*, Nov.-Dec. 1990, 47-48; ESA, "An Open Letter," *ESA Advocate*, Jan.-Feb. 1991, 13; Sider, "Global Rambo," 2; Jim Wallis, "Disrupting the Consensus," *Sojo*, Dec. 1990, 54; Jim Wallis, "A Pilgrimage for Peace," *Sojo*, Feb.-Mar. 1991, 4-7.

30. Patterson, *Restless Giant*, 230-38; "Leaders Wrestle with Faith and War," *CT*, Feb. 11, 1991, 50-51; "'Call to the Churches,'" *CC*, Feb. 27, 1991; Jim Wallis, "Where Do We Go from Here?," *Sojo*, May 1991, 4-5; Joan Chittister, "Are We Becoming What We Hate?," *Sojo*, Apr. 1991, 4; Jim Wallis, "A Neither Just nor Holy War," *Sojo*, Apr. 1991, 10-13; Ron Sider and L. Lamar Nisly, "A Just War or Just Another War?," *ESA Advocate*, Mar. 1991, 1-3; Ron Sider, "A New (and Improved?) World Order?," *ESA Advocate*, May 1991, 1-3.

31. Patterson, *Restless Giant*, 334-41, 399-402; Glen H. Stassen, "Nonviolence in Time of War," *Sojo*, July-Aug. 1999, 18-21; Sharon Pauling, "Ending Rwanda's Horror," *Sojo*, Aug. 1994, 9-10; Gerald Shenk, "Adding Fuel to the Fire," *Sojo*, July-Aug. 1999, 9-10; Jim Wallis, "United against War," *Sojo*, May-June 1998, 9-10; Jim Wallis, "No More Sanctions, No More Bombing," *Sojo*, Mar.-Apr. 1999, 7-8; Joe Nangle, "Rising Stakes in Israeli-Arab Stalemate," *Sojo*, May 1992,

32-33; Jeremy Milgrom, "A Sophisticated Colonialism," *Sojo*, Jan.-Feb. 1998, 12-13; Jim Wallis, "A Better Way to Fight Terrorism," *Sojo*, Nov.-Dec. 1998, 9-10.

32. Anderson, *Bush's Wars*, 47-92.

33. "Deny Them Their Victory," *Sojo*, Nov.-Dec. 2001, 26; Jim Wallis, "The Two Paths," *Sojomail*, Sept. 21, 2001, http://sojo.net/sojomail/2001/09/21 (Dec. 31, 2013); Jim Wallis, "What's Next," *Sojomail*, Sept. 24, 2001, http://sojo.net/sojomail/2001/09/24 (Dec. 31, 2013); Jim Wallis, "Telling the Truth," *Sojomail*, Sept. 26, 2001, http://sojo.net/sojomail/2001/09/26 (Dec. 31, 2013).

34. Jim Wallis, "Conscience in a Time of War," *Sojomail*, Oct. 12, 2001, http://sojo.net/sojomail/2001/10/12 (Dec. 31, 2013); Jim Wallis, "Justice Is Still the Goal," *WP*, Nov. 14, 2001; Jim Wallis, "A Call: Feed the People, Halt the Bombing, Honor Ramadan," *Sojomail*, Nov. 7, 2001, http://sojo.net/sojomail/2001/11/07 (Dec. 31, 2013); Jim Wallis, "Plans for a Wider War," *Sojomail*, Nov. 28, 2001, http://sojo.net/sojomail/2001/11/28 (Dec. 31, 2013).

35. Anderson, *Bush's Wars*, 93-119; Ron Sider, "Should We Attack Iraq?," *Prism*, Mar.-Apr. 2002, 36; David Cortright, "Why Not Attack Iraq?," *Sojo*, July-Aug., 2002, 15; "Disarm Iraq without War," Oct. 10, 2002, http://archive.sojo.net/index.cfm?action=action.US-UK_statement (June 1, 2013); Jim Wallis, "Disarm Iraq ... without War," *Sojo*, Nov.-Dec. 2002, 7-8; Jim Wallis, "Is Bush Deaf to Church Doubts on Iraq War?," *Boston Globe*, Dec. 9, 2002.

36. George Hunsinger, "We Must Oppose This War," *Sojo*, Mar.-Apr. 2003, 15; Jim Wallis, "Prophetic Leadership," *Sojo*, Jan.-Feb. 2003, 7-8; David Earle Anderson, "Not a Just or Moral War," *Sojo*, Jan.-Feb. 2003, 26-29; Jim Wallis, "A Momentous Choice," *Sojo*, Mar.-Apr. 2003, 7-8; Jim Wallis, "Meeting with Prime Minister Tony Blair," *Sojomail*, Feb. 20, 2003, http://sojo.net/sojomail/2003/02/20 (Dec. 31, 2013); Elisabeth Bumiller, "Religious Leaders Ask if Antiwar Call Is Heard," *NYT*, Mar. 10, 2003; Jim Wallis and John Bryson Chane, "There Is a Third Way," *WP*, Mar. 14, 2003; Anderson, *Bush's Wars*, 120-29; Williams, *God's Own Party*, 255-56.

37. Anderson, *Bush's Wars*, 131-86; Jim Wallis, "The Lessons of War," *Sojo*, May-June 2003, 7-8; "Antiwar Activists Are Left Unsure," *Los Angeles Times*, May 3, 2003; David Cortright, "Weapons of Mass Deception," *Sojo*, Sept.-Oct. 2003, 15; Duane Shank, "Why Sojourners Opposes an $87 Billion Blank Check for Iraq," *Sojomail*, Oct. 15, 2003, http://sojo.net/sojomail/2003/10/15 (Dec. 31, 2013); Jim Wallis, "Iraq: One Year Later," *Sojomail*, Mar. 18, 2004, http://sojo.net/sojomail/2004/03/18 (Dec. 31, 2013).

38. Jim Wallis, "Falsehoods and the Iraq War," *Sojo*, Jan. 2006, 5-6; Jim Wallis, "Iraq: the Tipping Point," *Sojo*, Sept.-Oct. 2007, 5-6; Jim Wallis, "Who Will Protect Us from Him?," *Sojo*, Nov. 2006, 5-6; Campolo, *Red Letter Christians*, 57-70; Sojourners, "A Call to Lament and Repent," Mar. 8, 2007, http://archive.sojo.net/action/alerts/080307_paths_of_peace.html (June 1, 2013); Gushee, *Future of Faith*, 253-70; Ted Olsen, "Where Jim Wallis Stands," *CT*, May 2008, 57; Wallis, *Great Awakening*, 244.

39. Ron Suskind, "Without a Doubt," *NYT Magazine*, Oct. 17, 2004; Anderson, *Bush's Wars*, 231; George W. Bush, "State of the Union," *NYT*, Jan. 21, 2004; Jim

Wallis, "Dangerous Religion," *Sojo*, Sept.-Oct. 2003, 20-26; Jim Wallis, "High Stakes for Church and State," *Sojo*, Nov. 2004, 12-19; Wallis, "Who Will Protect Us from Him?"; Wallis, *God's Politics*, 151-55; Jim Wallis, "Tonight We Begin to End the War," *Sojo*, June 2007, 5-6.

40. Jim Wallis, "A Call to Repentance," *Sojo*, Jan. 2008, 12-17.

41. Michaelson, "Human Rights," 5; Ron Sider, "Towards a Political Philosophy," *ESA Advocate*, Oct. 1988, 2; Sider, "New (and Improved?) World Order?," 2; Wallis, "Call to Repentance," 17. See also Michael Westmoreland-White, Glen H. Stassen, and David P. Gushee, "Disciples of the Incarnation," *Sojo*, May 1994, 26-30.

42. Sider, *Completely Pro-Life*, 156-57; Wallis, *Soul of Politics*, 109; Sider, *Christ and Violence*, 24-25; Ronald J. Sider, "The Risk of Peacemaking," *ESA Update*, May-June 1983, 4; Sider and Nisly, "Just War," 2. See also Reese, "Resistance and Hope," 68-75; and Sider and Taylor, *Nuclear Holocaust*, 95-158.

43. Ron Sider, "The Way of the Cross," *Prism*, Jan.-Feb. 2003, 36; Ron Sider, "To See the Cross," *TOS*, Feb. 1977, 19; Bill Kellerman, "Apologist of Power," *Sojo*, Mar. 1987, 15-20; John Alexander, "Political Realism," *TOS*, Oct. 1980, 10-13; Jim Rice, "The Pretense of Peacemaking," *Sojo*, Apr. 1987, 6; Sider and Taylor, *Nuclear Holocaust*, 61-81; Sider, *Completely Pro-Life*, 156-63; Wallis, *God's Politics*, 108-36; Campolo, *Speaking My Mind*, 155-62; Gushee, *Future of Faith*, 199-213.

44. Richard Mouw, "A Christian Reformed Teacher," in Wallis, *Peacemakers*, 130; Sider, *Scandal of Evangelical Politics*, 199; Wallis, *Faith Works*, 236; Sider and Taylor, *Nuclear Holocaust*, 333n1; Sider, "To See the Cross," 21; Sider, *Christ and Violence*, 44; Ron Sider, "Courageous Nonviolence," *CT*, Dec. 2007, 44; Wallis, *God's Politics*, 161.

45. Wallis, *God's Politics*, 191; Wallis, *Soul of Politics*, 73; Ronald J. Sider, "God's People Reconciling," Presentation at Mennonite World Conference, July 28, 1984, http://www.cpt.org/resources/writings/sider (Dec. 31, 2013); Wallis, *Great Awakening*, 76; Stassen, *Just Peacemaking*; Stassen, "Nonviolence in Time of War"; Wallis, *Faith Works*, 229-32; Sider, *Scandal of Evangelical Politics*, 205-7; Mark Olson, "Pacifism?," *TOS*, Nov. 1986, 2.

EPILOGUE

1. Al Tizon, "I Am Asian, Hear Me Roar!," *Prism*, Sept. 2009, 7; Soong-Chan Rah and Jason Mach, "Is the Emerging Church for Whites Only?," *Sojo*, May 2010, 16-19; Danny Duncan Collum, "America in Black and White," *Sojo*, Mar. 2009, 38; Michelle Alexander, "Cruel and Unusual," *Sojo*, Feb. 2011, 16-19; Jim Wallis, "Lament from a White Father," *Huffington Post*, July 15, 2013, http://www .huffingtonpost.com/jim-wallis/lament-from-a-white-fathe_b_3600320.html (Dec. 31, 2013); Lisa Sharon Harper, "'Fighting Words' from the Supreme Court," *Sojo*, Sept.-Oct. 2013, 14; Mimi Haddad, "Empowered by God," *Sojo*, Aug. 2009, 28-31; Anne Eggebroten, "The Persistence of Patriarchy," *Sojo*, July 2010, 22-24; Joan Chittister, "A 'Hostile Takeover' of Women Religious," *Sojo*, July 2012, 8-9; Molly Marsh, "Turning Despair into Hope," *Sojo*, Jan. 2010, 18-23; Jim Wallis, "Men Behaving Badly," *Sojo*, Aug. 2011, 7.

2. Ron Sider, "Open Letter to President Obama," *Prism*, Jan.-Feb. 2009, 40; Jim Wallis, "Abortion Common Ground," *God's Politics Blog*, July 31, 2009, http://sojo.net/blogs/2009/07/31/abortion-common-ground (Dec. 31, 2013); Jim Wallis, "Faith Principles for Health-Care Reform," *Sojo*, Nov. 2009, 7; "Pro-Life Christian Leaders Applaud Sen. Casey's Alternative Abortion Language," *Faith in Public Life*, Dec. 18, 2009, http://www.faithinpubliclife.org/newsroom/press/pro-life_christian_leaders_app/ (Dec. 31, 2013); Jim Wallis, "A Significant Step toward Health Reform in Spite of Poisonous Politics," *God's Politics Blog*, Mar. 23, 2010, http://sojo.net/blogs/2010/03/23/significant-step-toward-health-reform-spite-poisonous-politics (Dec. 31, 2013).

3. Ron Sider, "Evangelicals and Homosexuality," *Prism*, Nov.-Dec. 2012, 56; Laurie Goodstein, "Christian Leaders Unite on Political Issues," *NYT*, Nov. 20, 2009; Ron Sider, "Why Did I Sign?," *Prism*, Jan.-Feb. 2010, 48; Ron Sider, "Called to Love the Gay Community," *Prism*, Sept.-Oct. 2010, 40; ESA, "Oriented to Love: A Guide to Facilitating a Dialogue on Sexual Diversity in the Body of Christ," 2012, http://prism.wpengine.com/wp-content/uploads/2012/11/OrientedtoLoveGuide2012.pdf (Dec. 31, 2013); cover, *Prism*, Nov.-Dec. 2012.

4. Jeannie Choi, "Changes in Attitude," *Sojo*, July 2012, 30-35; Jim Wallis, "Equal Protection—for All," *Sojo*, Sept.-Oct. 2013, 7.

5. "A Shifting Landscape: A Decade of Change in American Attitudes about Same-Sex Marriage and LGBT Issues," Public Religion Research Institute, Feb. 26, 2014, http://publicreligion.org/research/2014/02/2014-lgbt-survey/ (Mar. 31, 2014); Jon Ward, "Evangelicals Face Growing Tension between Political and Personal Views of Marriage," *Huffington Post*, Mar. 26, 2013, http://www.huffingtonpost.com/2013/03/26/evangelicals-gay-marriage_n_2956917.html (Dec. 31, 2013).

6. Jim Wallis, "To Cut the Deficit, Cut Military Spending," *Sojo*, Apr. 2010, 7; Sojourners, "What Would Jesus Cut?," Feb. 28, 2011, http://sojo.net/press/what-would-jesus-cut-22 (Dec. 31, 2013); "A Call for Intergenerational Justice: A Christian Proposal for the American Debt Crisis," *Center for Public Justice*, Mar. 3, 2011, http://www.cpjustice.org/intergenerationaljustice (Dec. 31, 2013); Stephanie Samuel, "Leaders Offer a Christian Proposal on U.S. Debt Crisis," *Christian Post*, Mar. 3, 2011, http://www.christianpost.com/news/leaders-offer-a-christian-proposal-on-us-debt-crisis-49269/ (Dec. 31, 2013); Sider, *Fixing the Moral Deficit*; "A Circle of Protection," Apr. 21, 2011, http://go.sojo.net/site/DocServer/Circle_of_Protection_Statement.full.pdf (June 1, 2013); Tobin Grant, "Obama Meets with Christian Leaders over Budget," *CT Politics Blog*, July 21, 2011, http://blog.christianitytoday.com/ctpolitics/2011/07/obama_meets_wit_1.html (Dec. 31, 2013).

7. Jim Wallis, "Time to End This War," *Sojo*, Sept.-Oct. 2010, 7; Jim Wallis, "The Cost of War," *Sojo*, Mar. 2011, 7; David Cortright, "Finding the Way Out," *Sojo*, Mar. 2011, 17; Jim Wallis, "Iraq: It's Finally Over—and It Was Wrong," *Sojo*, Jan. 2012, 7; Lynne Hybels, "Stunned and Hopeful," *Sojo*, June 2012, 12; Churches for Middle East Peace, "Christians Support Bold Action for Holy Land Peace," June 4, 2009, http://action.cmep.org/t/4029/signUp.jsp?key=1013 (Dec. 31,

2013); Churches for Middle East Peace, "Letter from Heads of Denominations to President Obama," Aug. 30, 2010, http://www.cmep.org/content/letter-heads-denominations-president-obama-restart-direct-talks-August-30-2010 (Dec. 31, 2013). See also numerous articles on peacemaking in the Middle East in *Prism*, Mar.-Apr. 2012.

8. Wallis, *God's Politics*, xxvii; Larsen, "God's Gardeners"; Wilkinson, *Between God and Green*; Wallis, *Great Awakening*, 135-56; Sider, *Scandal of Evangelical Politics*, 209-18. See also, for example, David Gushee, "The Ultimate Ethical Issue?," *Prism*, Mar.-Apr. 2008, 4; Jim Ball, "Recipe for Disaster," *Sojo*, Dec. 2009, 10-11; Onleilove Alston, "Destroying West Virginia, One Mountain at a Time," *Sojo*, June 2010, 18-21; Rusty Pritchard, "The World Is Watching," *Prism*, Sept.-Oct. 2011, 7; and Jim Wallis, "A 'Historic Moment' on Climate Change?," *Sojo*, Mar. 2013, 7. For full issues devoted to environmental concerns, see *Sojo*, Apr. 2011; and *Prism*, July-Aug. 2011.

9. Ched Myers, "A House for All Peoples?," *Sojo*, Apr. 2006, 20-25; Sider, *Scandal of Evangelical Politics*, 225-26; Joel Hunter, "A More Noble Way," *Sojo*, Sept.-Oct. 2009, 16; Linda Espenshade, "It's Time, Mr. President," *Prism*, July-Aug. 2009, 36-38; Jim Wallis, "Arizona's Immigration Bill Is a Social and Racial Sin," *God's Politics Blog*, Apr. 4, 2010, http://sojo.net/blogs/2010/04/21/arizonas-immigration-bill-social-and-racial-sin (Dec. 31, 2013); Lisa Miller, "Why Are Evangelicals Supporting Immigration Reform?," *WP*, June 22, 2012, http://articles.washingtonpost.com/2012-06-22/national/35461786_1_immigration-reform-white-evangelicals-evangelical-base (Dec. 31, 2013); Dan Merica, "Obama Pushes Expedited Timetable on Immigration Reform in Meeting with Faith Leaders," *CNN Belief Blog*, Mar. 8, 2013, http://religion.blogs.cnn.com/2013/03/08/obama-pushes-expedited-timetable-on-immigration-reform-in-meeting-with-faith-leaders/ (Dec. 31, 2013). See also articles in *Sojo*, Mar. 2010.

10. Jim Wallis, "Defining 'Evangelicals' in an Election Year," *Sojo*, Feb. 2012, 7.

11. Al Tizon and Paul Alexander, "Mabuhay! Osiyo!," *Prism*, Summer 2013, 55.

Bibliography

ARCHIVAL COLLECTIONS

Evangelicals for Social Action Collection. Billy Graham Center. Wheaton, Ill.
Sojourners Collection. Wheaton College Special Collections. Wheaton, Ill.

PERIODICALS

ESA Advocate
ESA Update
Freedom Now
The Other Side
Post-American
Prism
Sojourners

BOOKS, ARTICLES, AND DISSERTATIONS

Alexander, John F. *Your Money or Your Life: A New Look at Jesus' View of Wealth and Power*. San Francisco: Harper and Row, 1986.
Anderson, Terry H. *Bush's Wars*. New York: Oxford University Press, 2011.
Audi, Robert, and Nicholas Wolterstorff. *Religion in the Public Square: The Place of Religious Convictions in Political Debate*. New York: Rowman and Littlefield, 1997.
Balmer, Randall. *Redeemer: The Life of Jimmy Carter*. New York: Basic Books, 2014.
Bellah, Robert N., Richard Madsen, William M. Sullivan, Ann Swidler, and Steven M. Tipton. *Habits of the Heart: Individualism and Commitment in American Life*. Berkeley: University of California Press, 1985.
Bendroth, Margaret Lamberts. *Fundamentalism and Gender: 1875 to the Present*. New Haven: Yale University Press, 1993.

Bentley, William H. *The National Black Evangelical Association: Reflections on the Evolution of a Concept of Ministry.* Chicago: self-published, 1979.

Bivins, Jason C. *The Fracture of Good Order: Christian Antiliberalism and the Challenge to American Politics.* Chapel Hill: University of North Carolina Press, 2003.

Cahill, Sean. *Same-Sex Marriage in the United States: Focus on the Facts.* Lanham, Md.: Lexington Books, 2004.

Campolo, Tony. *Red Letter Christians: A Citizen's Guide to Faith and Politics.* Ventura, Calif.: Regal, 2008.

——. *Speaking My Mind: The Radical Evangelical Prophet Tackles the Tough Issues Christians Are Afraid to Face.* Nashville: W Publishing, 2004.

Carenen, Caitlin. *The Fervent Embrace: Liberal Protestants, Evangelicals, and Israel.* New York: New York University Press, 2012.

Carpenter, Joel A. *Revive Us Again: The Reawakening of American Fundamentalism.* New York: Oxford University Press, 1997.

Carter, Stephen L. *The Culture of Disbelief: How American Law and Politics Trivialize Religious Devotion.* New York: Basic Books. 1993.

Chilton, David. *Productive Christians in an Age of Guilt Manipulators.* Tyler, Texas: Institute for Christian Economics, 1981.

Claiborne, Shane. *The Irresistible Revolution: Living as an Ordinary Radical.* Grand Rapids, Mich.: Zondervan, 2006.

Clark, Robert F. *Victory Deferred: The War on Global Poverty (1945-2003).* Lanham, Md.: University Press of America, 2005.

Clouse, Robert G., Robert D. Linder, and Richard V. Pierard, eds. *The Cross and the Flag.* Carol Stream, Ill.: Creation House, 1972.

——. *Protest and Politics: Christianity and Contemporary Affairs.* Greenwood, S.C.: Attic Press, 1968.

Cochran, Pamela. *Evangelical Feminism: A History.* New York: New York University Press, 2005.

Coffman, Elesha J. *The Christian Century and the Rise of the Protestant Mainline.* New York: Oxford University Press, 2013.

Collins, Kenneth J. *Power, Politics and the Fragmentation of Evangelicalism: From the Scopes Trial to the Obama Administration.* Downers Grove, Ill.: InterVarsity Press, 2012.

Culverson, Donald R. *Contesting Apartheid: U.S. Activism, 1960-1987.* Boulder, Colo.: Westview Press, 1999.

Davis, Flora. *Moving the Mountain: The Women's Movement in America since 1960.* Urbana: University of Illinois Press, 1999.

Dayton, Donald W. *Discovering an Evangelical Heritage.* New York: Harper and Row, 1976.

Deberg, Betty A. *Ungodly Women: Gender and the First Wave of American Fundamentalism.* Macon, Ga.: Mercer University Press, 2000.

Eberle, Christopher. *Religious Conviction in Liberal Politics.* New York: Cambridge University Press, 2002.

Emerson, Michael O., and Christian Smith. *Divided by Faith: Evangelical Religion and the Problem of Race in America.* New York: Oxford University Press, 2000.

Evans, Sara M. *Tidal Wave: How Women Changed America at Century's End.* New York: Free Press, 2003.

Falwell, Jerry. *Listen, America!* Garden City, N.Y.: Doubleday, 1980.

Findlay, James F. *Church People in the Struggle: The National Council of Churches and the Black Freedom Movement, 1950-1970.* New York: Oxford University Press, 1993.

Fowler, Robert Booth. *A New Engagement: Evangelical Political Thought, 1966-1976.* Grand Rapids, Mich.: Eerdmans, 1982.

Gallagher, Sally K. *Evangelical Identity and Gendered Family Life.* New Brunswick, N.J.: Rutgers University Press, 2003.

Gay, Craig M. *With Liberty and Justice for Whom? The Recent Evangelical Debate over Capitalism.* Grand Rapids, Mich.: Eerdmans, 1991.

Gilbreath, Edward. *Reconciliation Blues: A Black Evangelical's Inside View of White Christianity.* Downers Grove, Ill.: InterVarsity Press, 2006.

Gish, Arthur G. *The New Left and Christian Radicalism.* Grand Rapids, Mich.: Eerdmans, 1970.

Griffin-Nolan, Ed. *Witness for Peace: A Story of Resistance.* Louisville: Westminster/John Knox Press, 1991.

Grounds, Vernon. *Evangelicalism and Social Responsibility.* Scottdale, Pa.: Herald Press, 1969.

Gundry, Patricia. *Woman Be Free!* Grand Rapids, Mich.: Zondervan, 1977.

Gushee, David P. *The Future of Faith: The Public Witness of the Evangelical Center.* Waco, Texas: Baylor University Press, 2008.

Gutterman, David S. *Prophetic Politics: Christian Social Movements and American Democracy.* Ithaca, N.Y.: Cornell University Press, 2005.

Hardesty, Nancy. *Women Called to Witness: Evangelical Feminism in the Nineteenth Century.* Knoxville: University of Tennessee Press, 1999.

Harper, Lisa Sharon. *Evangelical Does Not Equal Republican ... or Democrat.* New York: New Press, 2008.

Hartley, Benjamin L. *Evangelicals at a Crossroads: Revivalism and Social Reform in Boston, 1860-1910.* Durham: University of New Hampshire Press, 2011.

Hatfield, Mark O. *Conflict and Conscience.* Waco, Texas: Word, 1971.

Henry, Carl F. H. *The Uneasy Conscience of Modern Fundamentalism.* Grand Rapids, Mich.: Eerdmans, 1947.

Herman, Didi. *The Antigay Agenda: Orthodox Vision and the Christian Right.* Chicago: University of Chicago Press, 1997.

Hirshman, Linda. *Victory: The Triumphant Gay Revolution.* New York: Harper, 2012.

Hollinger, Dennis P. *Individualism and Social Ethics: An Evangelical Syncretism.* Lanham, Md.: University Press of America, 1983.

Hull, N. E. H., and Peter Charles Hoffer. Roe v. Wade: *The Abortion Rights Controversy in American History.* Lawrence: University Press of Kansas, 2001.

Hulsether, Mark. *Building a Protestant Left:* Christianity and Crisis *Magazine, 1941-1993.* Knoxville: University of Tennessee Press, 1999.

Hunter, James Davison. *To Change the World: The Irony, Tragedy, and Possibility of Christianity in the Late Modern World*. New York: Oxford University Press, 2010.

Jenkins, Philip. *Decade of Nightmares: The End of the Sixties and the Making of Eighties America*. New York: Oxford University Press, 2006.

Jones, Jeffrey McClain. "Ronald Sider and Radical Evangelical Political Theology." Ph.D. diss., Northwestern University and Garrett-Evangelical Theological Seminary, 1990.

Kazin, Michael. *A Godly Hero: The Life of William Jennings Bryan*. New York: Knopf, 2006.

LaHaye, Beverly. *I Am a Woman by God's Design*. Old Tappan, N.J.: Revell, 1980.

LaHaye, Tim. *The Unhappy Gays: What Everyone Should Know about Homosexuality*. Wheaton, Ill.: Tyndale, 1978.

Larsen, David Kenneth. "God's Gardeners: American Protestant Evangelicals Confront Environmentalism, 1967-2000." Ph.D. diss., University of Chicago Divinity School, 2001.

Lienesch, Michael. *Redeeming America: Piety and Politics in the New Christian Right*. Chapel Hill: University of North Carolina Press, 1993.

Lincoln, C. Eric, and Lawrence H. Mamiya. *The Black Church in the African-American Experience*. Durham: Duke University Press, 1990.

Lindsay, D. Michael. *Faith in the Halls of Power*. New York: Oxford University Press, 2007.

Lindsell, Harold. *Free Enterprise: A Judeo-Christian Defense*. Wheaton, Ill.: Tyndale, 1982.

Loveland, Anne C. *American Evangelicals and the U.S. Military, 1942-1993*. Baton Rouge: Louisiana State University Press, 1996.

Luker, Kristin. *Abortion and the Politics of Motherhood*. Berkeley: University of California Press, 1984.

Magnuson, Norris A. *Salvation in the Slums: Evangelical Social Work, 1865-1920*. Grand Rapids, Mich.: Baker, 1990.

Marsden, George M. *Fundamentalism and American Culture*. New York: Oxford University Press, 2006.

——. *Understanding Fundamentalism and Evangelicalism*. Grand Rapids, Mich.: Eerdmans, 1991.

Martin, William. *With God on Our Side: The Rise of the Religious Right in America*. New York: Broadway Books, 2005.

Mayer, Jeremy D. *Running on Race: Racial Politics in Presidential Campaigns, 1960-2000*. New York: Random House, 2002.

Miller, Steven P. *The Age of Evangelicalism: America's Born-Again Years*. New York: Oxford University Press, 2014.

Moberg, David O. *The Great Reversal: Evangelism versus Social Concern*. Philadelphia: Lippincott, 1972.

——. *Inasmuch: Christian Social Responsibility in the Twentieth Century*. Grand Rapids, Mich.: Eerdmans, 1965.

Mouw, Richard J. *Political Evangelism*. Grand Rapids, Mich.: Eerdmans, 1973.

Mulhall, Stephen, and Adam Swift. *Liberals and Communitarians*. 2nd ed. Oxford: Blackwell, 1996.

Nash, Ronald H. *Social Justice and the Christian Church*. Milford, Mich.: Mott Media, 1983.

———. *Why the Left Is Not Right: The Religious Left: Who They Are and What They Believe*. Grand Rapids, Mich.: Zondervan, 1996.

Neuhaus, Richard John. *The Naked Public Square: Religion and Democracy in America*. Grand Rapids, Mich.: Eerdmans, 1984.

Pannell, William E. *My Friend, the Enemy*. Waco, Texas: Word, 1968.

Patterson, James T. *Restless Giant: The United States from Watergate to Bush v. Gore*. New York: Oxford University Press, 2005.

Pierard, Richard V. *The Unequal Yoke: Evangelical Christianity and Political Conservatism*. Philadelphia: Lippincott, 1970.

Quebedeaux, Richard. *The Worldly Evangelicals*. New York: Harper and Row, 1978.

———. *The Young Evangelicals: Revolution in Orthodoxy*. New York: Harper and Row, 1974.

Reese, Boyd. "Resistance and Hope: The Interplay of Theological Synthesis, Biblical Interpretation, Political Analysis, and Praxis in the Christian Radicalism of 'Sojourners' Magazine." Ph.D. diss., Temple University, 1991.

Ryan. Alan. *The Making of Modern Liberalism*. Princeton: Princeton University Press, 2012.

Scanzoni, Letha, and Nancy Hardesty. *All We're Meant to Be: A Biblical Approach to Women's Liberation*. Waco, Texas: Word, 1974.

Scanzoni, Letha, and Virginia Mollenkott. *Is the Homosexual My Neighbor?* San Francisco: Harper and Row, 1978.

Schaeffer, Franky, ed. *Is Capitalism Christian? Toward a Christian Perspective on Economics*. Westchester, Ill.: Crossway Books, 1985.

Schaller, Michael. *Right Turn: American Life in the Reagan-Bush Era, 1980-1992*. New York: Oxford University Press, 2007.

Schlafly, Phyllis. *The Power of the Positive Woman*. New Rochelle, N.Y.: Arlington House, 1977.

Schmidt, Jean Miller. *Souls or the Social Order: The Two-Party System in American Protestantism*. New York: Carlson Publishing, 1991.

Settje, David E. *Faith and War: How Christians Debated the Cold and Vietnam Wars*. New York: New York University Press, 2011.

Shields, Jon A. *The Democratic Virtues of the Christian Right*. Princeton: Princeton University Press, 2009.

Sider, Ronald J. *Christ and Violence*. Scottsdale, Pa.: Herald Press, 1979.

———. *Completely Pro-Life: Building a Consistent Stance*. Downers Grove, Ill.: InterVarsity Press, 1987.

———. *Fixing the Moral Deficit: A Balanced Way to Balance the Budget*. Downers Grove, Ill.: IVP Books, 2012.

———. *Just Generosity: A New Vision for Overcoming Poverty in America*. Grand Rapids, Mich.: Baker Books, 1999.

———. *Nonviolence: The Invincible Weapon*. Dallas: Word, 1989.

———. *Rich Christians in an Age of Hunger: A Biblical Study*. Downers Grove, Ill.: InterVarsity Press, 1977.

———. *Rich Christians in an Age of Hunger: A Biblical Study*. 2nd ed. Downers Grove, Ill.: InterVarsity Press, 1984.

———. *Rich Christians in an Age of Hunger: Moving from Affluence to Generosity*. 4th ed. Nashville: Word, 1997.

———. *Rich Christians in an Age of Hunger: Moving from Affluence to Generosity*. 5th ed. Nashville: Thomas Nelson, 2005.

———. *The Scandal of Evangelical Politics: Why Are Christians Missing the Chance to Really Change the World?* Grand Rapids, Mich.: Baker Books, 2008.

Sider, Ronald J., ed. *The Chicago Declaration*. Carol Stream, Ill.: Creation House, 1974.

———. *Living More Simply: Biblical Principles and Practical Models*. Downers Grove, Ill.: InterVarsity Press, 1980.

Sider, Ronald J., and Diane Knippers, eds., *Toward an Evangelical Public Policy: Political Strategies for the Health of the Nation*. Grand Rapids, Mich.: Baker Books, 2005.

Sider, Ronald J., and Richard Taylor. *Nuclear Holocaust and Christian Hope: A Book for Christian Peacemakers*. New York: Paulist Press, 1982.

Skinner, Tom. *Words of Revolution*. Grand Rapids, Mich.: Zondervan, 1970.

Smith, Christian. *The Emergence of Liberation Theology: Radical Religion and Social Movement Theory*. Chicago: University of Chicago Press, 1991.

———. *Resisting Reagan: The U.S. Central American Peace Movement*. Chicago: University of Chicago Press, 1996.

Smith, Timothy L. *Revivalism and Social Reform: American Protestantism on the Eve of the Civil War*. Baltimore: Johns Hopkins University Press, 1980.

Stassen, Glen H., ed. *Just Peacemaking: Ten Practices for Abolishing War*. Cleveland: Pilgrim Press, 1998.

Stricker, Frank. *Why America Lost the War on Poverty—and How to Win It*. Chapel Hill: University of North Carolina Press, 2007.

Stringfellow, William. *An Ethic for Christians and Other Aliens in a Strange Land*. Waco, Texas: Word, 1973.

Sullivan, Amy. *The Party Faithful: How and Why Democrats Are Closing the God Gap*. New York: Scribner, 2008.

Swartz, David R. *Moral Minority: The Evangelical Left in an Age of Conservatism*. Philadelphia: University of Pennsylvania Press, 2012.

Thiemann, Ronald F. *Constructing a Public Theology: The Church in a Pluralistic Culture*. Louisville: Westminster/John Knox Press, 1991.

Tong, Rosemarie. *Feminist Thought: A More Comprehensive Introduction*. Boulder, Colo.: Westview Press, 2009.

Wallis, Jim. *Agenda for Biblical People*. New York: Harper and Row, 1976.

———. *The Call to Conversion: Recovering the Gospel for These Times*. San Francisco: Harper and Row, 1981.

———. *Faith Works: How to Live Your Beliefs and Ignite Positive Social Change*. New York: Random House, 2005.

———. *God's Politics: Why the Right Gets It Wrong and the Left Doesn't Get It*. San Francisco: HarperSanFrancisco, 2005.

———. *The Great Awakening: Reviving Faith and Politics in a Post-Religious Right America*. New York: HarperOne, 2008.

———. *On God's Side: What Religion Forgets and Politics Hasn't Learned about Serving the Common Good*. Grand Rapids, Mich.: Brazos Press, 2013.

———. *Rediscovering Values: On Wall Street, Main Street, and Your Street*. New York: Howard Books, 2010.

———. *Revive Us Again: A Sojourner's Story*. Nashville: Abingdon Press, 1983.

———. *The Soul of Politics: A Practical and Prophetic Vision for Change*. New York: New Press, 1994.

———. *Who Speaks for God? An Alternative to the Religious Right—A New Politics of Compassion, Community, and Civility*. New York: Delacorte Press, 1996.

Wallis, Jim, ed. *Peacemakers: Christian Voices from the New Abolitionist Movement*. San Francisco: Harper and Row, 1983.

———. *The Rise of Christian Conscience: The Emergence of a Dramatic Renewal Movement in Today's Church*. San Francisco: Harper and Row, 1987.

———. *Waging Peace: A Handbook for the Struggle to Abolish Nuclear Weapons*. San Francisco: Harper and Row, 1982.

Wallis, Jim, and Charles E. Gutenson. *Living God's Politics: A Guide to Putting Your Faith into Action*. San Francisco: HarperSanFrancisco, 2006.

Wallis, Jim, and Joyce Hollyday, eds. *Cloud of Witnesses*. Maryknoll, N.Y.: Orbis Books, 1991.

———. *Crucible of Fire: The Church Confronts Apartheid*. Maryknoll, N.Y.: Orbis Books, 1989.

Weber, Timothy P. *On the Road to Armageddon: How Evangelicals Became Israel's Best Friend*. Grand Rapids, Mich.: Baker Academic, 2004.

Wilkinson, Katharine K. *Between God and Green: How Evangelicals are Cultivating a Middle Ground on Climate Change*. New York: Oxford University Press, 2012.

Williams, Daniel K. *God's Own Party: The Making of the Christian Right*. New York: Oxford University Press, 2010.

Wilson, William Julius. *The Declining Significance of Race: Blacks and Changing American Institutions*. Chicago: University of Chicago Press, 1978.

Wuthnow, Robert. *The Restructuring of American Religion: Society and Faith since World War II*. Princeton: Princeton University Press, 1988.

Yoder, John Howard. *The Politics of Jesus*. Grand Rapids, Mich.: Eerdmans, 1972.

Young, Michael P. *Bearing Witness against Sin: The Evangelical Birth of the American Social Movement*. Chicago: University of Chicago Press, 2006.

Index

Chilton, David, 220
Chittister, Joan, 123
Christian Century (magazine), 25, 31, 32
Christianity and Crisis (magazine), 25, 31, 32
Christianity Today (magazine), 8-9, 16, 25, 32, 45, 105, 124, 175
Christians for Biblical Equality, 120
Civil rights movement, 26, 29, 31, 43, 77
Claiborne, Shane, 13, 230, 273, 274
Clark, Fred, 64
Clinton, Bill, 89, 147, 148, 153-54, 155, 156, 158, 226-27, 258
Clinton, Hillary, 117, 153
Clouse, Robert, 218
Coffin, William Sloane, 178, 179, 262
Cold War, 84, 219, 237-52
Collum, Danny (Duncan), 82, 90, 96, 97, 184, 210-20 passim, 232, 233, 244, 245, 250, 256
Communal living, 215
Communism, 9, 32, 64, 84, 135, 220-21, 222, 235, 239, 240, 243-45, 249, 250-51. *See also* Cold War
Cone, James, 83, 96
Contras, 245, 246-47, 249-50
Creation care, 21-22, 275

Daughters of Sarah (magazine), 107, 108, 111, 120, 121, 122, 123
Day, Dorothy, 19, 242
Dayton, Donald, 7, 111, 174
Dayton, Lucille Sider, 111
Death penalty, 1, 129, 137, 140, 158, 160, 162
Delk, Yvonne, 88, 122
Democratic Party, 66, 114, 138, 149, 155-60, 220, 227
Dobson, James, 10, 71, 154, 156, 196

El Salvador, 244-50
Environmentalism, 21-22, 275
Equal Rights Amendment (ERA), 106, 107, 112-14, 116, 125, 131, 153
Escobar, Samuel, 47

Evangelical and Ecumenical Women's Caucus, 120
Evangelical Committee for Aid and Development (CEPAD), 247, 248
Evangelical Environmental Network, 15, 22
Evangelicals Concerned, 169, 170
Evangelicals for McGovern, 45-46, 238
Evangelicals for Social Action (ESA), 2, 14-20, 51, 276-77; founding of, 10; on racial issues, 85-99 passim, 270; on feminism, 117-25, 152-53, 270-71; on abortion and pro-life position, 138-40, 150-55, 160-61; on LGBT issues, 180-83, 185-86, 193-95, 272; on poverty and economic justice, 211-33 passim; on nationalism and militarism, 243, 250, 256, 274-75
Evangelical social activism: in nineteenth century, 5-7; and individualistic social ethic in twentieth century, 7-9, 24, 28-29, 96-97; renewed by contemporary progressive evangelicalism, 9-10, 23-52; of Religious Right, 10-11
Evangelical theology of liberation, 203-10, 211, 212, 225-26, 230, 233
Evangelical Women's Caucus, 107, 108, 120, 168

Fager, Charles, 132, 135
Faith-based initiatives, 200, 228, 229
Falwell, Jerry, 2-3, 10, 18, 31, 51, 70, 85, 112, 131, 136, 167, 183-84, 214, 239, 240, 254-55
Feminism: nineteenth-century evangelical support for, 103; modern movement, 104-6, 111-17, 125-27, 128, 130-31
Feminist theology, 123-25
Finney, Charles Grandison, 5-6, 103
First Amendment, religion clauses of, 72-73
First Things (magazine), 25

McCain, John, 160, 230

McGovern, George, 45, 218

McLaren, Brian, 13, 273

Michaelson, Wes. *See* Granberg-Michaelson, Wesley

Minnery, Tom, 187

Moberg, David, 42, 45, 47

Mollenkott, Virginia, 108, 110, 111, 114, 123, 168, 169, 178, 179, 182

Mondale, Walter, 157, 219

Monsma, Stephen, 61

Moral Majority, 51, 52, 85, 138

Morrison, Melanie, 191

Mott, Stephen, 47, 58, 59, 60, 61, 107

Mouw, Richard, 43, 46, 47, 192, 267

Nash, Ronald, 214, 220

National Association of Evangelicals, 8, 12, 89, 239, 243

National Black Evangelical Association, 42, 93, 94

National Council of Churches, 28

National Organization of Women (NOW), 111-12, 125, 130

Native Americans, 86-87, 91

Neuhaus, Richard John, 25, 70, 154, 257

New Left, 15, 35, 37, 38, 43, 44, 50, 237

Nicaragua, 244-50

Niebuhr, H. Richard, 68

Niebuhr, Reinhold, 25, 42, 267

Nixon, Richard, 32, 33, 38, 45, 218, 237

Nonviolence, 266-69

Noriega, Manuel, 251-52

Nuclear weapons, 15, 137, 139, 140, 142, 145, 150, 219, 241-43

Obama, Barack, 13, 90-92, 160, 230, 271, 273, 274, 275, 276

Obamacare, 271

Olson, Mark, 66, 79-80, 133-34, 142, 169, 170, 171-73, 219, 269

Operation Rescue, 145, 156

Ortega, Daniel, 247, 250

The Other Side (magazine), 2, 4, 14-20, 31-32, 40-47, 77; as successor

to *Freedom Now*, 9, 31; on racial issues, 79-100 passim; on feminism, 106, 108, 111, 113, 117-24; on abortion, 132-35, 141-44, 160; on LGBT issues, 168-74, 185, 188-90, 273; on poverty and economic justice, 204-31 passim; on nationalism and militarism, 240-43, 248, 251, 256

Ozard, Dwight, 198

Pacifism, 266-69

Palestinians. *See* Israeli-Palestinian conflict

Palmer, Phoebe, 6, 103

Panama, 251-52

Pannell, Bill, 29, 41, 47, 77, 80, 82-83, 211

Patient Protection and Affordable Care Act, 271

Patriotism, criticism of, 37-38, 51, 241, 265

Pavlischek, Keith, 153-54, 193-94

Peacemaking, 267-69

People's Christian Coalition. *See* Post-Americans; Sojourners (organization)

Perkins, John, 42, 47, 77, 79, 80, 82, 85, 230

Pierard, Richard, 42, 45, 47

Pinnock, Clark, 36, 37, 44, 209-10, 251

Pledge of Resistance, 248-50

Polter, Julie, 124, 127, 147, 148

Post-American (magazine), 9, 14, 34, 37-47 passim, 78, 101, 106, 107-8, 211. See also *Sojourners* (magazine)

Post-Americans, 9, 33-34, 36-40, 77-78, 101, 203, 237-39. *See also* Sojourners (organization)

Potter, Wyn Wright, 47, 94

Premillennial dispensationalism, 8, 254-56

Public theology: definition of, 56

—as developed by progressive evangelicals, 56-65; and liberalism, 66-70;

as similar to Religious Right, 70-71; critics of, 71; and separation of church and state, 71-73; and racism, 73, 100; and feminism, 73, 126-27; and abortion and pro-life position, 73, 160-61; and LGBT issues, 73, 175, 184, 195-98; and poverty and economic justice, 73-74, 233-34; and nationalism and militarism, 74, 265-69

Quebedeaux, Richard, 110

"Radical evangelicals," 15, 18, 32
Rauschenbusch, Walter, 42
Rawls, John, 65, 66, 67, 69
Reagan, Ronald, 10, 81-85, 97, 114, 116, 157, 183, 218-19, 231-32, 243, 244-50
Red Letter Christians, 13, 19, 277
Reed, Ralph, 154, 156
Reese, Boyd, 47, 111
Reformed Journal, 15, 25
Religious Right, 2-4, 19, 51-52, 85, 99; development of, 10-11, 31; criticism of progressive evangelicals, 18; public theology, 70-71; on feminism, 111-13, 116; on abortion, 131-32, 138, 154; on LGBT issues, 167, 175, 180, 181, 183, 184, 187, 193, 196; on economic policies, 214, 215, 219-20; on nationalism and militarism, 239, 243, 249; support for Israel, 254-55
Republican Party, 81, 83, 112, 138, 155-60, 226-27, 232; supported by Religious Right, 2-3, 10, 52, 99, 155-56
Rice, Jim, 193, 248
Right On (magazine), 15, 25, 47
Rivers, Eugene, 88
Robertson, Pat, 70, 116, 249
Roe v. Wade, 128, 130, 131, 132, 136, 145, 151, 152
Roman Catholics. *See* Catholics
Roos, Joe, 47, 175-76, 242

Same-sex marriage, 164, 172-73, 187, 194-98, 272-73
Scanzoni, Letha, 105, 106, 108, 109, 110, 113, 132, 168, 169, 172, 178, 182
Schaeffer, Francis, 131
Schaeffer, Franky, 220, 251
Schlafly, Phyllis, 112, 131, 167
Shank, Duane, 60, 263
Sider, Ron, 3, 10, 11, 12, 13, 14-18, 42, 276; differentiation from Religious Right and political left, 3, 4; and Evangelicals for McGovern, 45-46; and Thanksgiving Workshop on Evangelicals and Social Concern, 46, 47, 50, 51; on public theology of community, 55-72 passim; on racial issues, 78, 84, 87, 91-92, 94, 98; on feminism, 119-20, 125, 126; on abortion and pro-life position, 132, 150-55, 156, 158-60, 271; on LGBT issues, 180-83, 185-86, 190, 193-98, 272; on poverty and economic justice, 203-33 passim, 273-74; on nationalism and militarism, 239, 247, 251-68 passim
Simple living, 215
Simpson, O. J., 88
Skinner, Tom, 41, 45, 77, 80
Smedes, Lewis, 47
Social Gospel, 8, 24, 27-28, 40
Socialism, 219-20
Social justice, progressive evangelicals' definition of, 61-65
Sojourners (magazine), 9, 14-15, 19-20; on racial issues, 80-100 passim, 270; on feminism, 108, 111, 113-14, 117-24, 146, 270-71; on abortion and pro-life position, 132-33, 135-38, 144-49, 160-61; on LGBT issues, 174-80, 184, 190-93, 272; on poverty and economic justice, 204-34 passim, 273-74; on nationalism and militarism, 237-68 passim, 274. See also *Post-American*

Made in the USA
San Bernardino, CA
04 August 2019